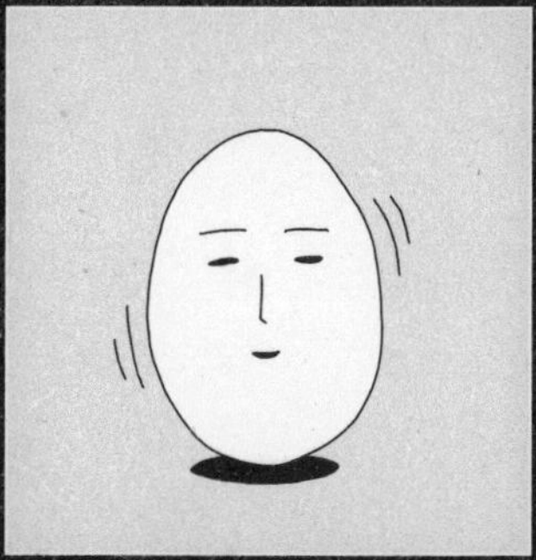

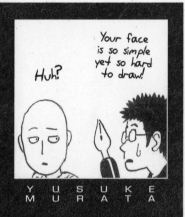

ONE

One-Punch Man first appeared on the web, and we tried our hardest to bring you the best possible book. I hope you enjoy it!

—ONE

Manga creator ONE began *One-Punch Man* as a webcomic, which quickly went viral, garnering over 10 million hits. In addition to *One-Punch Man*, ONE writes and draws the series *Mob Psycho 100* and *Makai no Ossan*.

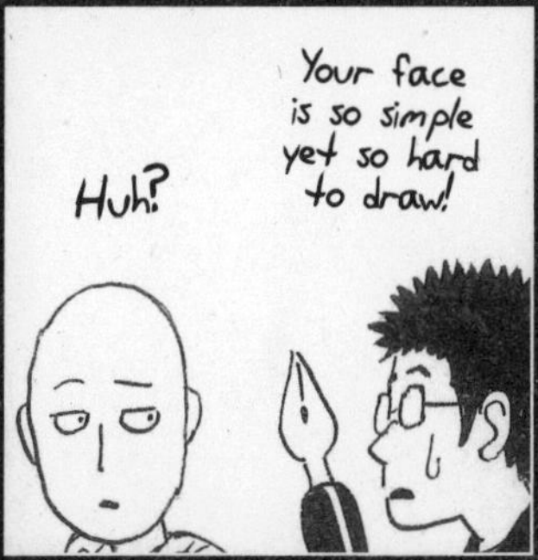
Your face is so simple yet so hard to draw!
Huh?

YUSUKE MURATA

Finally, the graphic novel! You can't re-draw a printed book the way you can a webcomic, so I was meticulous about it. Enjoy!

—Yusuke Murata

A highly decorated and skilled artist best known for his work on *Eyeshield 21*, Yusuke Murata won the 122nd Hop Step Award (1995) for *Partner* and placed second in the 51st Akatsuka Award (1998) for *Samui Hanashi*.

ONE-PUNCH MAN | 01
ONE + YUSUKE MURATA

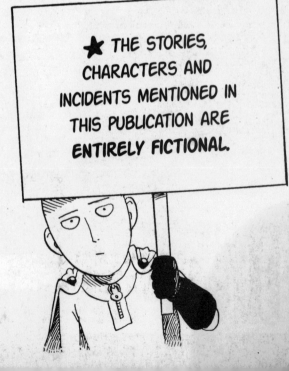

★ THE STORIES, CHARACTERS AND INCIDENTS MENTIONED IN THIS PUBLICATION ARE ENTIRELY FICTIONAL.

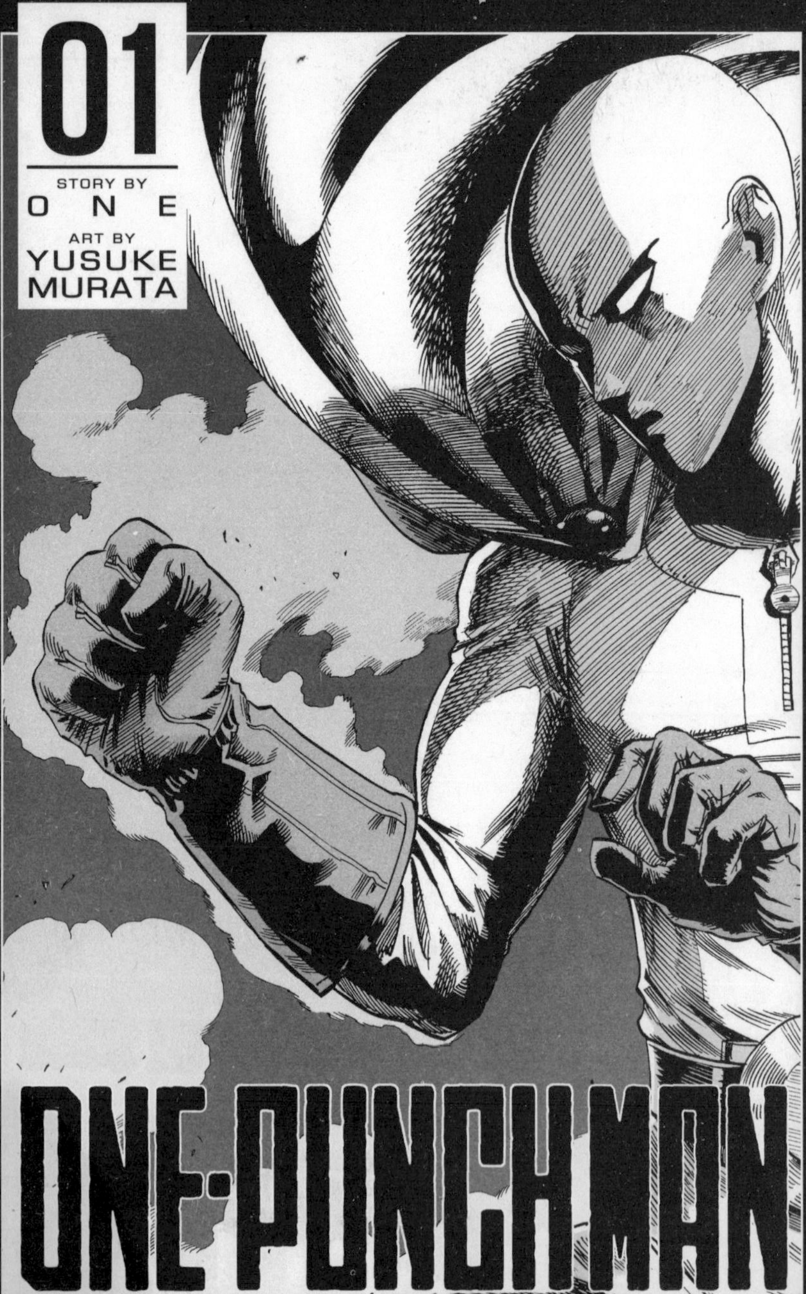
01
STORY BY
ONE
ART BY
YUSUKE
MURATA
ONE-PUNCH MAN

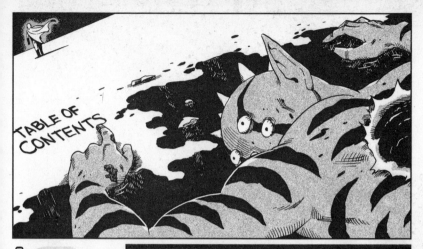

TABLE OF CONTENTS

CONTENTS

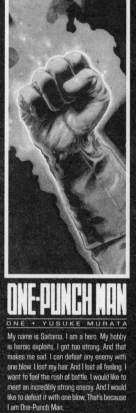

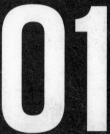

01
ONE PUNCH

PUNCH 1:
One Punch _____ 5

PUNCH 2:
Crab and Job Hunting _____ 27

PUNCH 3:
Walking Disaster _____ 43

PUNCH 4:
Subterraneans of Darkness _____ 65

PUNCH 5:
Itch Explosion _____ 91

PUNCH 6:
Saitama _____ 113

PUNCH 7:
A Mysterious Attack _____ 137

PUNCH 8:
This Guy? _____ 153

BONUS MANGA:
200 Yen _____ 177

ONE-PUNCH MAN
ONE + YUSUKE MURATA

My name is Saitama. I am a hero. My hobby is heroic exploits. I got too strong. And that makes me sad. I can defeat any enemy with one blow. I lost my hair And I lost all feeling. I want to feel the rush of battle. I would like to meet an incredibly strong enemy. And I would like to defeat it with one blow. That's because I am One-Punch Man.

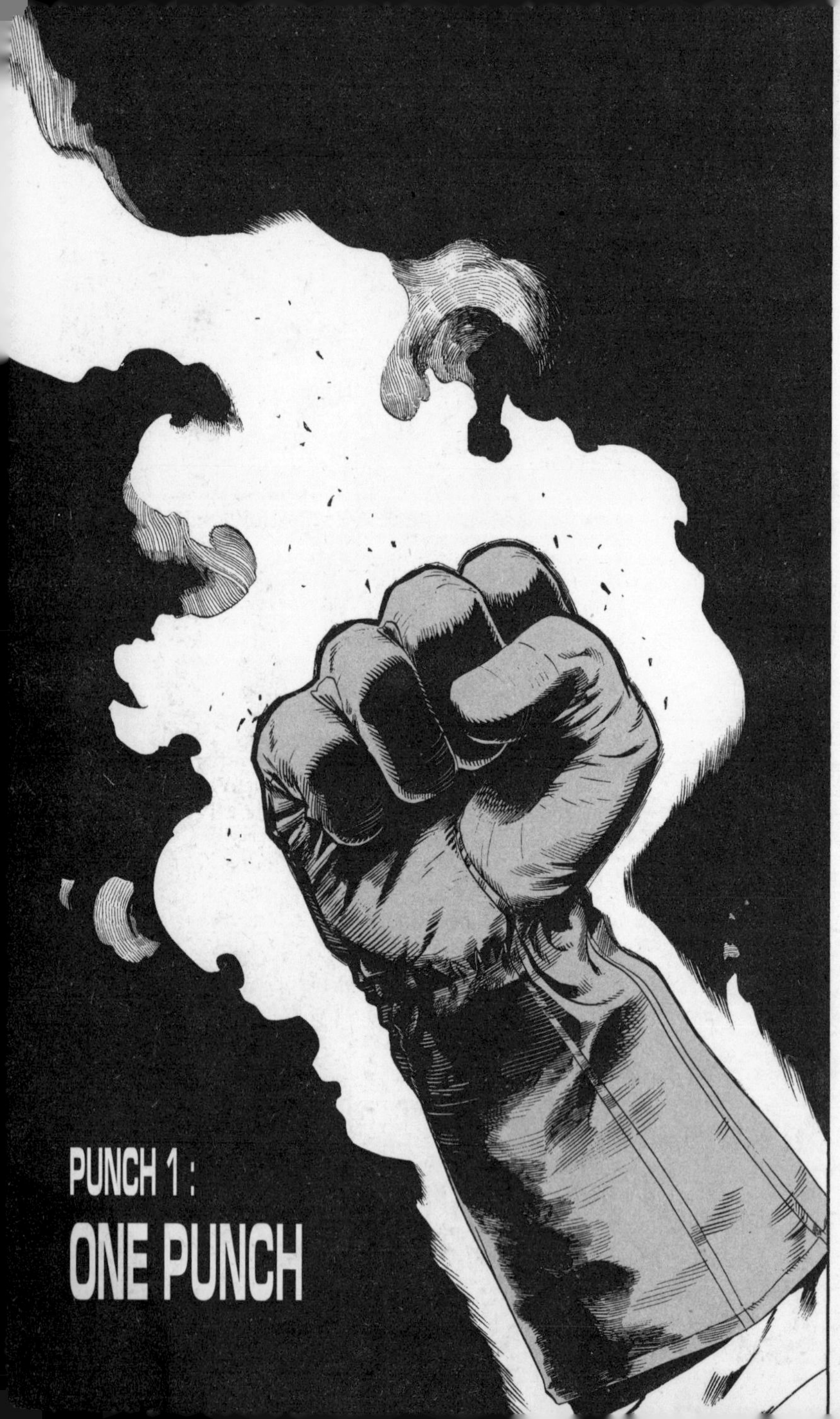
PUNCH 1:
ONE PUNCH

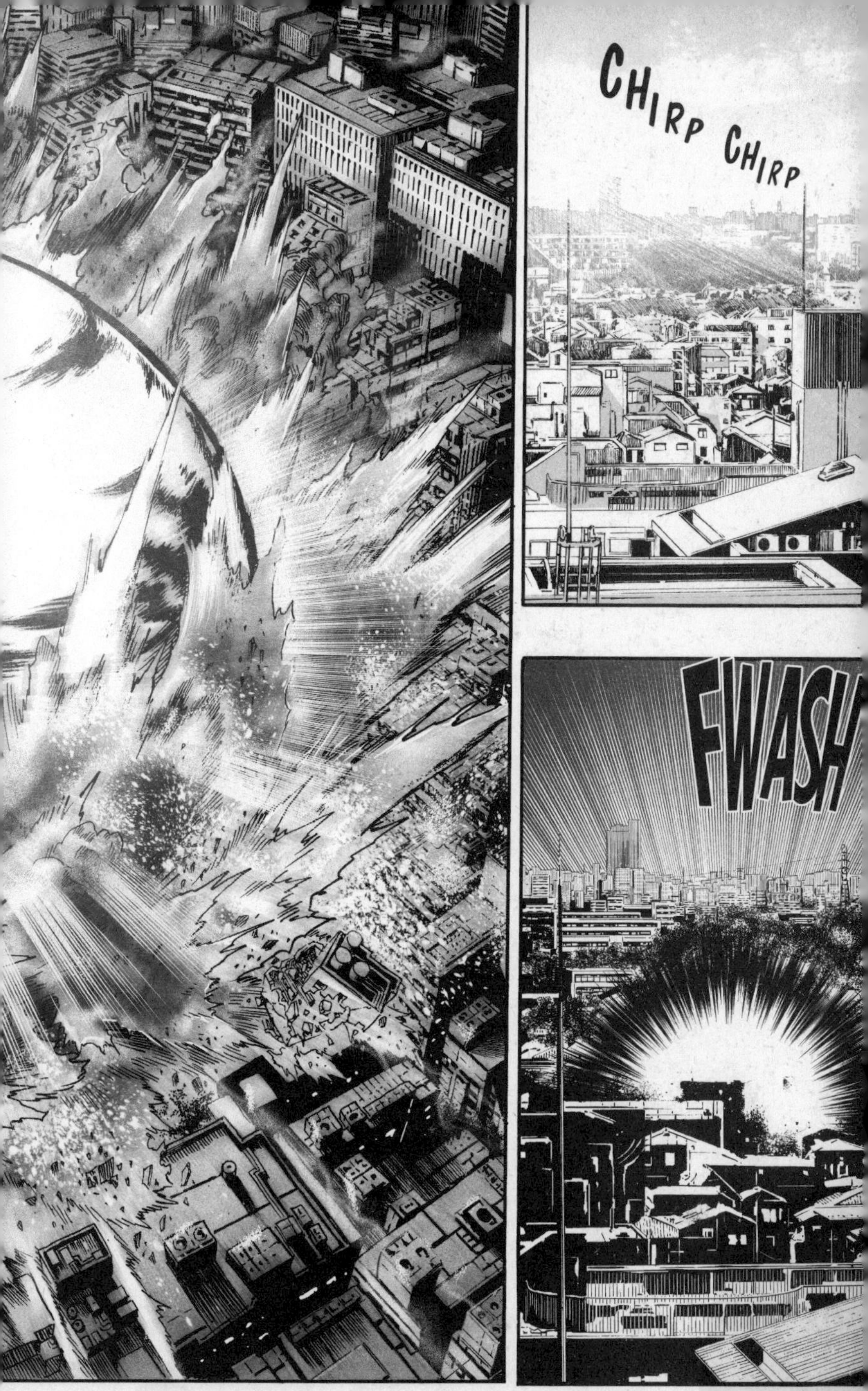
CHIRP CHIRP
FWASH

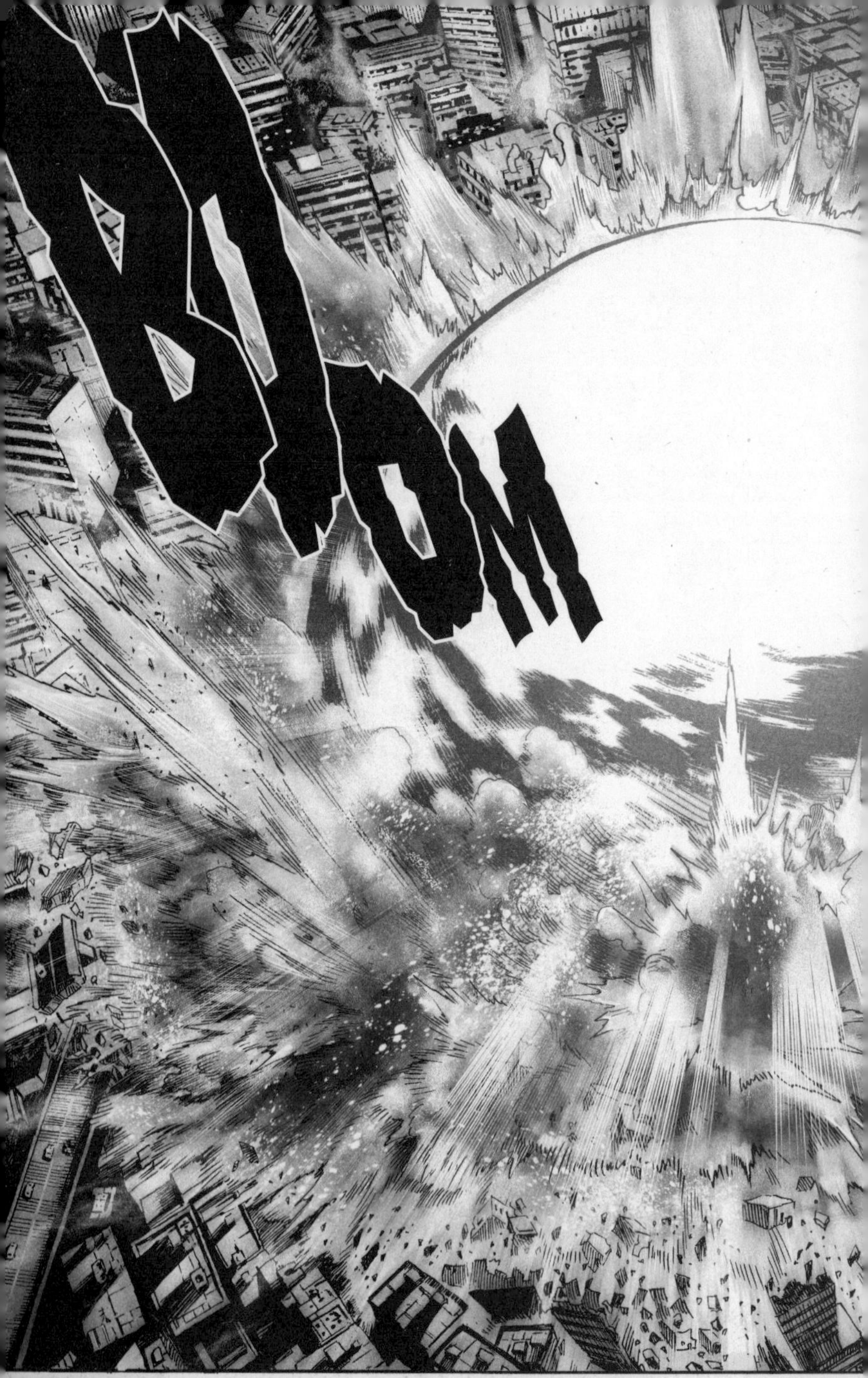
BOOM

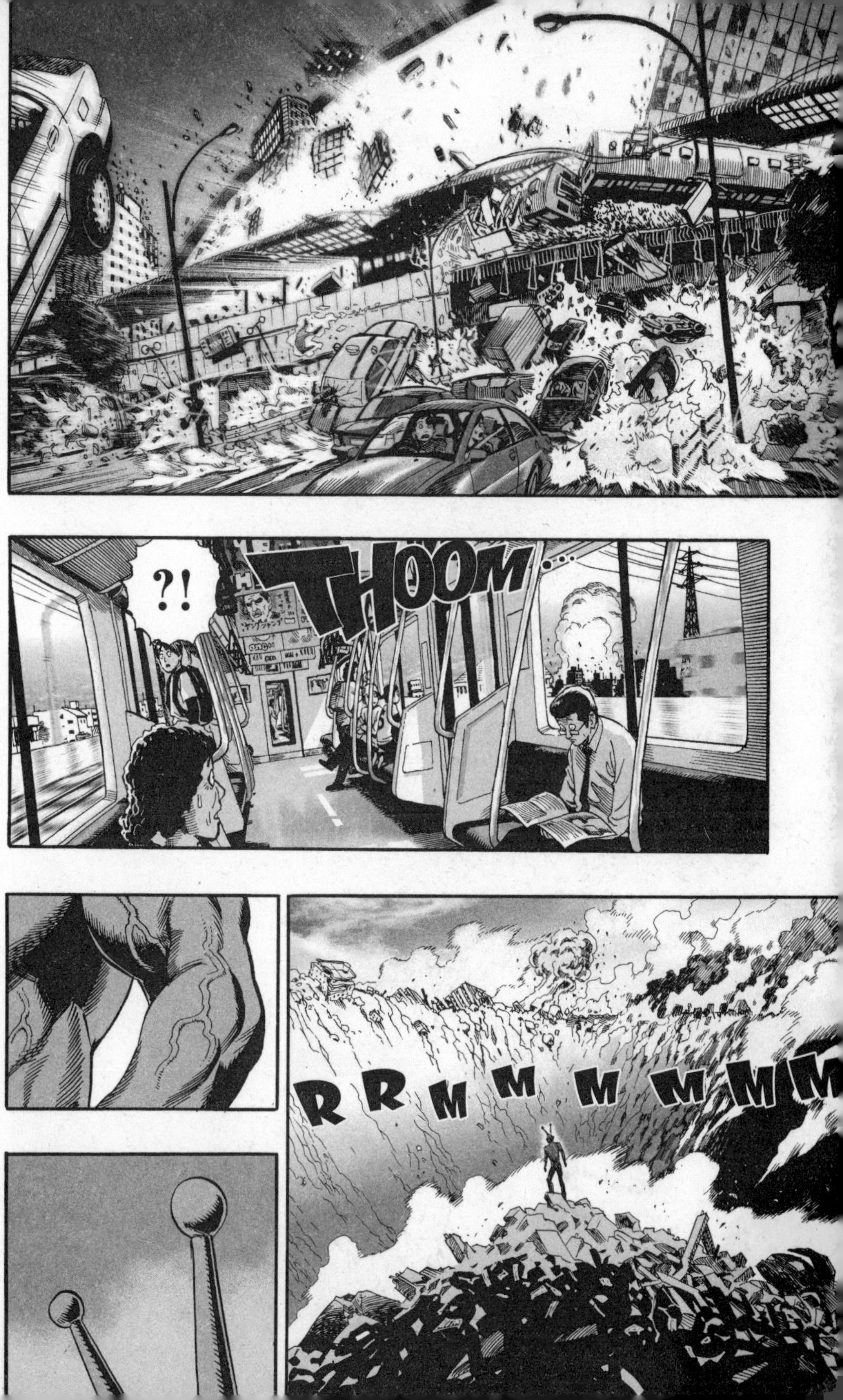
THOOM...
?!
RRMMMMMM

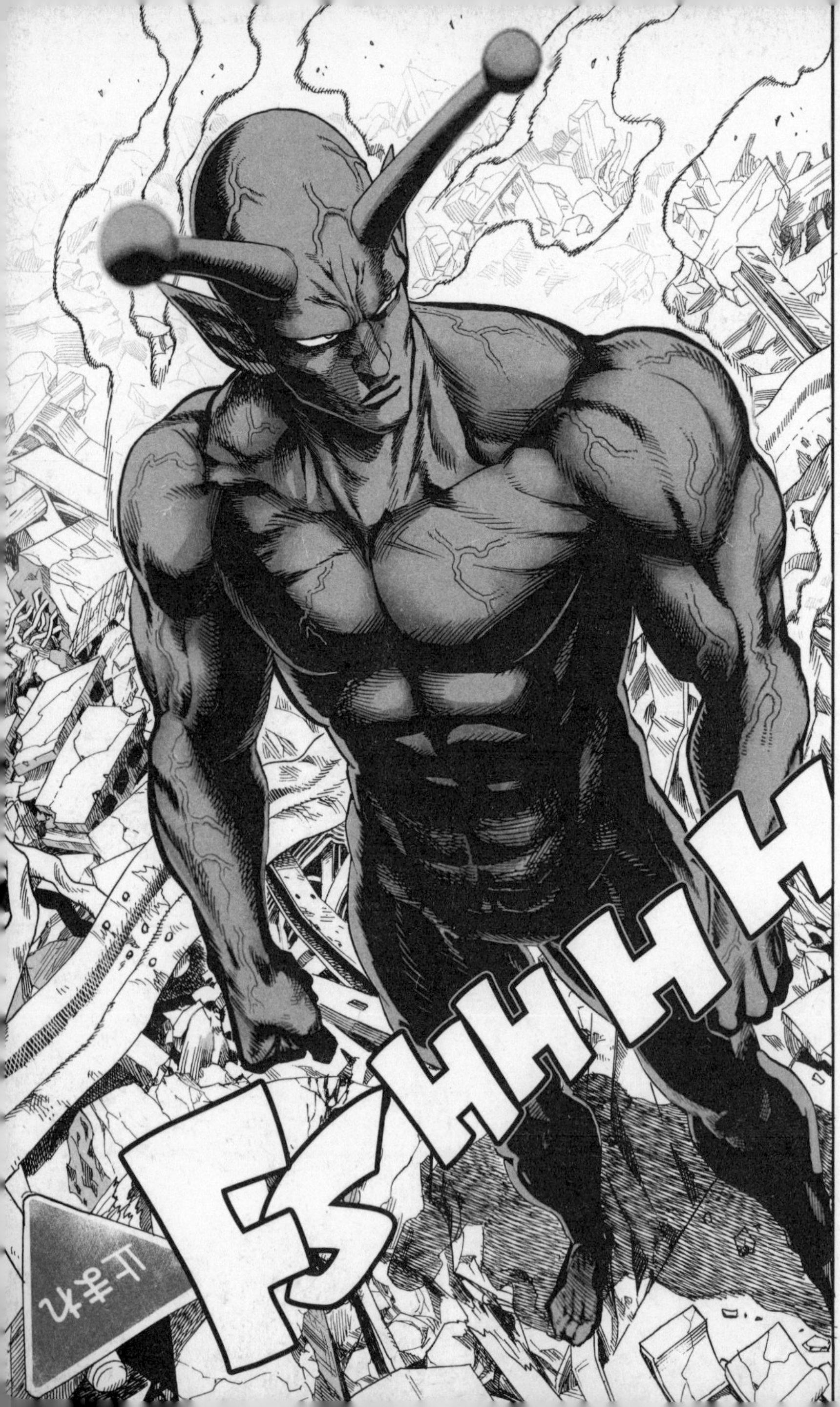
FSHHHHH
止まれ

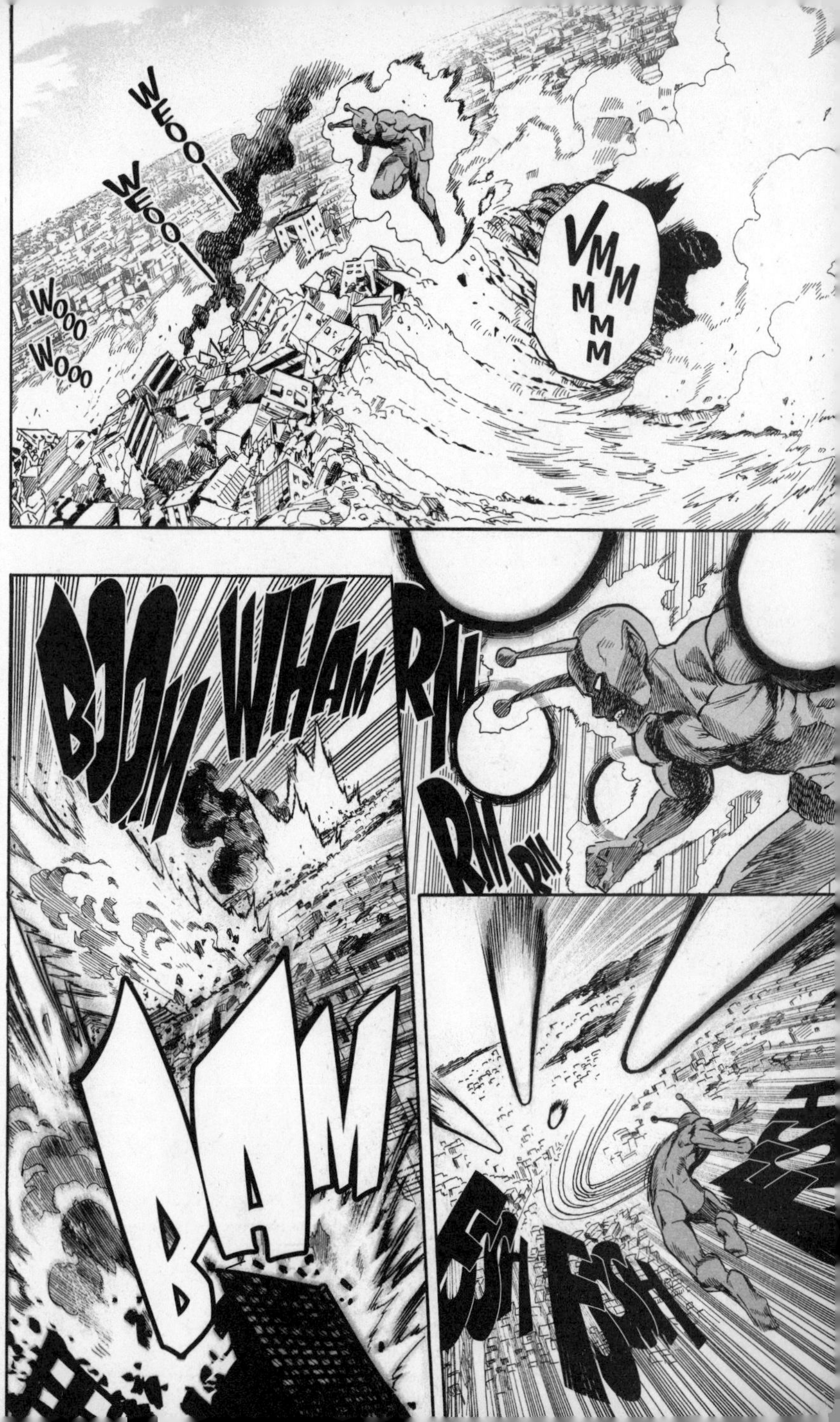
VMMMMMMM
WEOO
WEOO
WOOO
WOOO
RM
RM
RM
WHAM
BOOM
FSH
FSH
BAM

READ THIS WAY

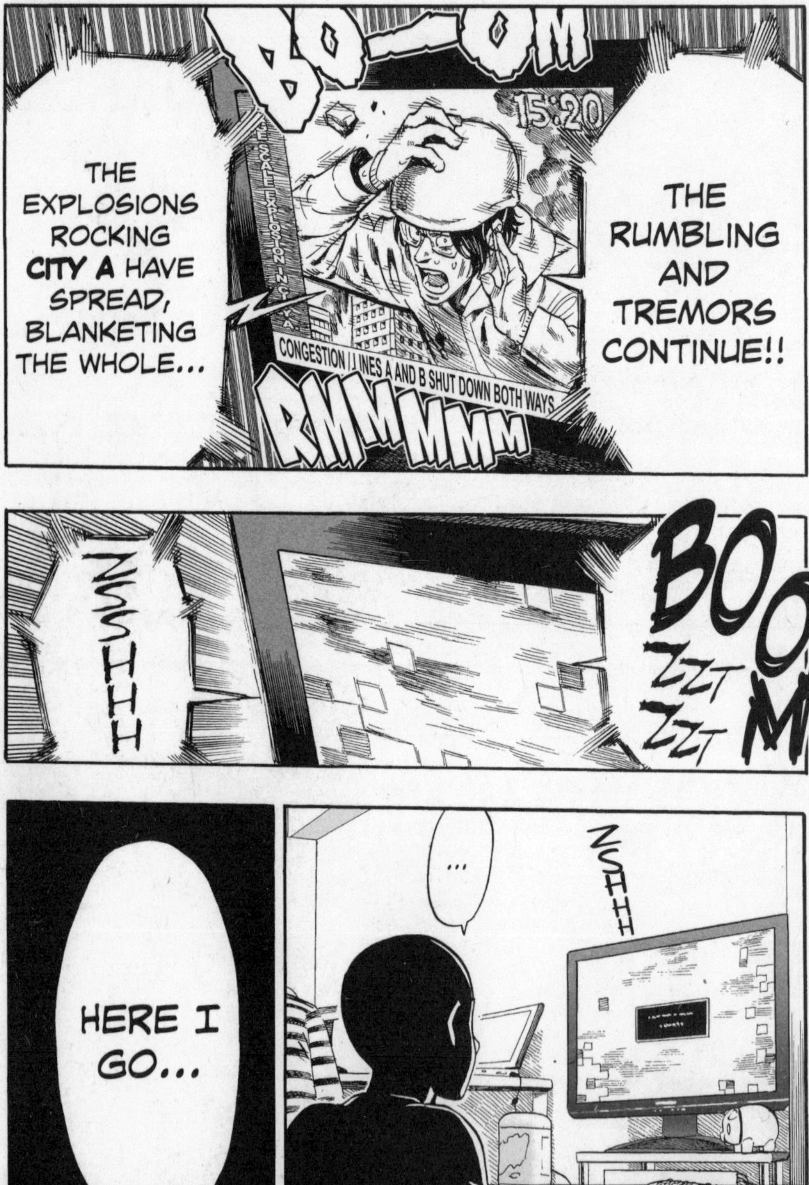
BO—OM
15:20
THE RUMBLING AND TREMORS CONTINUE!!
E SCALE EXPLOSION IN CITY A.
CONGESTION / LINES A AND B SHUT DOWN BOTH WAYS
RMMMMMM
THE EXPLOSIONS ROCKING **CITY A** HAVE SPREAD, BLANKETING THE WHOLE...
BOOOM
ZZZT ZZZT
ZSHHH
...
ZSHHH
HERE I GO...

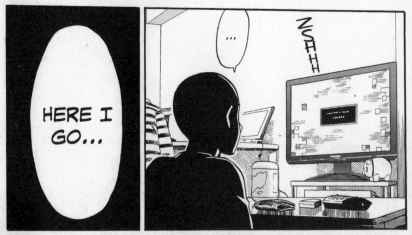

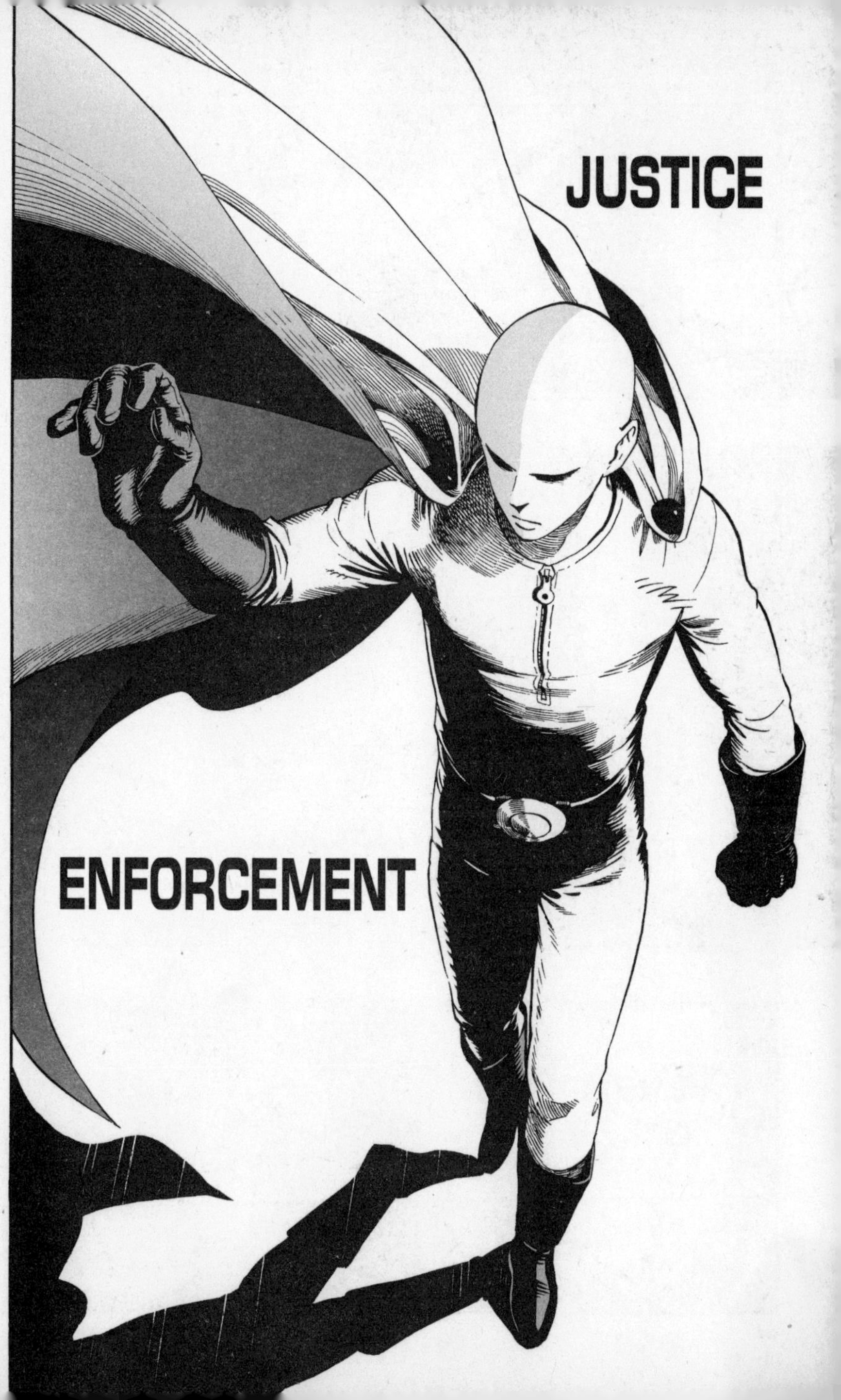
JUSTICE
ENFORCEMENT

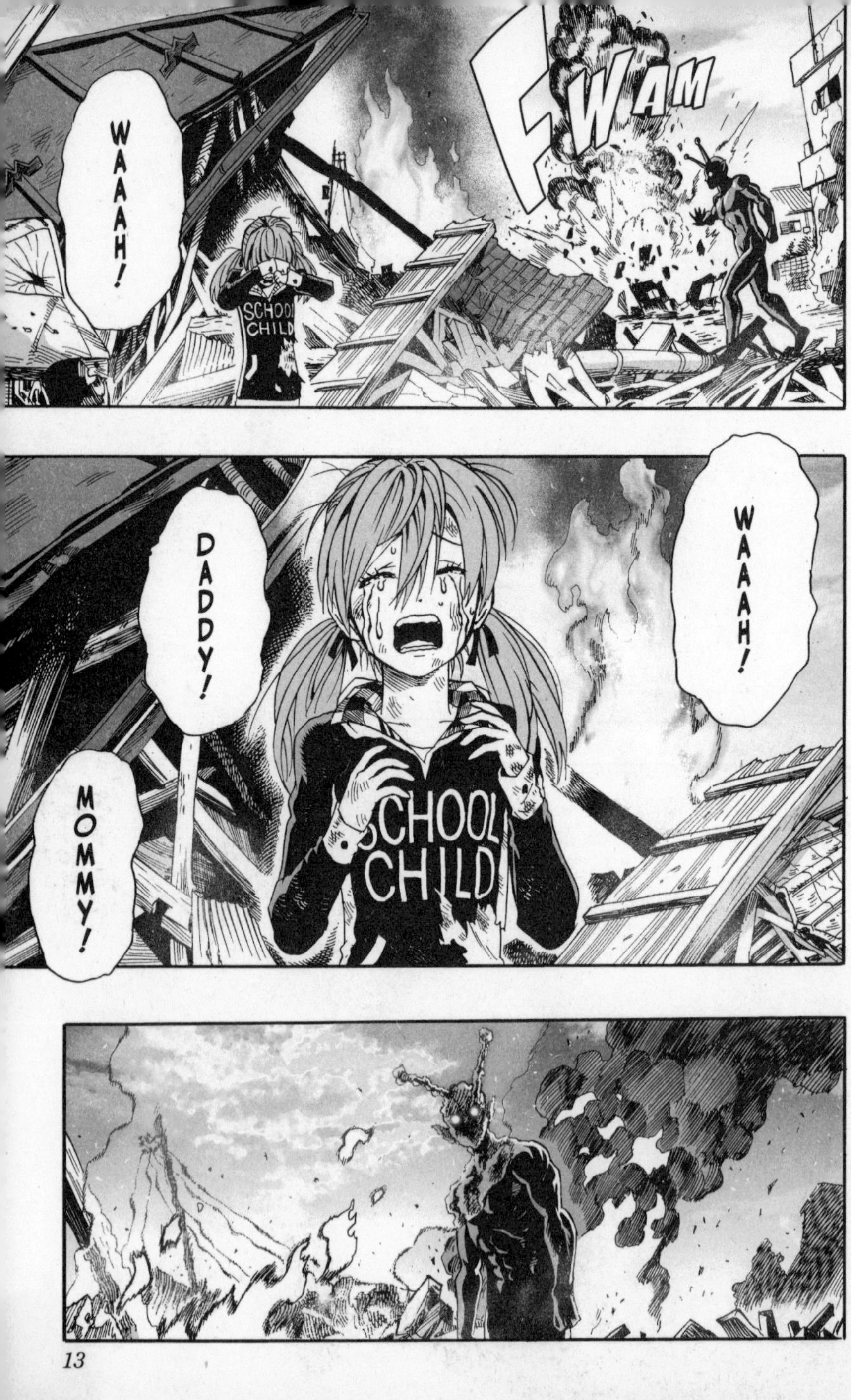
FWAM
WAAAAH!
WAAAAH!
DADDY!
MOMMY!

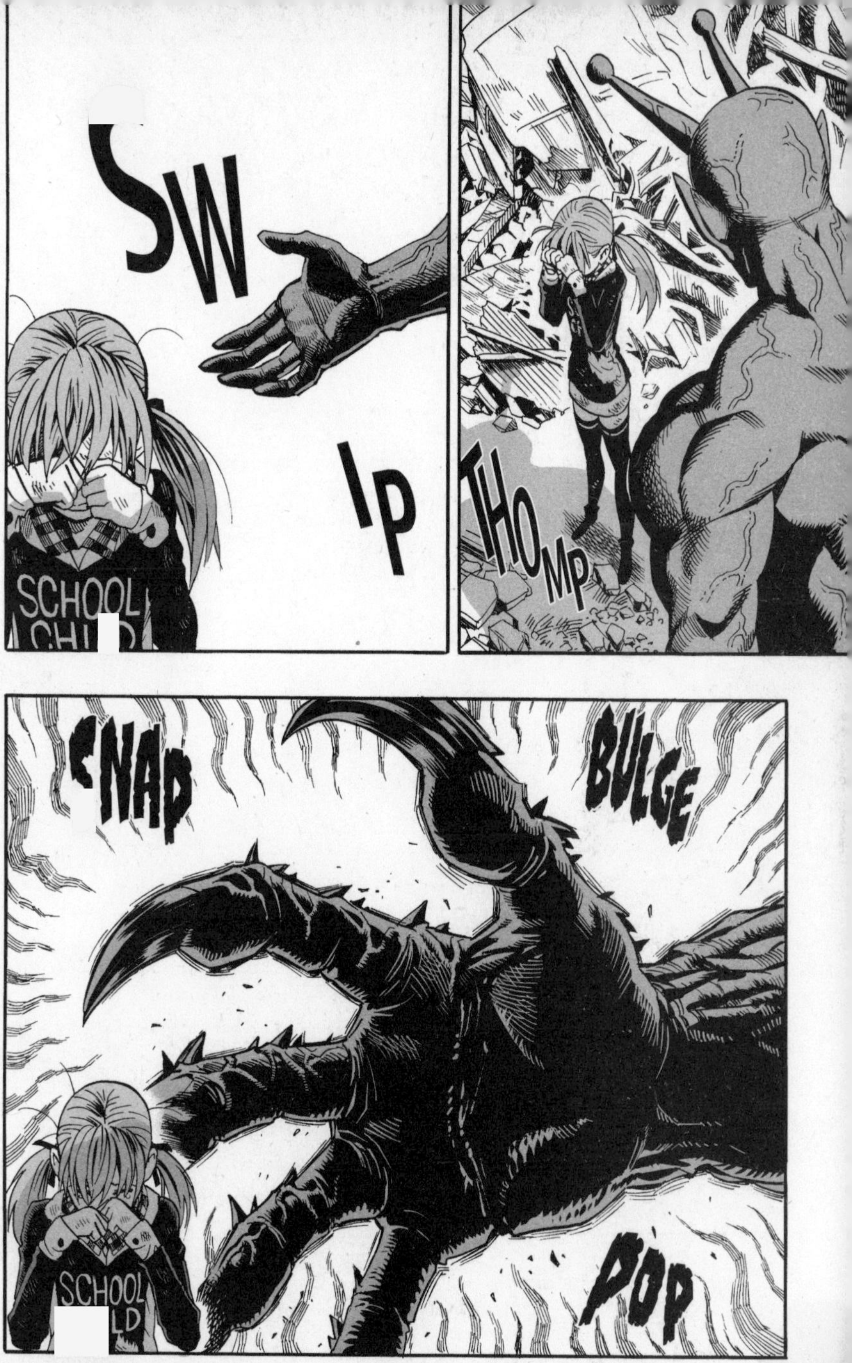
THOMP
SWIP
SCHOOL
BULGE
SNAP
SCHOOL
POP

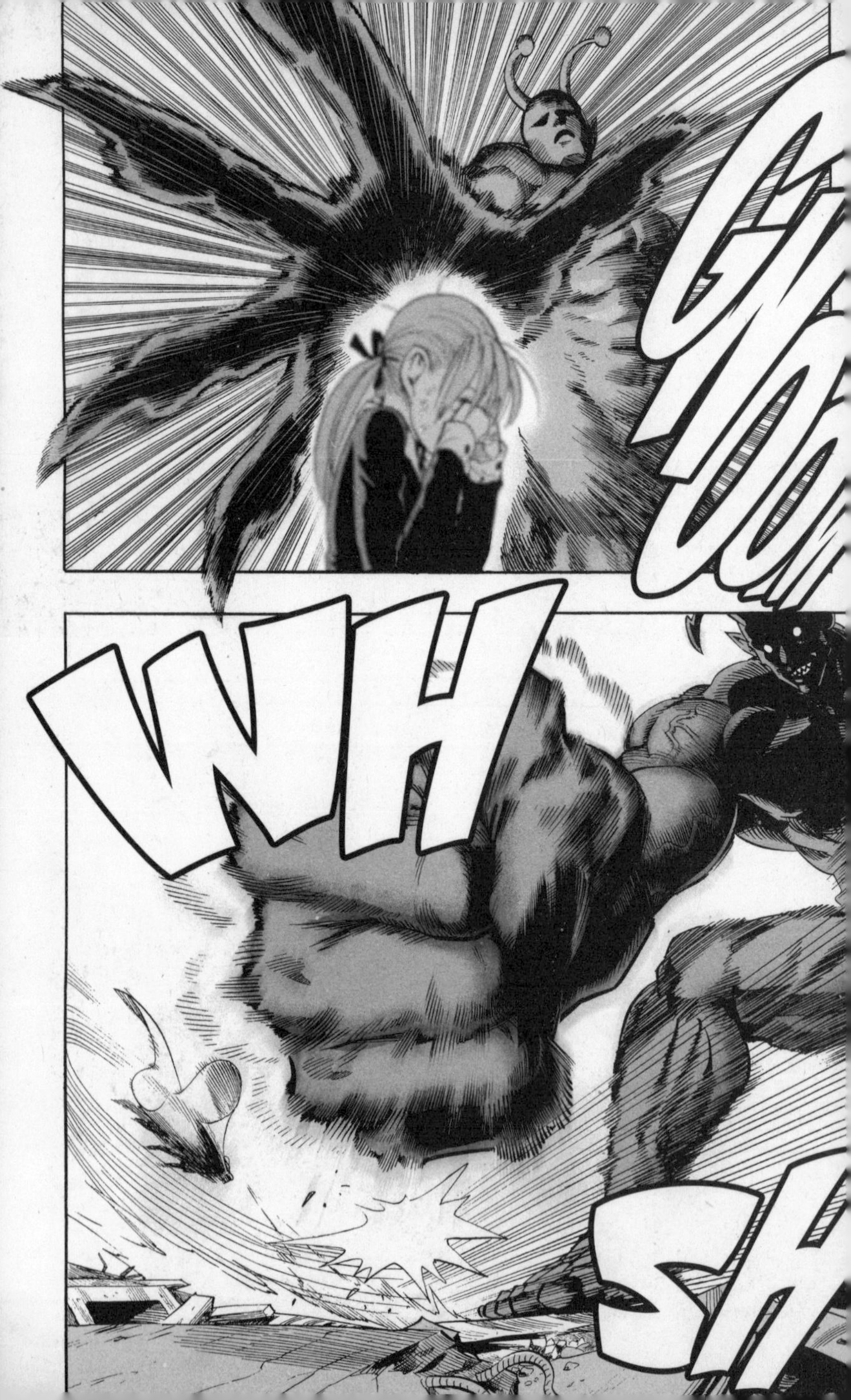
WH
SH

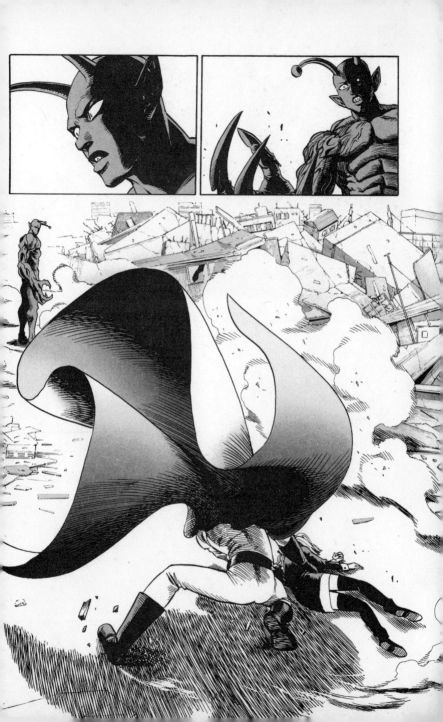

READ THIS WAY

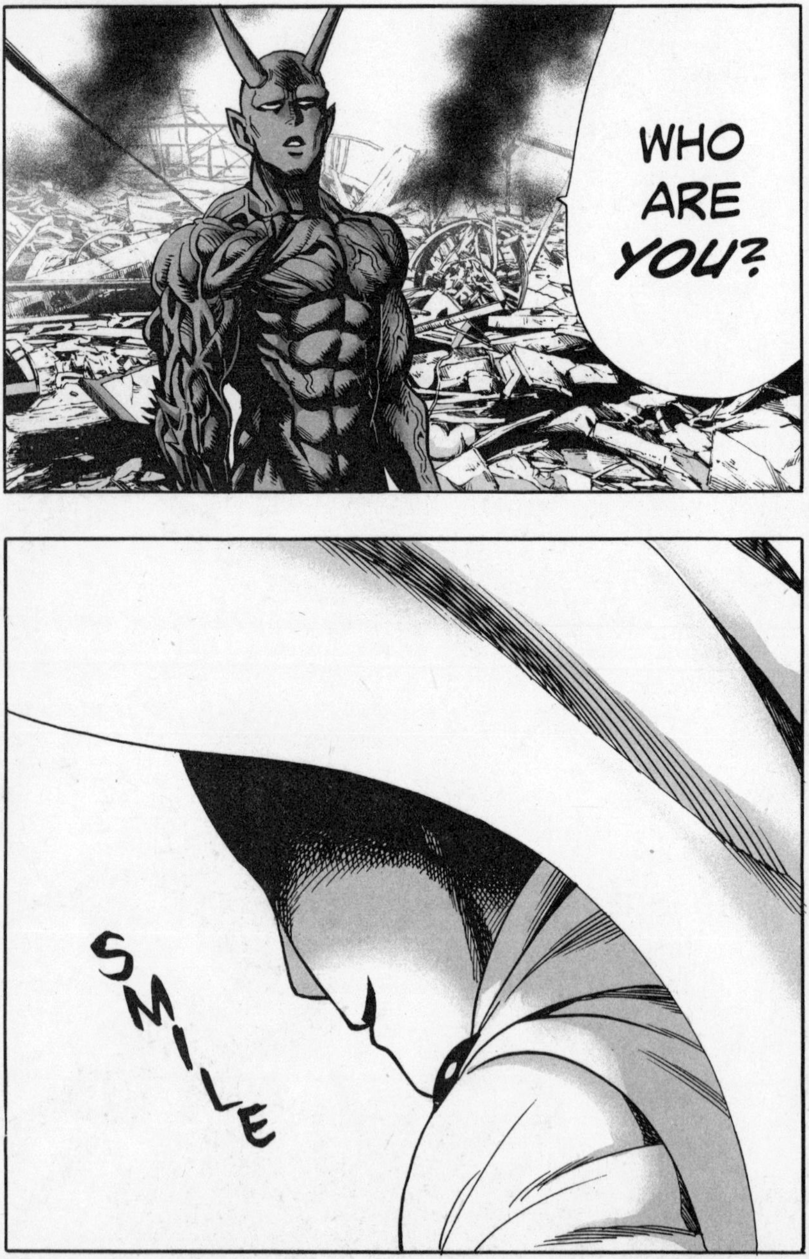
WHO ARE YOU?
SMILE

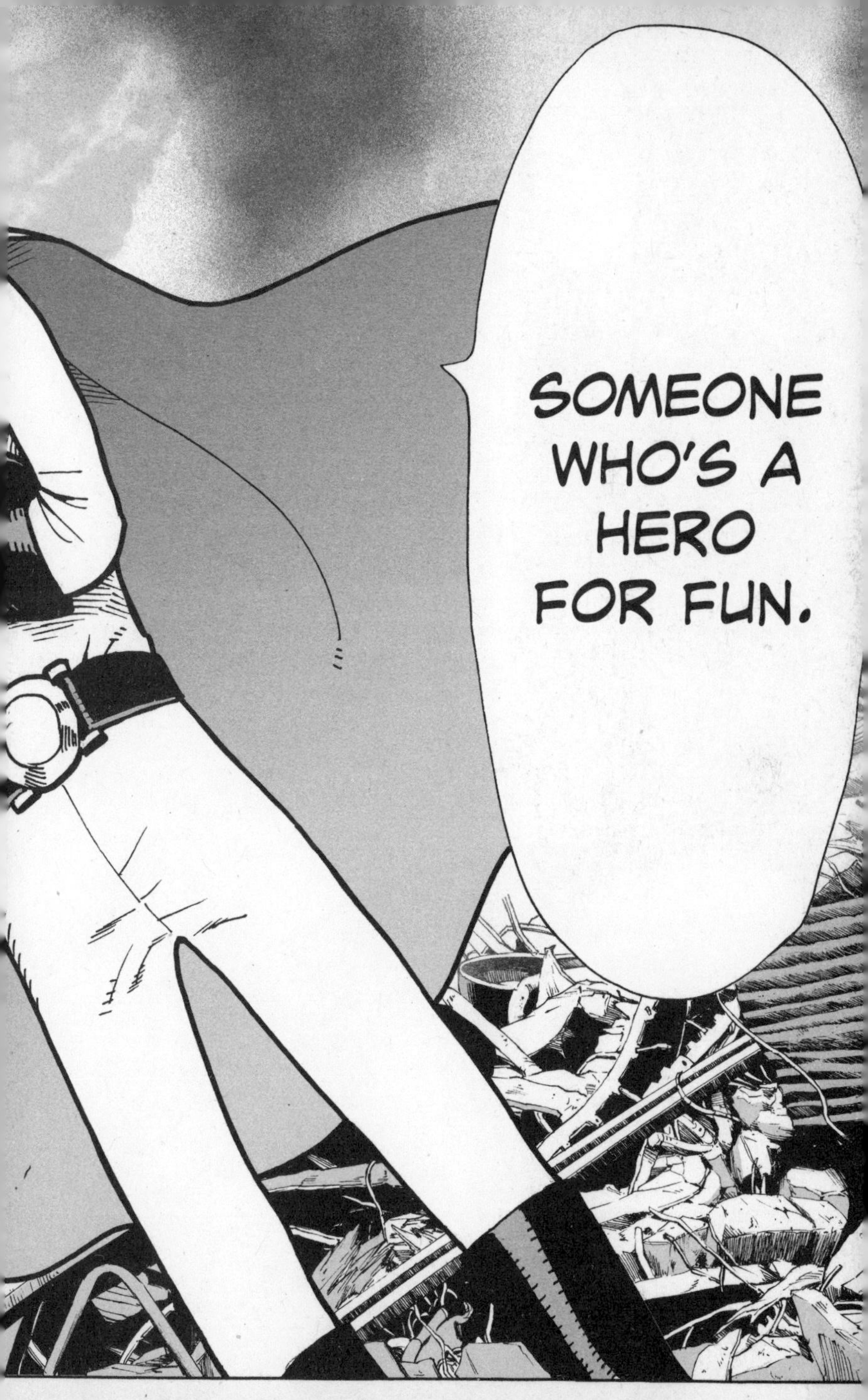
SOMEONE WHO'S A HERO FOR FUN.

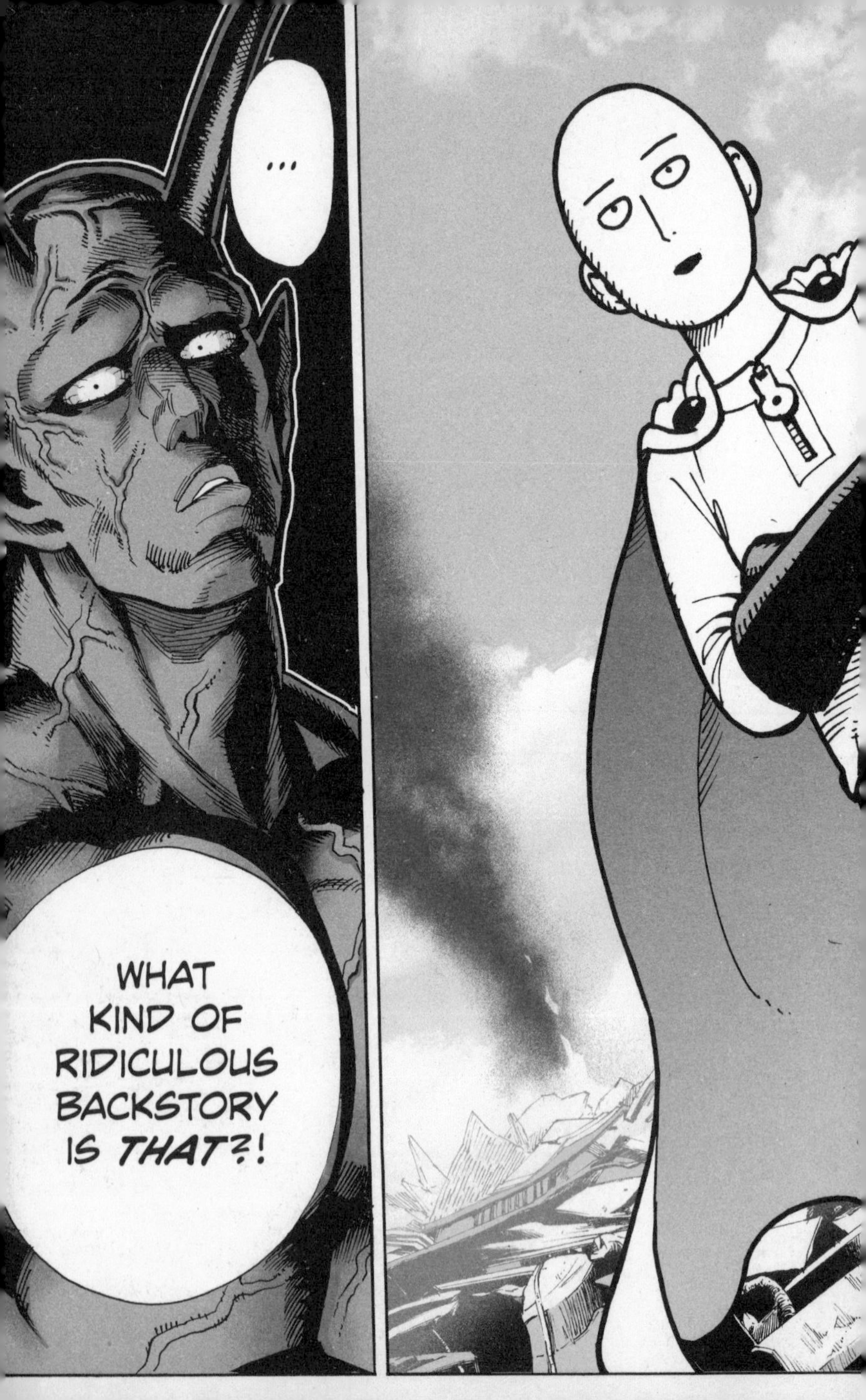
...
WHAT KIND OF RIDICULOUS BACKSTORY IS *THAT*?!

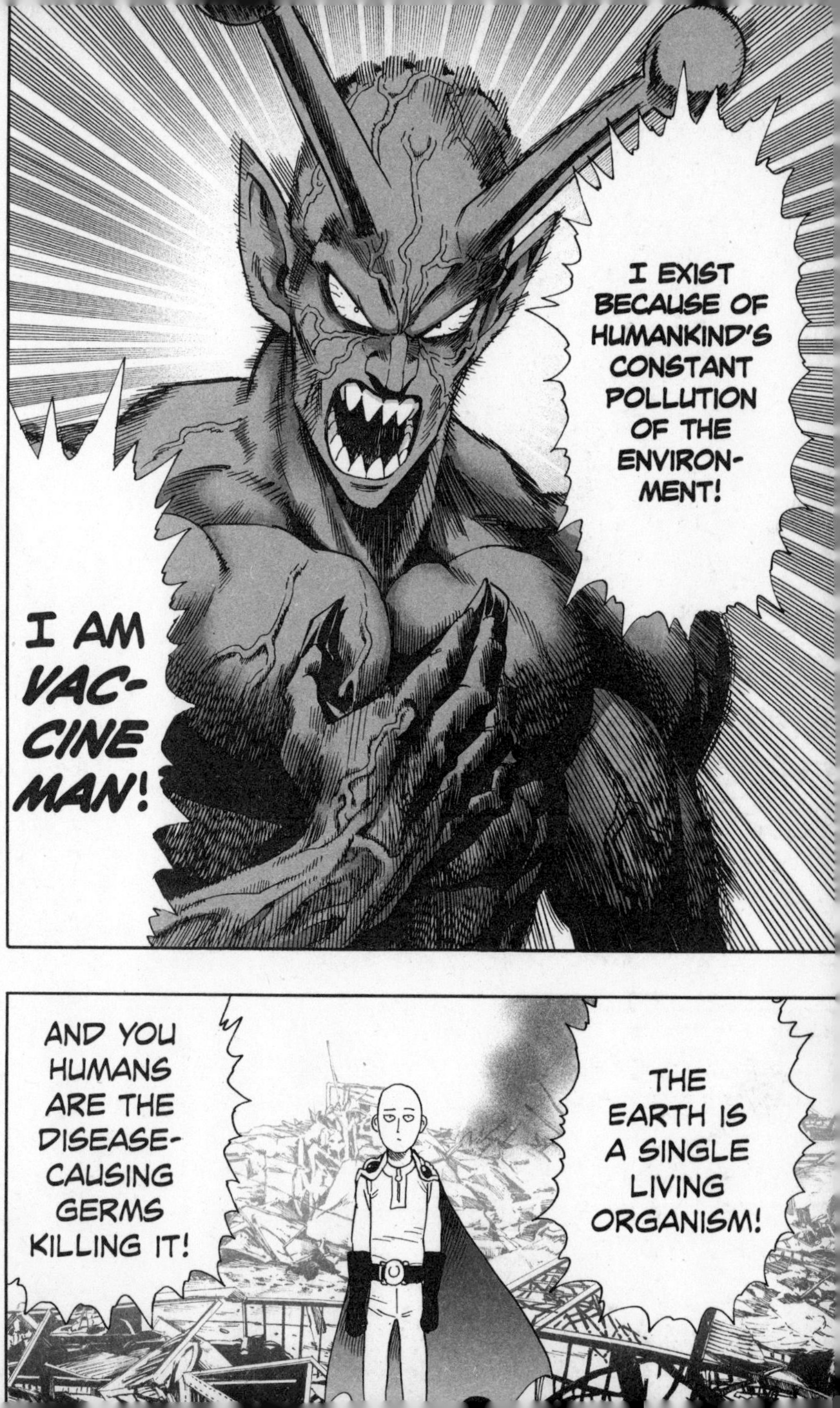
I EXIST BECAUSE OF HUMANKIND'S CONSTANT POLLUTION OF THE ENVIRON-MENT!
I AM VAC-CINE MAN!
THE EARTH IS A SINGLE LIVING ORGANISM!
AND YOU HUMANS ARE THE DISEASE-CAUSING GERMS KILLING IT!

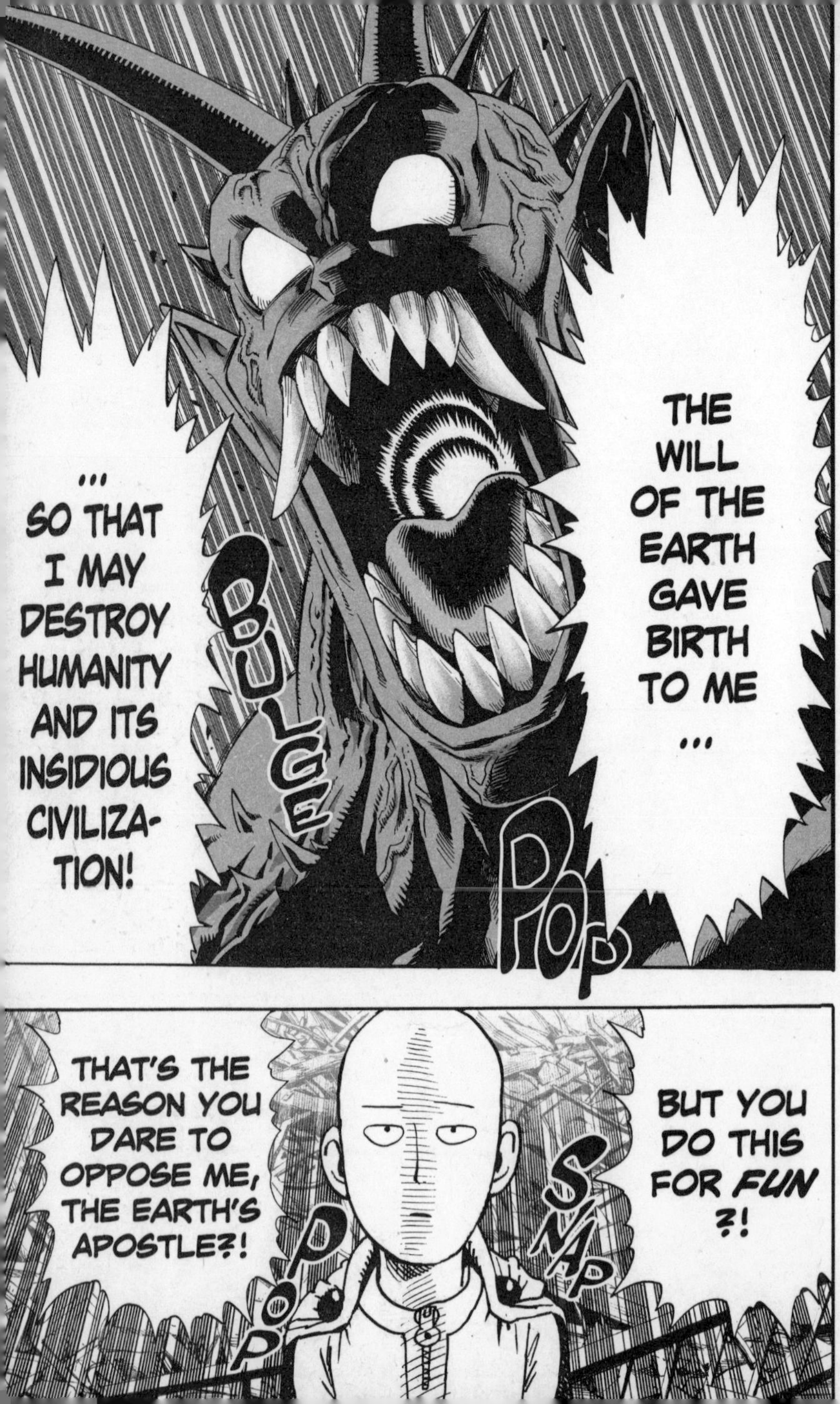
THE WILL OF THE EARTH GAVE BIRTH TO ME ...
... SO THAT I MAY DESTROY HUMANITY AND ITS INSIDIOUS CIVILIZA-TION!
BULGE
POP
BUT YOU DO THIS FOR *FUN* ?!
THAT'S THE REASON YOU DARE TO OPPOSE ME, THE EARTH'S APOSTLE?!
SNAP
POP

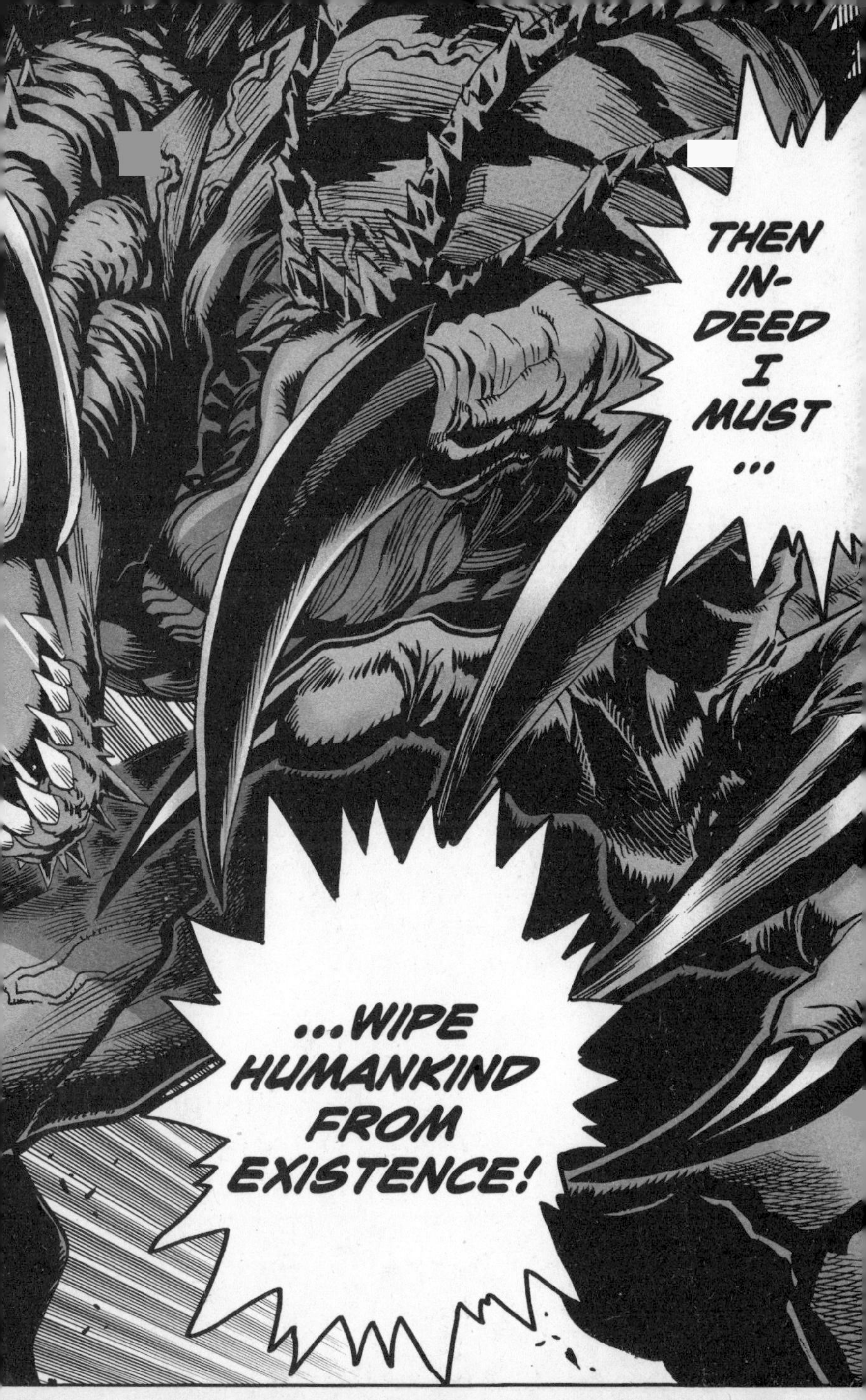
THEN IN-DEED I MUST ...
...WIPE HUMANKIND FROM EXISTENCE!

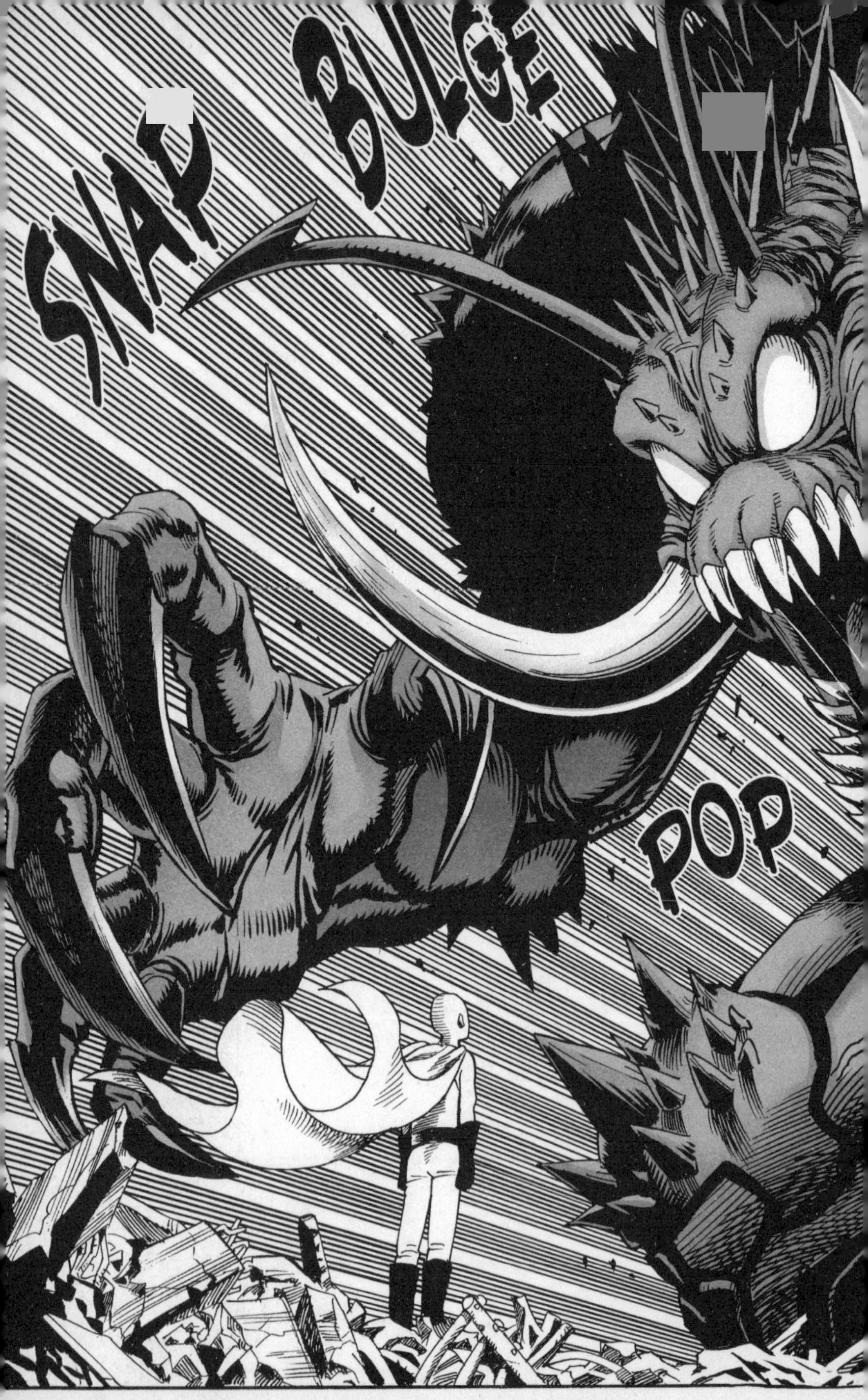
BULGE
SNAP
POP

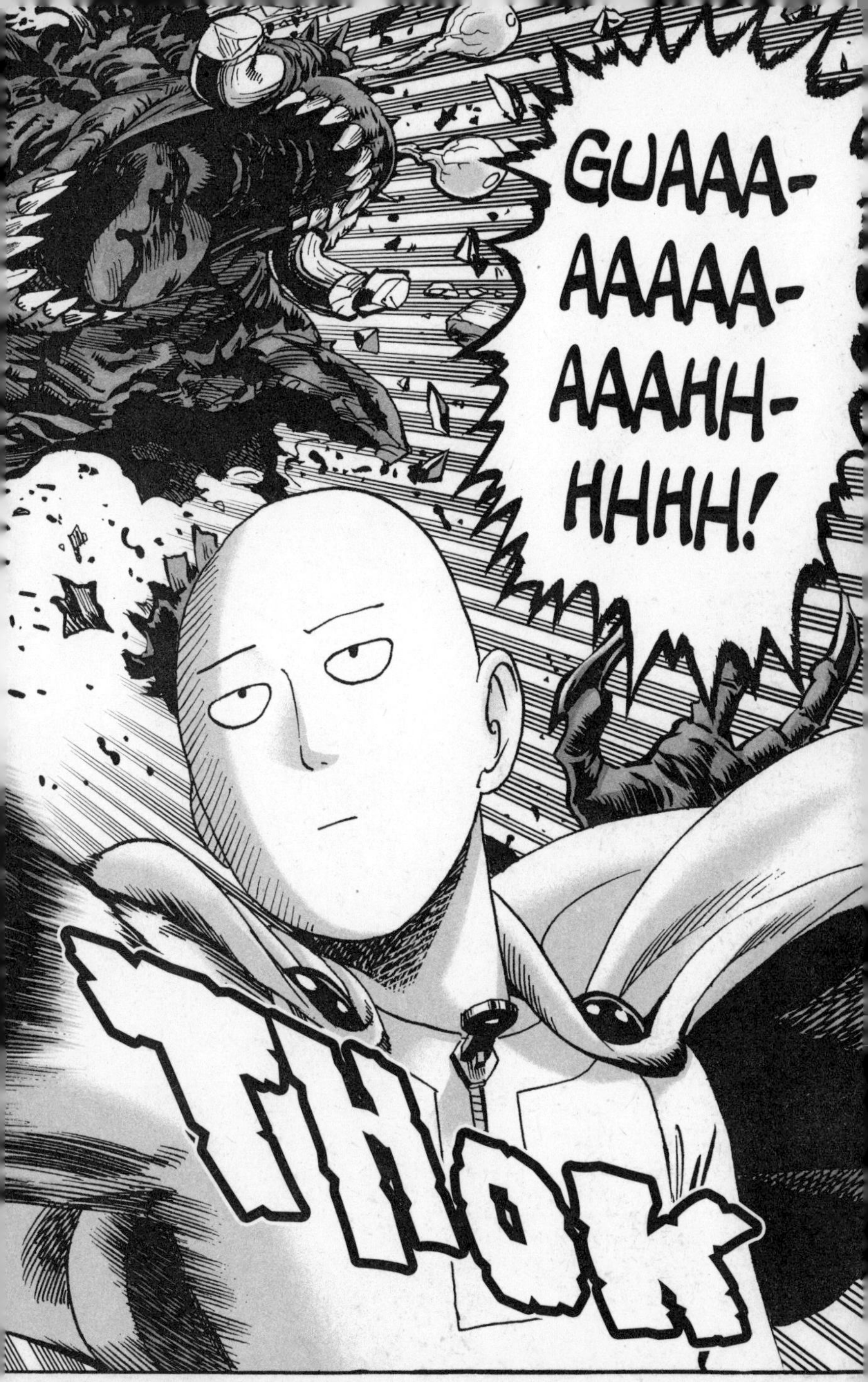
GUAAA-
AAAAA-
AAAHH-
HHHH!
THOK

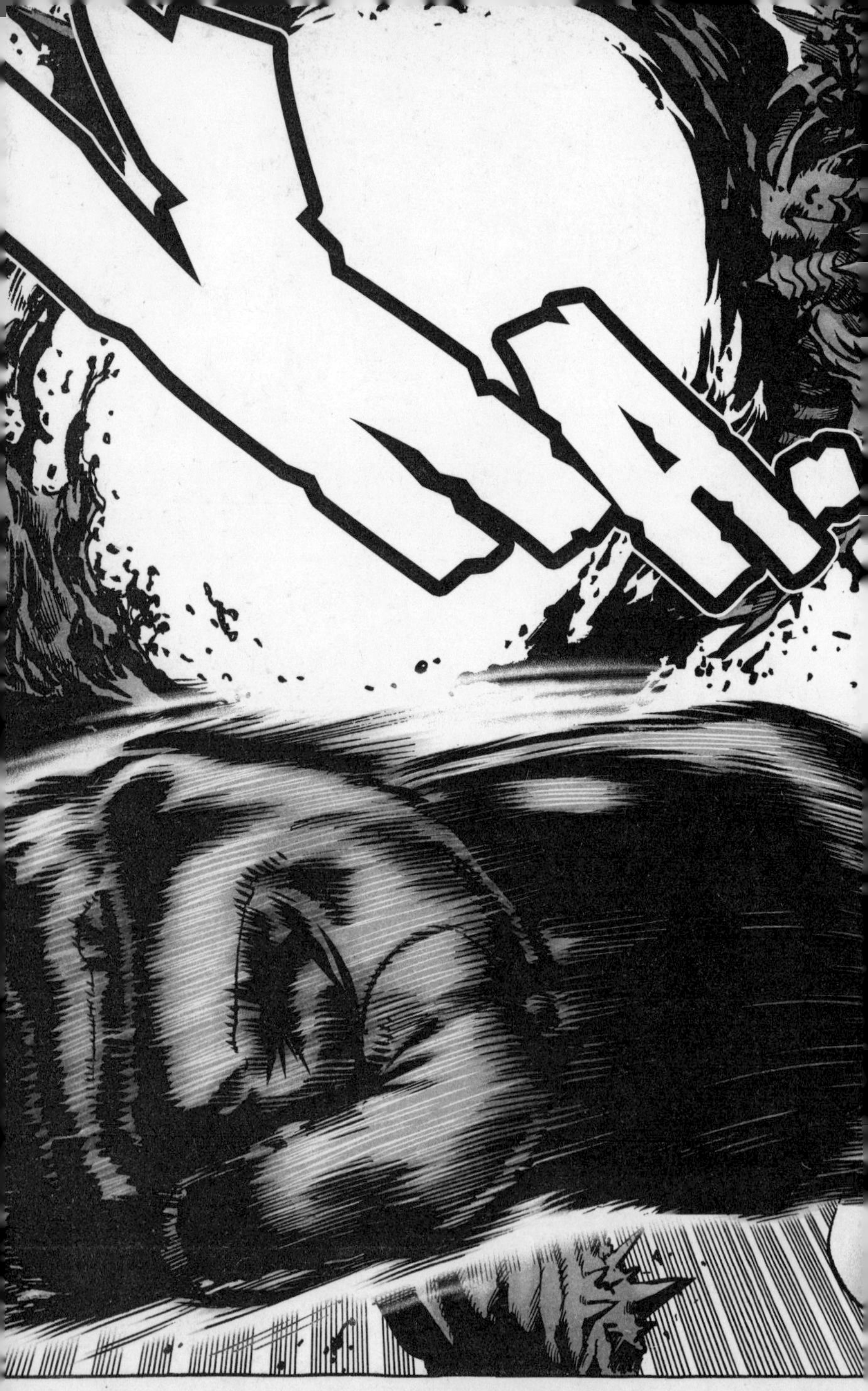

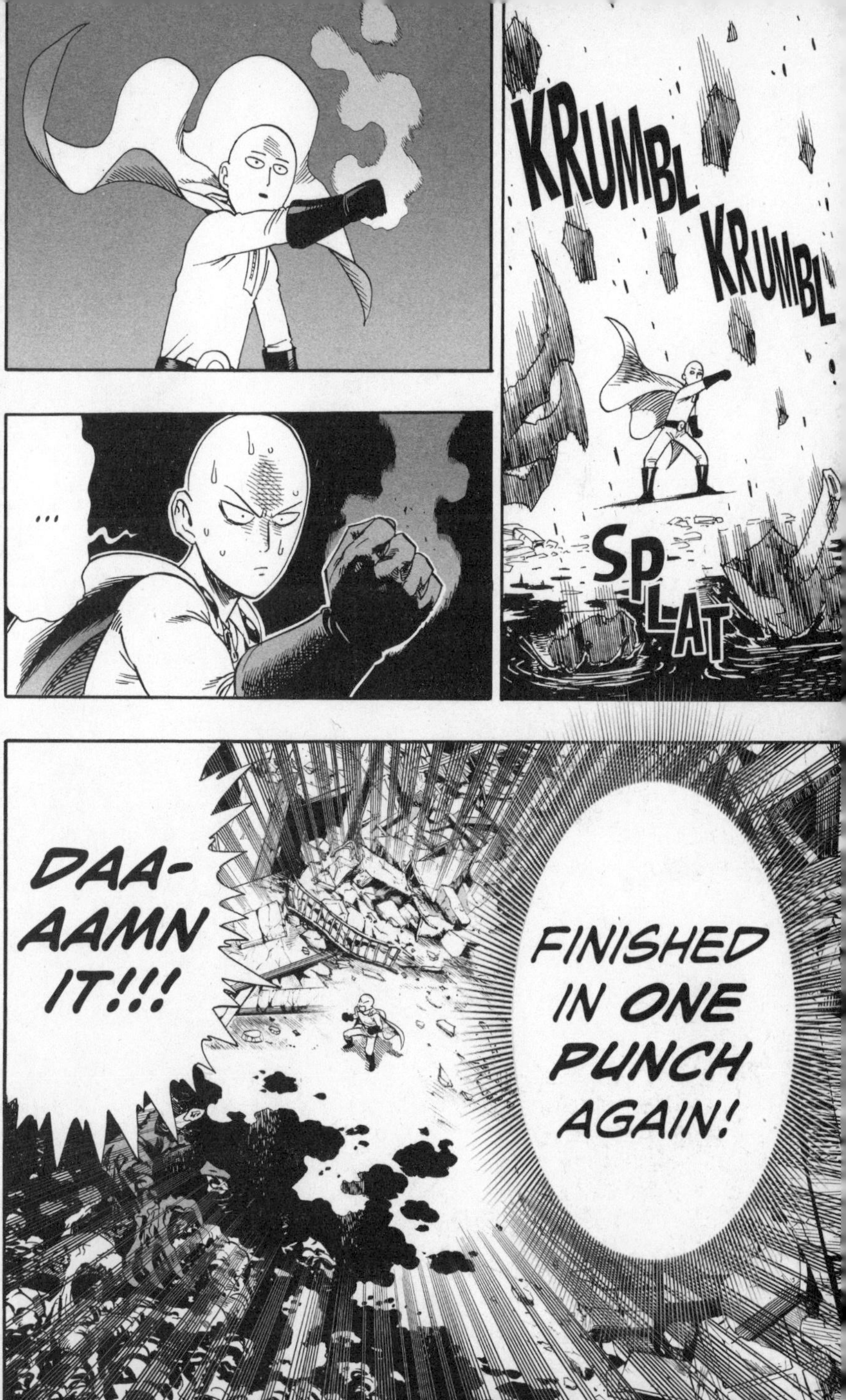
KRUMBL
KRUMBL
SPLAT
...
FINISHED IN ONE PUNCH AGAIN!
DAA-AAMN IT!!!

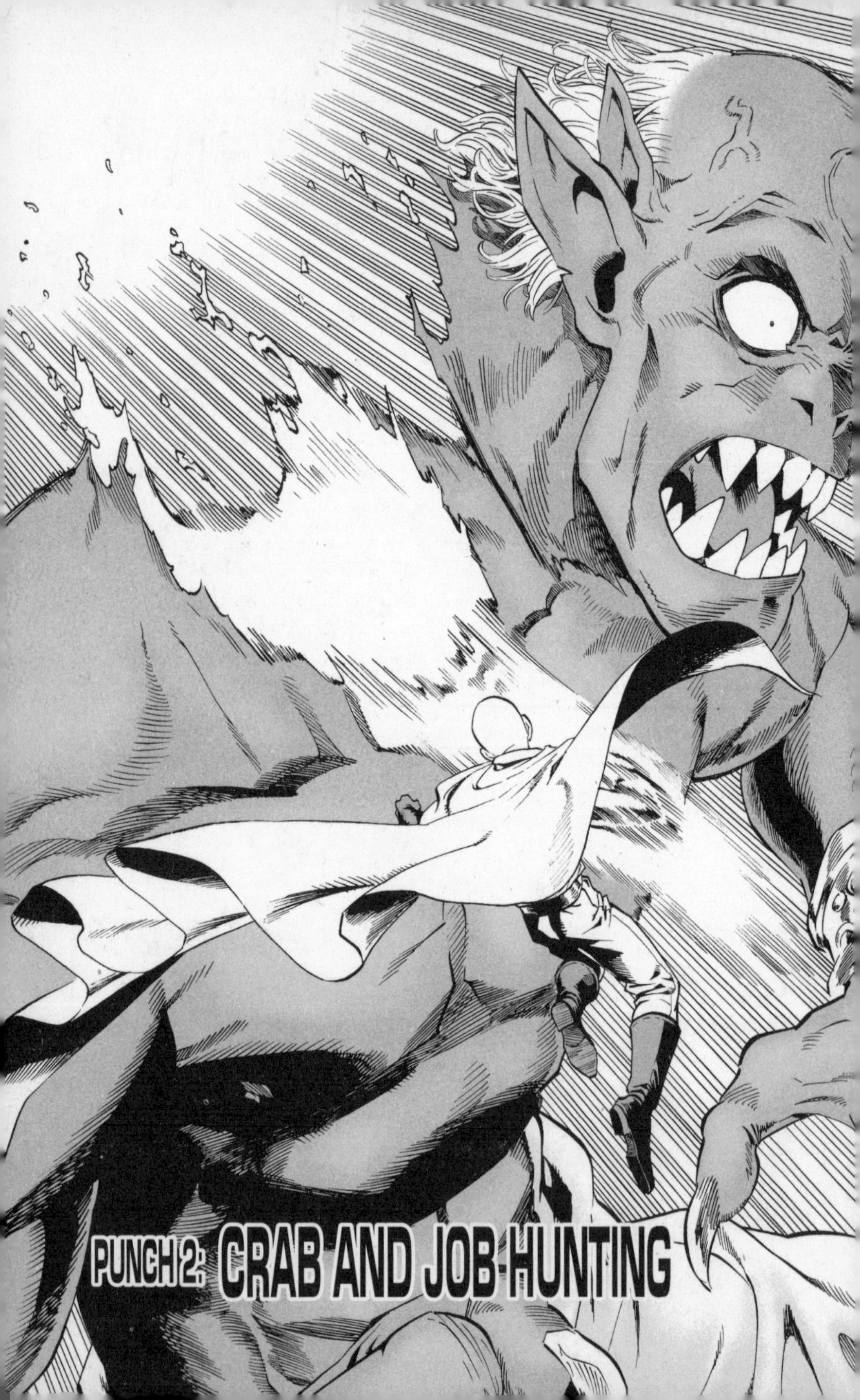
PUNCH 2: CRAB AND JOB HUNTING

THREE YEARS EARLIER

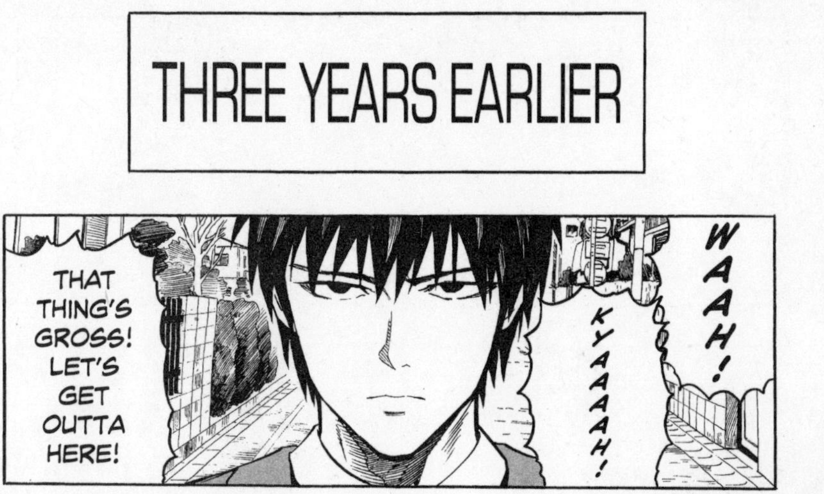

WAAAH!
KYAAAAAH!
THAT THING'S GROSS! LET'S GET OUTTA HERE!

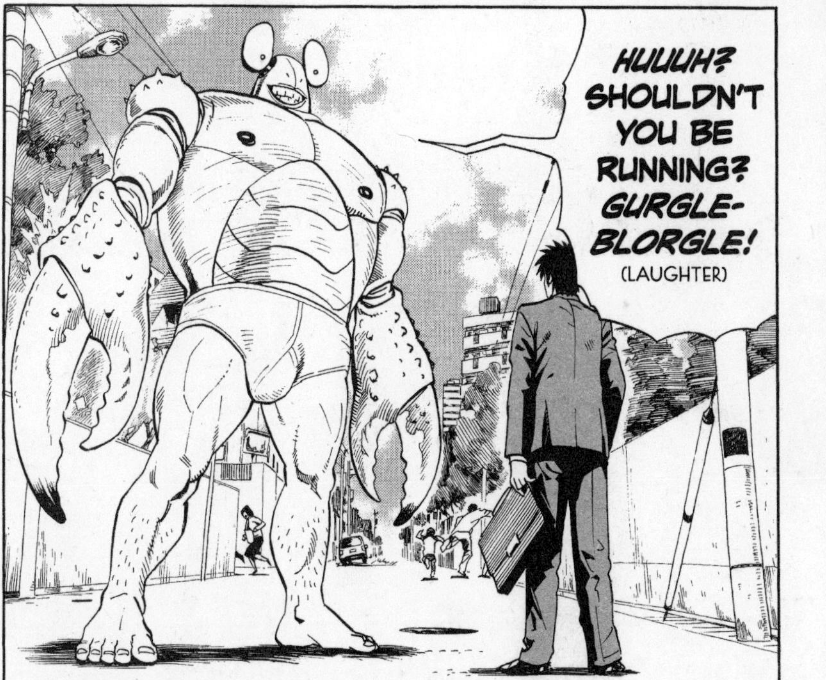

HUUUH? SHOULDN'T YOU BE RUNNING? GURGLE-BLORGLE!
(LAUGHTER)

READ THIS WAY

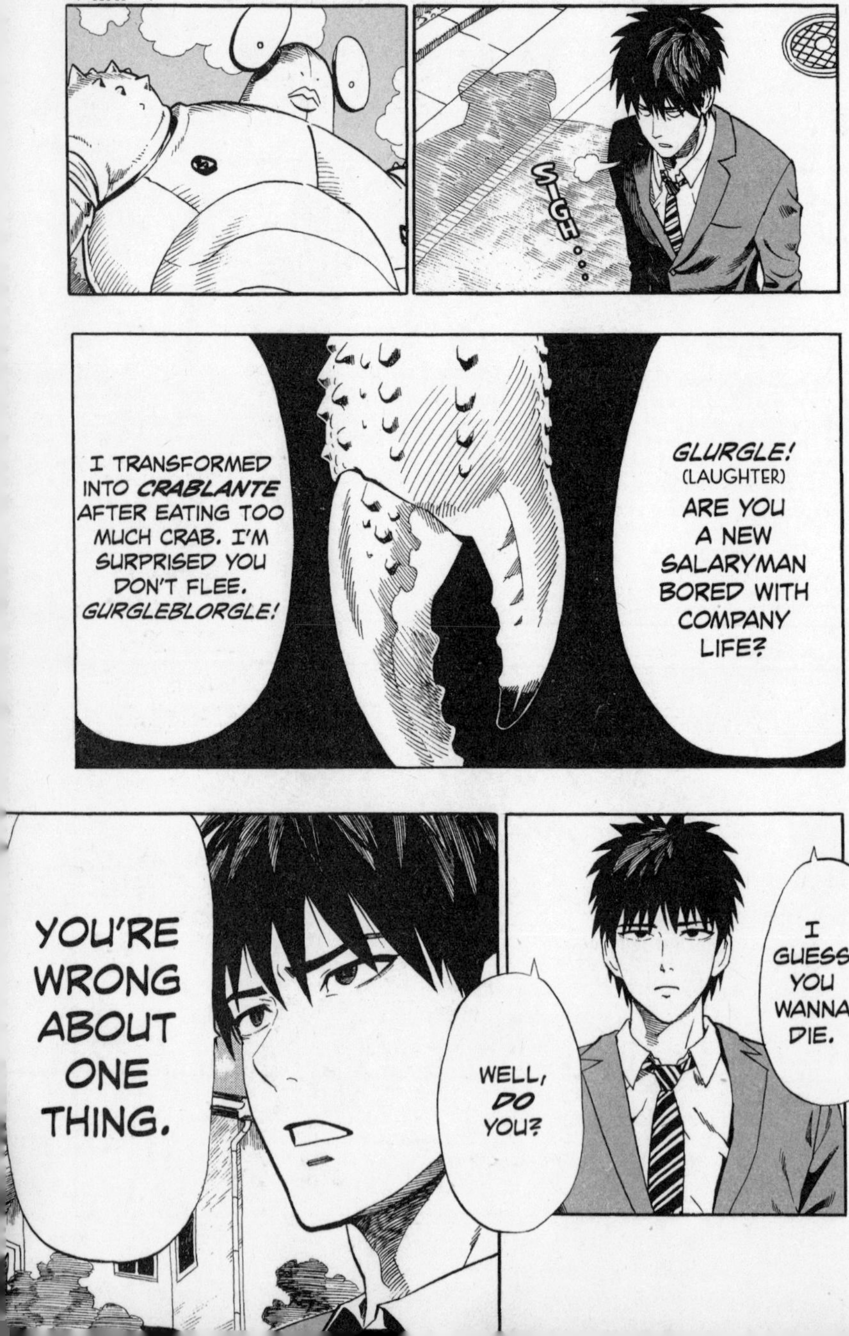
SIGH...
GLURGLE! (LAUGHTER) ARE YOU A NEW SALARYMAN BORED WITH COMPANY LIFE?
I TRANSFORMED INTO CRABLANTE AFTER EATING TOO MUCH CRAB. I'M SURPRISED YOU DON'T FLEE. GURGLEBLORGLE!
I GUESS YOU WANNA DIE.
WELL, DO YOU?
YOU'RE WRONG ABOUT ONE THING.

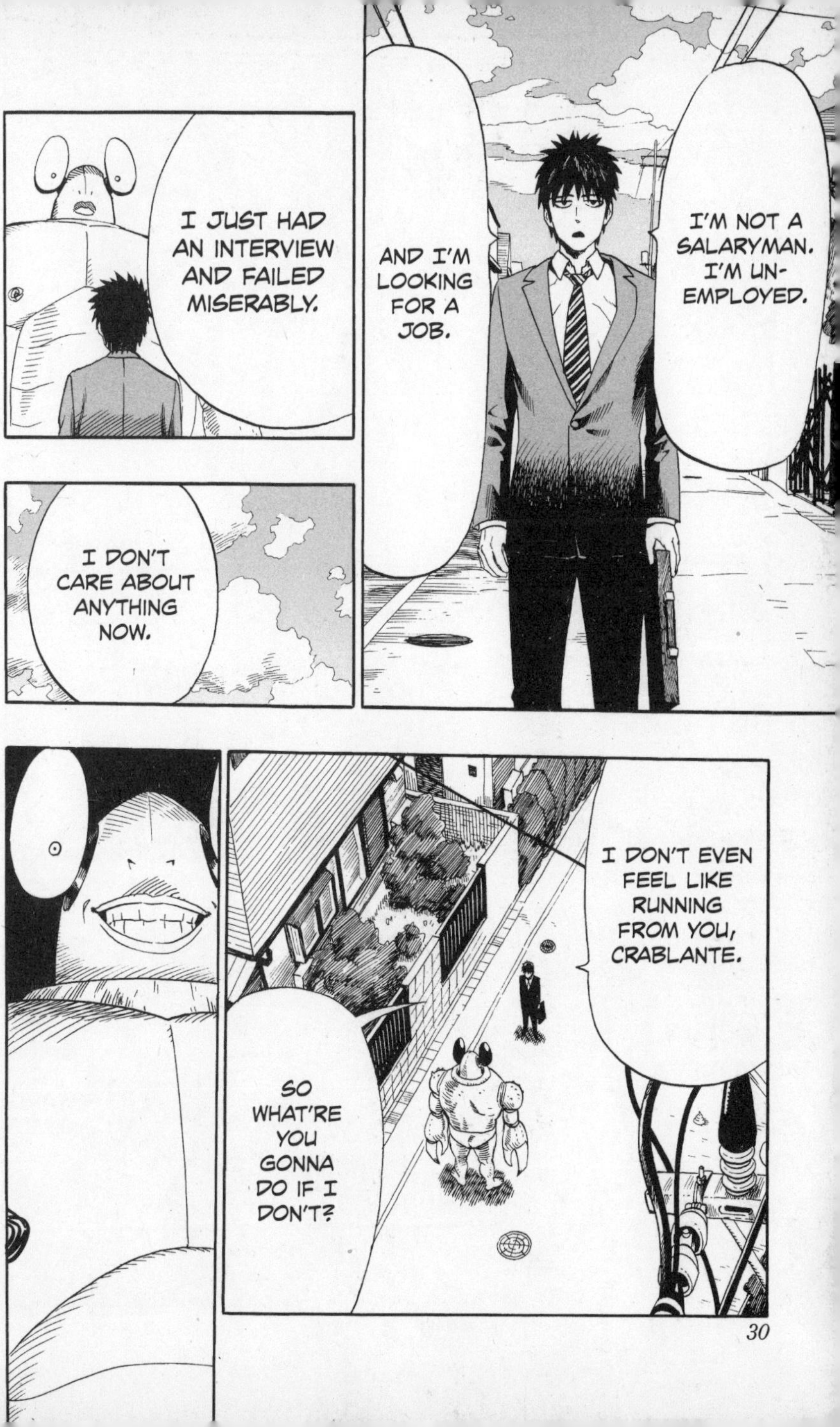
I'M NOT A SALARYMAN. I'M UN-EMPLOYED.
AND I'M LOOKING FOR A JOB.
I JUST HAD AN INTERVIEW AND FAILED MISERABLY.
I DON'T CARE ABOUT ANYTHING NOW.
I DON'T EVEN FEEL LIKE RUNNING FROM YOU, CRABLANTE.
SO WHAT'RE YOU GONNA DO IF I DON'T?

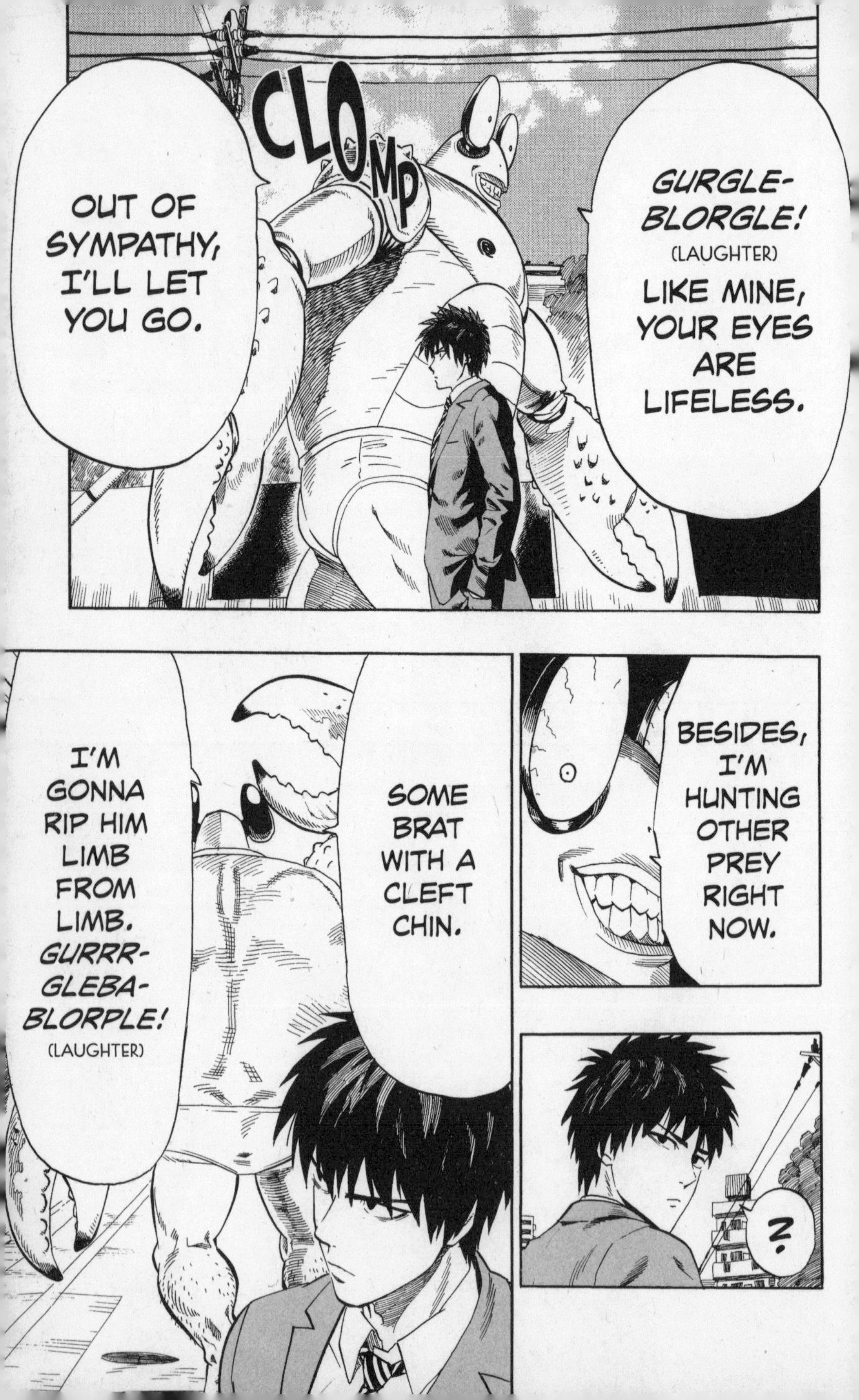
GURGLE-BLORGLE! (LAUGHTER) LIKE MINE, YOUR EYES ARE LIFELESS.
CLOMP
OUT OF SYMPATHY, I'LL LET YOU GO.
BESIDES, I'M HUNTING OTHER PREY RIGHT NOW.
?
SOME BRAT WITH A CLEFT CHIN.
I'M GONNA RIP HIM LIMB FROM LIMB. GURRR-GLEBA-BLORPLE! (LAUGHTER)

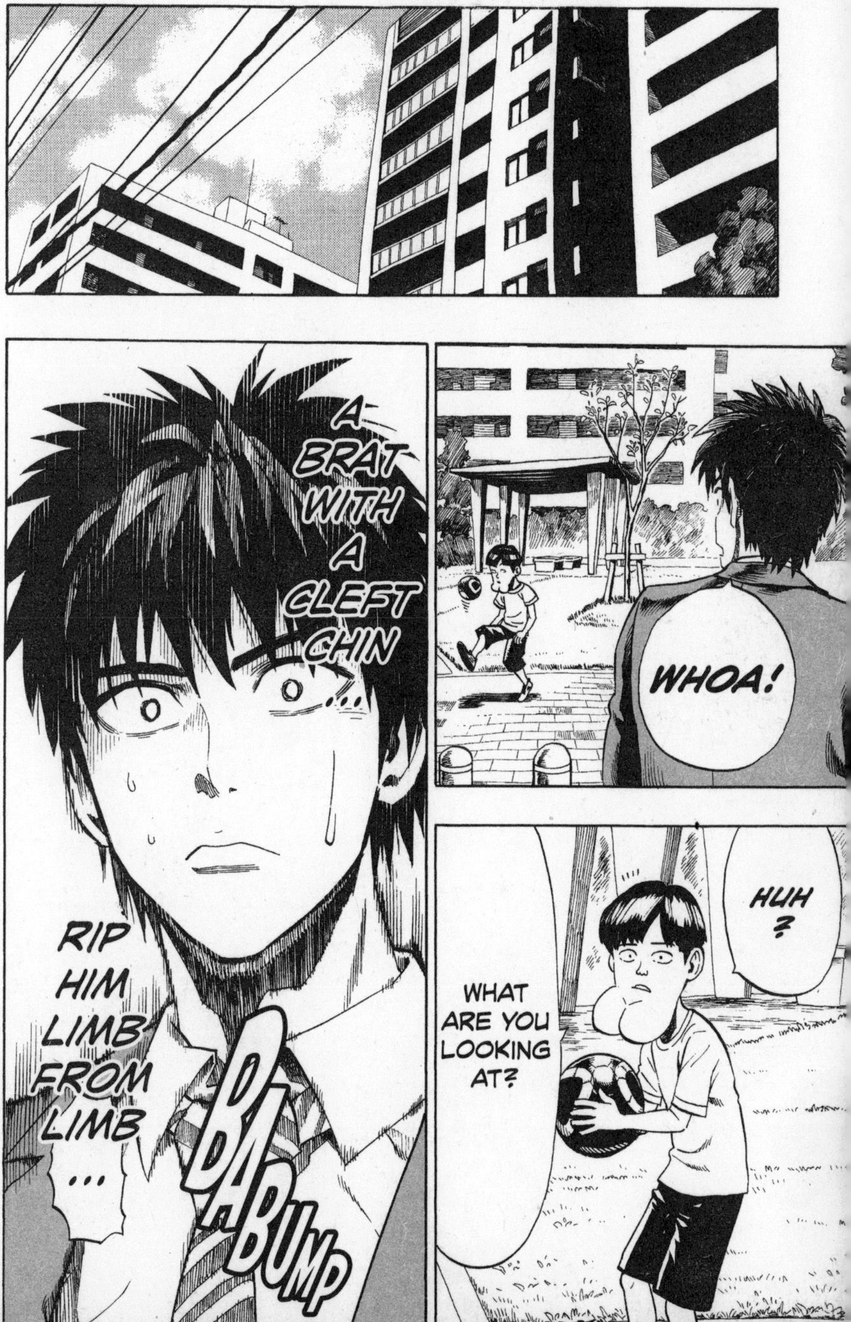
WHOA!
HUH?
WHAT ARE YOU LOOKING AT?
A BRAT WITH A CLEFT CHIN...
RIP HIM LIMB FROM LIMB...
BADABUMP

READ THIS WAY

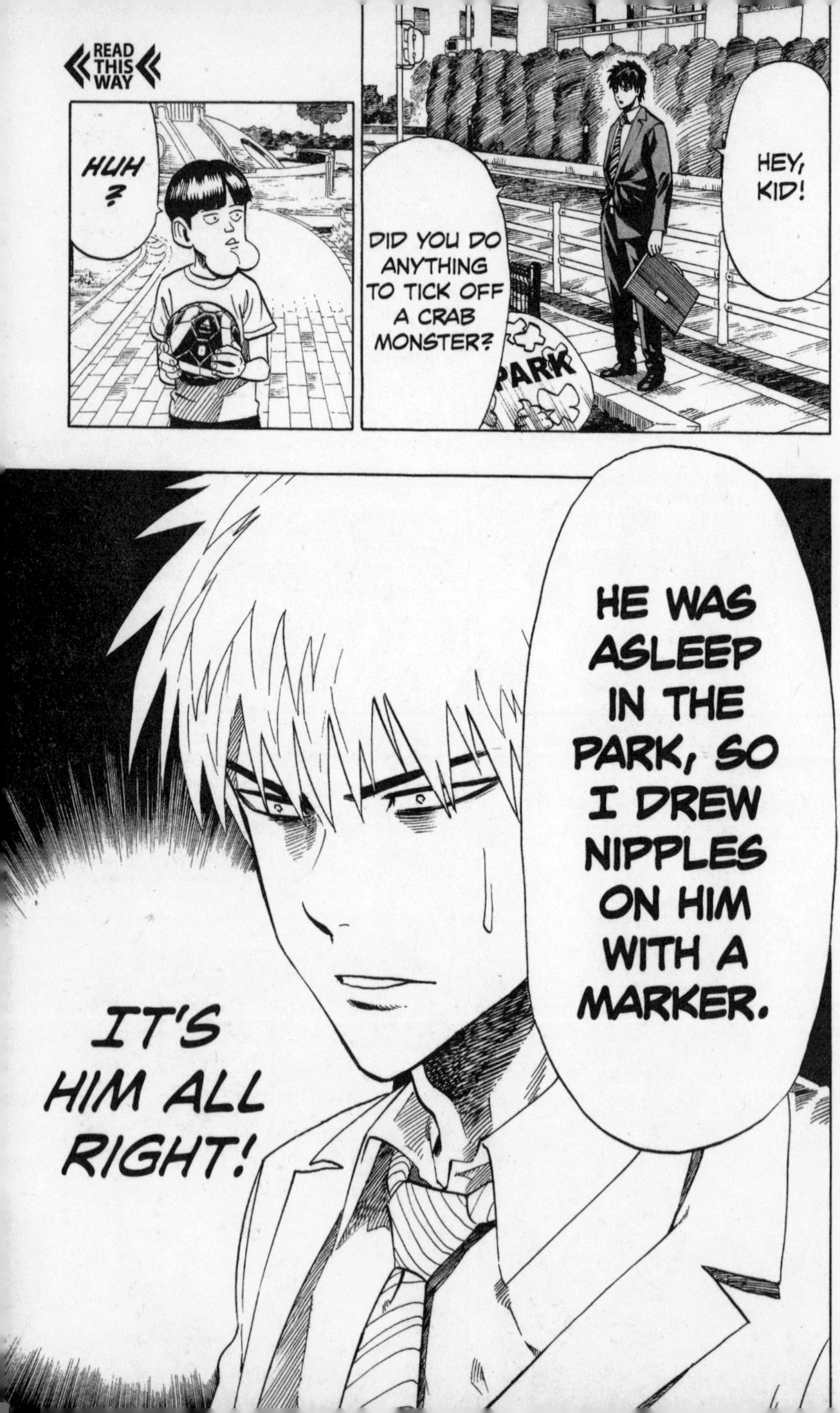
HEY, KID!
DID YOU DO ANYTHING TO TICK OFF A CRAB MONSTER?
PARK
HUH?
HE WAS ASLEEP IN THE PARK, SO I DREW NIPPLES ON HIM WITH A MARKER.
IT'S HIM ALL RIGHT!

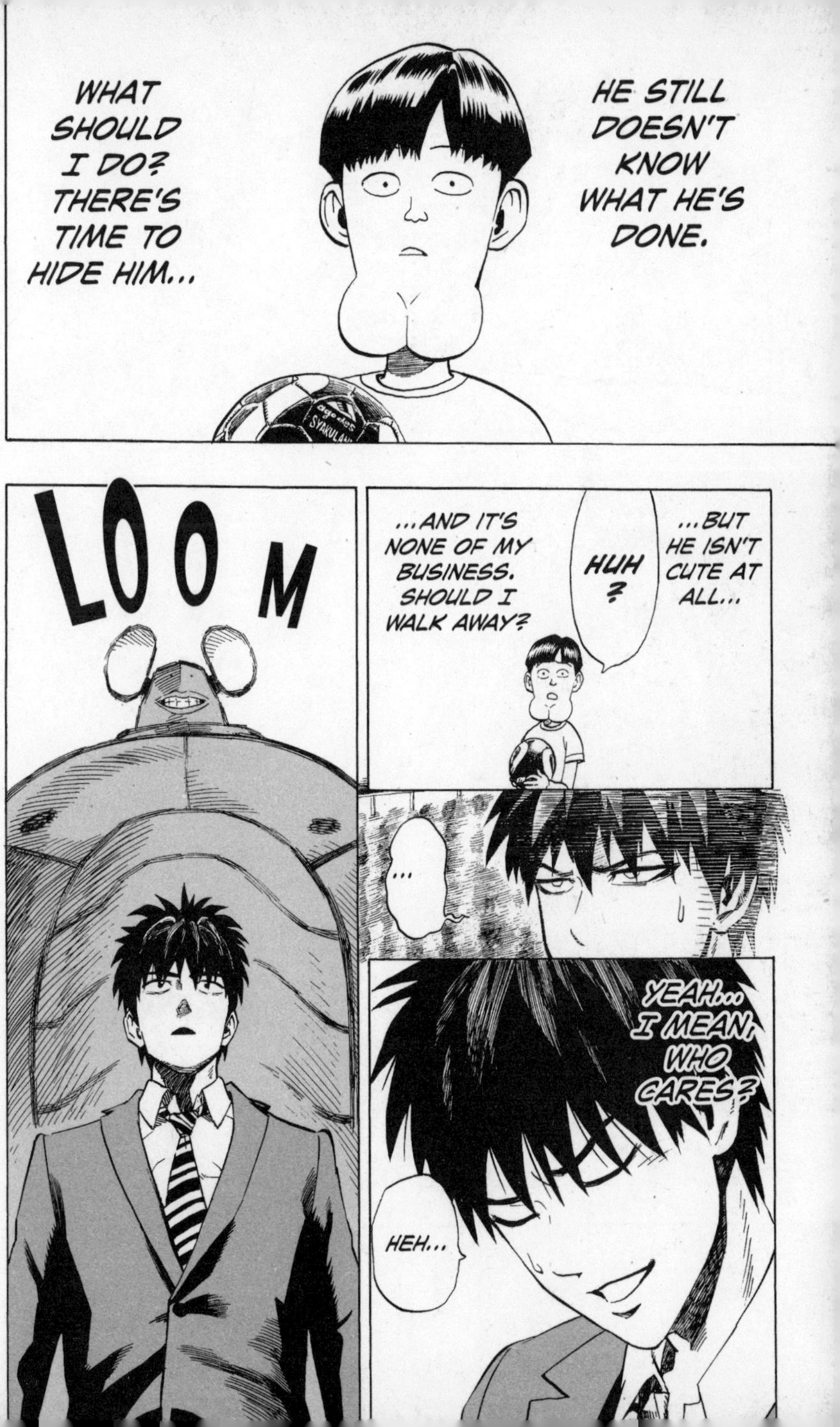
HE STILL DOESN'T KNOW WHAT HE'S DONE.
WHAT SHOULD I DO? THERE'S TIME TO HIDE HIM...
...BUT HE ISN'T CUTE AT ALL...
HUH?
...AND IT'S NONE OF MY BUSINESS. SHOULD I WALK AWAY?
...
YEAH... I MEAN, WHO CARES?
HEH...
LOOM

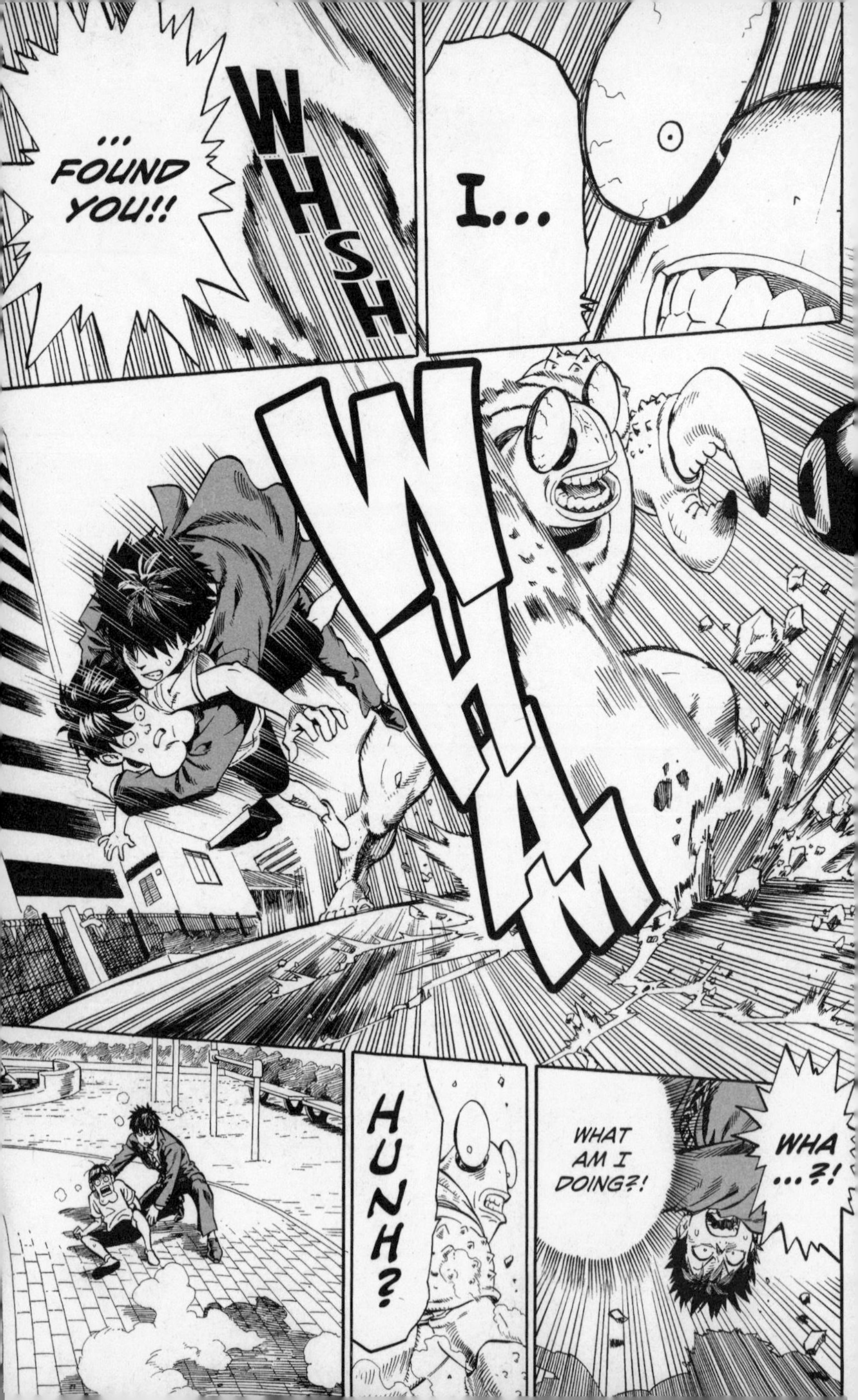
I...
WHSH
... FOUND YOU!!
WHAM
WHA ...?!
WHAT AM I DOING?!
HUNH?

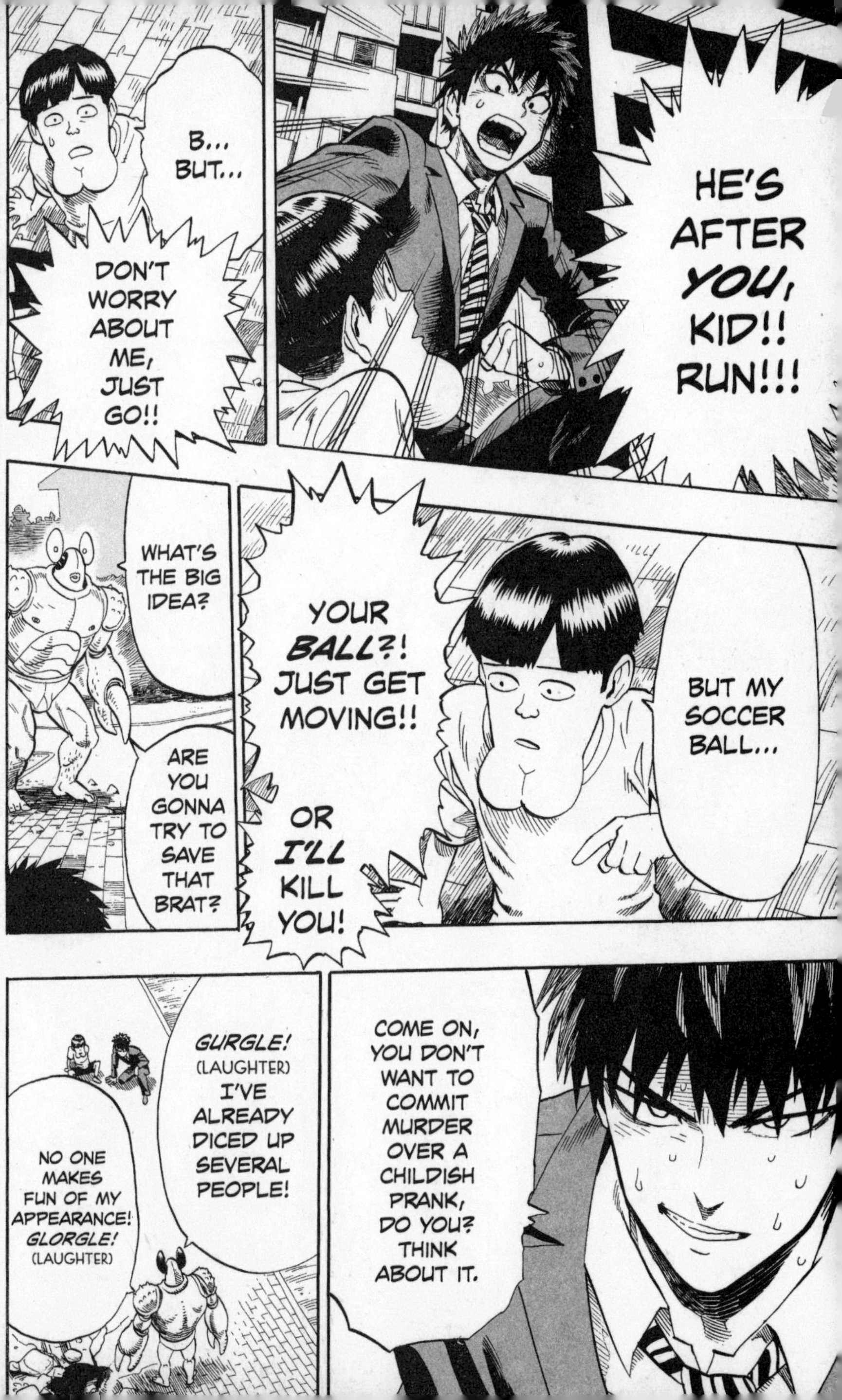
HE'S AFTER YOU, KID!! RUN!!!
B... BUT...
DON'T WORRY ABOUT ME, JUST GO!!
BUT MY SOCCER BALL...
YOUR BALL?! JUST GET MOVING!!
OR I'LL KILL YOU!
WHAT'S THE BIG IDEA?
ARE YOU GONNA TRY TO SAVE THAT BRAT?
COME ON, YOU DON'T WANT TO COMMIT MURDER OVER A CHILDISH PRANK, DO YOU? THINK ABOUT IT.
GURGLE! (LAUGHTER) I'VE ALREADY DICED UP SEVERAL PEOPLE!
NO ONE MAKES FUN OF MY APPEARANCE! GLORGLE! (LAUGHTER)

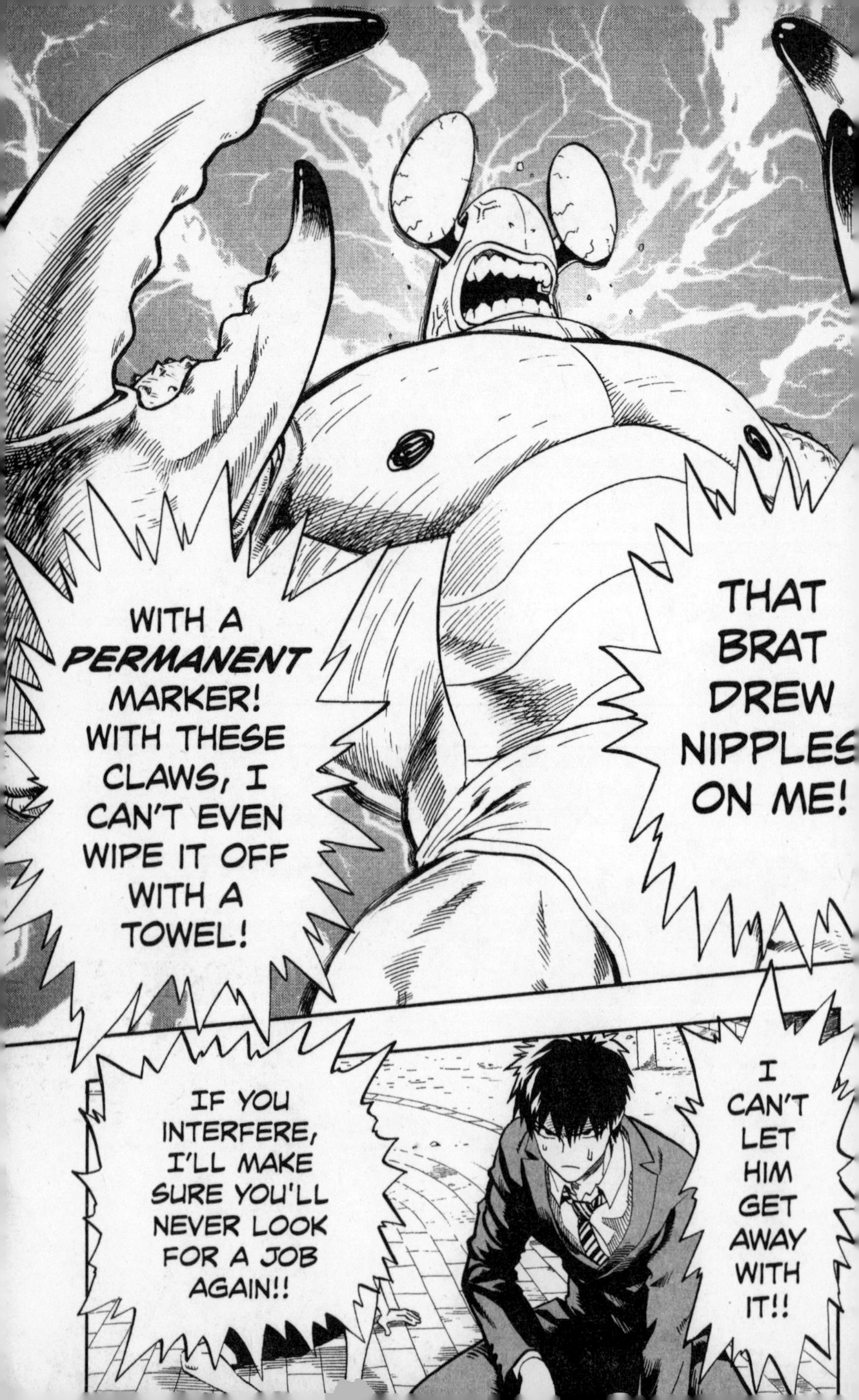
THAT BRAT DREW NIPPLES ON ME!
WITH A *PERMANENT* MARKER! WITH THESE CLAWS, I CAN'T EVEN WIPE IT OFF WITH A TOWEL!
I CAN'T LET HIM GET AWAY WITH IT!!
IF YOU INTERFERE, I'LL MAKE SURE YOU'LL NEVER LOOK FOR A JOB AGAIN!!

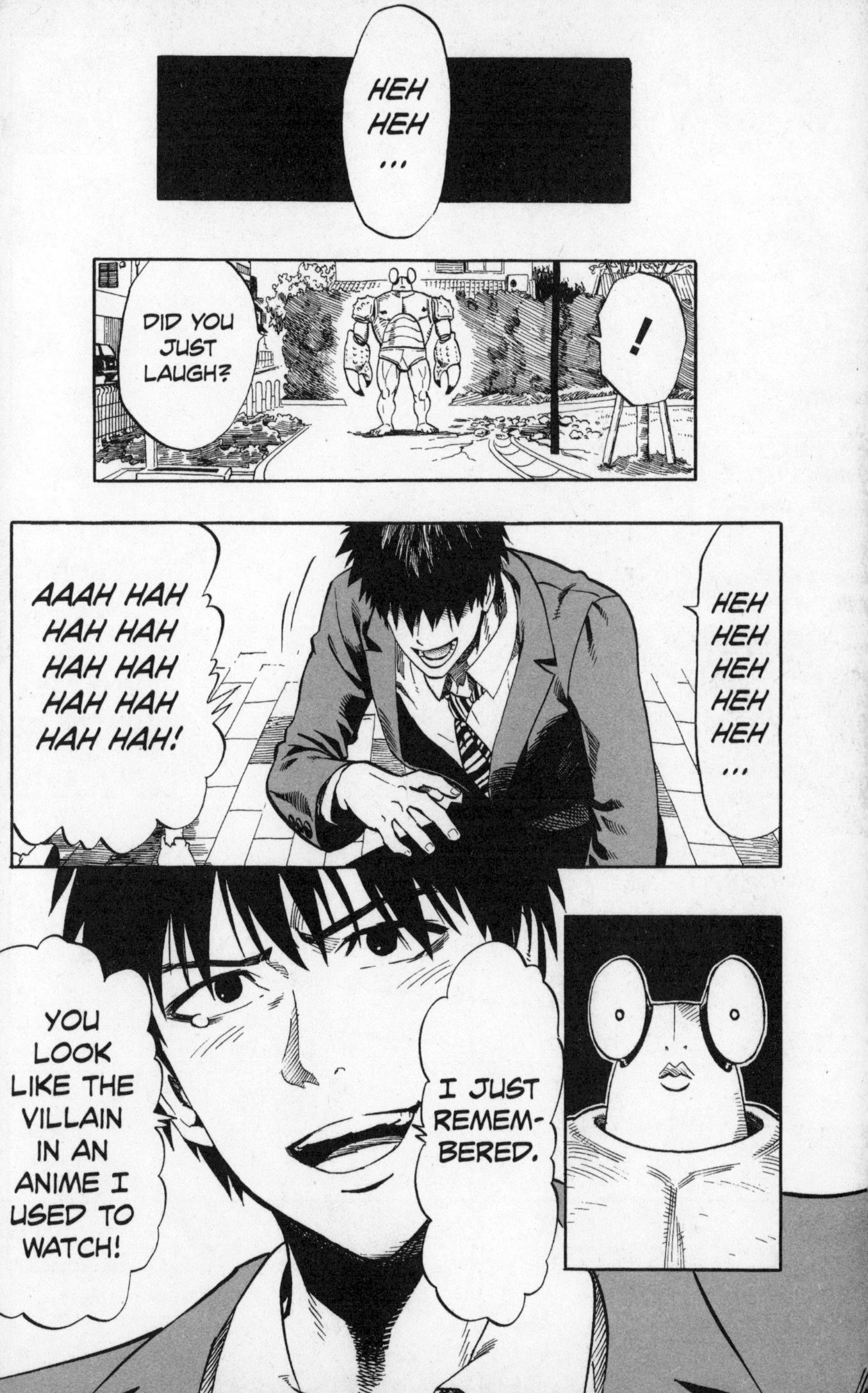
HEH HEH ...
!
DID YOU JUST LAUGH?
HEH HEH HEH HEH HEH ...
AAAH HAH HAH HAH HAH HAH HAH HAH HAH HAH!
I JUST REMEM-BERED.
YOU LOOK LIKE THE VILLAIN IN AN ANIME I USED TO WATCH!

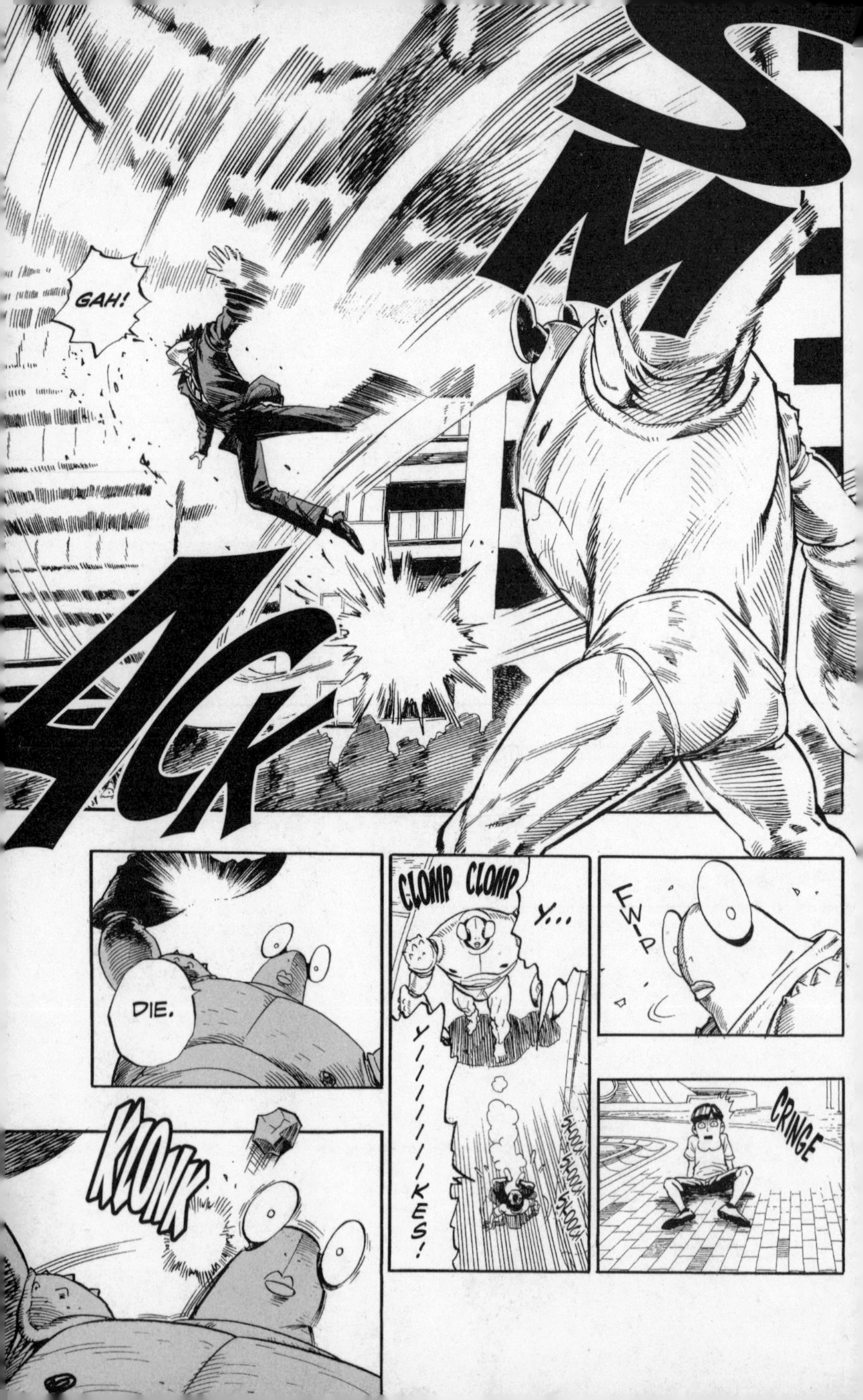
SMACK
GAH!
FWIP
CRINGE
CLOMP CLOMP
Y...
Y//////KES!
DIE.
KLONK

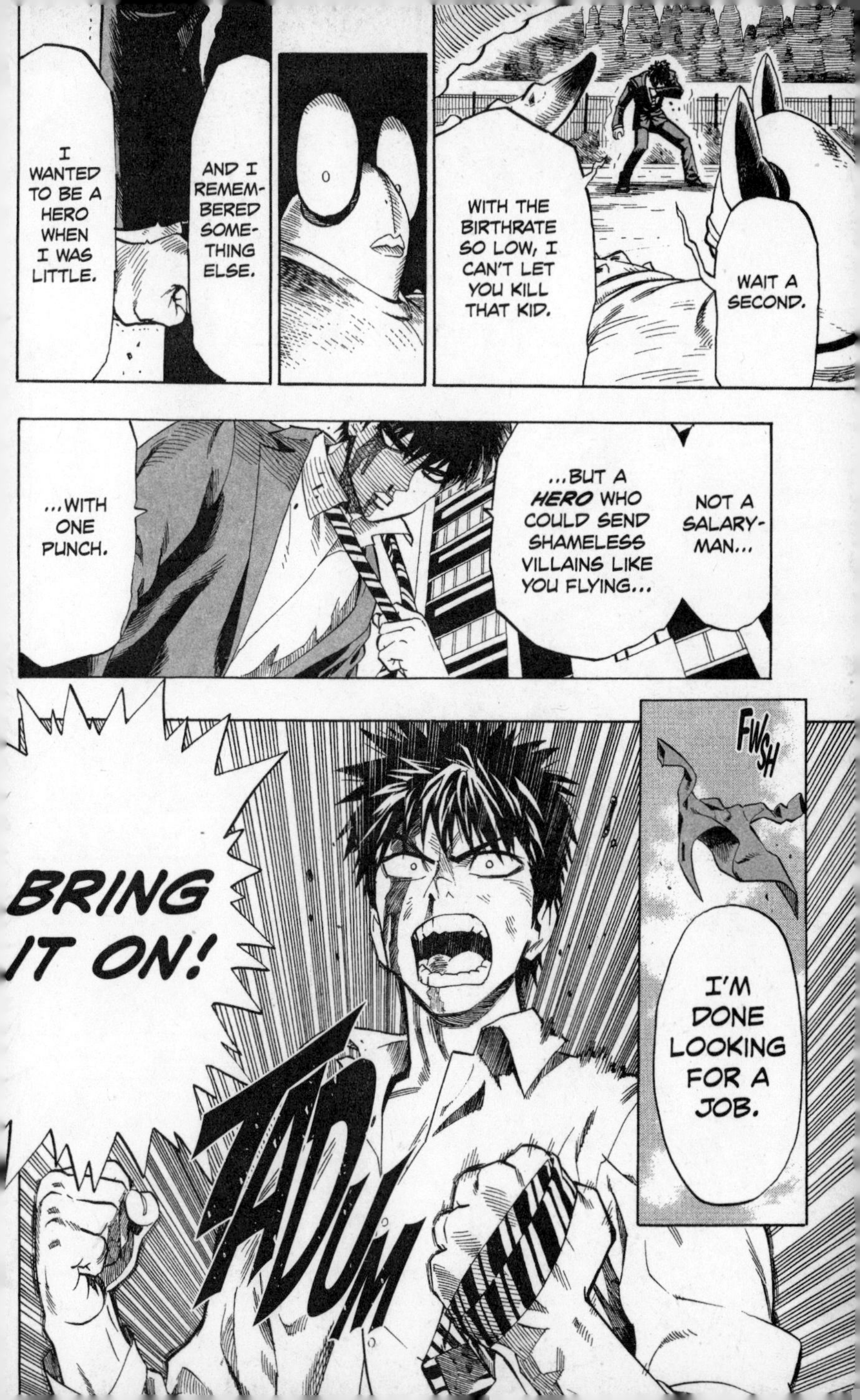
WAIT A SECOND.
WITH THE BIRTHRATE SO LOW, I CAN'T LET YOU KILL THAT KID.
AND I REMEMBERED SOMETHING ELSE.
I WANTED TO BE A HERO WHEN I WAS LITTLE.
NOT A SALARYMAN...
...BUT A *HERO* WHO COULD SEND SHAMELESS VILLAINS LIKE YOU FLYING...
...WITH ONE PUNCH.
FWSH
I'M DONE LOOKING FOR A JOB.
BRING IT ON!
TADOM

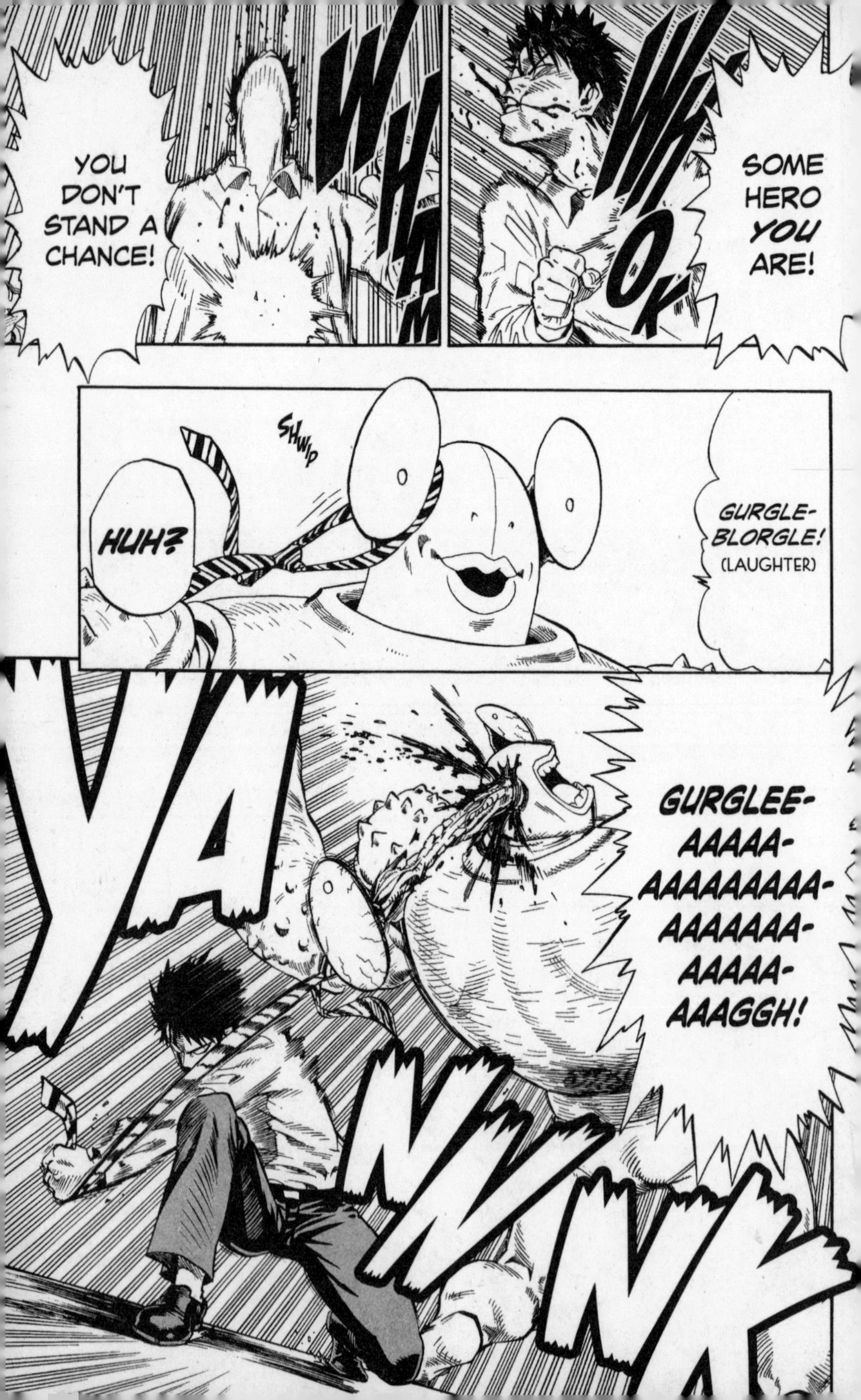
SOME HERO YOU ARE!
WHOK
WHAM
YOU DON'T STAND A CHANCE!
GURGLE-BLORGLE! (LAUGHTER)
SHWIP
HUH?
GURGLEE-AAAAA-AAAAAAAAA-AAAAAAA-AAAAA-AAAGGH!

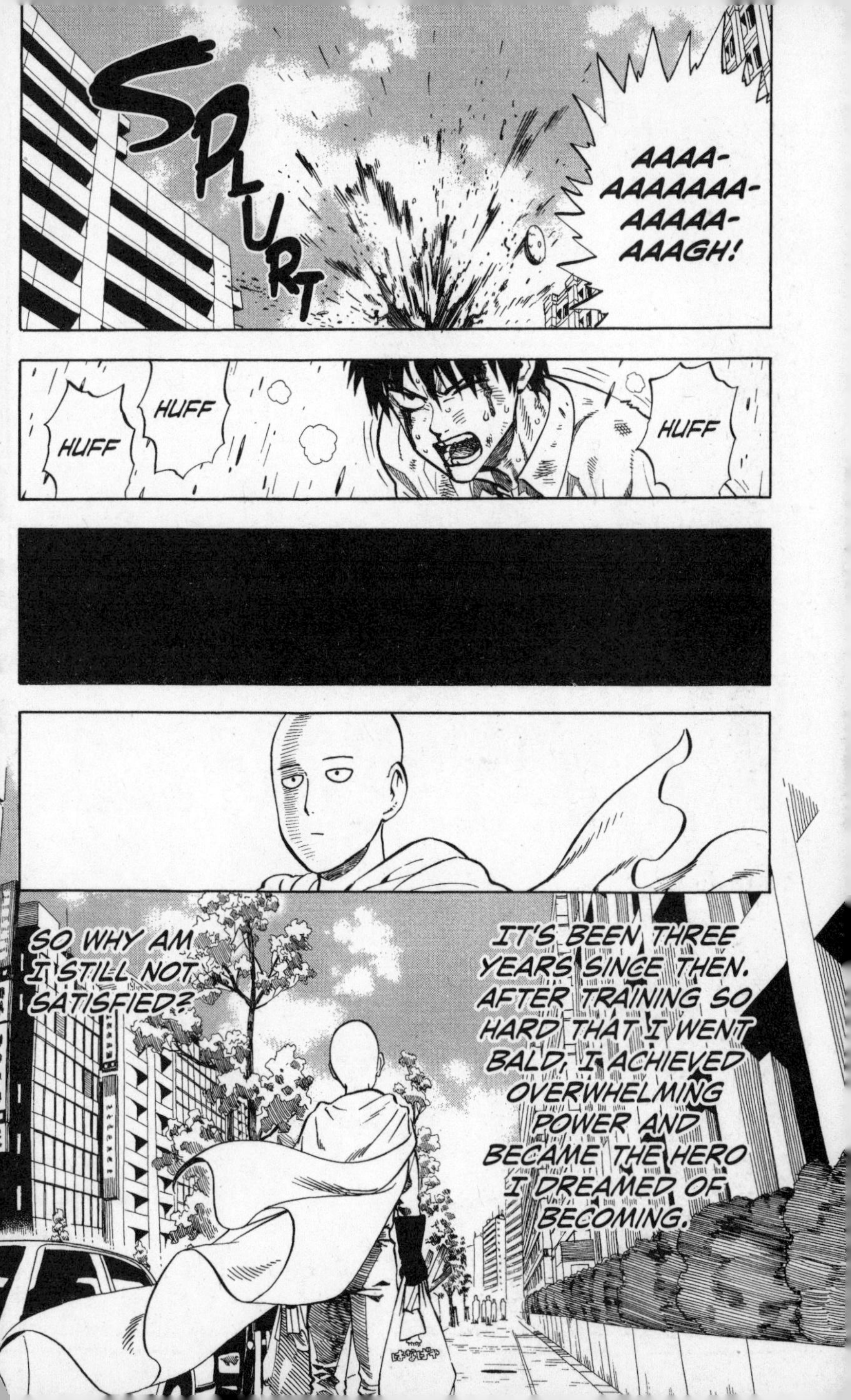
AAAA-
AAAAAAA-
AAAAA-
AAAGH!
SPLURT
HUFF
HUFF
HUFF
IT'S BEEN THREE YEARS SINCE THEN. AFTER TRAINING SO HARD THAT I WENT BALD, I ACHIEVED OVERWHELMING POWER AND BECAME THE HERO I DREAMED OF BECOMING.
SO WHY AM I STILL NOT SATISFIED?

PUNCH 3: WALKING DISASTER

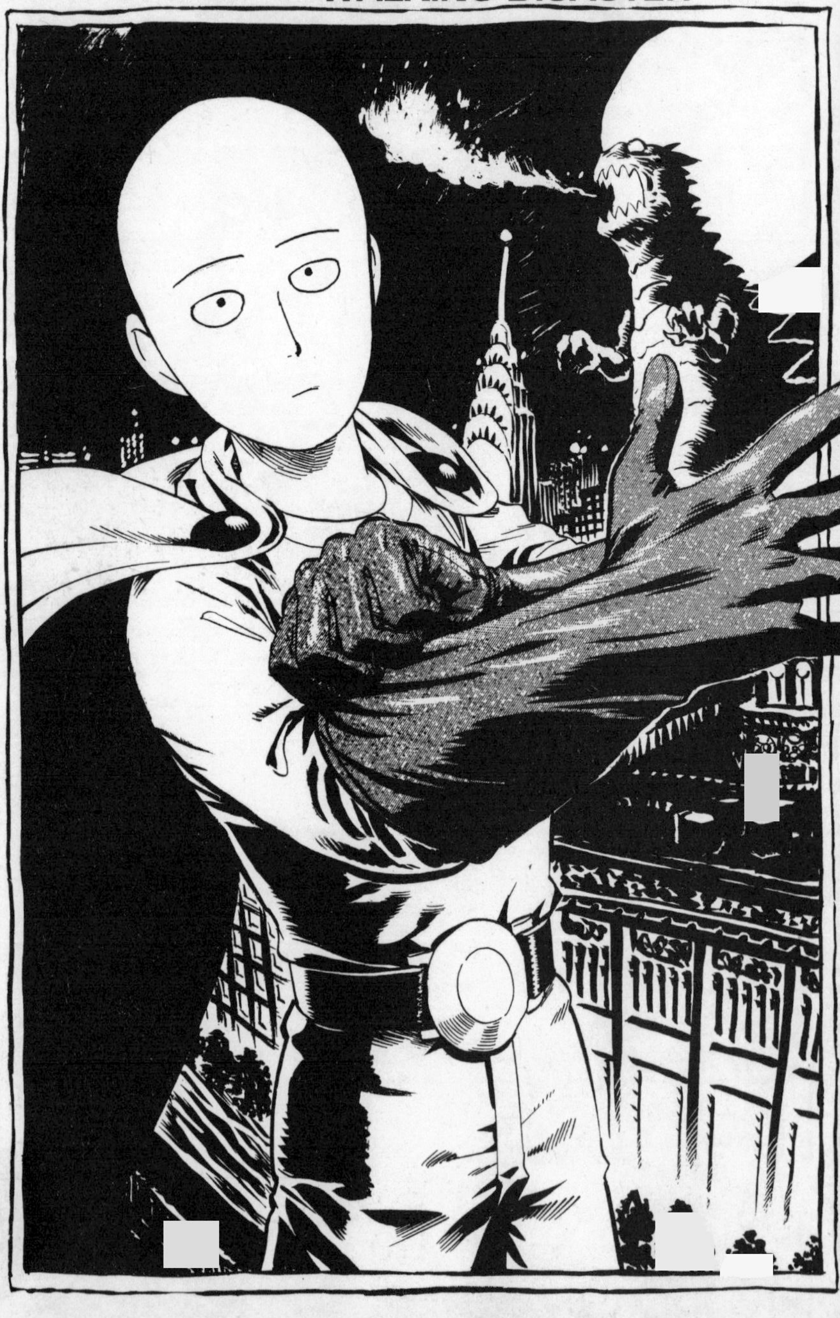

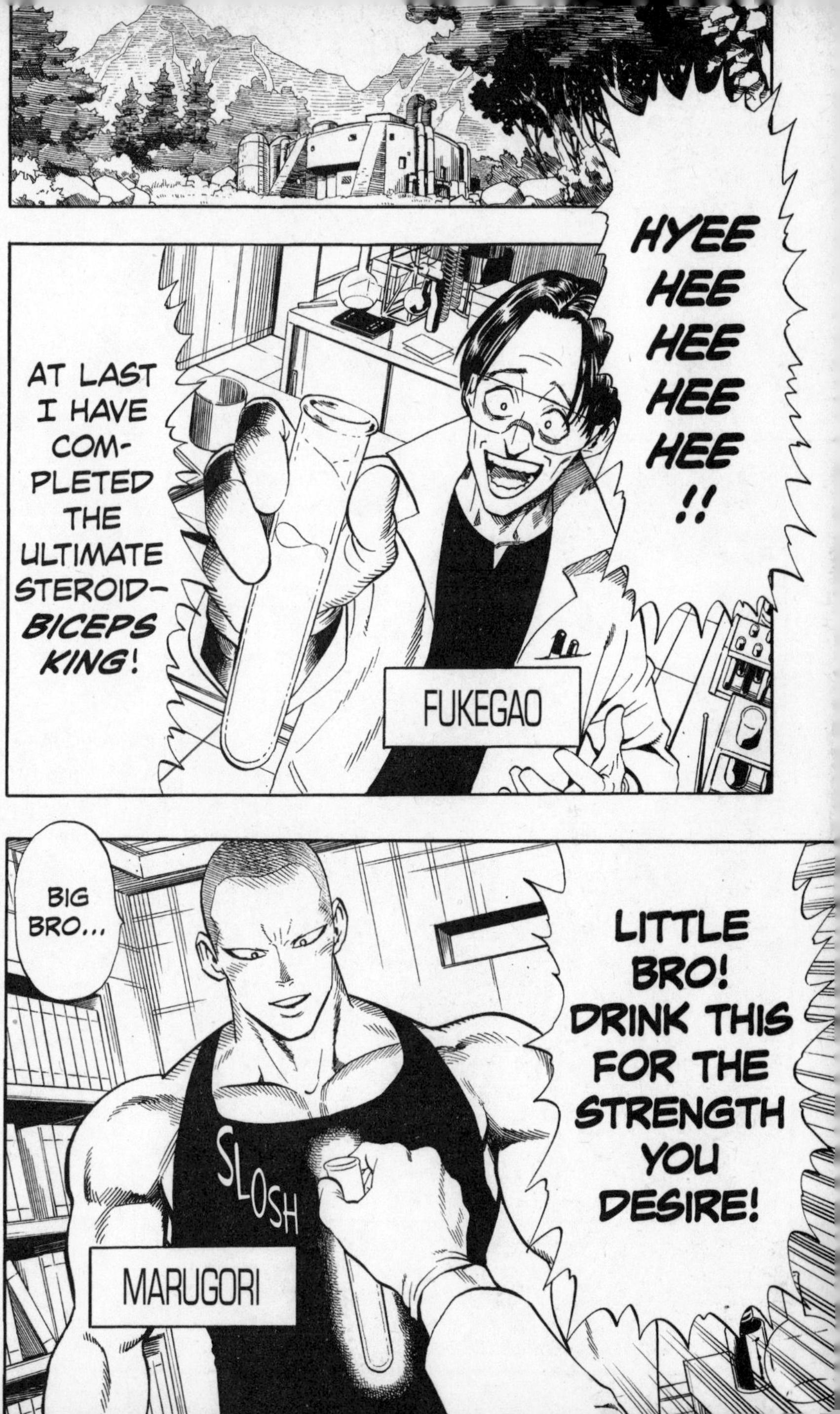
HYEE HEE HEE HEE HEE!!
AT LAST I HAVE COMPLETED THE ULTIMATE STEROID—BICEPS KING!
FUKEGAO
LITTLE BRO! DRINK THIS FOR THE STRENGTH YOU DESIRE!
BIG BRO...
SLOSH
MARUGORI

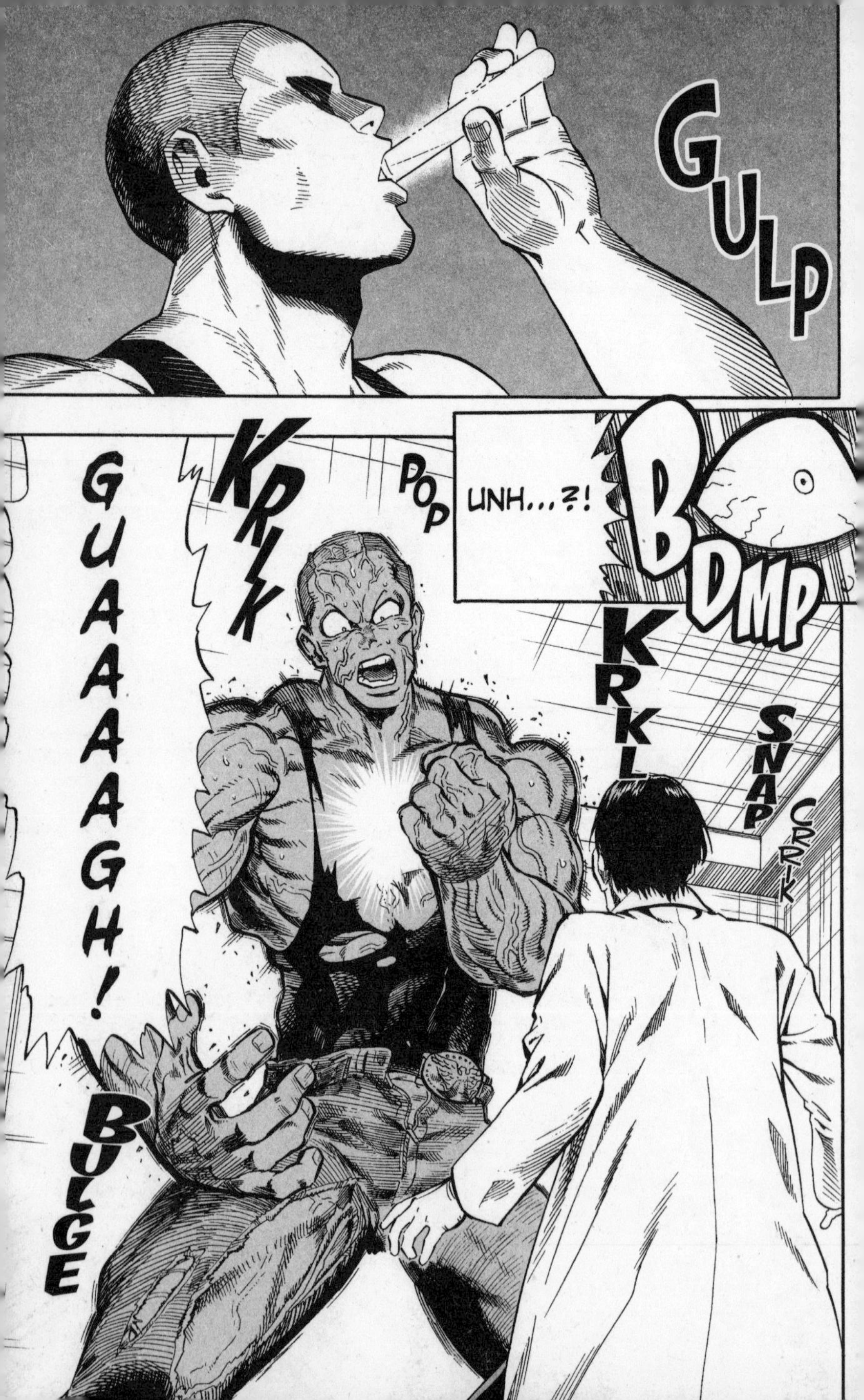
GULP
BDMP
UNH...?!
POP
KRIK
GUAAAAAGH!
KRKL
SNAP
CRRIK
BULGE

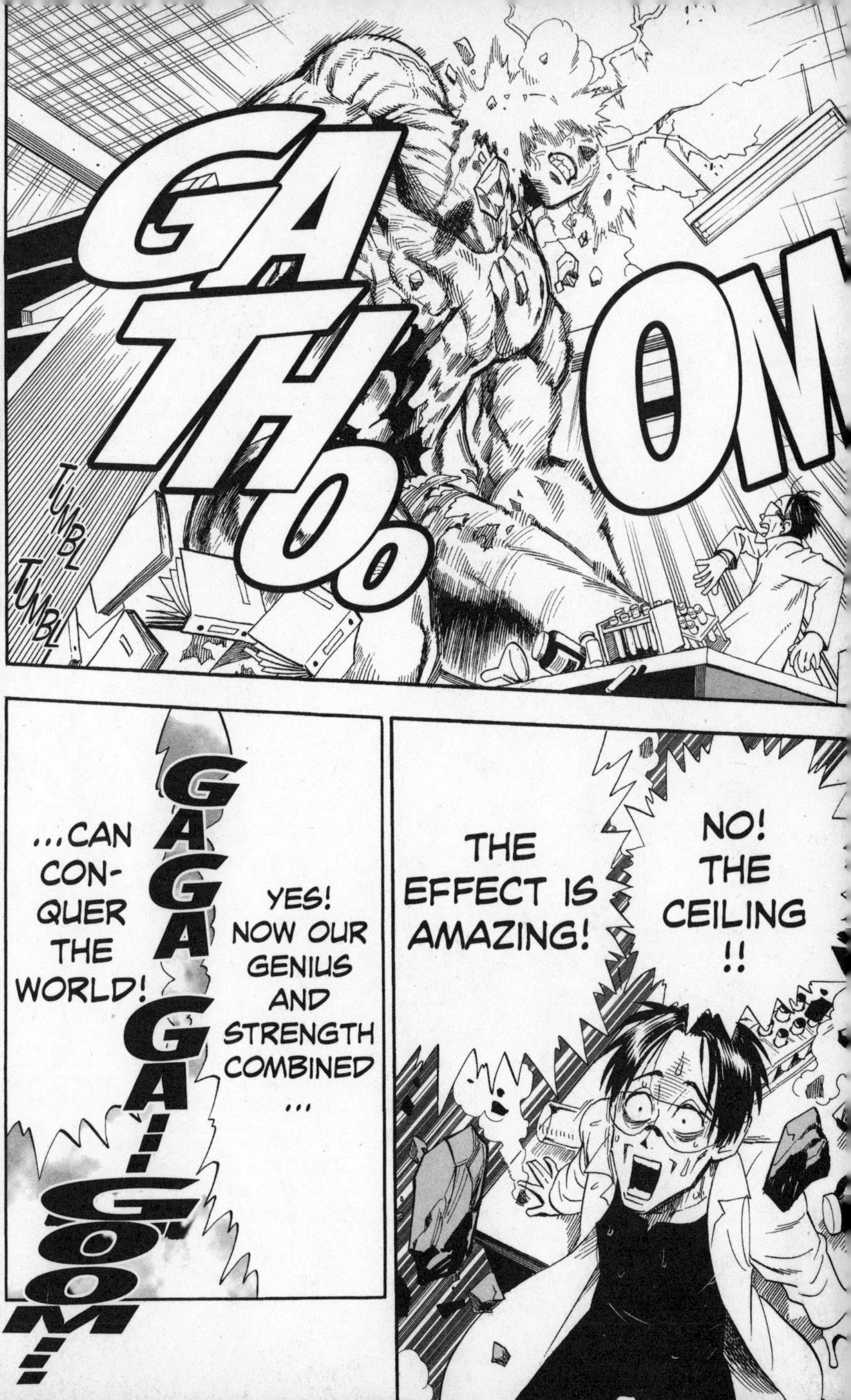
GATHOOOM
TUMBL TUMBL
NO! THE CEILING !!
THE EFFECT IS AMAZING!
YES! NOW OUR GENIUS AND STRENGTH COMBINED ...
...CAN CONQUER THE WORLD!
GAGAGA GOOM!!

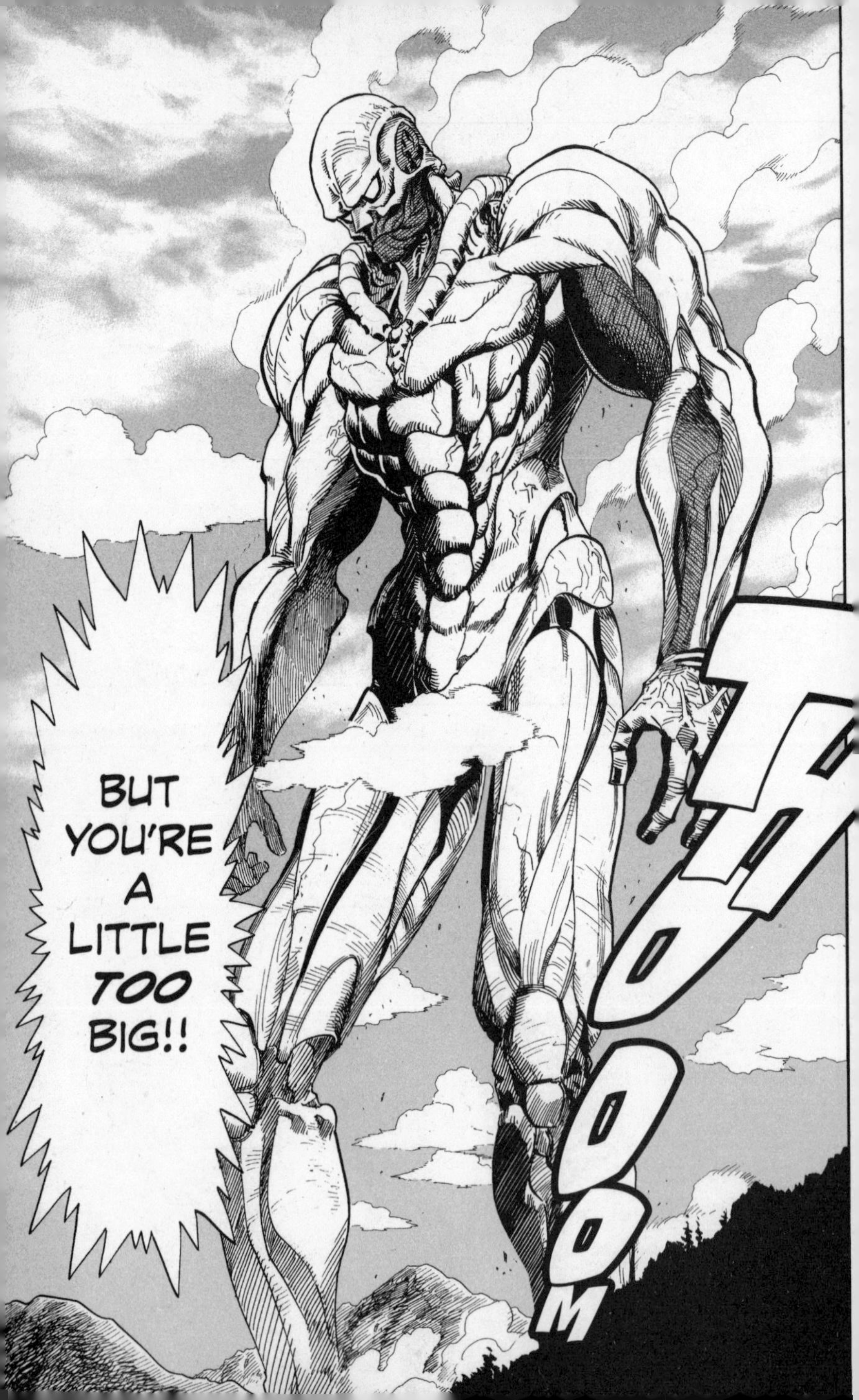
BUT YOU'RE A LITTLE *TOO* BIG!!

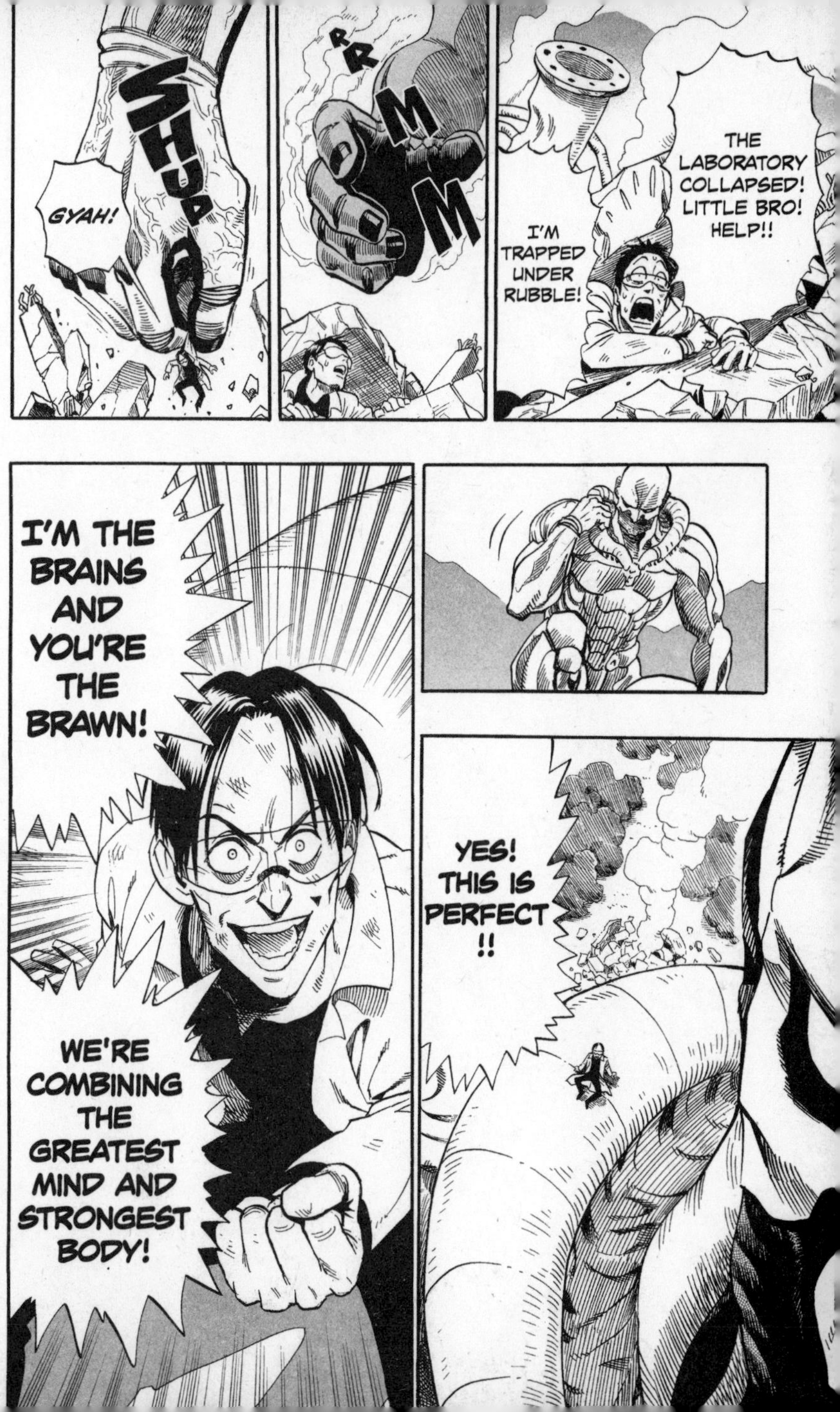
THE LABORATORY COLLAPSED! LITTLE BRO! HELP!!
I'M TRAPPED UNDER RUBBLE!
RRMM
SHUD
GYAH!
YES! THIS IS PERFECT!!
I'M THE BRAINS AND YOU'RE THE BRAWN!
WE'RE COMBINING THE GREATEST MIND AND STRONGEST BODY!

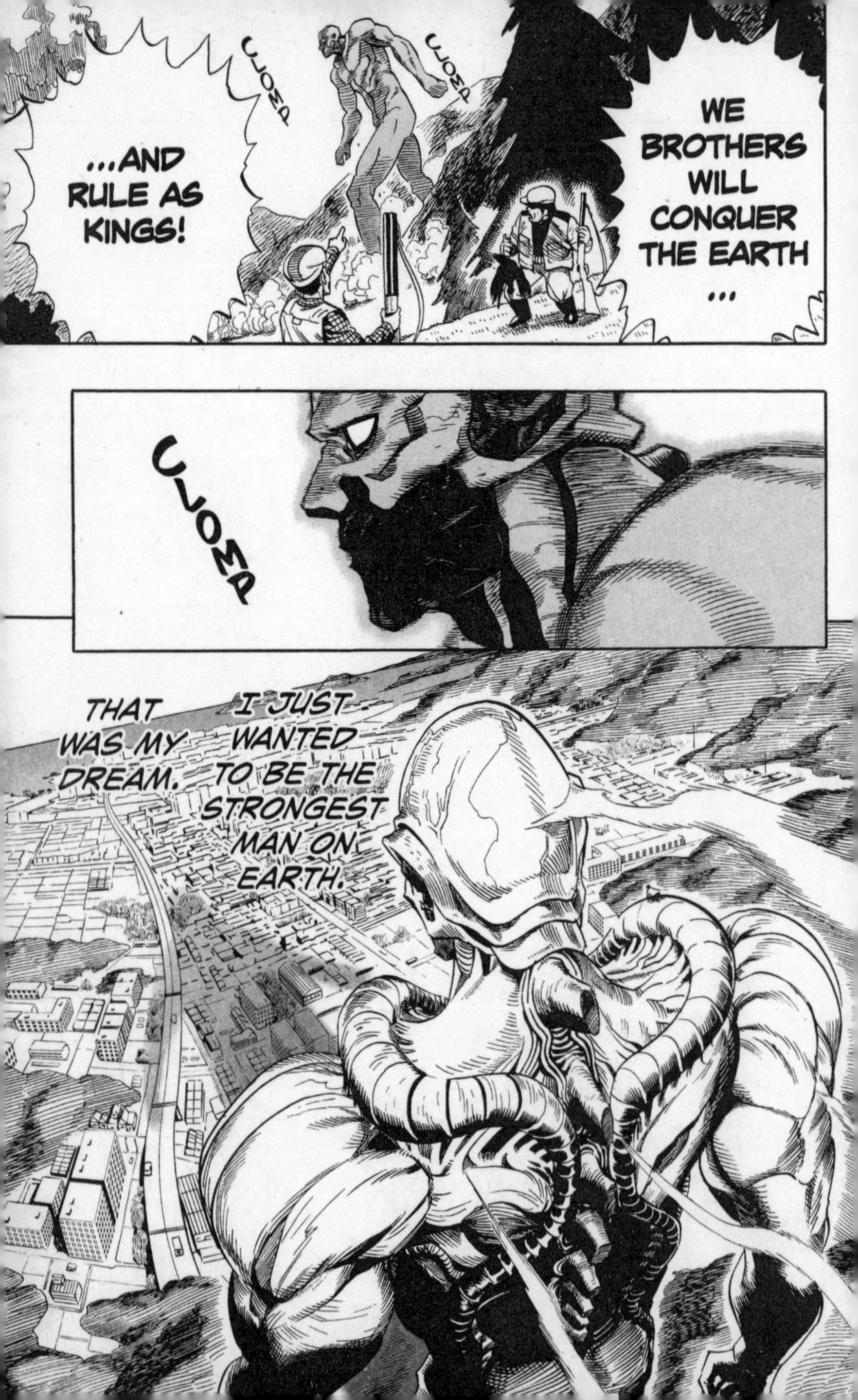
WE BROTHERS WILL CONQUER THE EARTH ...
CLOMP
CLOMP
...AND RULE AS KINGS!
CLOMP
I JUST WANTED TO BE THE STRONGEST MAN ON EARTH.
THAT WAS MY DREAM.

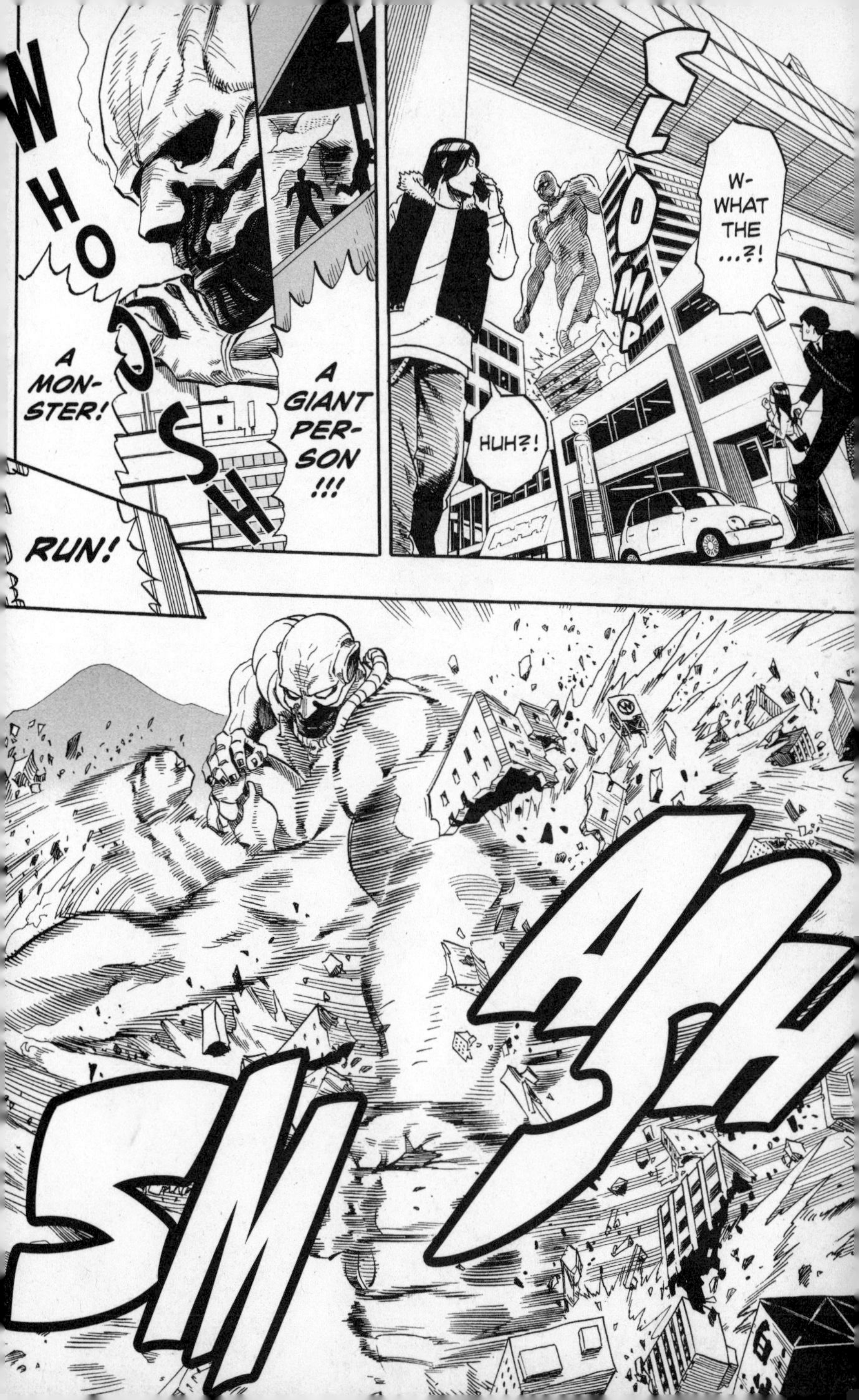
CLOMP
W-WHAT THE ...?!
HUH?!
A GIANT PERSON!!!
WHOOSH
A MONSTER!
RUN!
SMAH

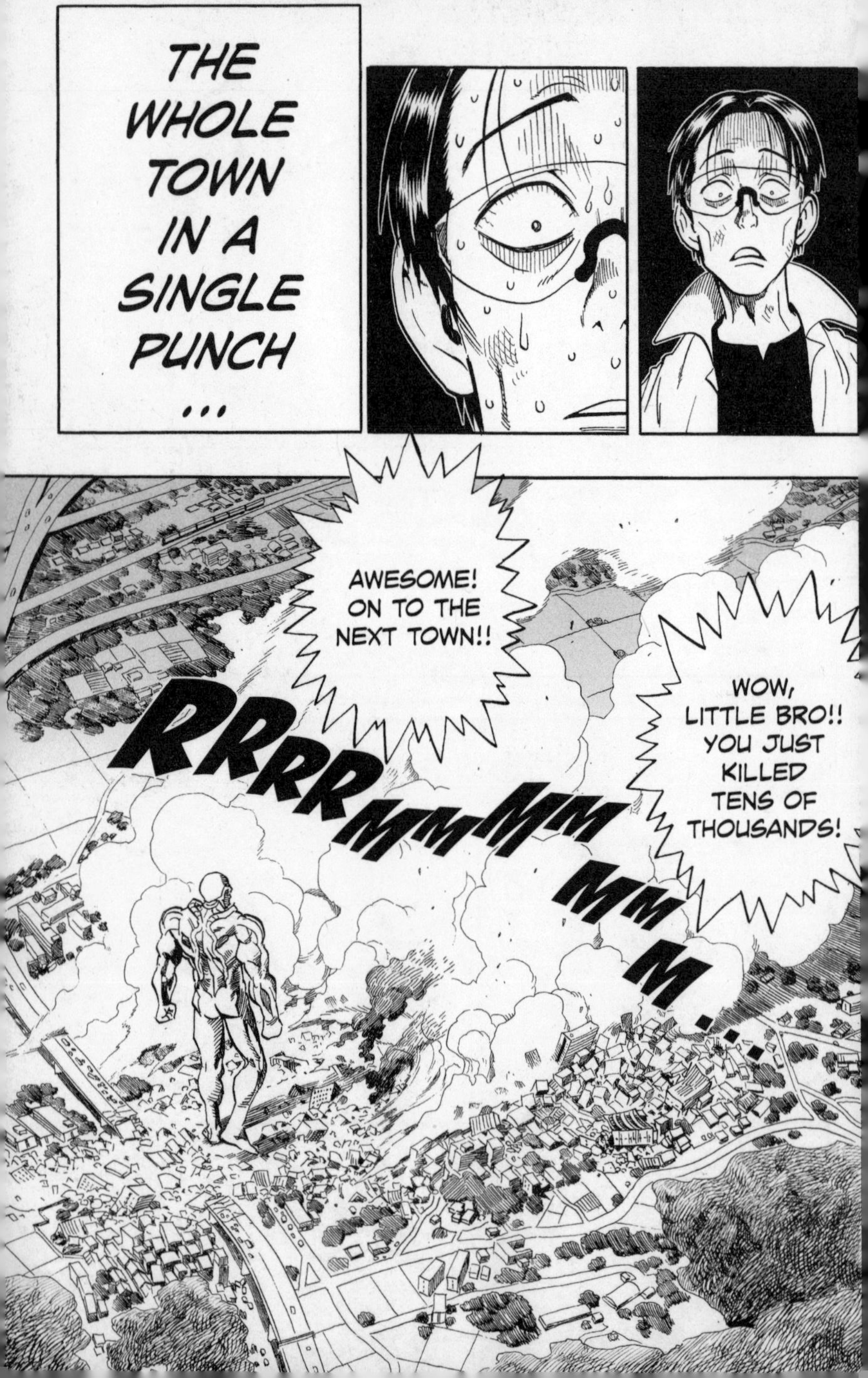
THE WHOLE TOWN IN A SINGLE PUNCH ...
WOW, LITTLE BRO!! YOU JUST KILLED TENS OF THOUSANDS!
AWESOME! ON TO THE NEXT TOWN!!
RRRRMMMMMMMM...

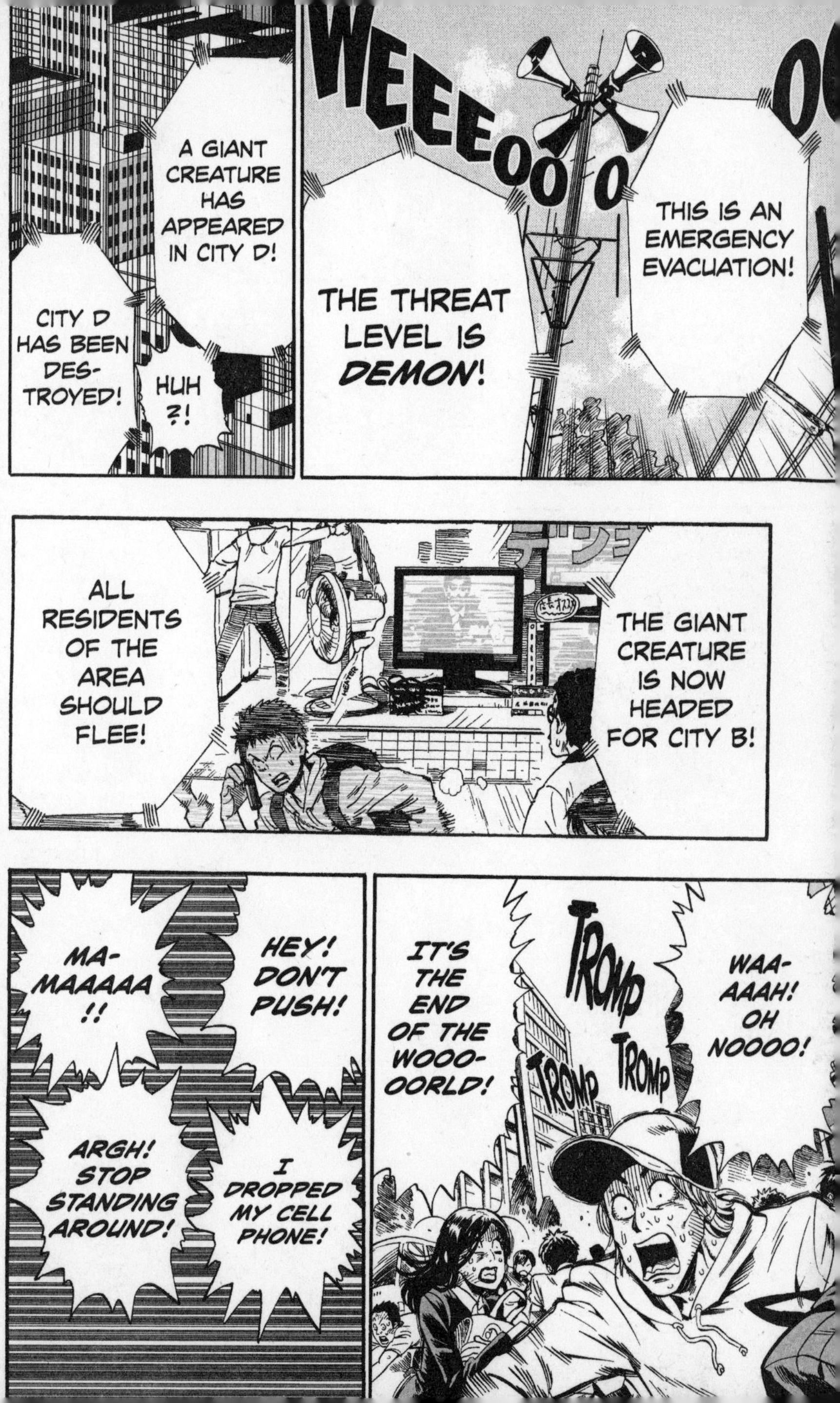
WEEEOOO O OO
THIS IS AN EMERGENCY EVACUATION!
THE THREAT LEVEL IS *DEMON*!
A GIANT CREATURE HAS APPEARED IN CITY D!
CITY D HAS BEEN DES-TROYED!
HUH ?!
THE GIANT CREATURE IS NOW HEADED FOR CITY B!
HEATER
ALL RESIDENTS OF THE AREA SHOULD FLEE!
WAA-AAAH! OH NOOOO!
TROMP
TROMP
TROMP
IT'S THE END OF THE WOOO-OORLD!
HEY! DON'T PUSH!
MA-MAAAAA!!
I DROPPED MY CELL PHONE!
ARGH! STOP STANDING AROUND!

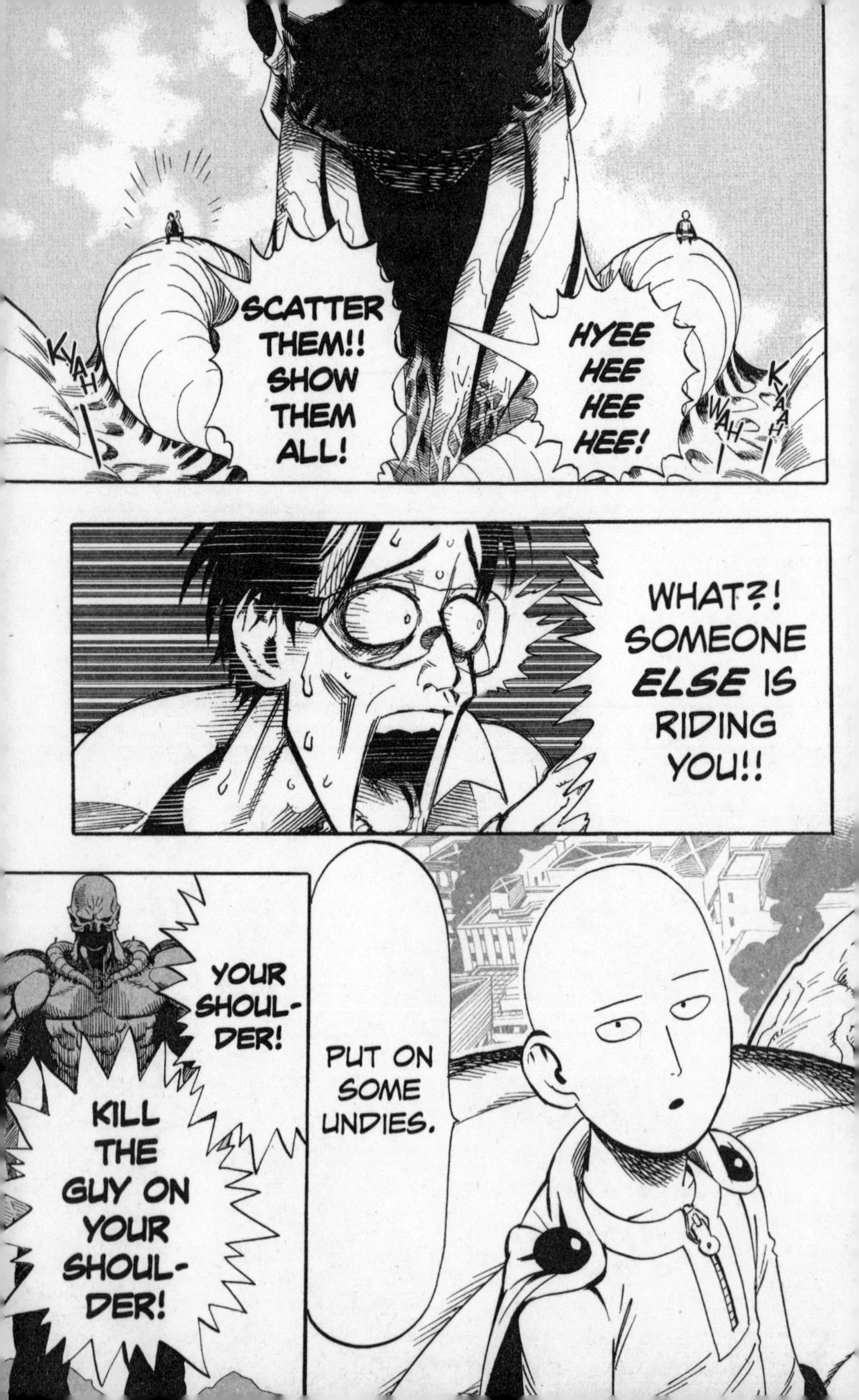
KYAAH
WAH
HYEE HEE HEE HEE!
SCATTER THEM!! SHOW THEM ALL!
KYAAH
WHAT?! SOMEONE *ELSE* IS RIDING YOU!!
PUT ON SOME UNDIES.
YOUR SHOUL-DER!
KILL THE GUY ON YOUR SHOUL-DER!

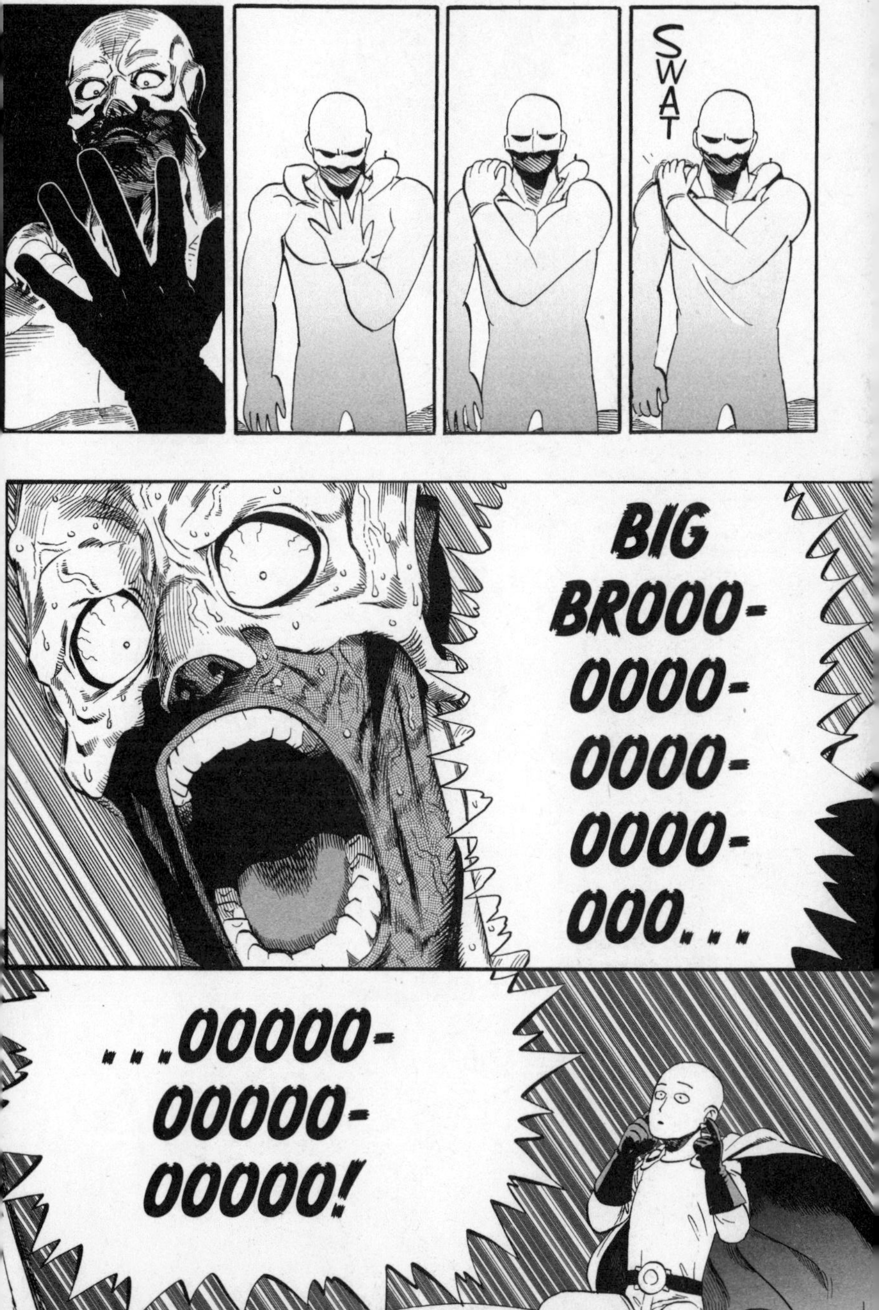
SWAT
BIG BROOO-OOOO-OOOO-OOOO-OOO...
...OOOOO-OOOOO-OOOOO!

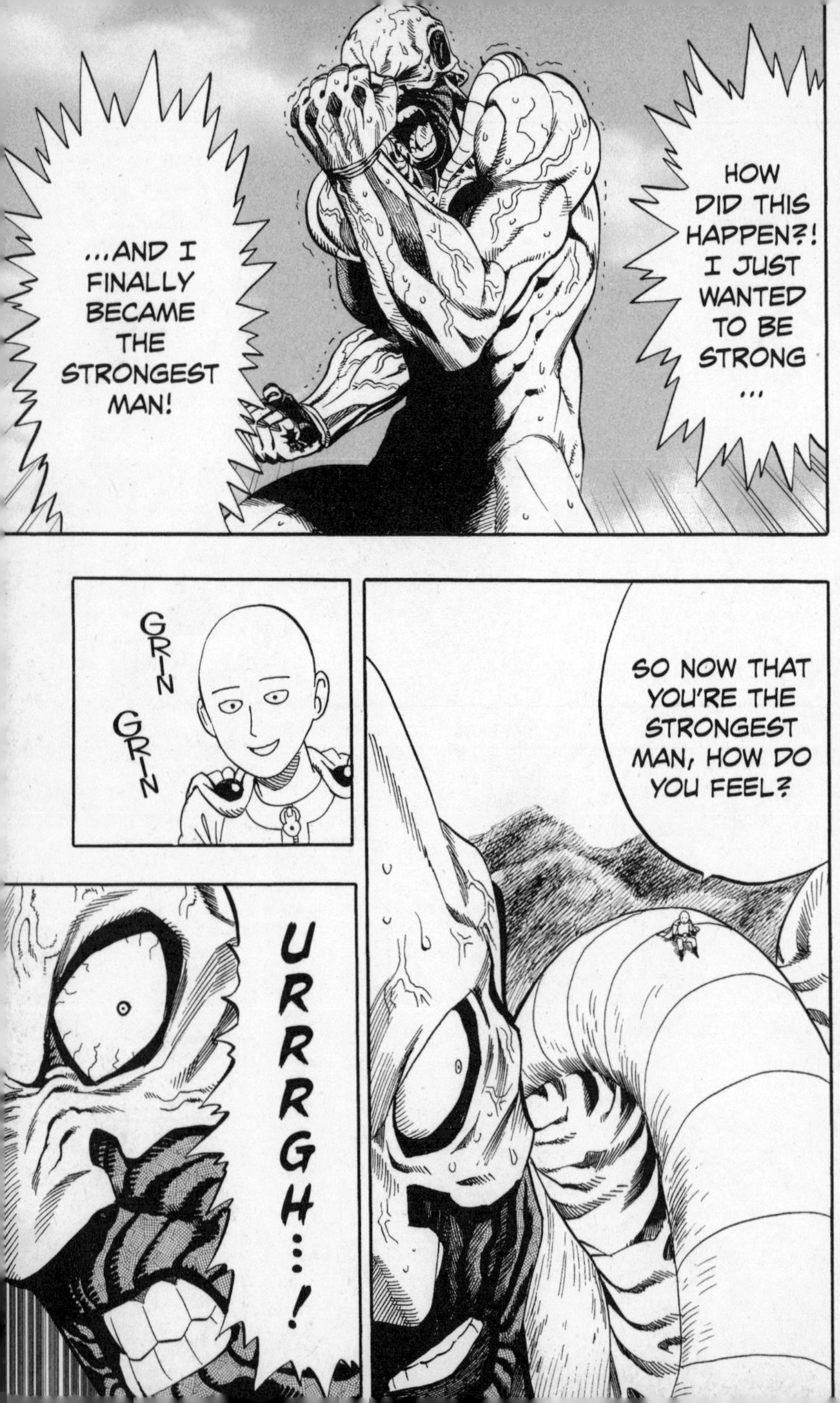
HOW DID THIS HAPPEN?! I JUST WANTED TO BE STRONG...
...AND I FINALLY BECAME THE STRONGEST MAN!
SO NOW THAT YOU'RE THE STRONGEST MAN, HOW DO YOU FEEL?
GRIN GRIN
URRRGH...!

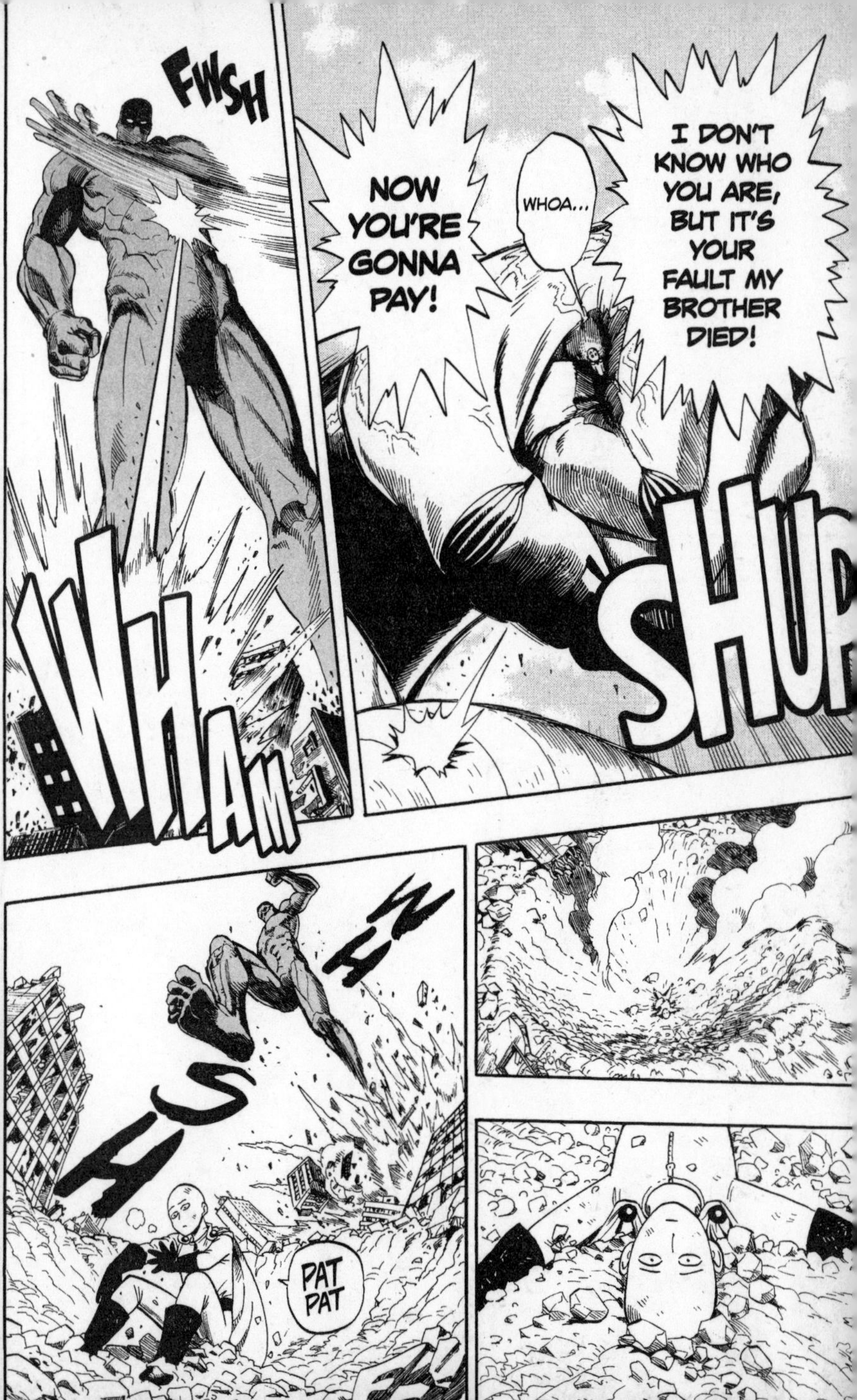
I DON'T KNOW WHO YOU ARE, BUT IT'S YOUR FAULT MY BROTHER DIED!
WHOA...
NOW YOU'RE GONNA PAY!
SHUP
FWISH
WHAM
PAT PAT

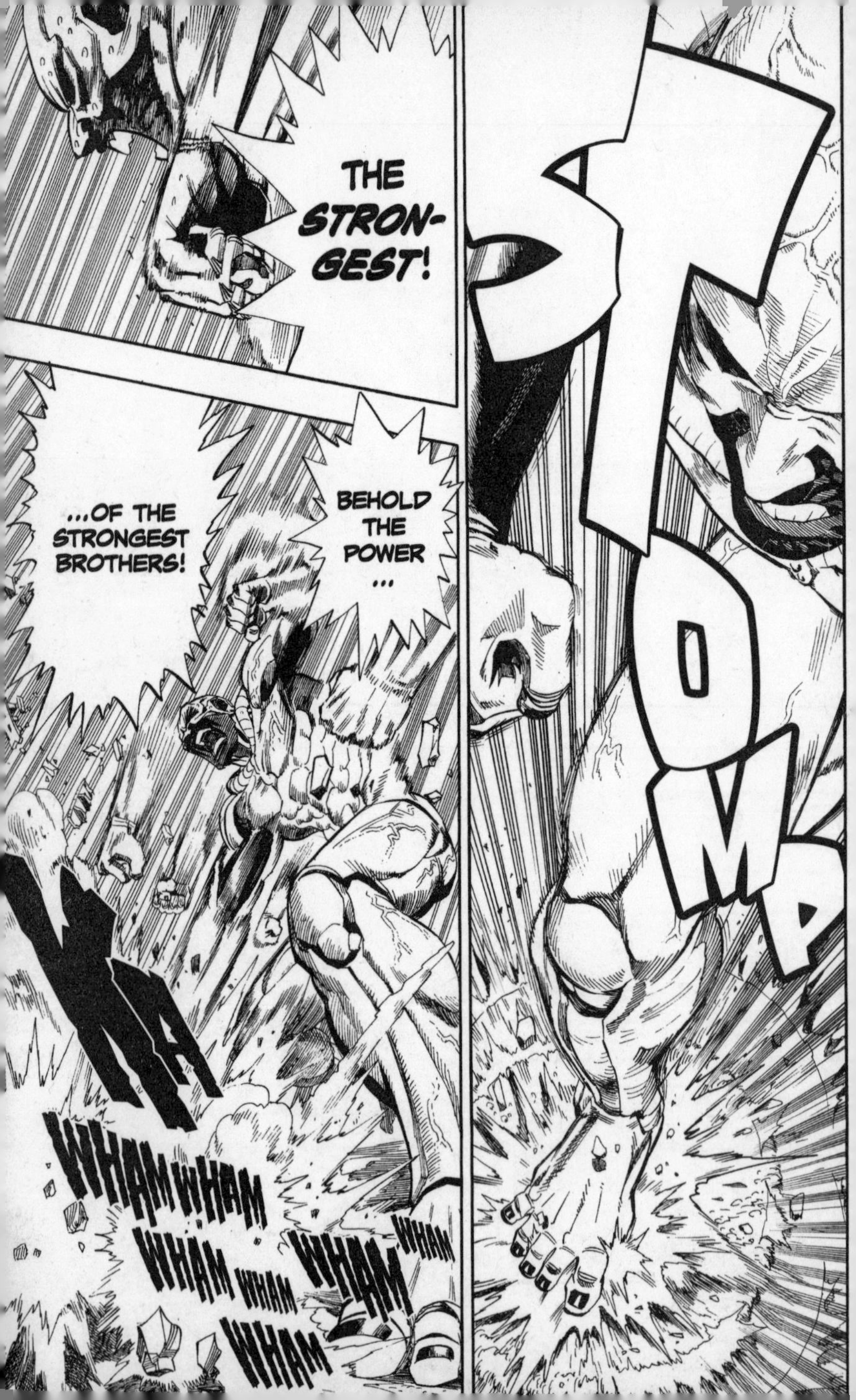
STOMP
THE STRONGEST!
BEHOLD THE POWER...
...OF THE STRONGEST BROTHERS!
WHAM WHAM
WHAM WHAM
WHAM WHAM WHAM
WHAM

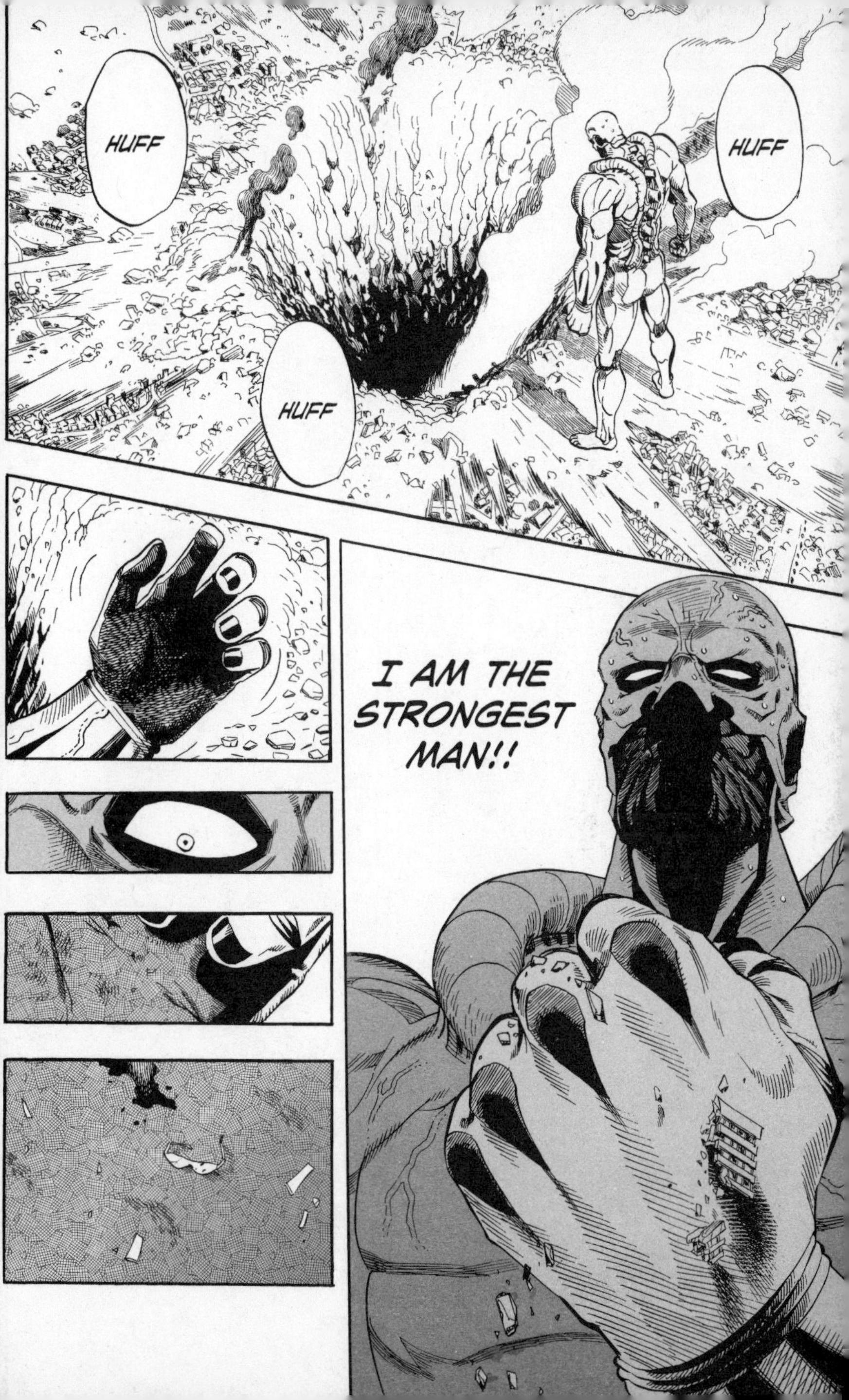
HUFF
HUFF
HUFF
I AM THE STRONGEST MAN!!

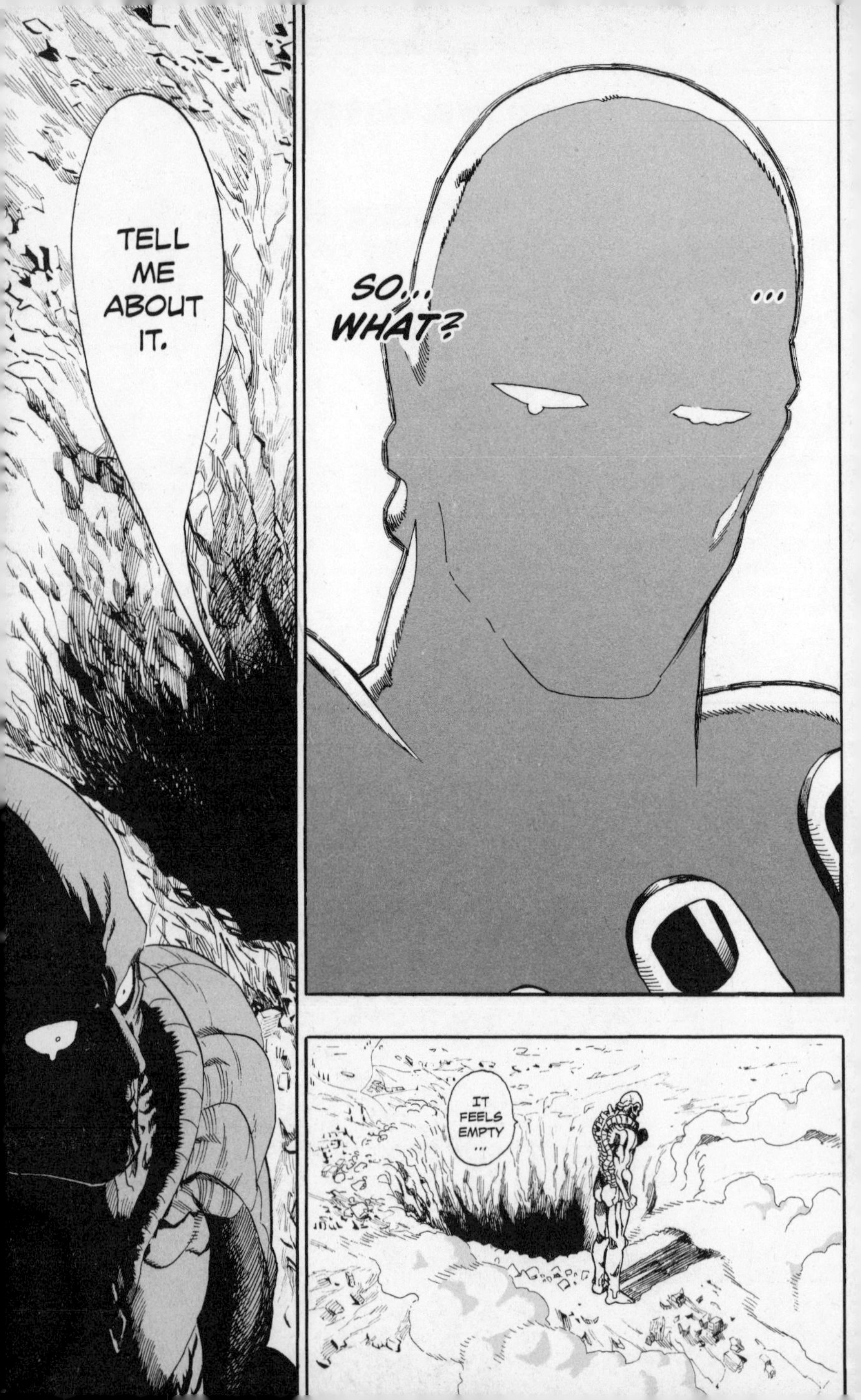
...
SO... WHAT?
IT FEELS EMPTY ...
TELL ME ABOUT IT.

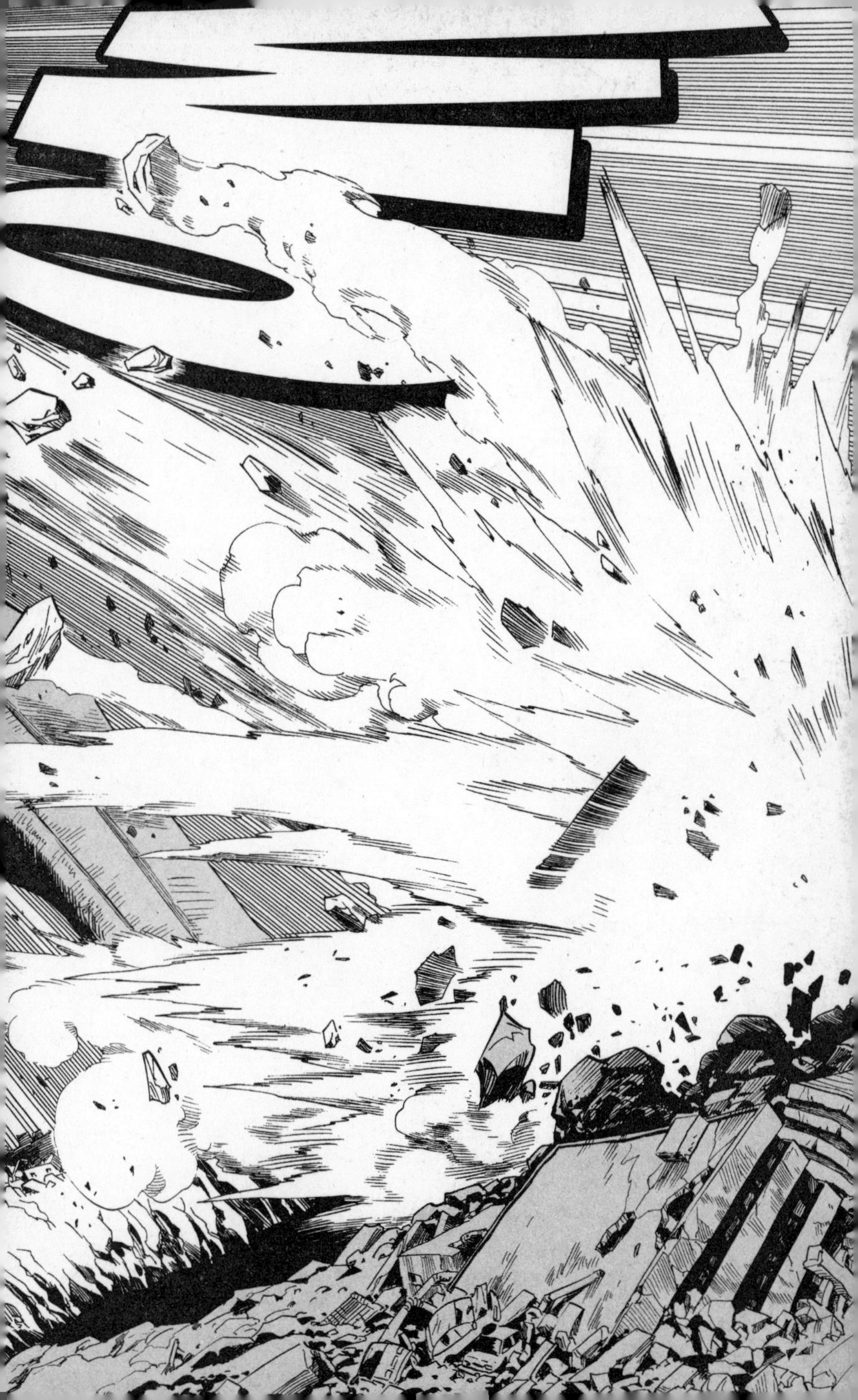

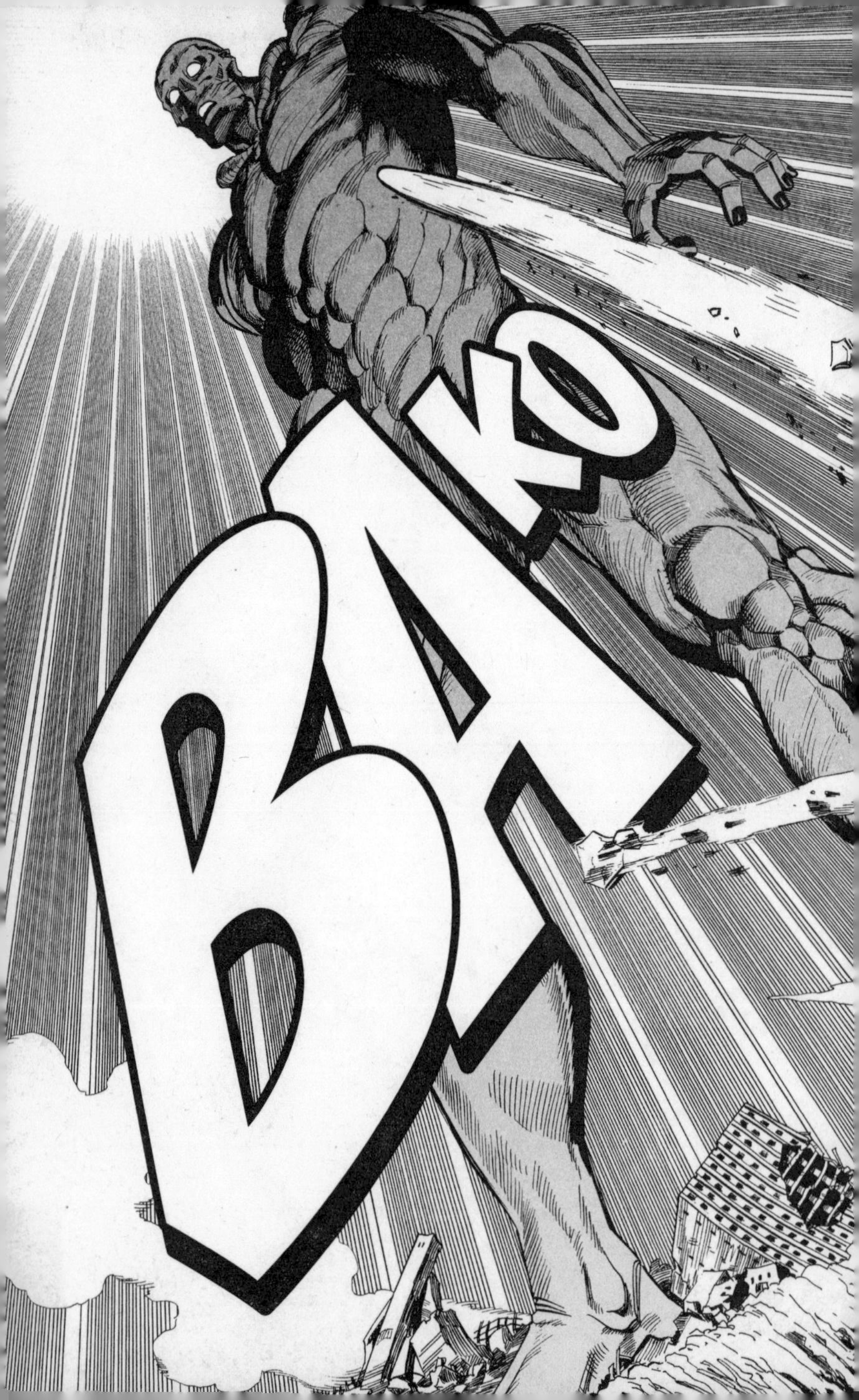
BAKO

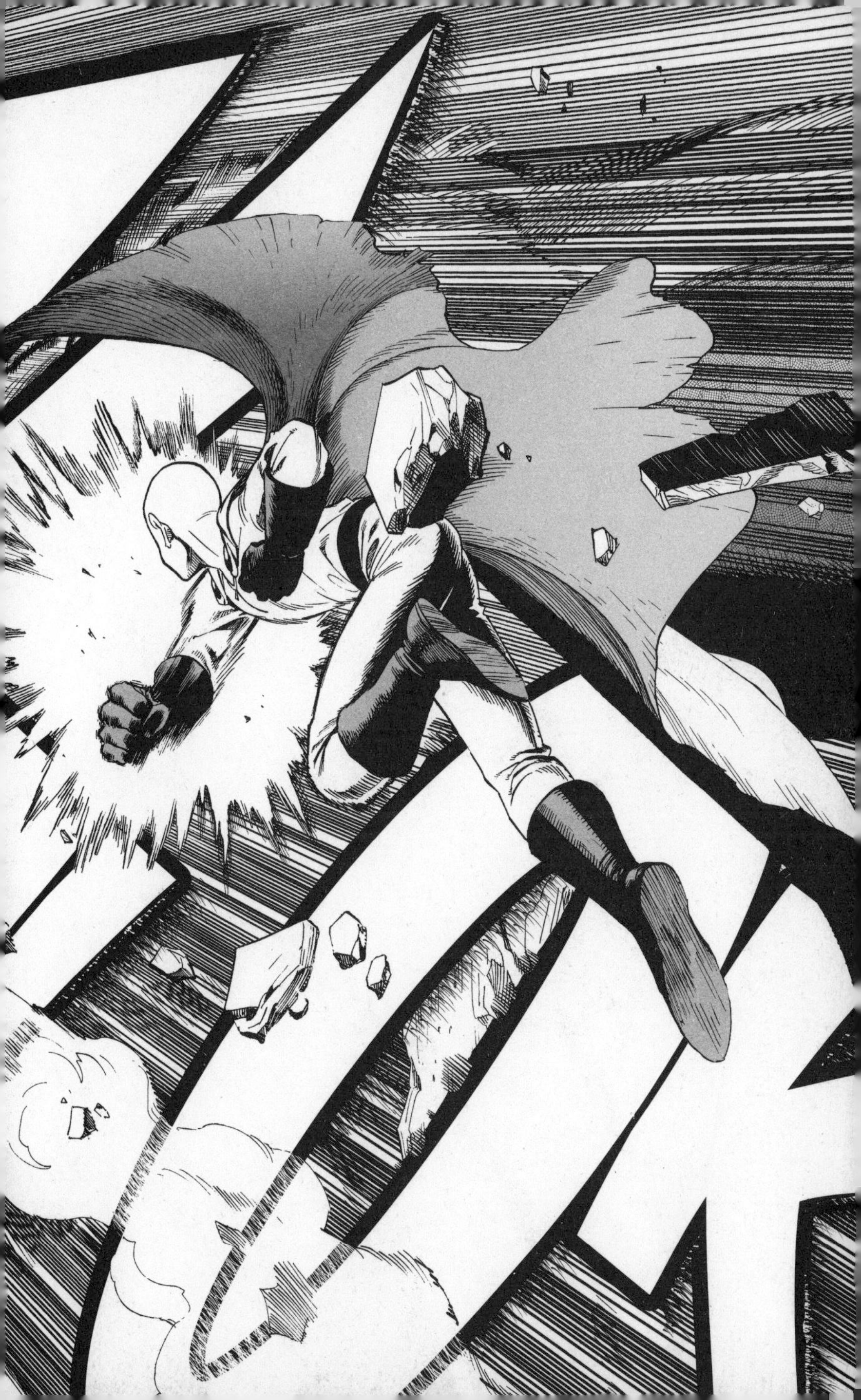

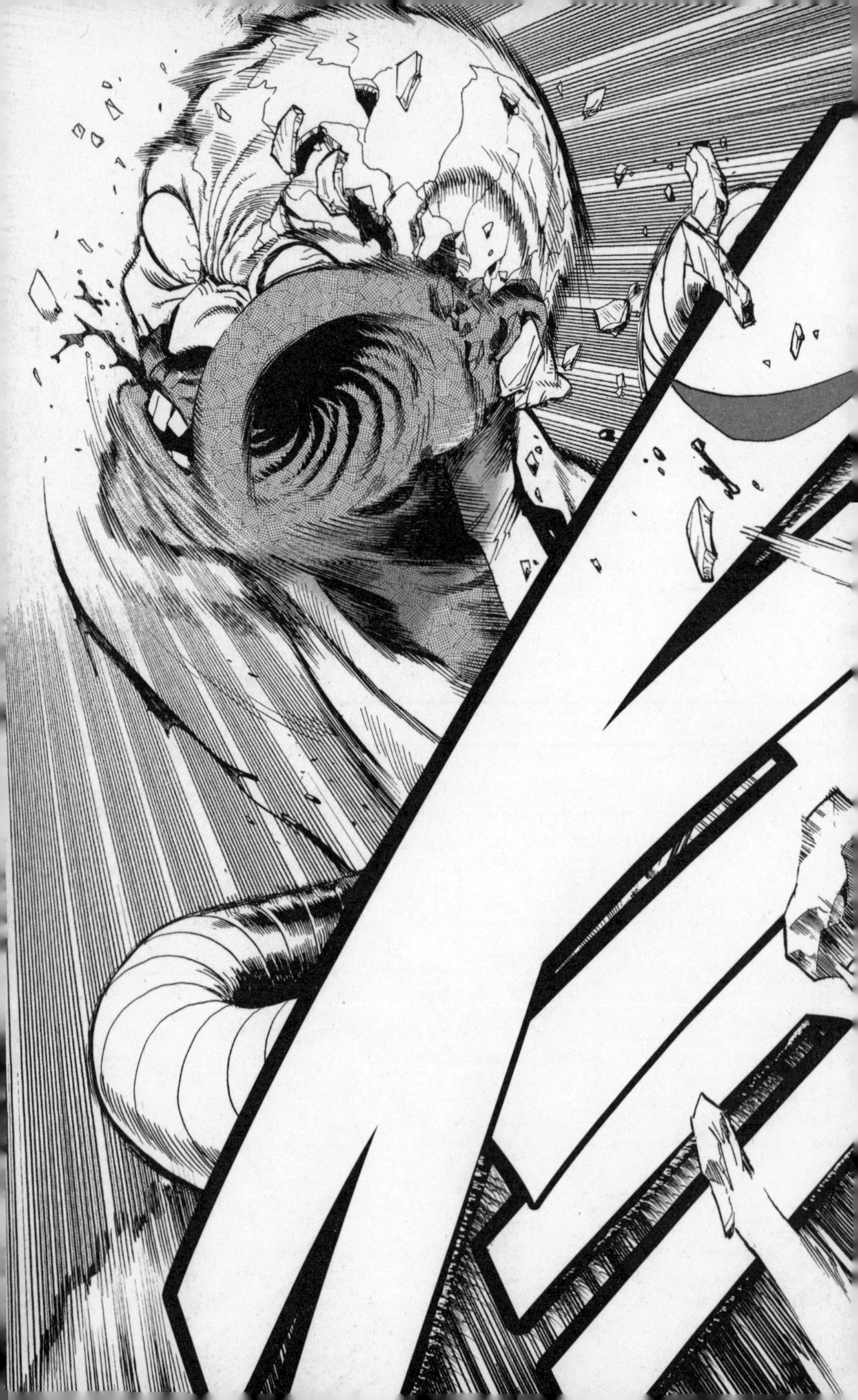

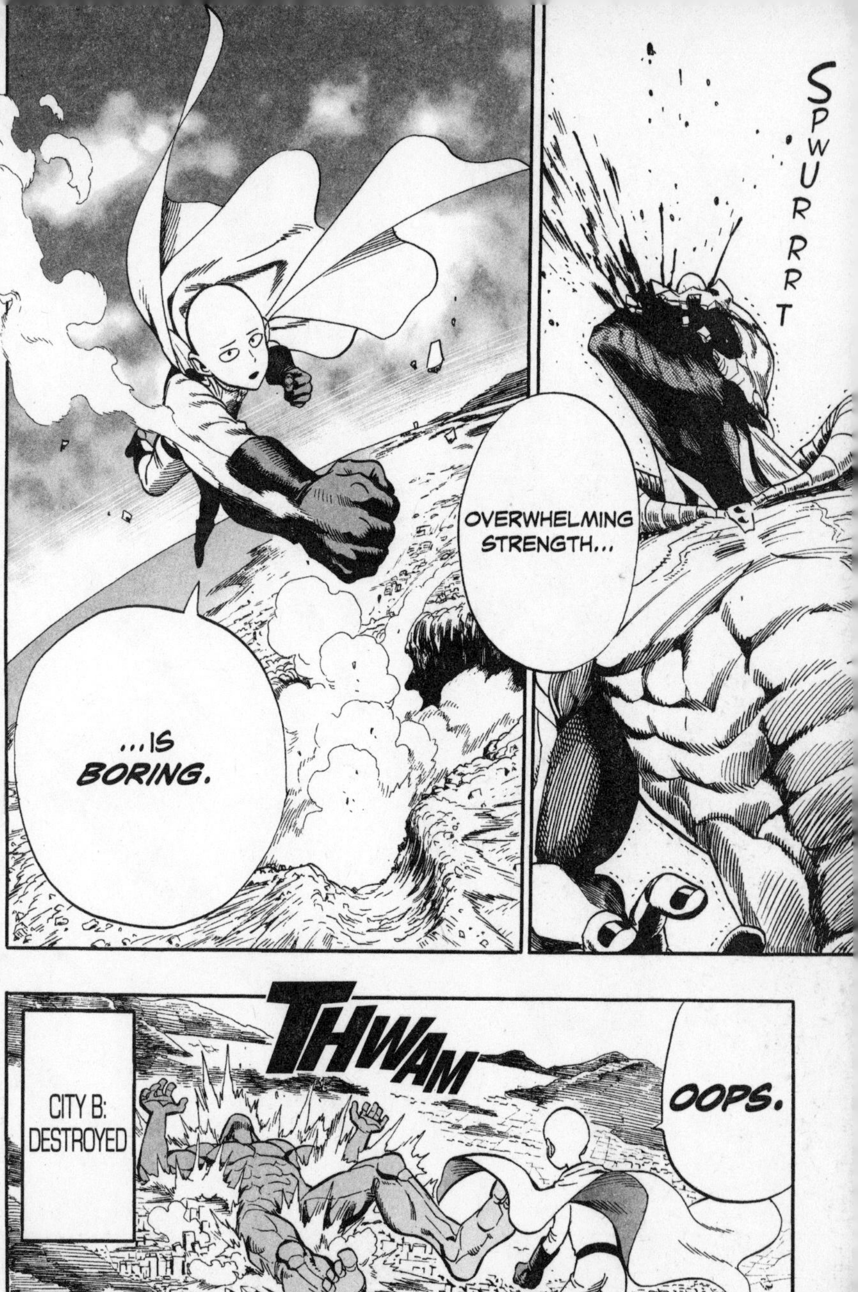
SPWURRRT
OVERWHELMING STRENGTH...
...IS BORING.
OOPS.
THWAM
CITY B: DESTROYED

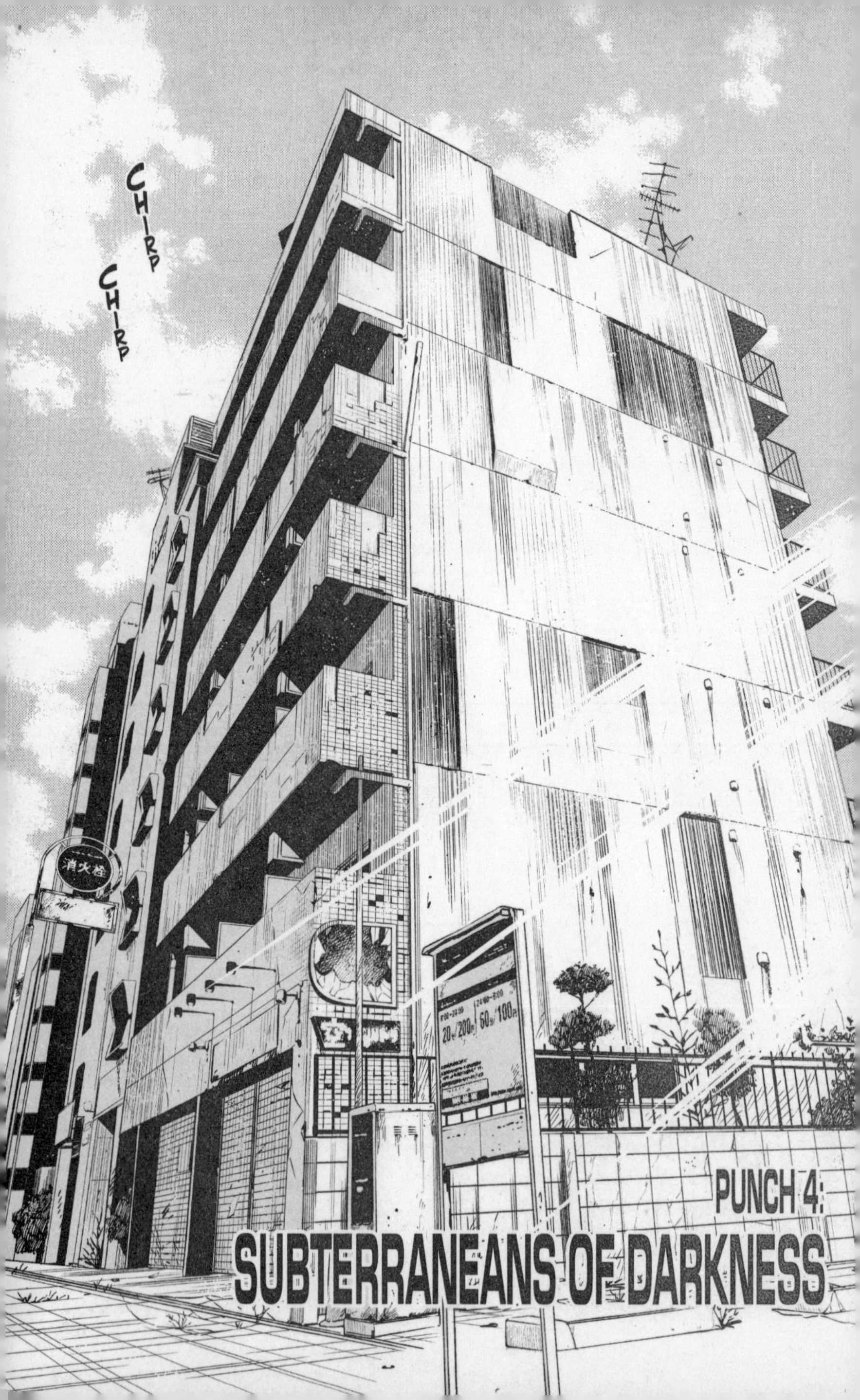
CHIRP
CHIRP
消火栓
PUNCH 4:
SUBTERRANEANS OF DARKNESS

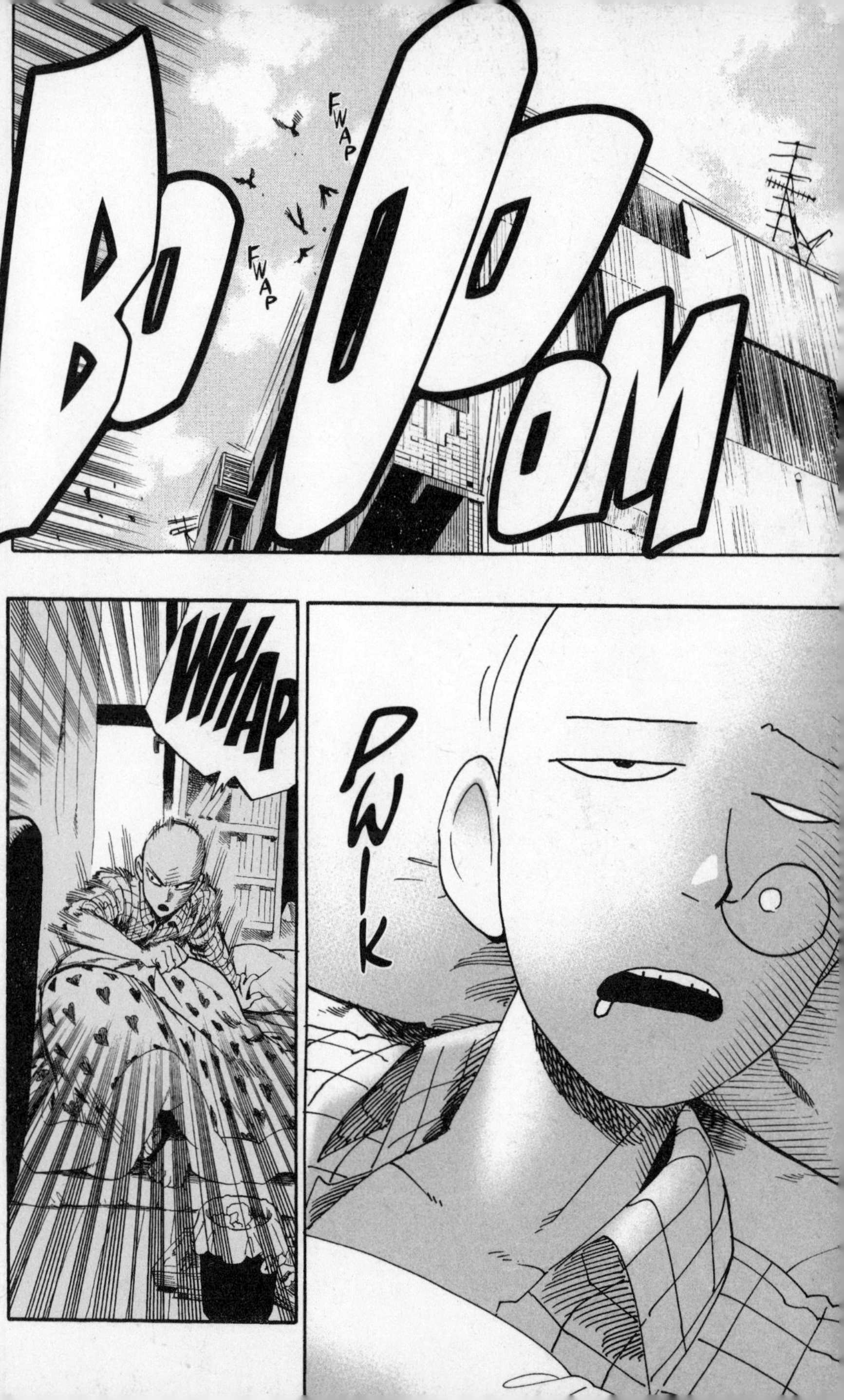
BOOOOM
FWAP
FWAP
PWIK
WHAP

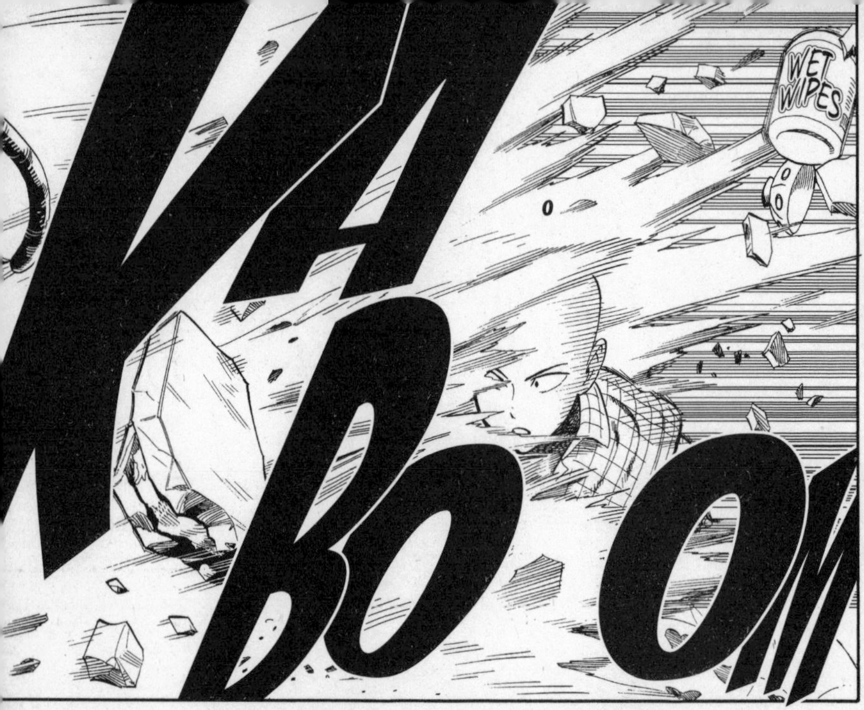
WET WIPES
BOOM
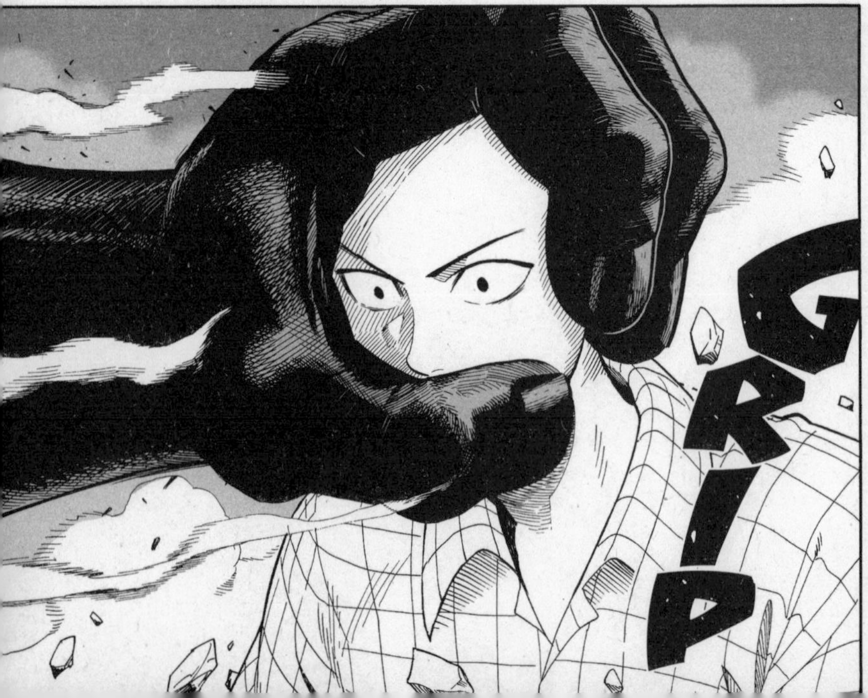
GRIP

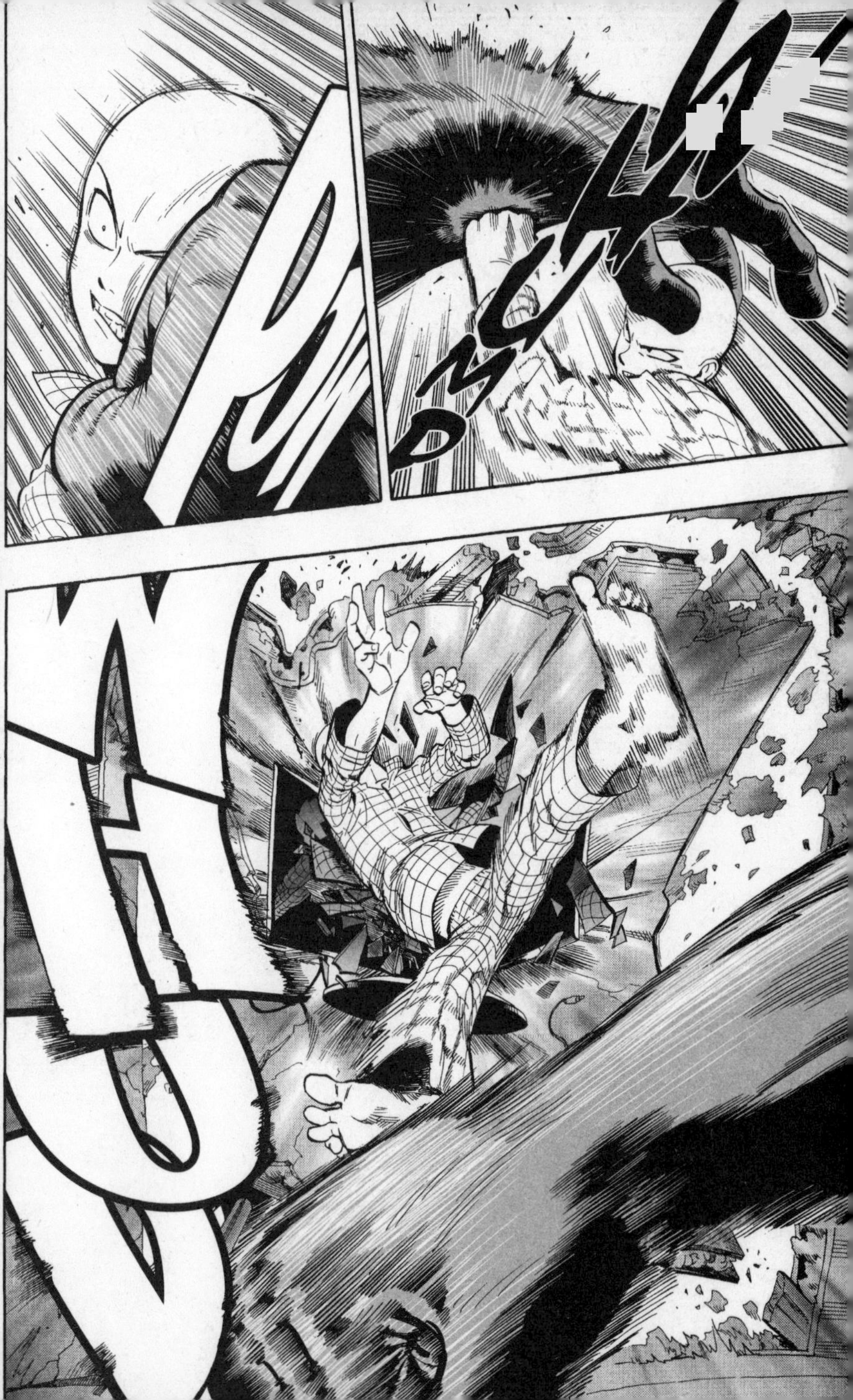

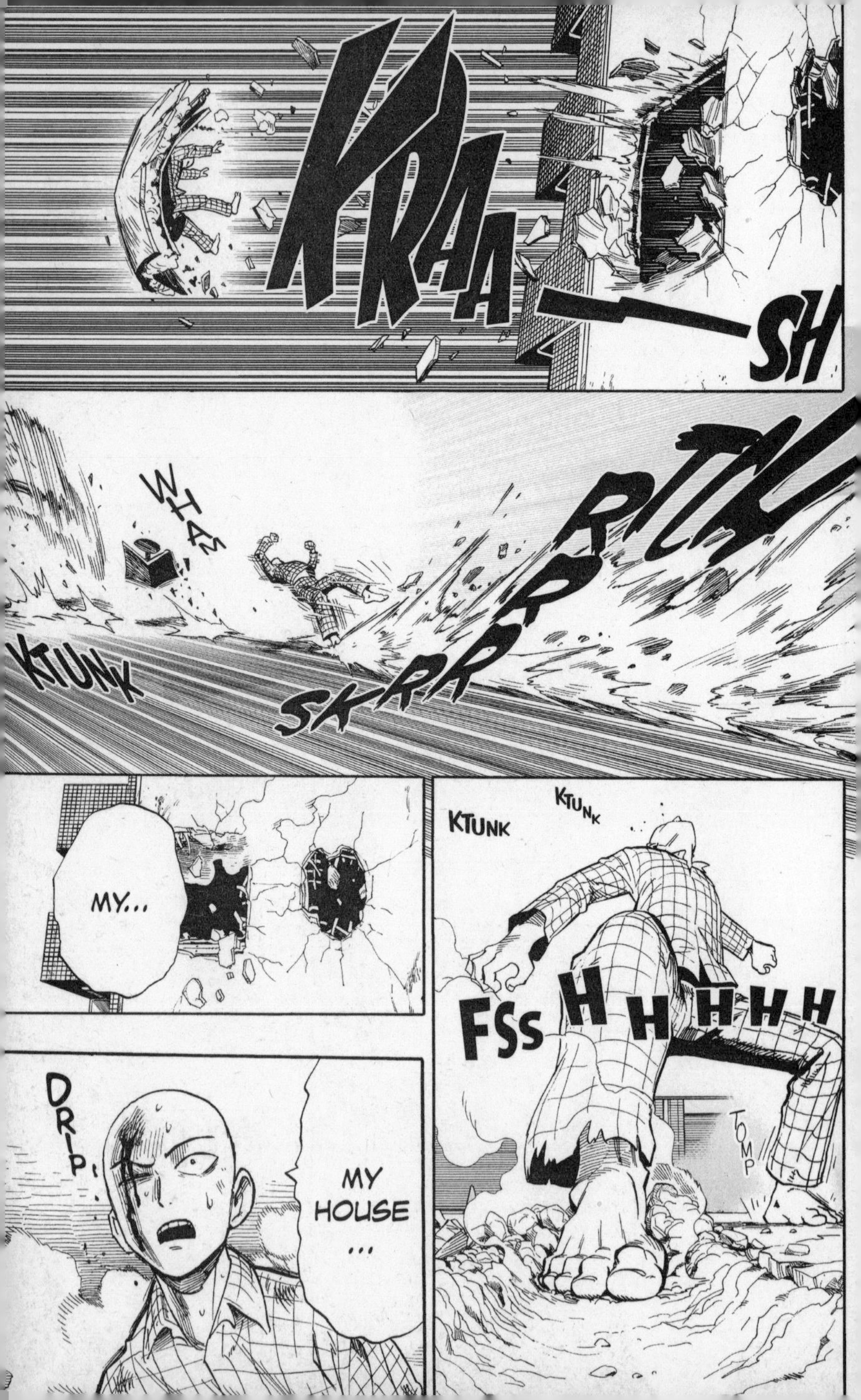
KRAA—SH
SKRRRRITCH
WHAM
KTUNK
KTUNK
KTUNK
FSSHHHHH
TOMP
MY...
DRIP
MY HOUSE ...

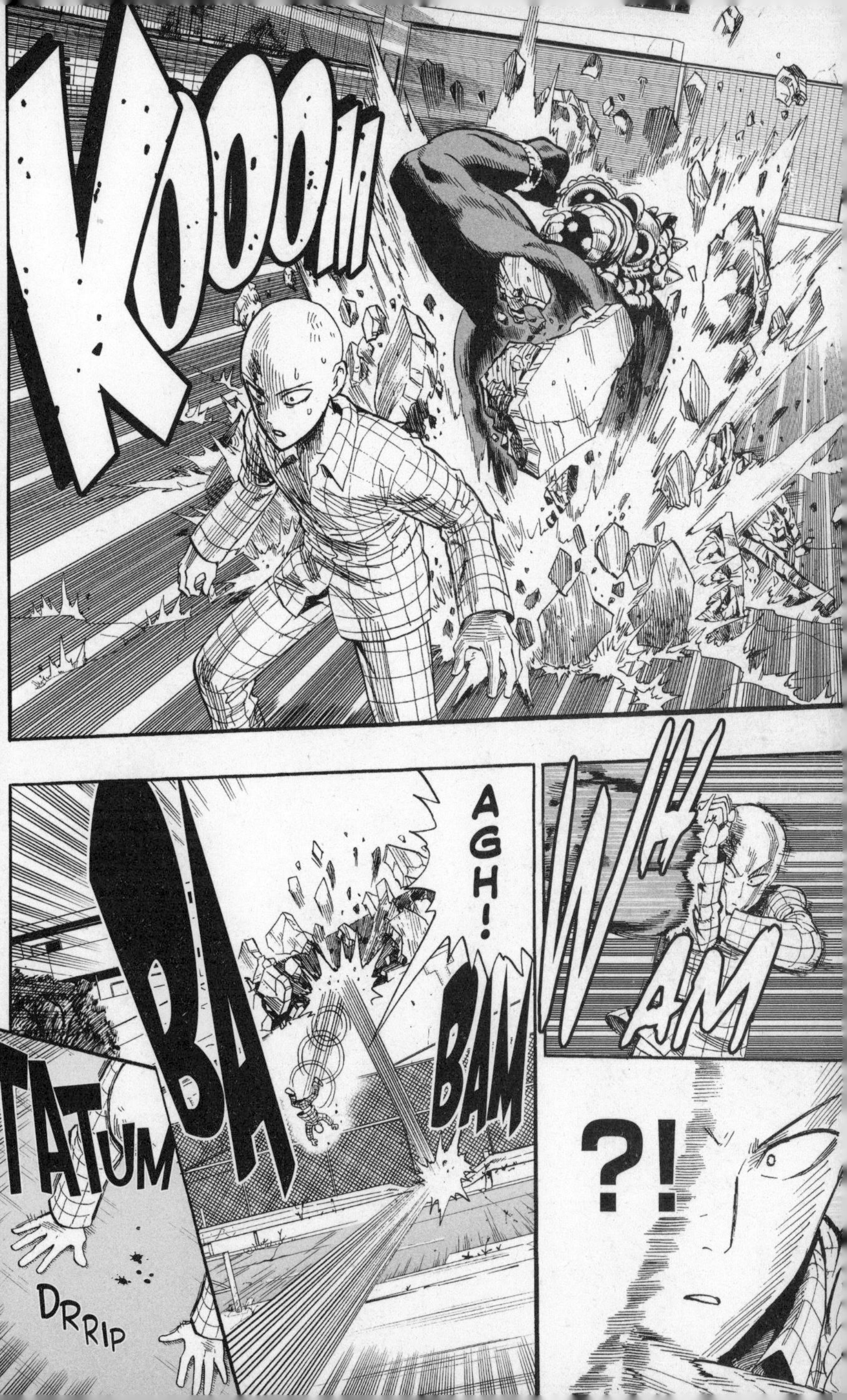
KOOOM
WHAM
?!
AGH!
BAM
BA
TATUM
DRRIP

READ THIS WAY

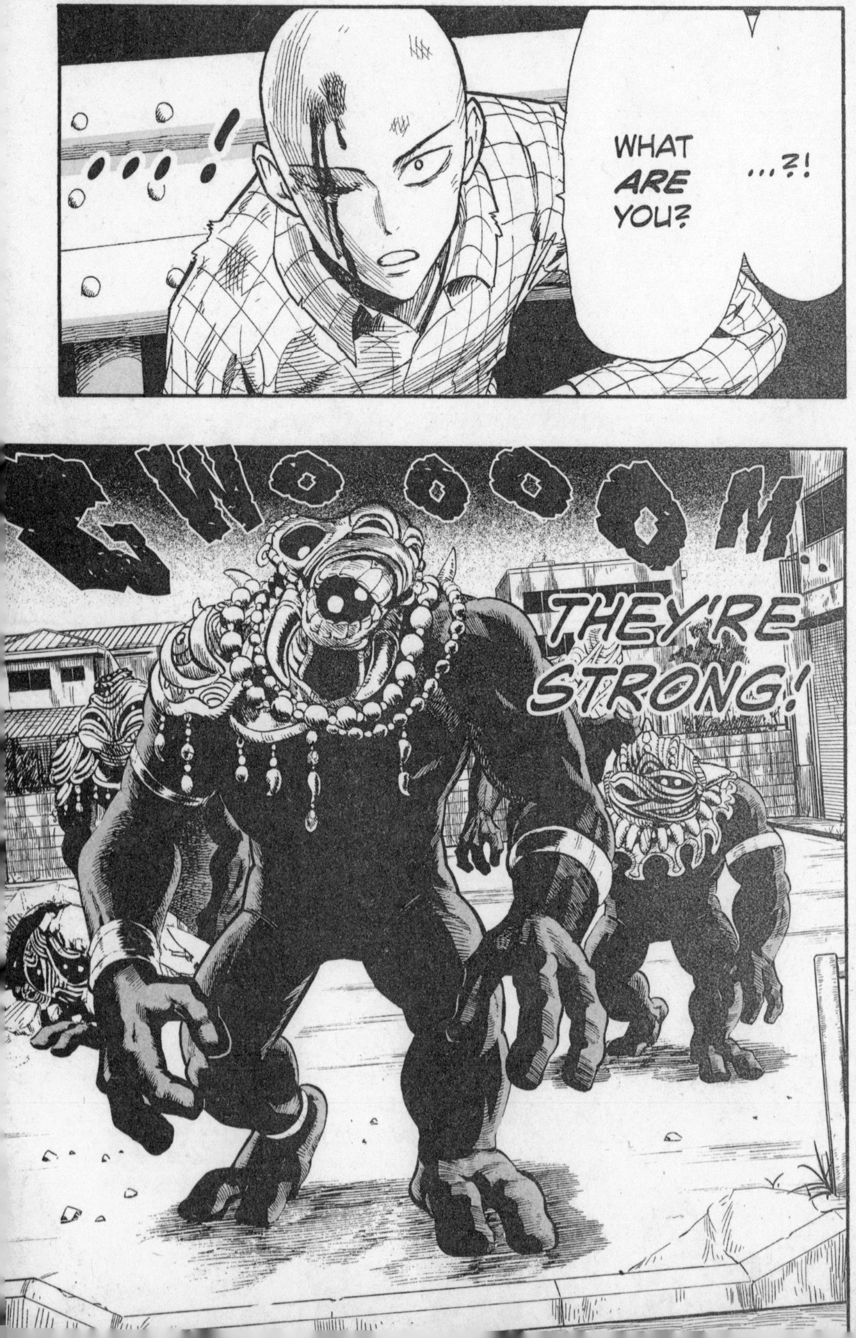
WHAT ARE YOU? ...?!
...!
GWOOOOOM
THEY'RE STRONG!

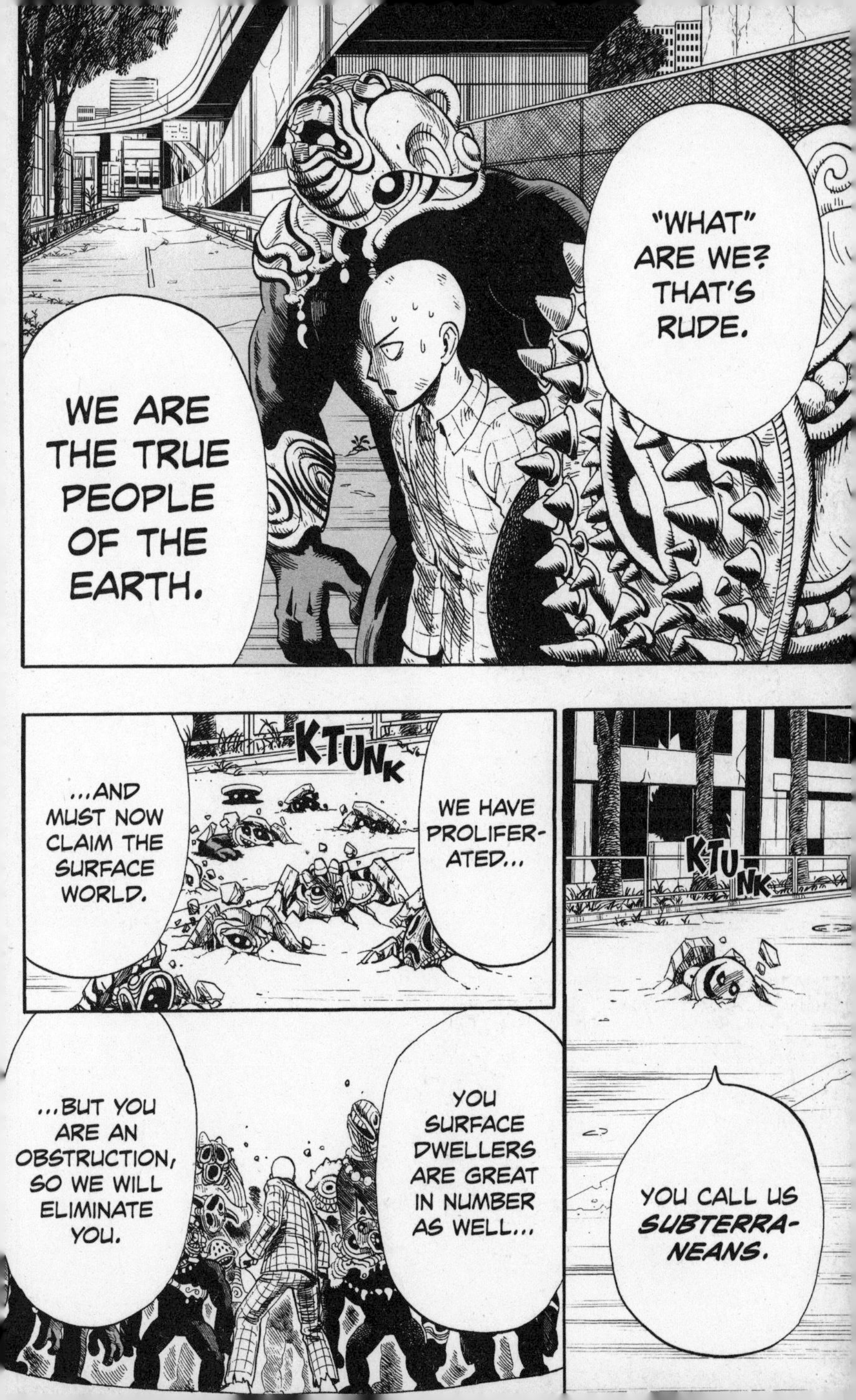
"WHAT" ARE WE? THAT'S RUDE.
WE ARE THE TRUE PEOPLE OF THE EARTH.
KTUNK
YOU CALL US *SUBTERRANEANS*.
KTUNK
WE HAVE PROLIFERATED...
...AND MUST NOW CLAIM THE SURFACE WORLD.
YOU SURFACE DWELLERS ARE GREAT IN NUMBER AS WELL...
...BUT YOU ARE AN OBSTRUCTION, SO WE WILL ELIMINATE YOU.

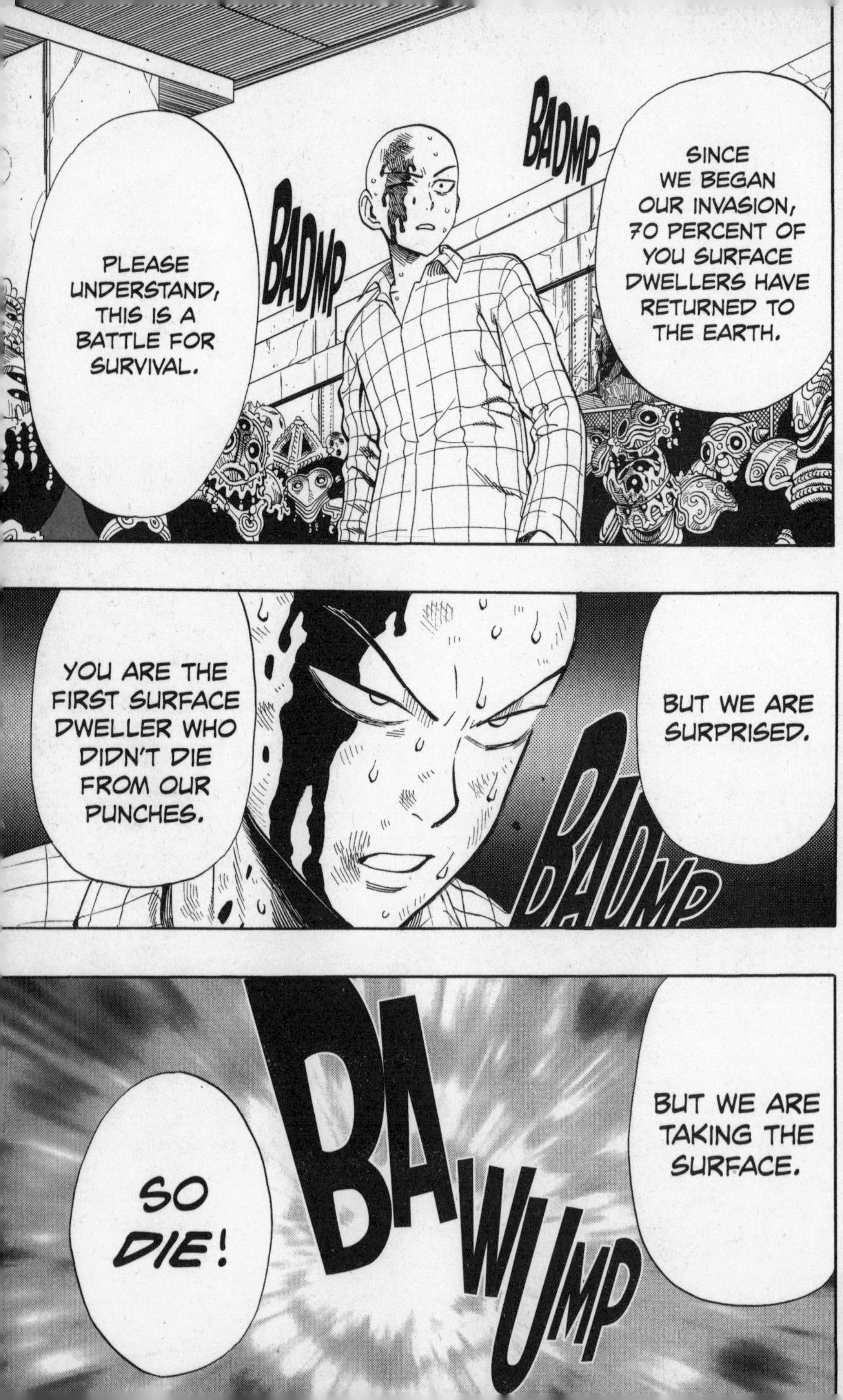
SINCE WE BEGAN OUR INVASION, 70 PERCENT OF YOU SURFACE DWELLERS HAVE RETURNED TO THE EARTH.
BADMP
BADMP
PLEASE UNDERSTAND, THIS IS A BATTLE FOR SURVIVAL.
BUT WE ARE SURPRISED.
BADUMP
YOU ARE THE FIRST SURFACE DWELLER WHO DIDN'T DIE FROM OUR PUNCHES.
BUT WE ARE TAKING THE SURFACE.
BAWUMP
SO *DIE*!

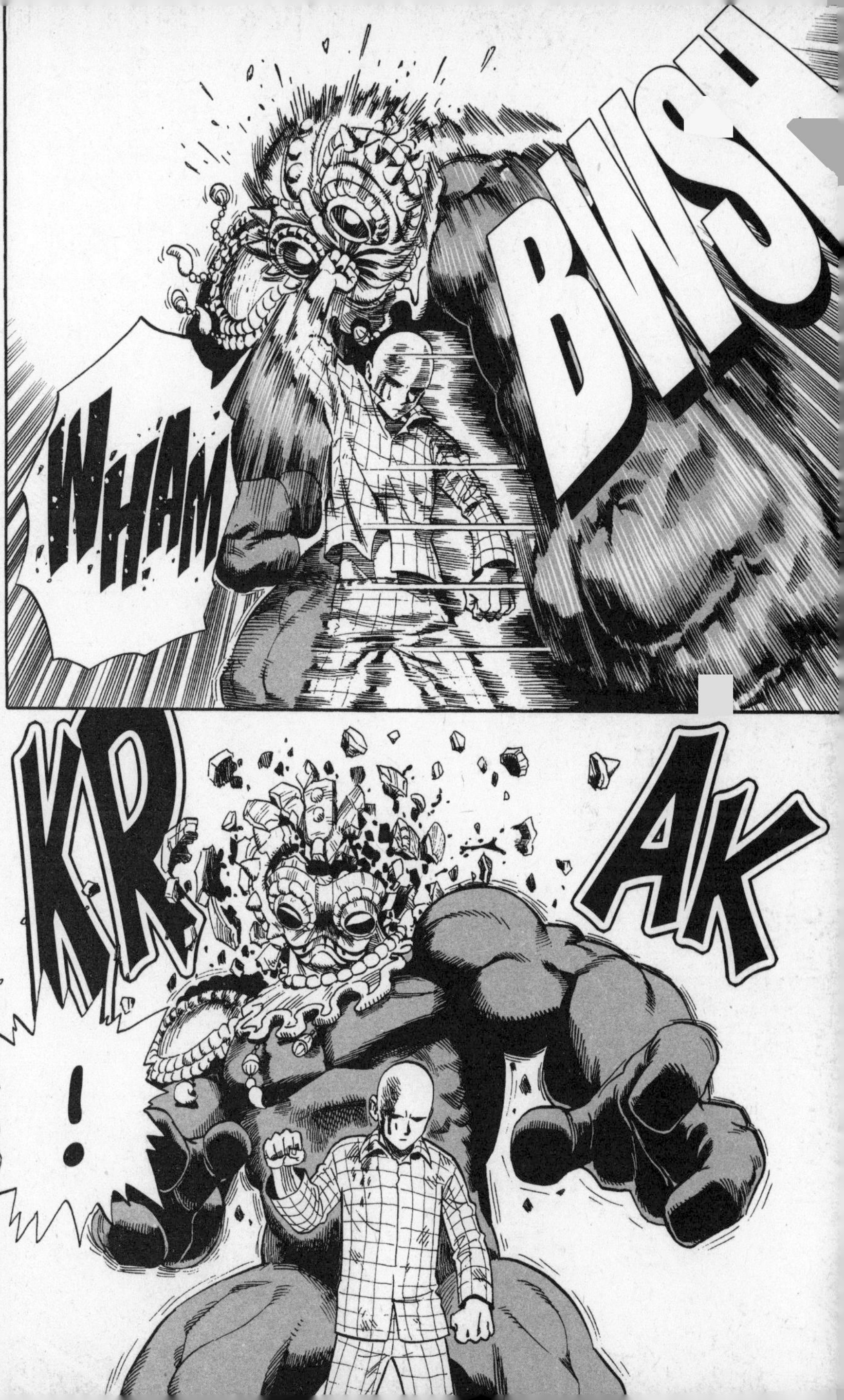
BWSH!
WHAM
KRAK
!

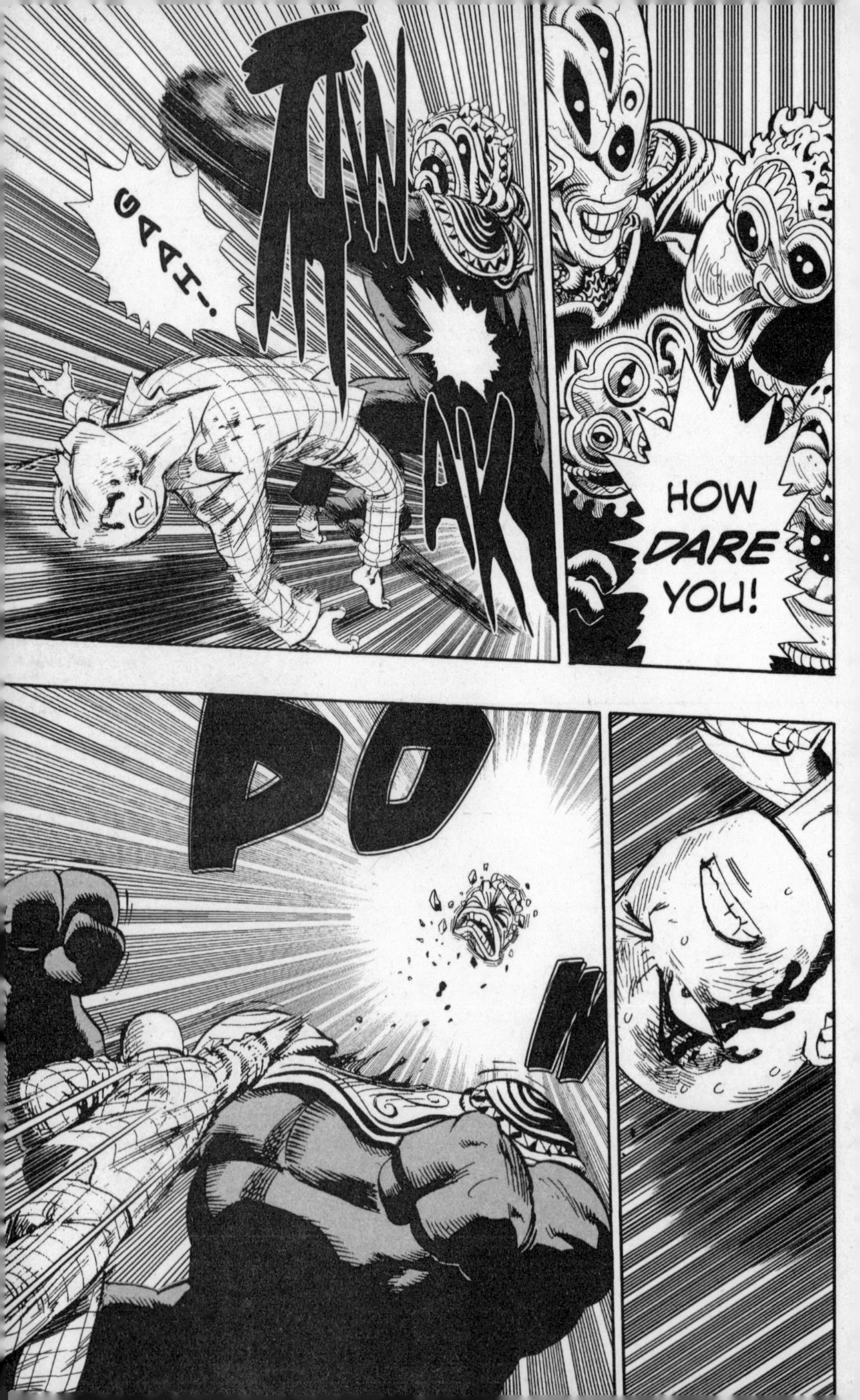
HOW DARE YOU!
GAAH!!

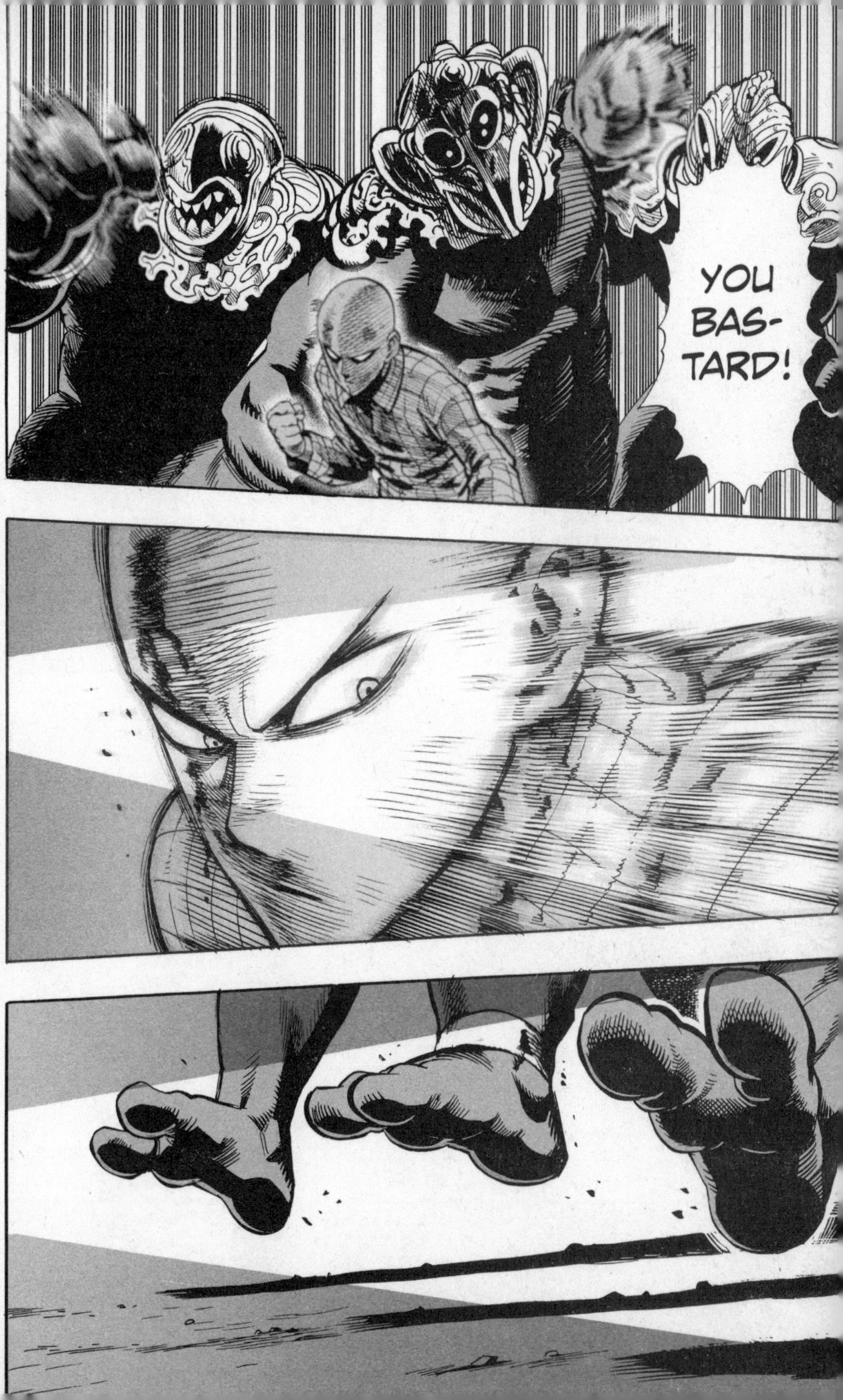
YOU BAS- TARD!

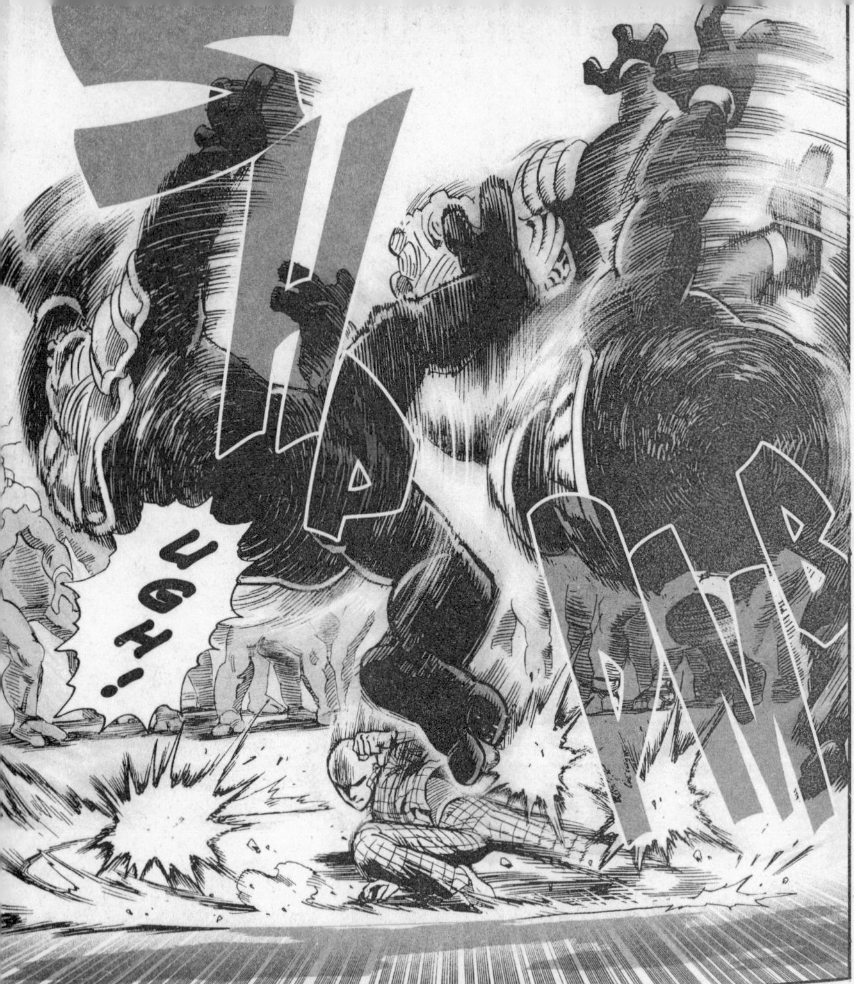
UGH!
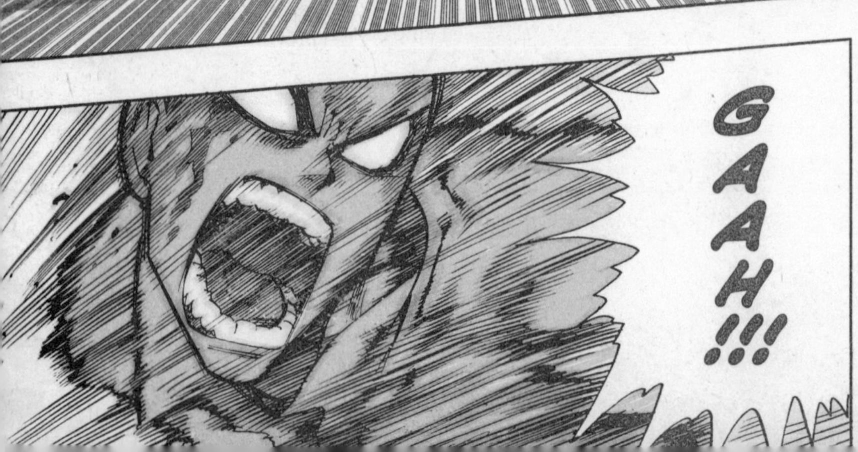
GAAH!!!

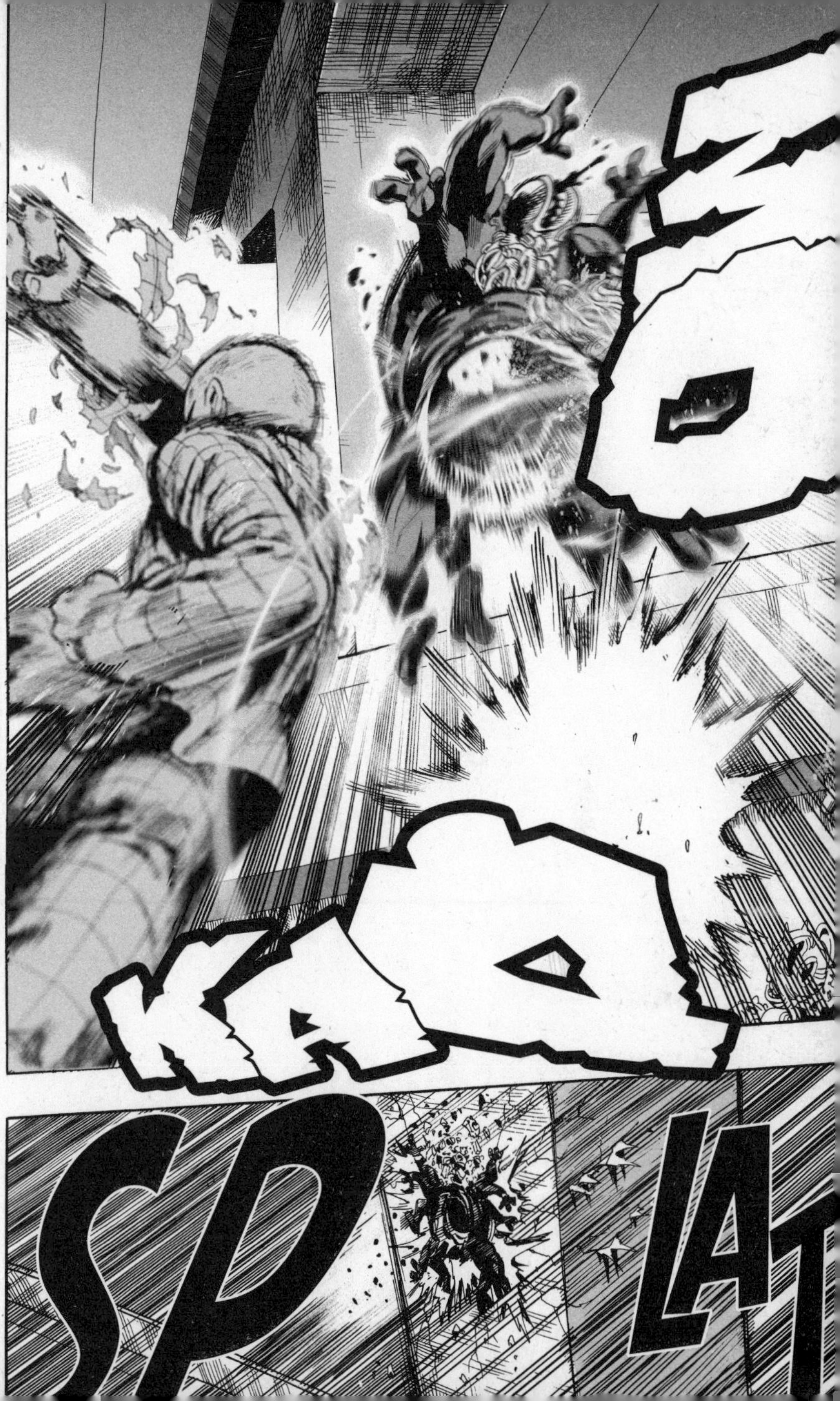
KA
SPLAT

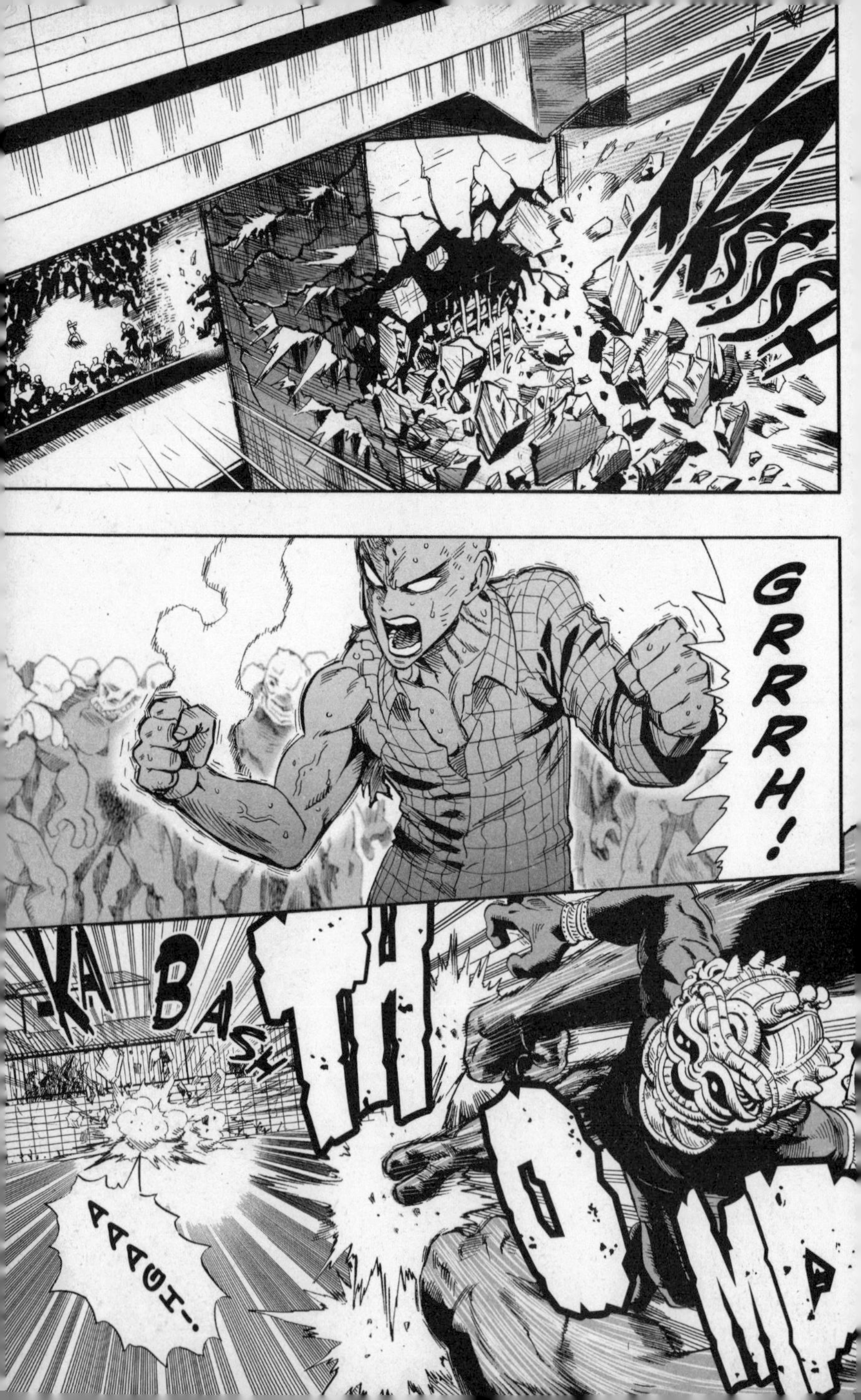
KRSSH
GRRRH!
THOMP
KA-BASH
AAAGH!

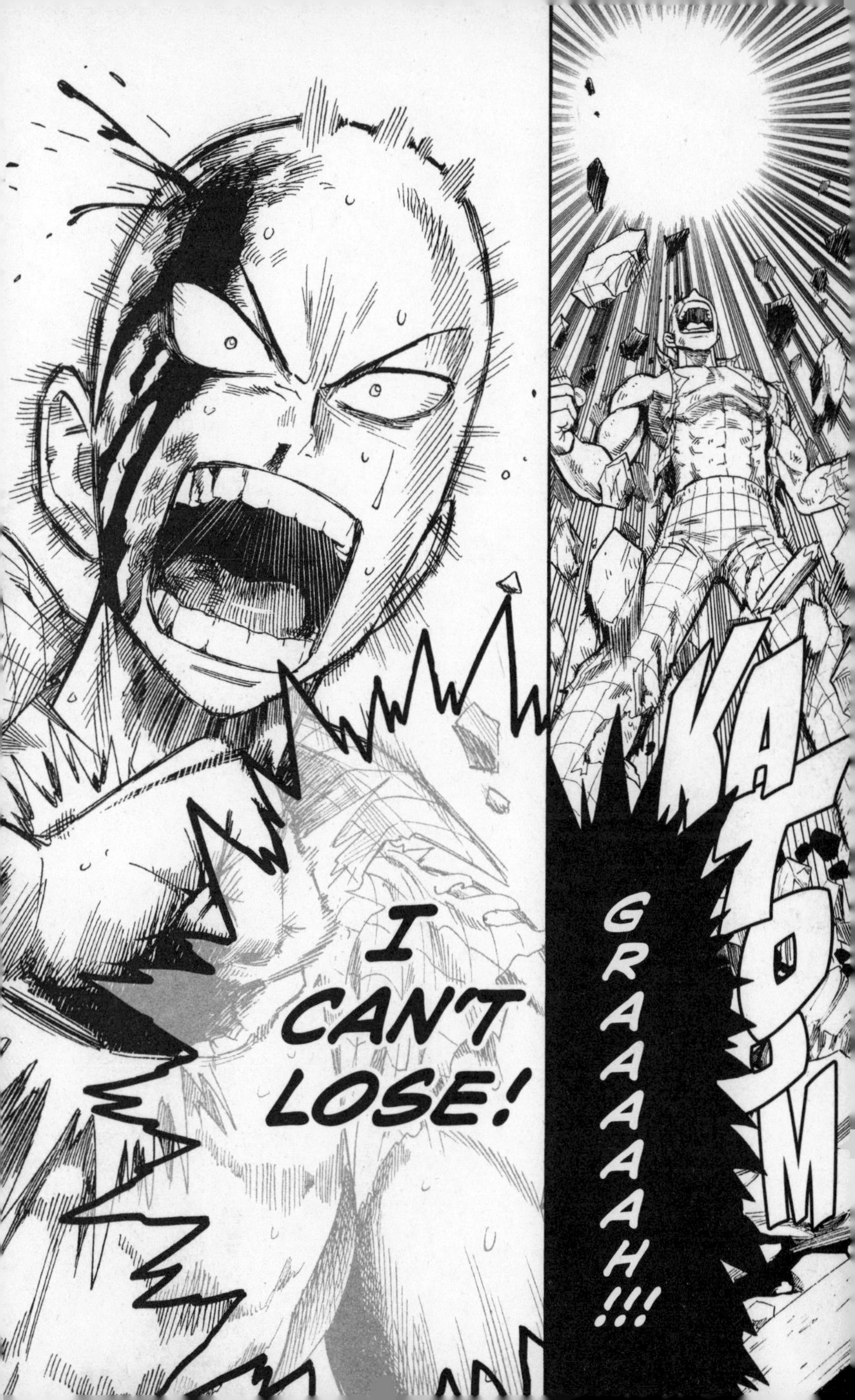
KABOOM
GRAAAAAH!!!
I CAN'T LOSE!

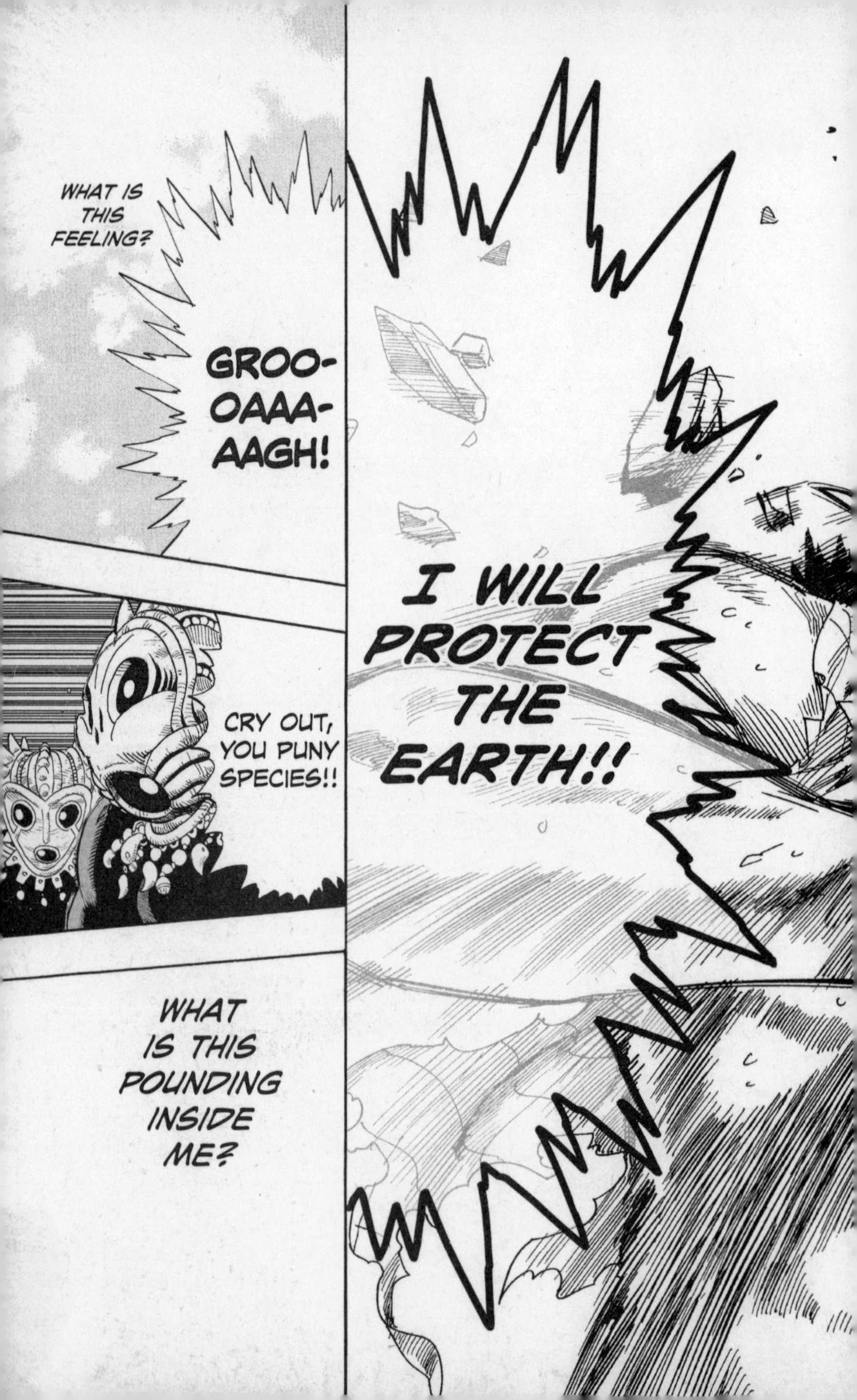
I WILL PROTECT THE EARTH!!
WHAT IS THIS FEELING?
GROO-OAAA-AAGH!
CRY OUT, YOU PUNY SPECIES!!
WHAT IS THIS POUNDING INSIDE ME?

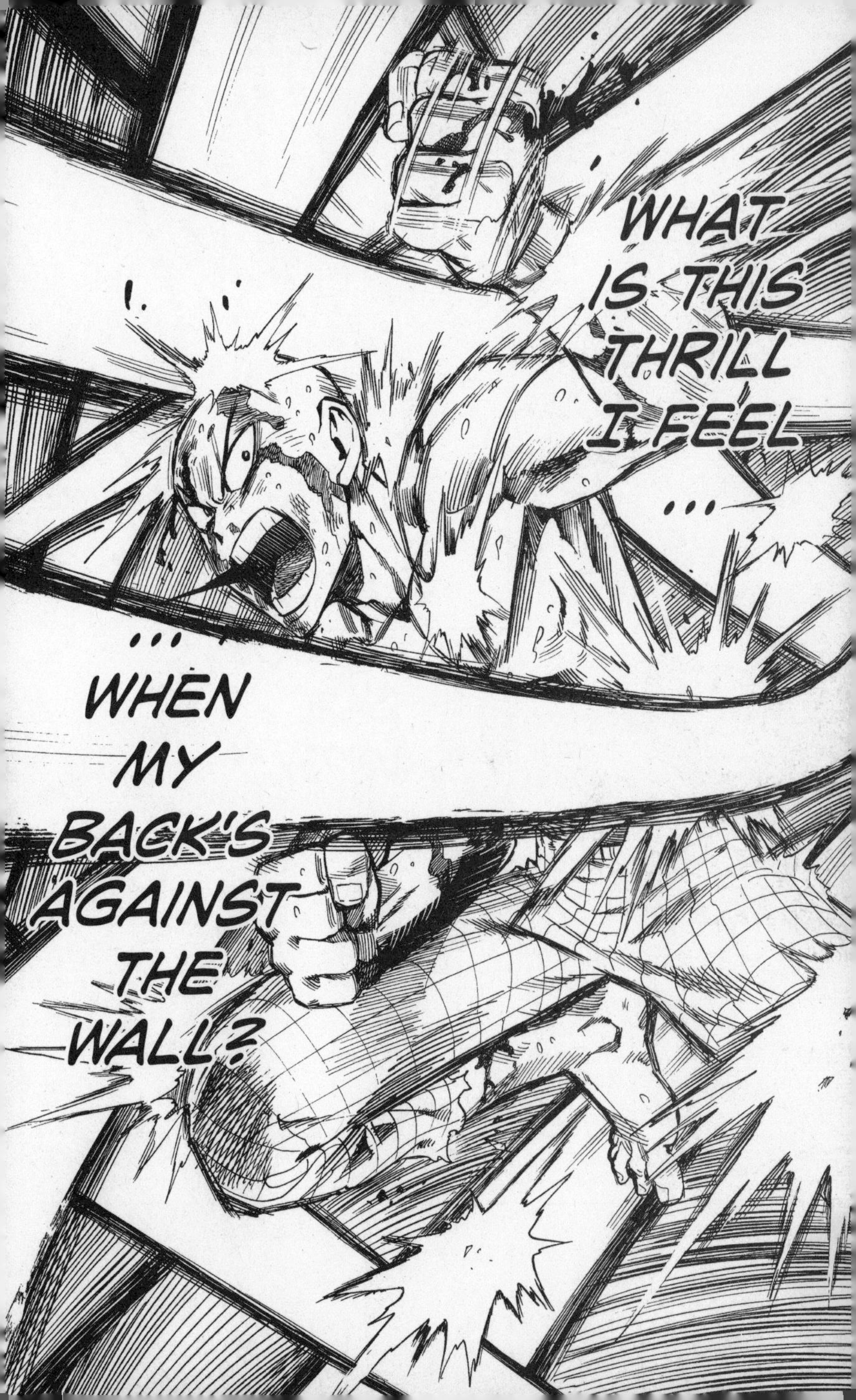
!
WHAT IS THIS THRILL I FEEL ...
... WHEN MY BACK'S AGAINST THE WALL?

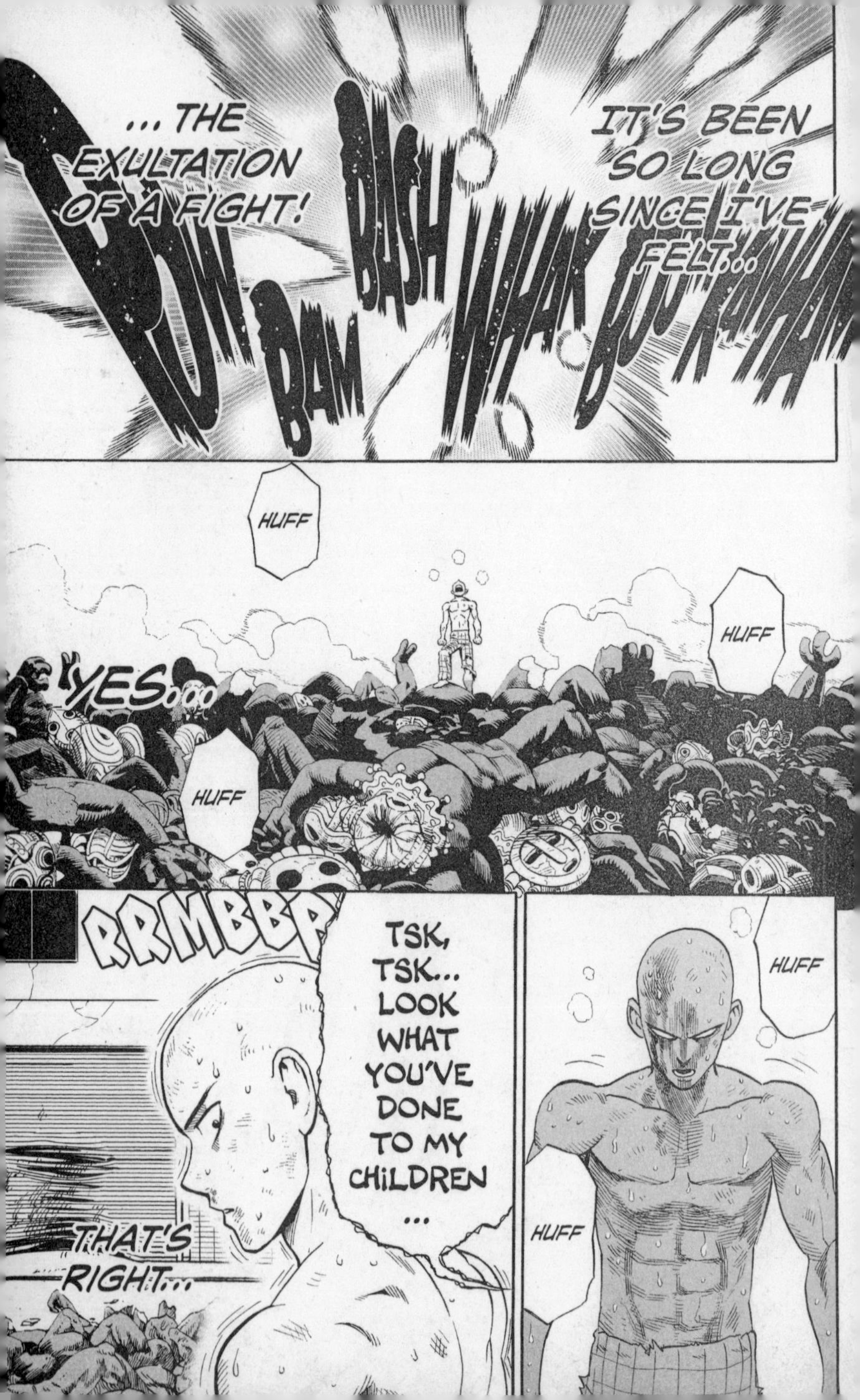
IT'S BEEN SO LONG SINCE I'VE FELT...
...THE EXULTATION OF A FIGHT!
WHAK
BASH
BAM
POW
HUFF
HUFF
YES...
HUFF
HUFF
HUFF
RRMBBR
TSK, TSK... LOOK WHAT YOU'VE DONE TO MY CHILDREN...
THAT'S RIGHT...

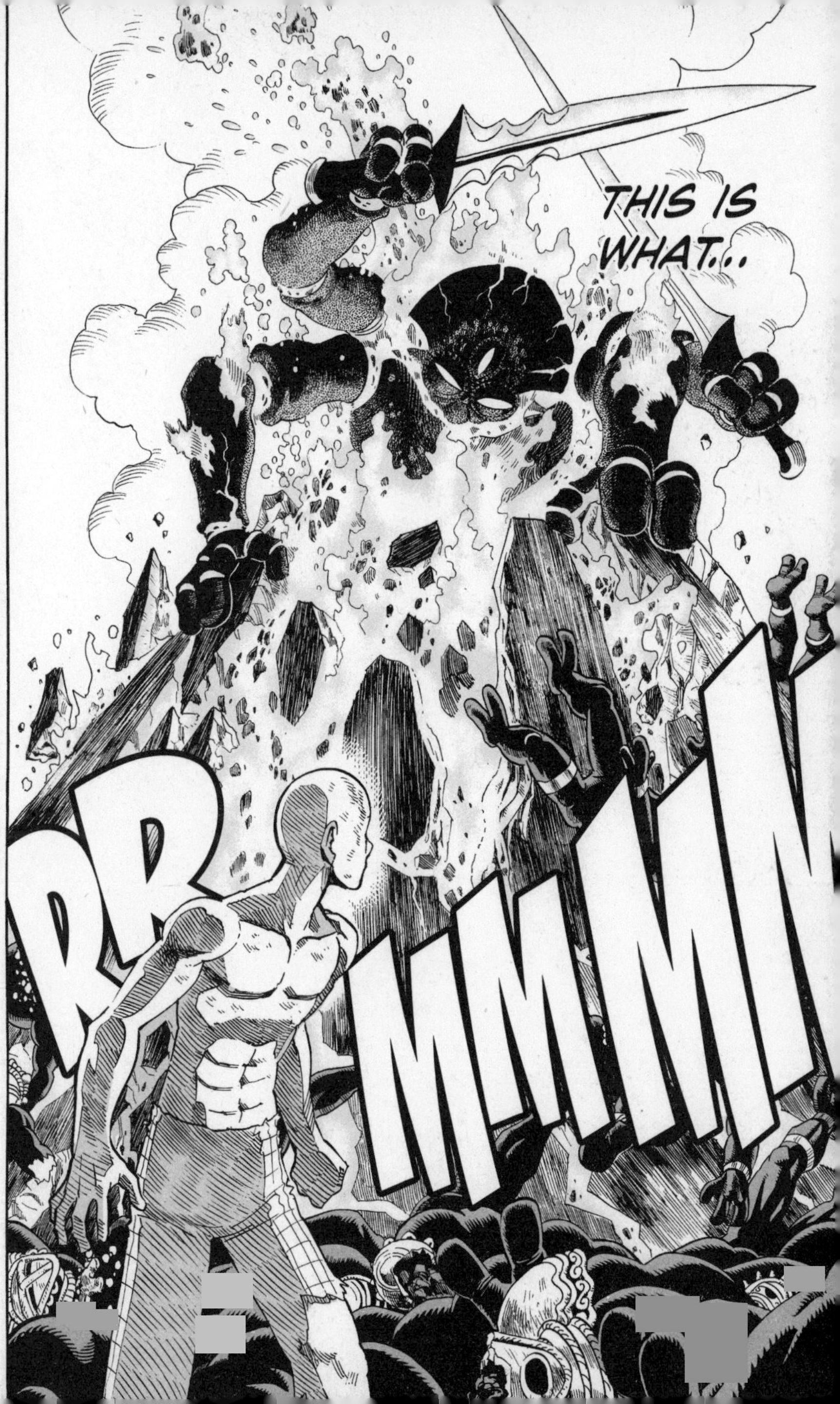
THIS IS WHAT...
RRMMMM

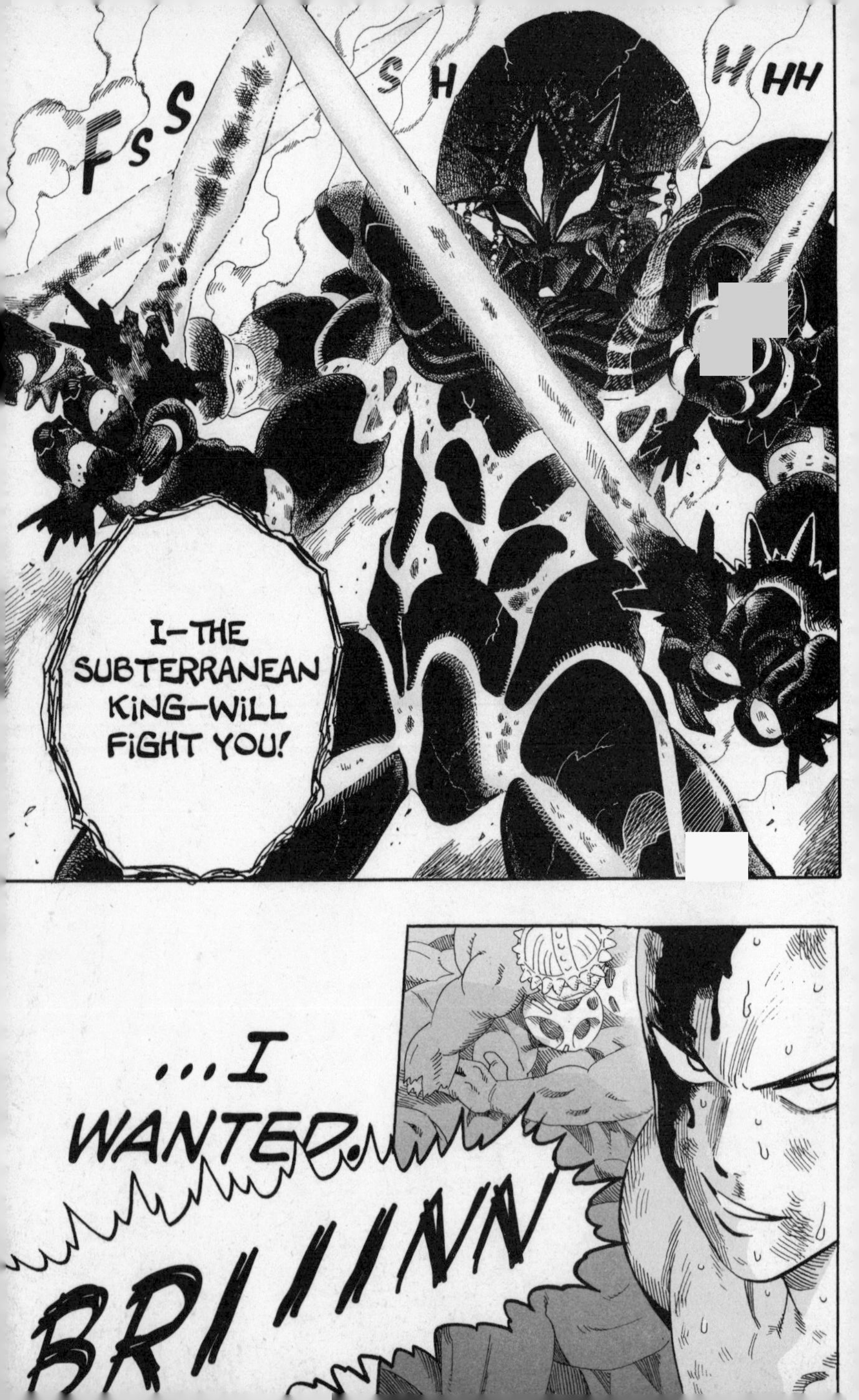
FsS
SHHHH
I—THE SUBTERRANEAN KiNG—WiLL FiGHT YOU!
...I WANTED...
BRIIINN

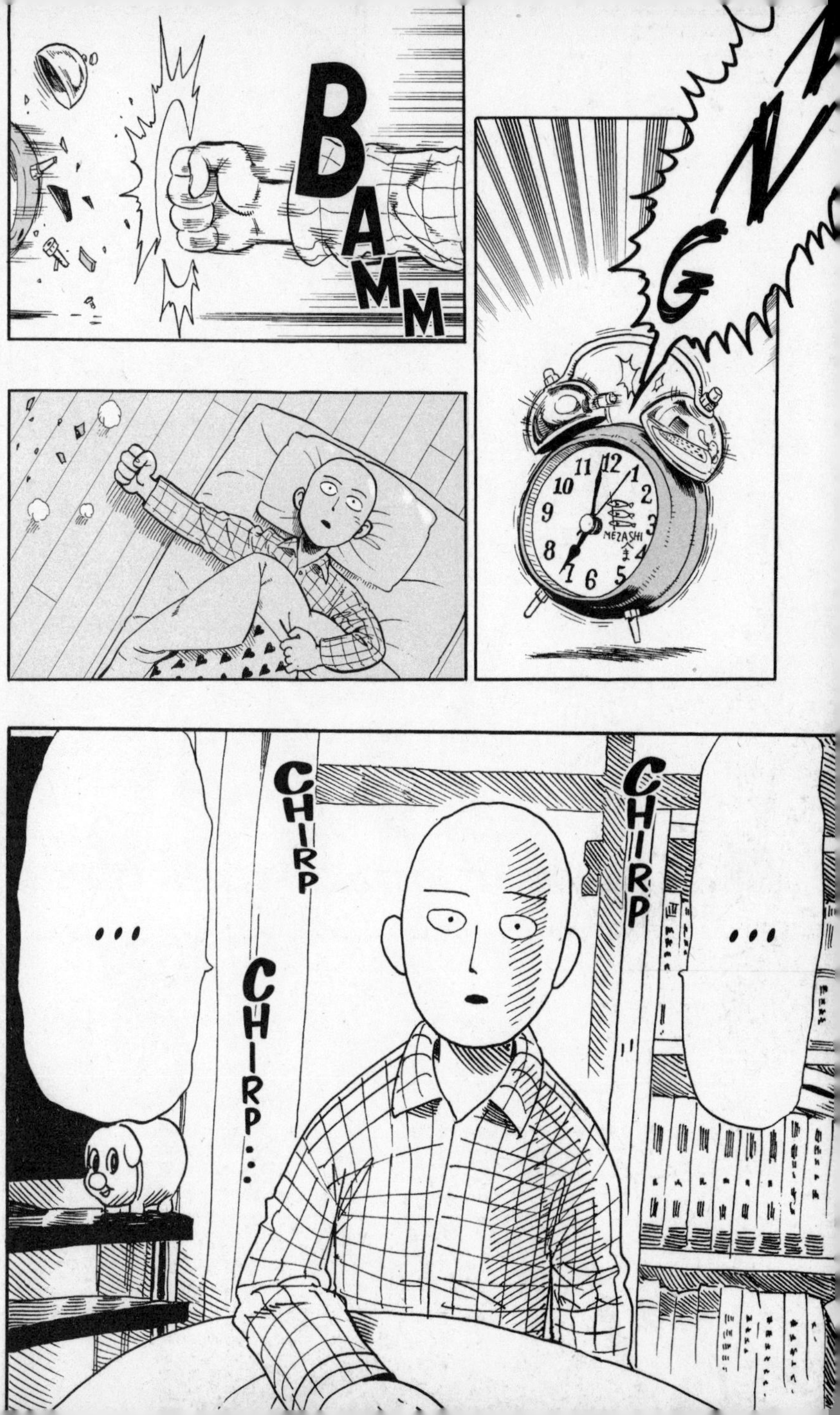
NNG
MEZASHI
BAMM
CHIRP
CHIRP
...
CHIRP
CHIRP...
...

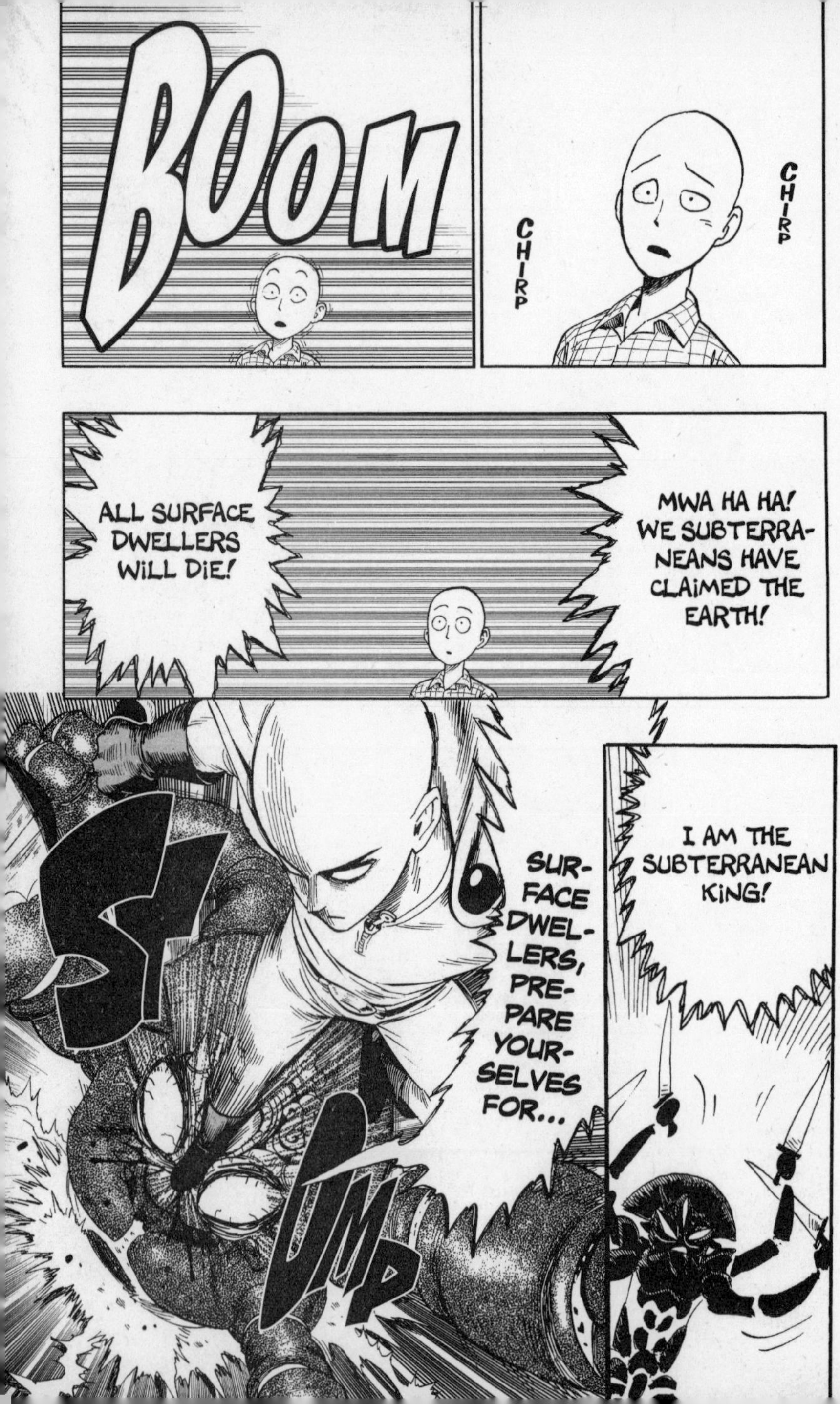
CHIRP
CHIRP
BOOM
MWA HA HA! WE SUBTERRANEANS HAVE CLAIMED THE EARTH!
ALL SURFACE DWELLERS WILL DIE!
I AM THE SUBTERRANEAN KING!
SURFACE DWELLERS, PREPARE YOURSELVES FOR...

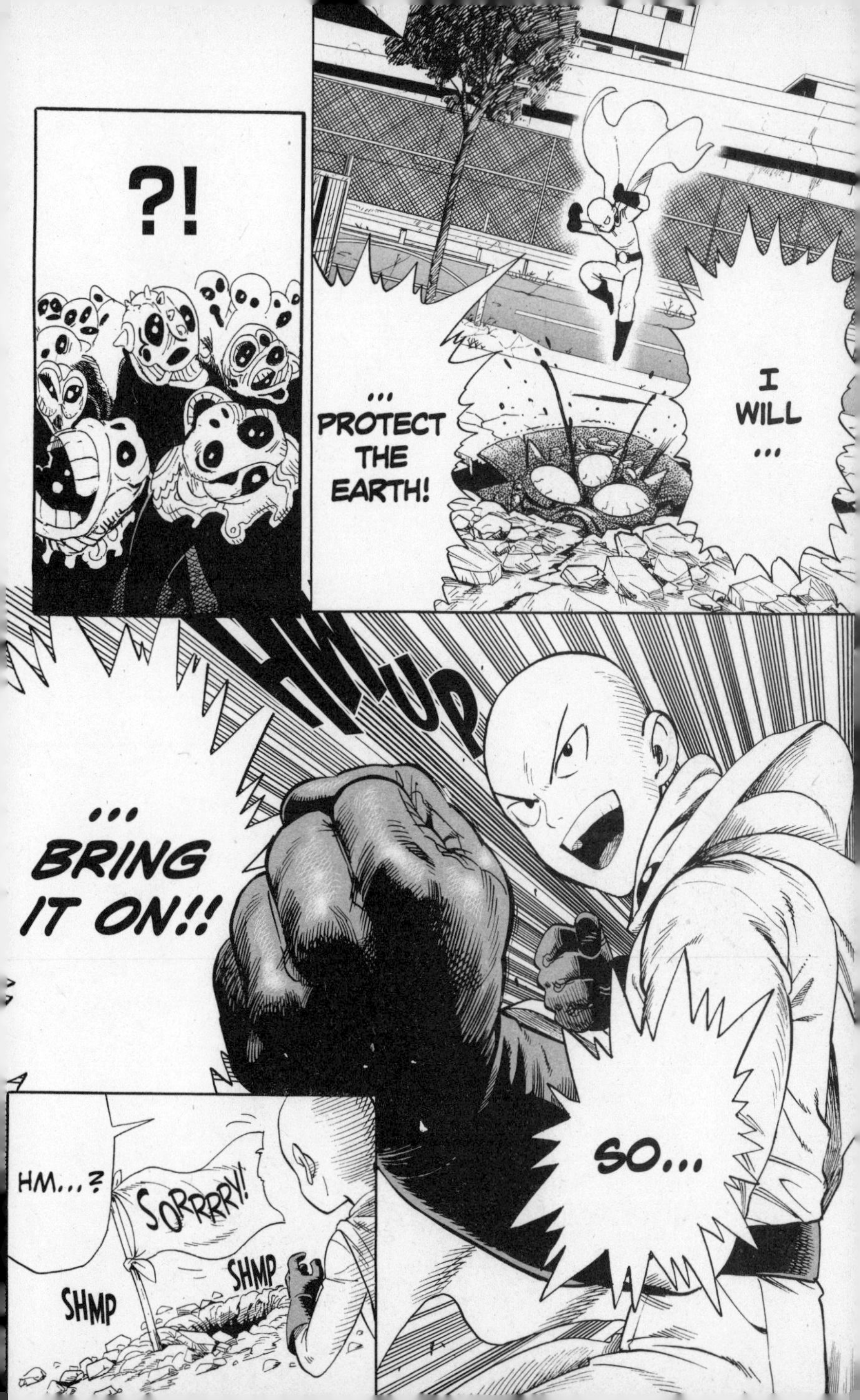

I WILL ...
... PROTECT THE EARTH!
?!
HWUP
SO...
... BRING IT ON!!
HM...?
SORRRRY!
SHMP
SHMP

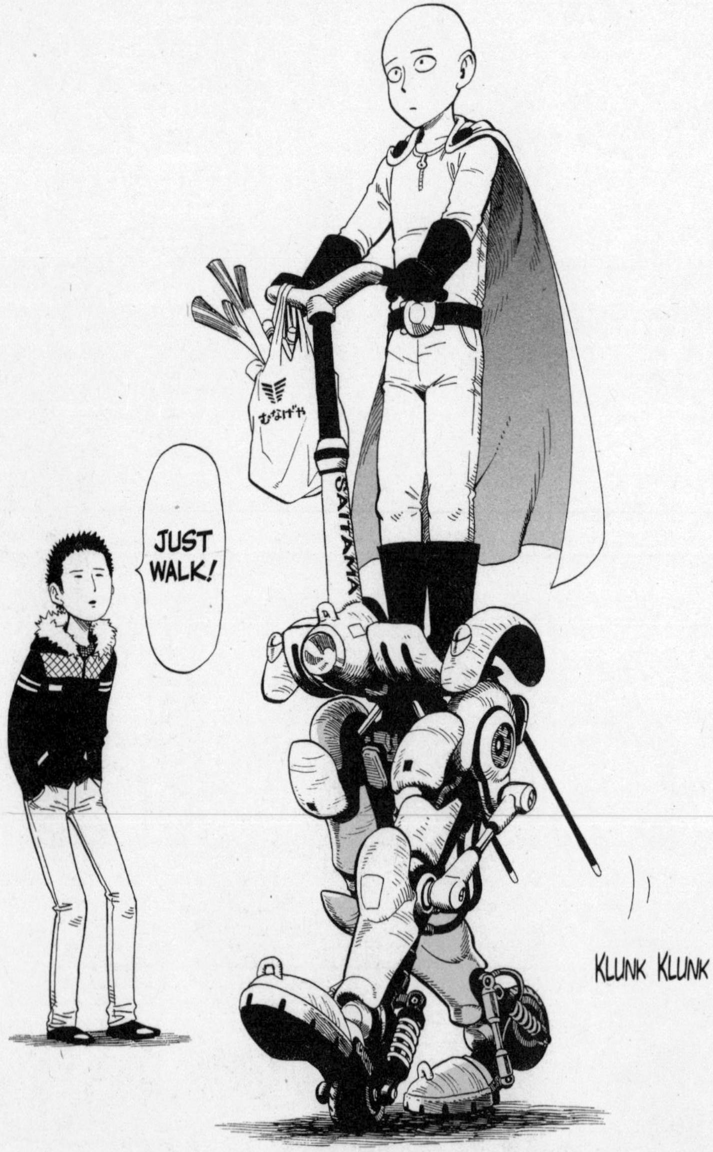
JUST WALK!
KLUNK KLUNK

ONE-PUNCH MAN 01

STORY by ONE &
ART by YUSUKE MURATA

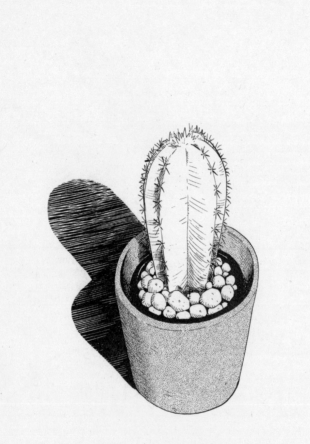

PUNCH 5:
ITCH EXPLOSION

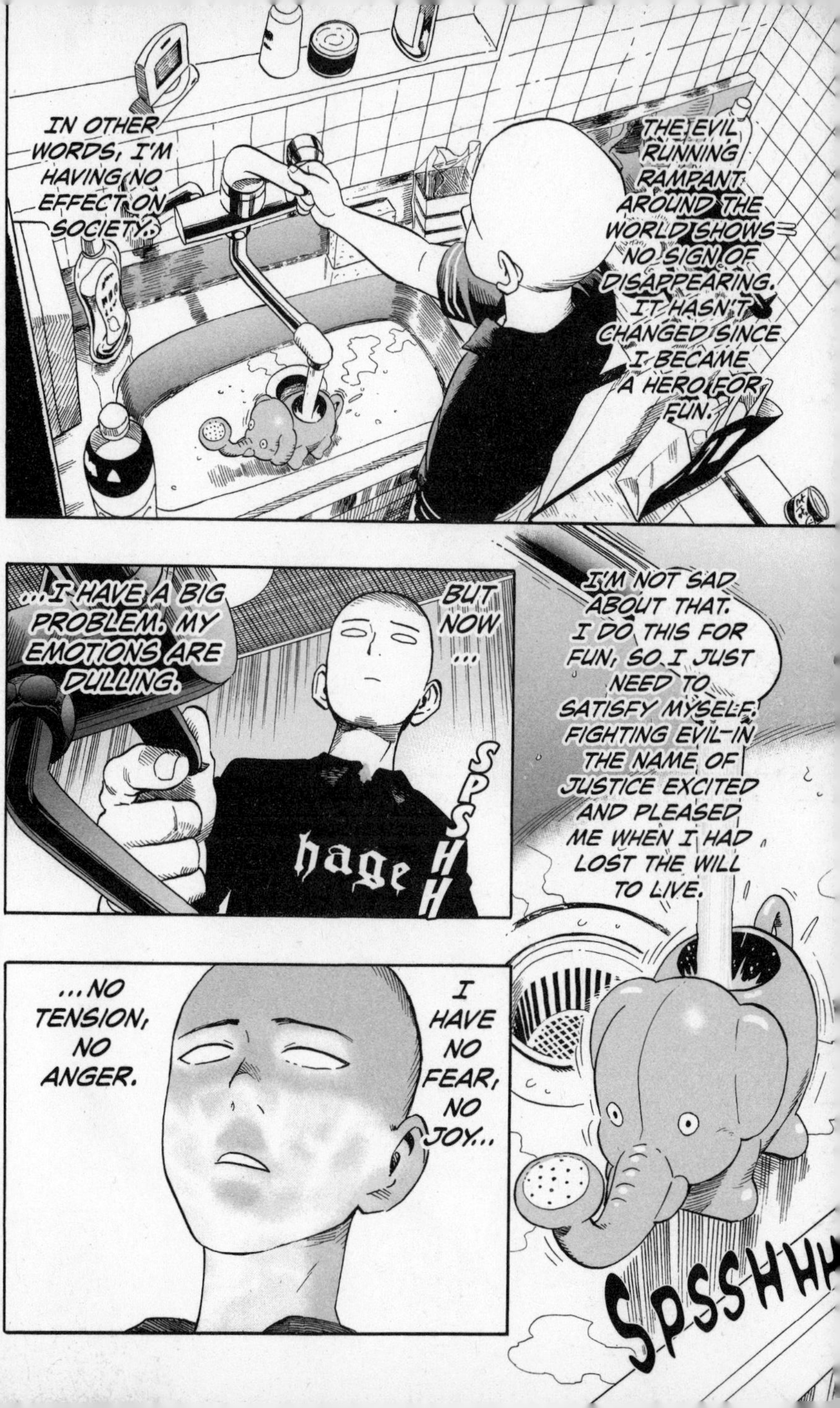
THE EVIL RUNNING RAMPANT AROUND THE WORLD SHOWS NO SIGN OF DISAPPEARING. IT HASN'T CHANGED SINCE I BECAME A HERO FOR FUN.
IN OTHER WORDS, I'M HAVING NO EFFECT ON SOCIETY.
I'M NOT SAD ABOUT THAT. I DO THIS FOR FUN, SO I JUST NEED TO SATISFY MYSELF. FIGHTING EVIL IN THE NAME OF JUSTICE EXCITED AND PLEASED ME WHEN I HAD LOST THE WILL TO LIVE.
SPSSHHH
BUT NOW...
...I HAVE A BIG PROBLEM. MY EMOTIONS ARE DULLING.
hage
SPSHHH
I HAVE NO FEAR, NO JOY...
...NO TENSION, NO ANGER.

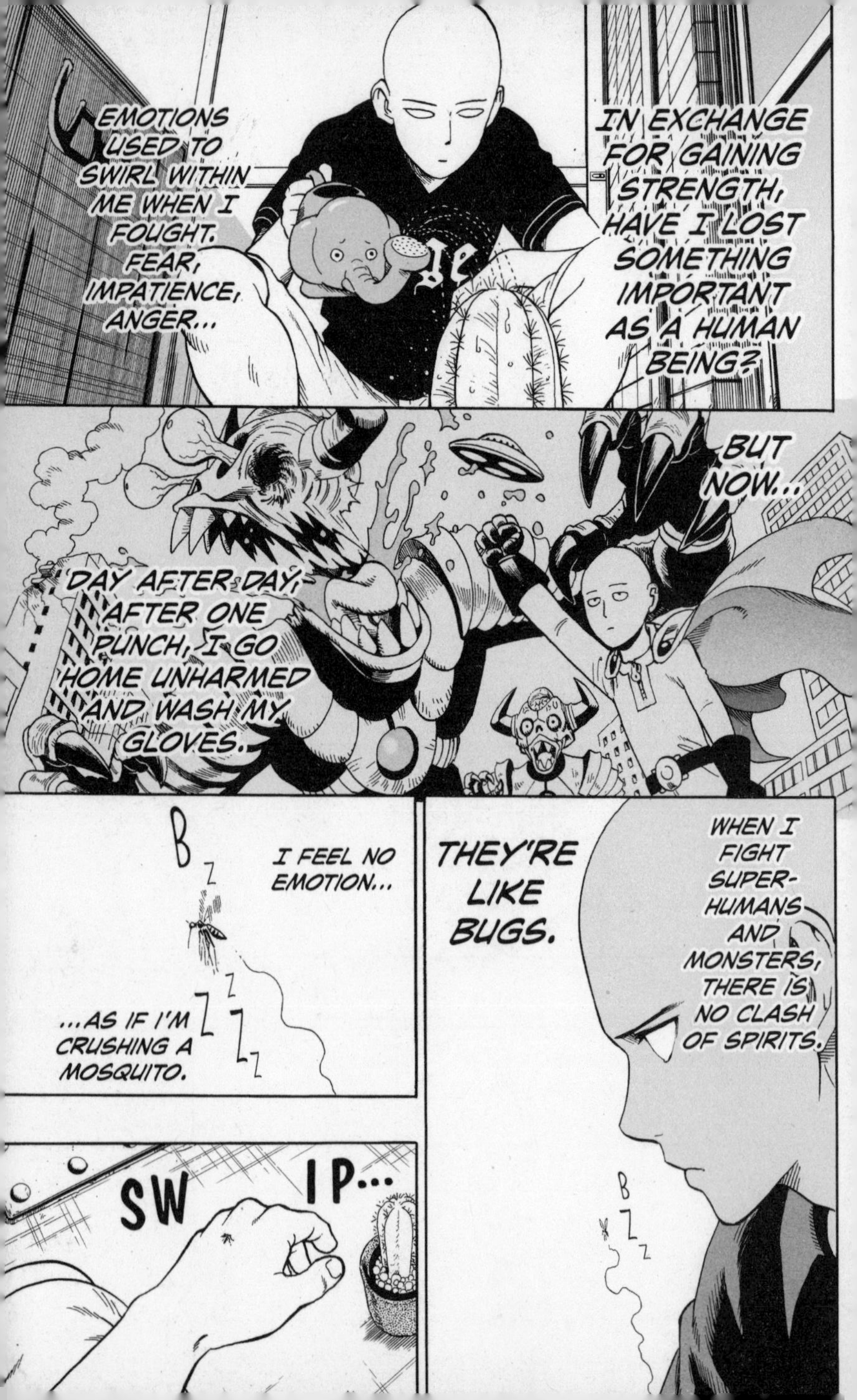
IN EXCHANGE FOR GAINING STRENGTH, HAVE I LOST SOMETHING IMPORTANT AS A HUMAN BEING?
EMOTIONS USED TO SWIRL WITHIN ME WHEN I FOUGHT. FEAR, IMPATIENCE, ANGER...
BUT NOW...
DAY AFTER DAY, AFTER ONE PUNCH, I GO HOME UNHARMED AND WASH MY GLOVES.
WHEN I FIGHT SUPER-HUMANS AND MONSTERS, THERE IS NO CLASH OF SPIRITS.
THEY'RE LIKE BUGS.
BZZ
BZZZZZ
I FEEL NO EMOTION...
...AS IF I'M CRUSHING A MOSQUITO.
SW IP...

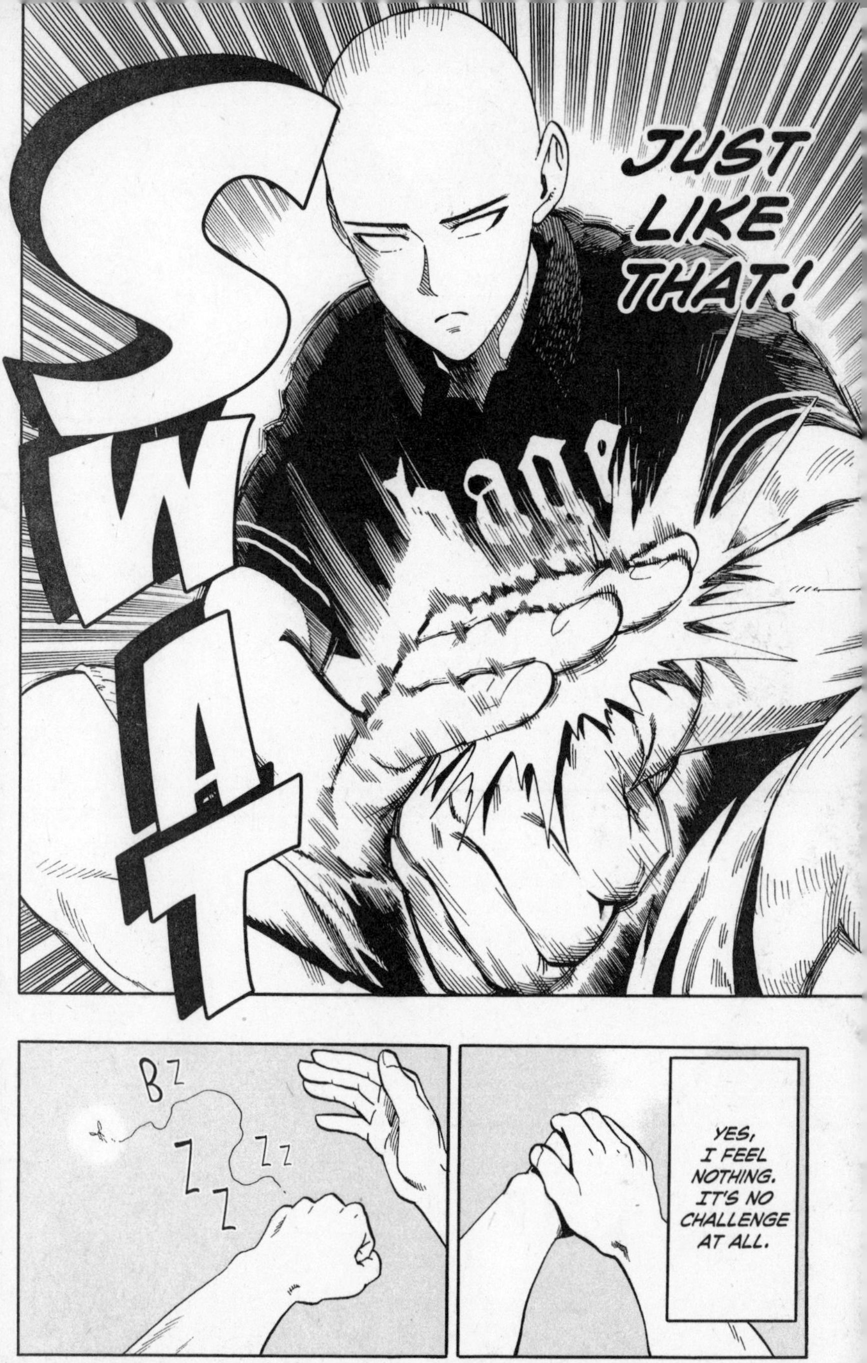
JUST LIKE THAT!
SWAT
YES, I FEEL NOTHING. IT'S NO CHALLENGE AT ALL.
BZZZZZ

READ THIS WAY

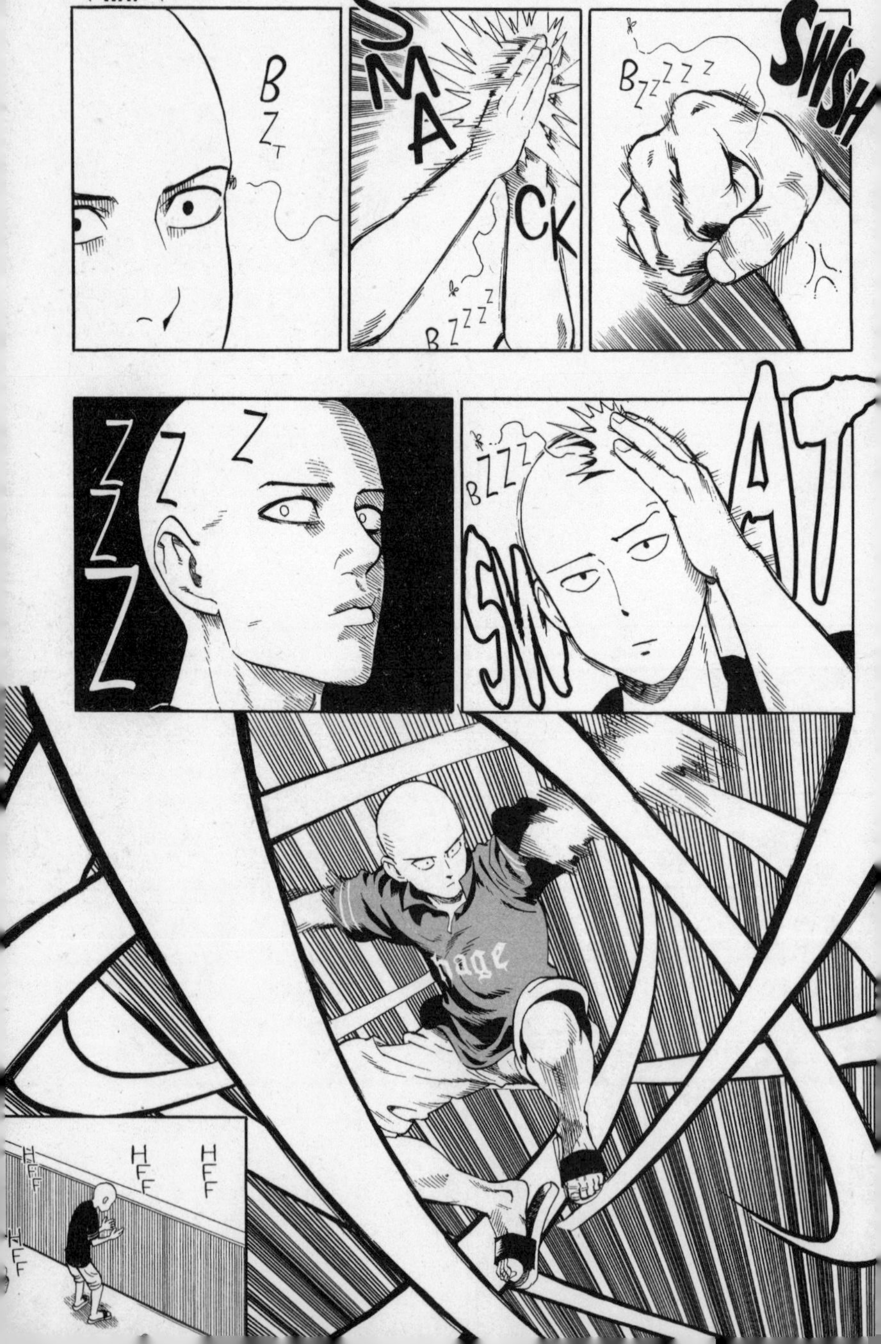
SWSH
BZZZZZ
SMACK
BZZZZ
BZZT
BZZZ
AT
SW
ZZZZZ
hage
HFF
HFF
HFF
HFF

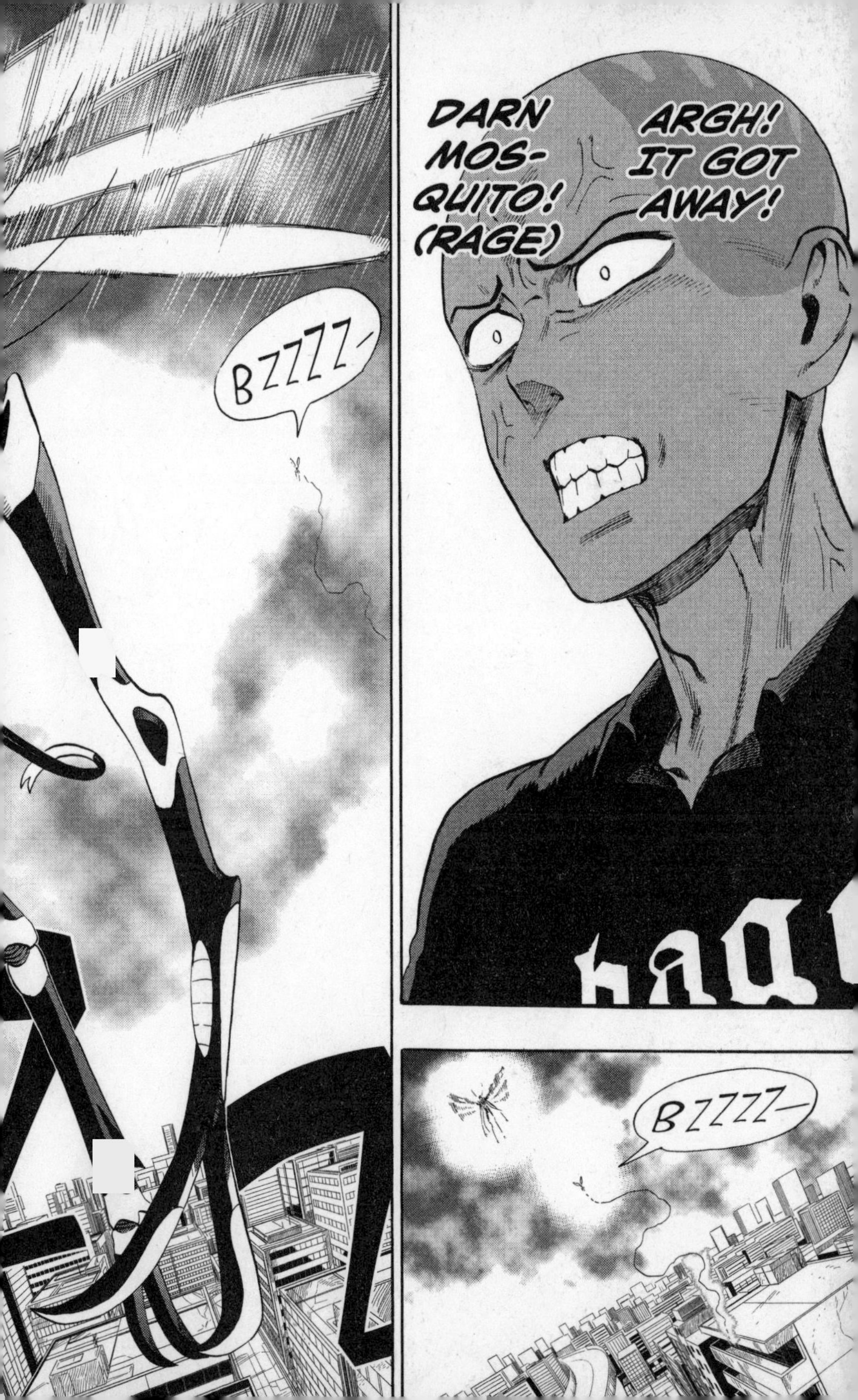
ARGH! IT GOT AWAY!
DARN MOS-QUITO! (RAGE)
BZZZZ—
BZZZZZ—

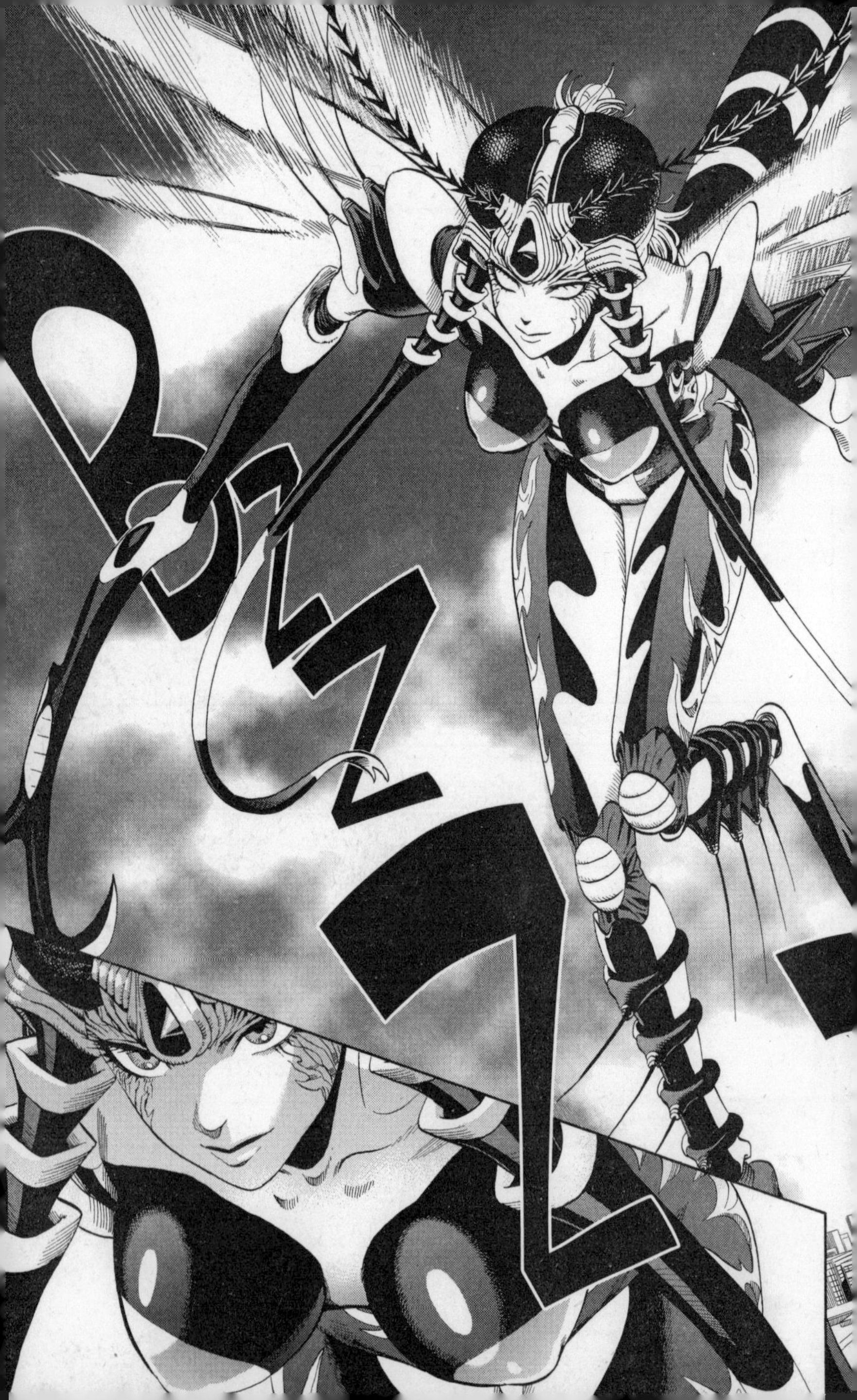
BZZZZ

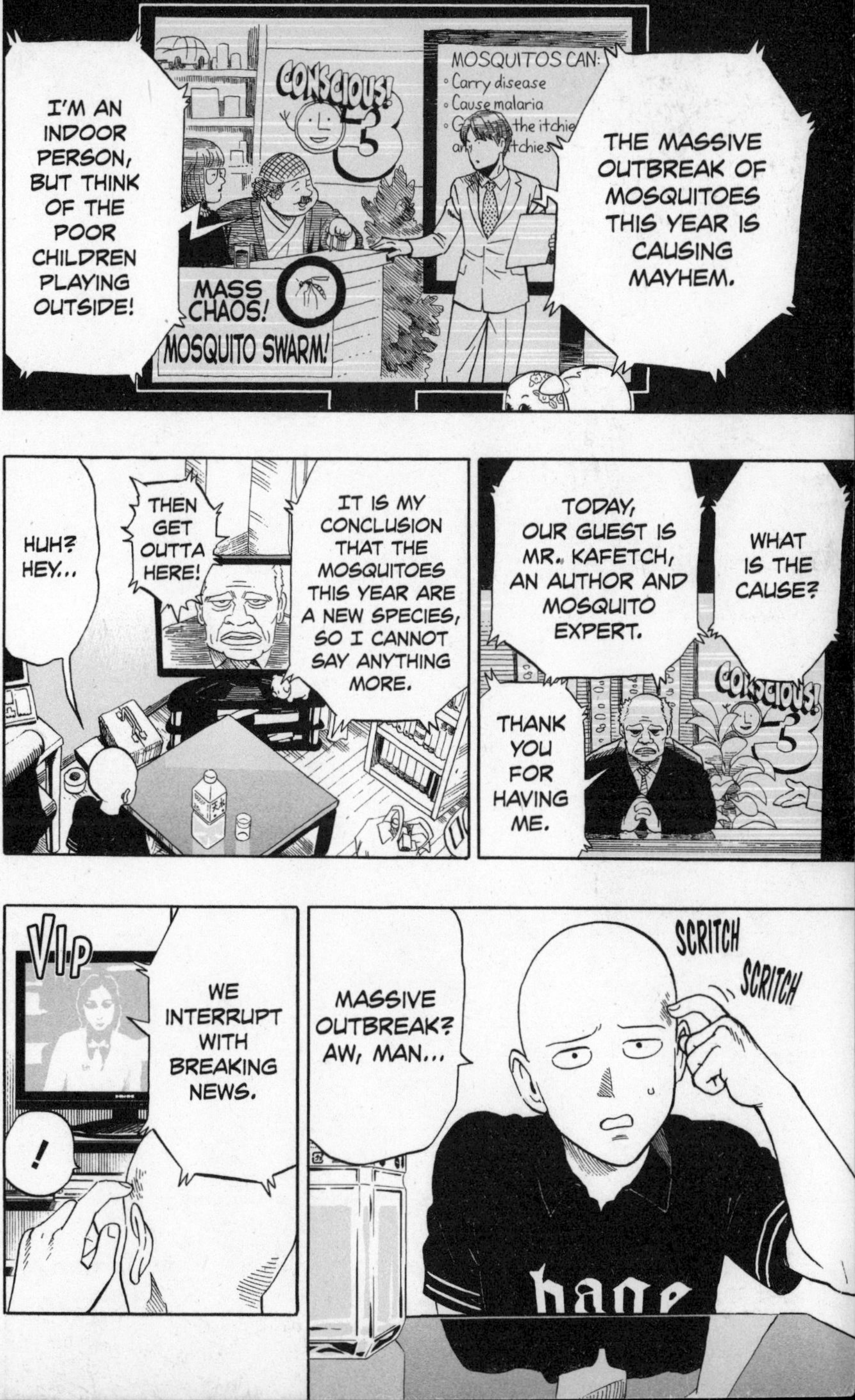
THE MASSIVE OUTBREAK OF MOSQUITOES THIS YEAR IS CAUSING MAYHEM.
MOSQUITOS CAN:
◦ Carry disease
◦ Cause malaria
CONSCIOUS! 3
I'M AN INDOOR PERSON, BUT THINK OF THE POOR CHILDREN PLAYING OUTSIDE!
MASS CHAOS!
MOSQUITO SWARM!
WHAT IS THE CAUSE?
TODAY, OUR GUEST IS MR. KAFETCH, AN AUTHOR AND MOSQUITO EXPERT.
CONSCIOUS! 3
THANK YOU FOR HAVING ME.
IT IS MY CONCLUSION THAT THE MOSQUITOES THIS YEAR ARE A NEW SPECIES, SO I CANNOT SAY ANYTHING MORE.
THEN GET OUTTA HERE!
HUH? HEY...
SCRITCH
SCRITCH
MASSIVE OUTBREAK? AW, MAN...
VIP
WE INTERRUPT WITH BREAKING NEWS.
!

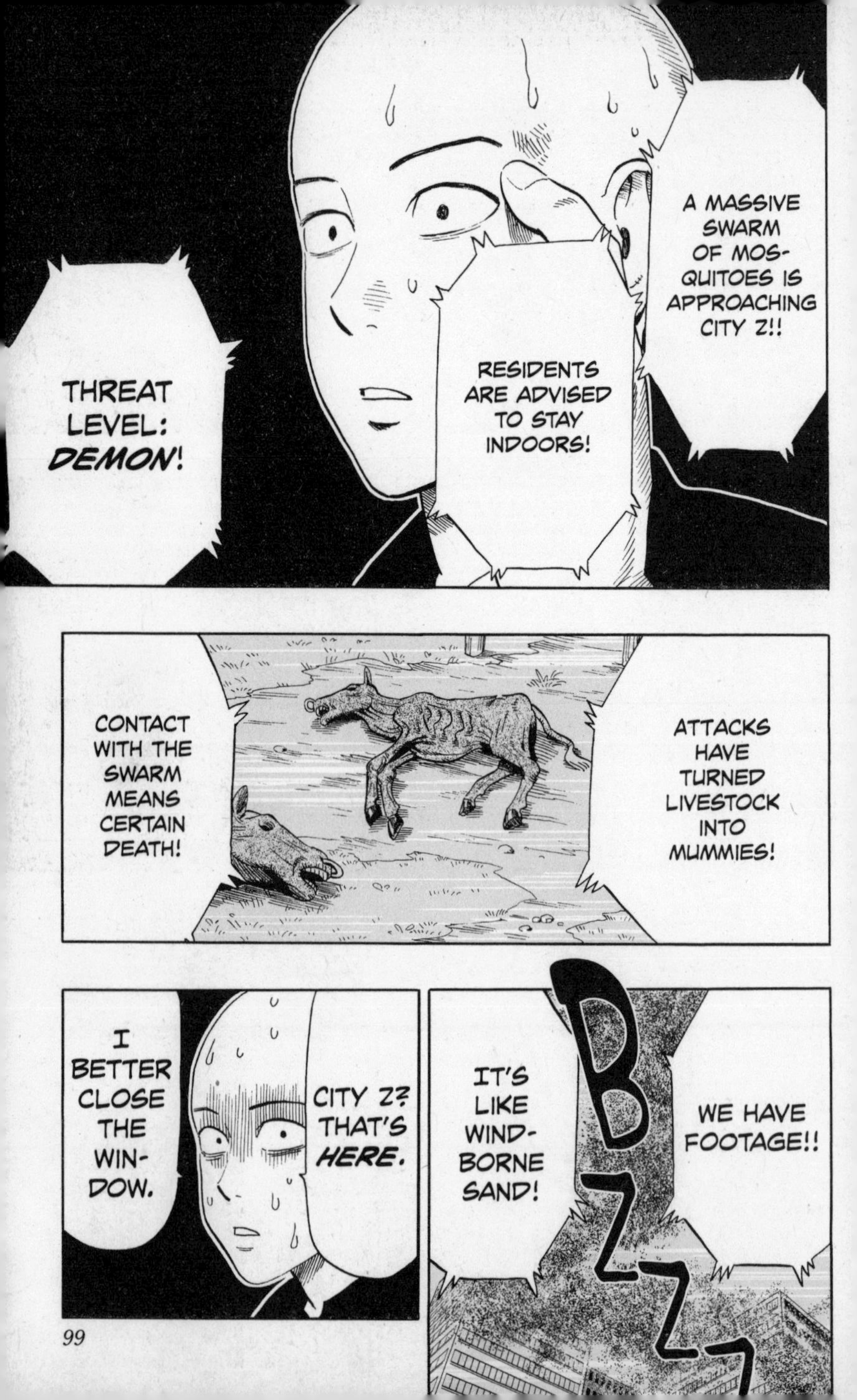
A MASSIVE SWARM OF MOS-QUITOES IS APPROACHING CITY Z!!
RESIDENTS ARE ADVISED TO STAY INDOORS!
THREAT LEVEL: *DEMON*!
ATTACKS HAVE TURNED LIVESTOCK INTO MUMMIES!
CONTACT WITH THE SWARM MEANS CERTAIN DEATH!
WE HAVE FOOTAGE!!
BZZZ
IT'S LIKE WIND-BORNE SAND!
CITY Z? THAT'S *HERE*.
I BETTER CLOSE THE WIN-DOW.

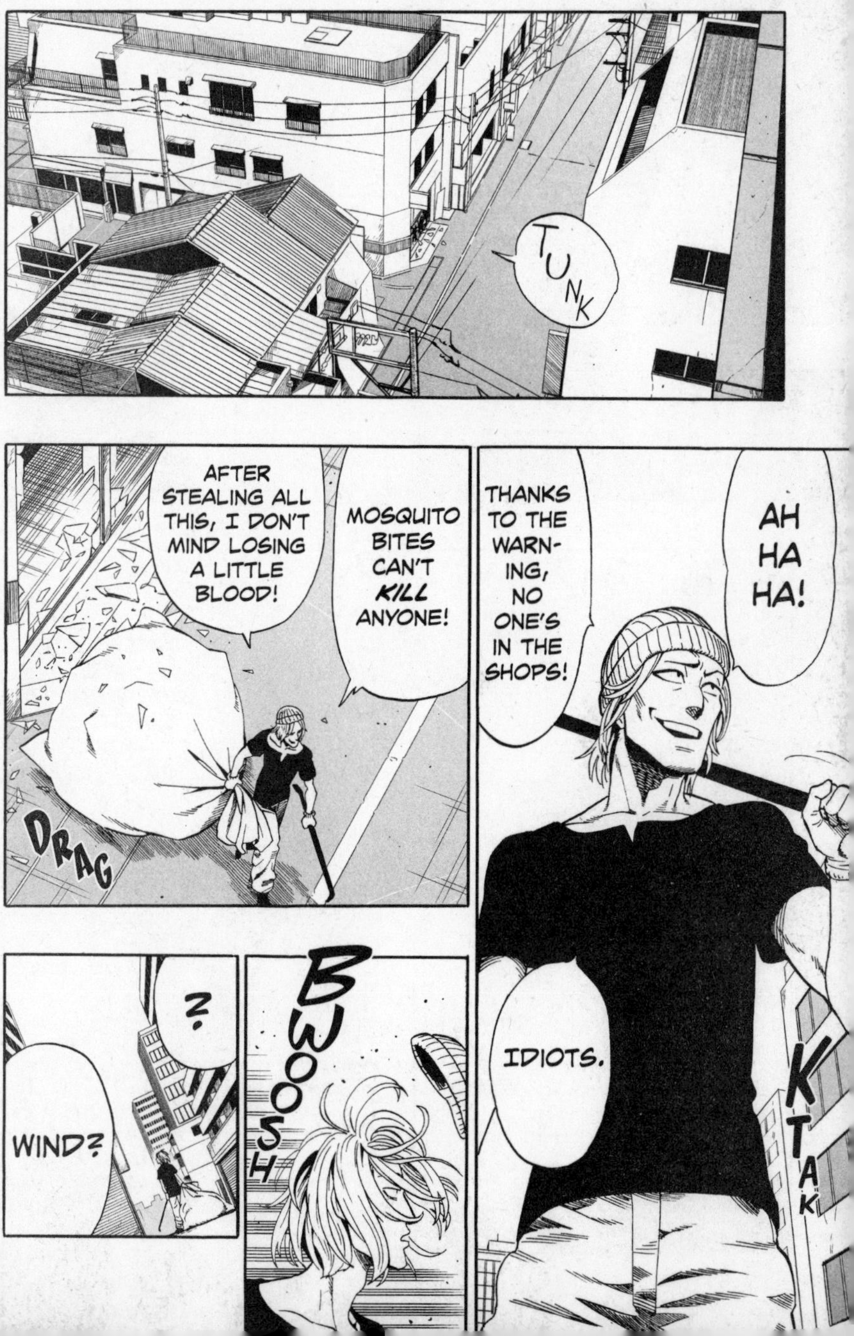
TUNK
AH HA HA!
THANKS TO THE WARNING, NO ONE'S IN THE SHOPS!
IDIOTS.
KTAK
MOSQUITO BITES CAN'T KILL ANYONE!
AFTER STEALING ALL THIS, I DON'T MIND LOSING A LITTLE BLOOD!
DRAG
BWOOSH
?
WIND?

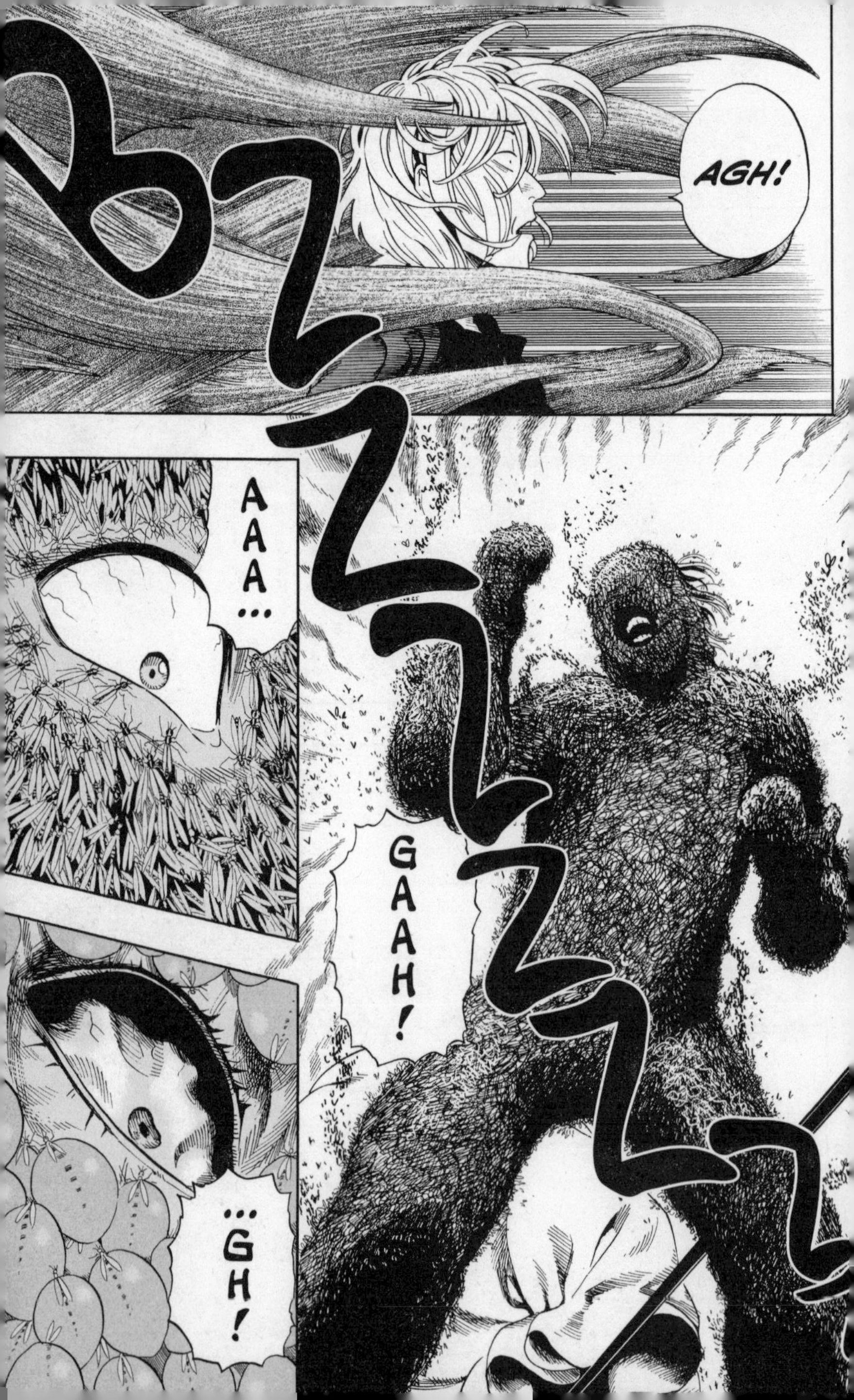
AGH!
GAAH!
AAA...
..GH!

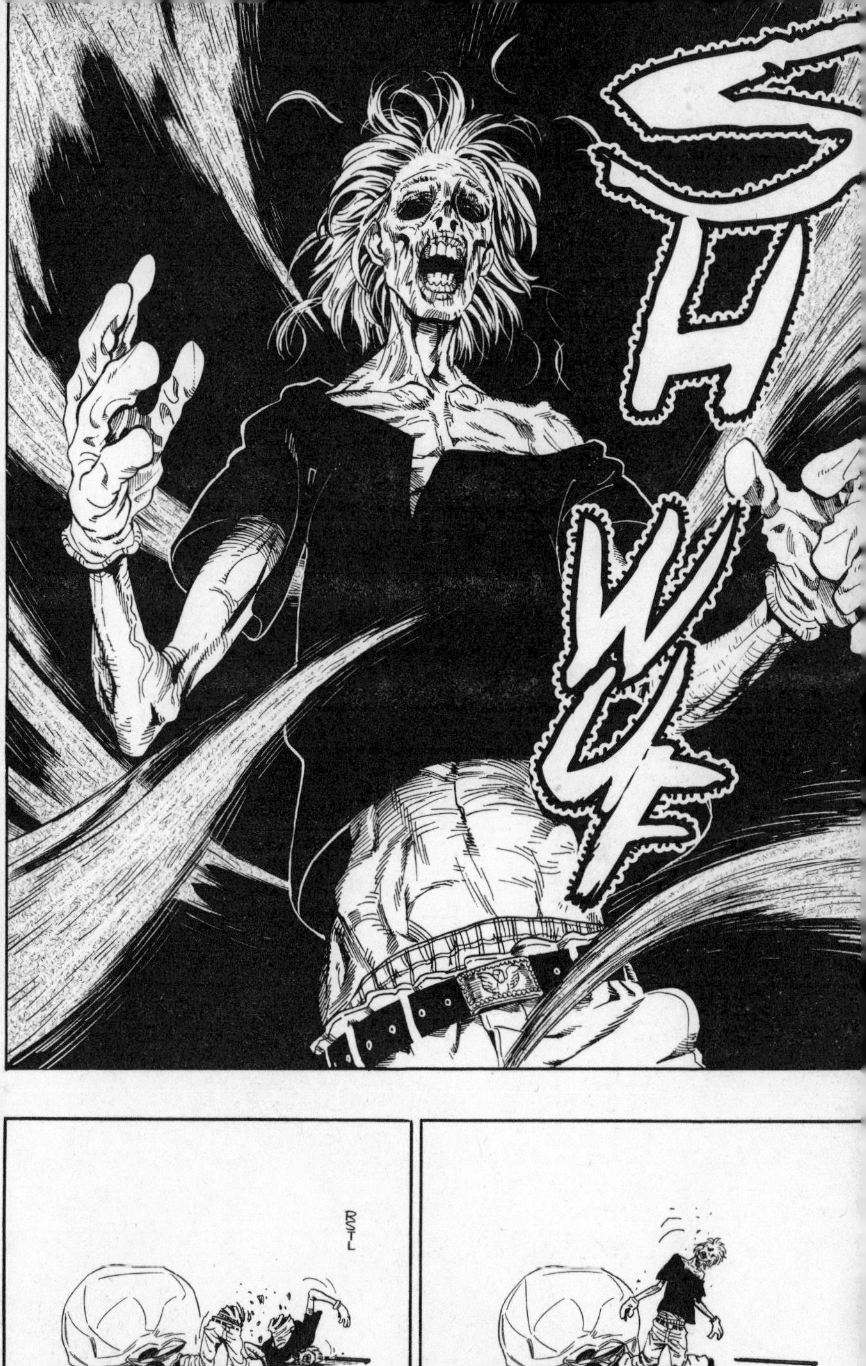
SHWF
RSTL

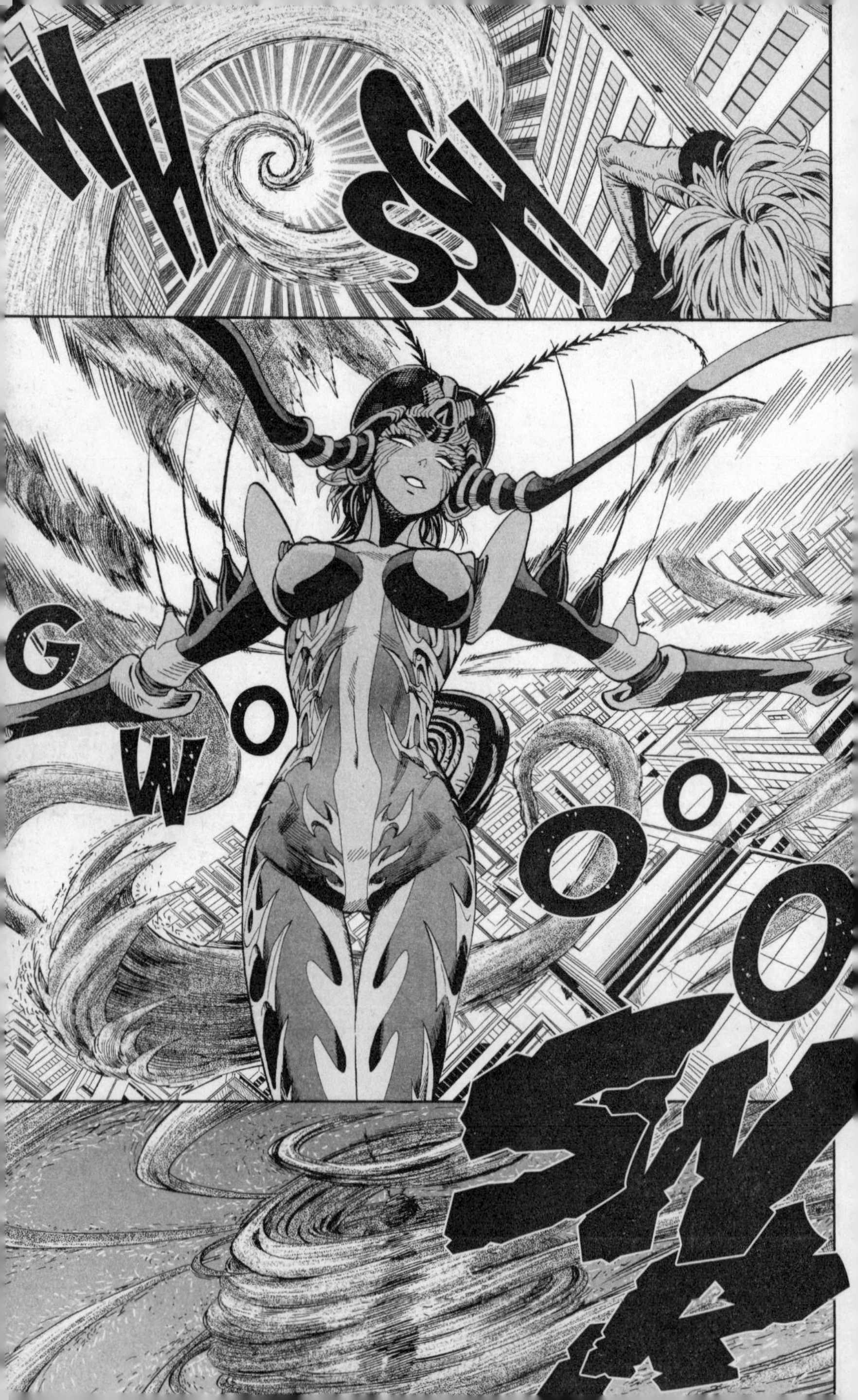
WH SH
GWOOOOO

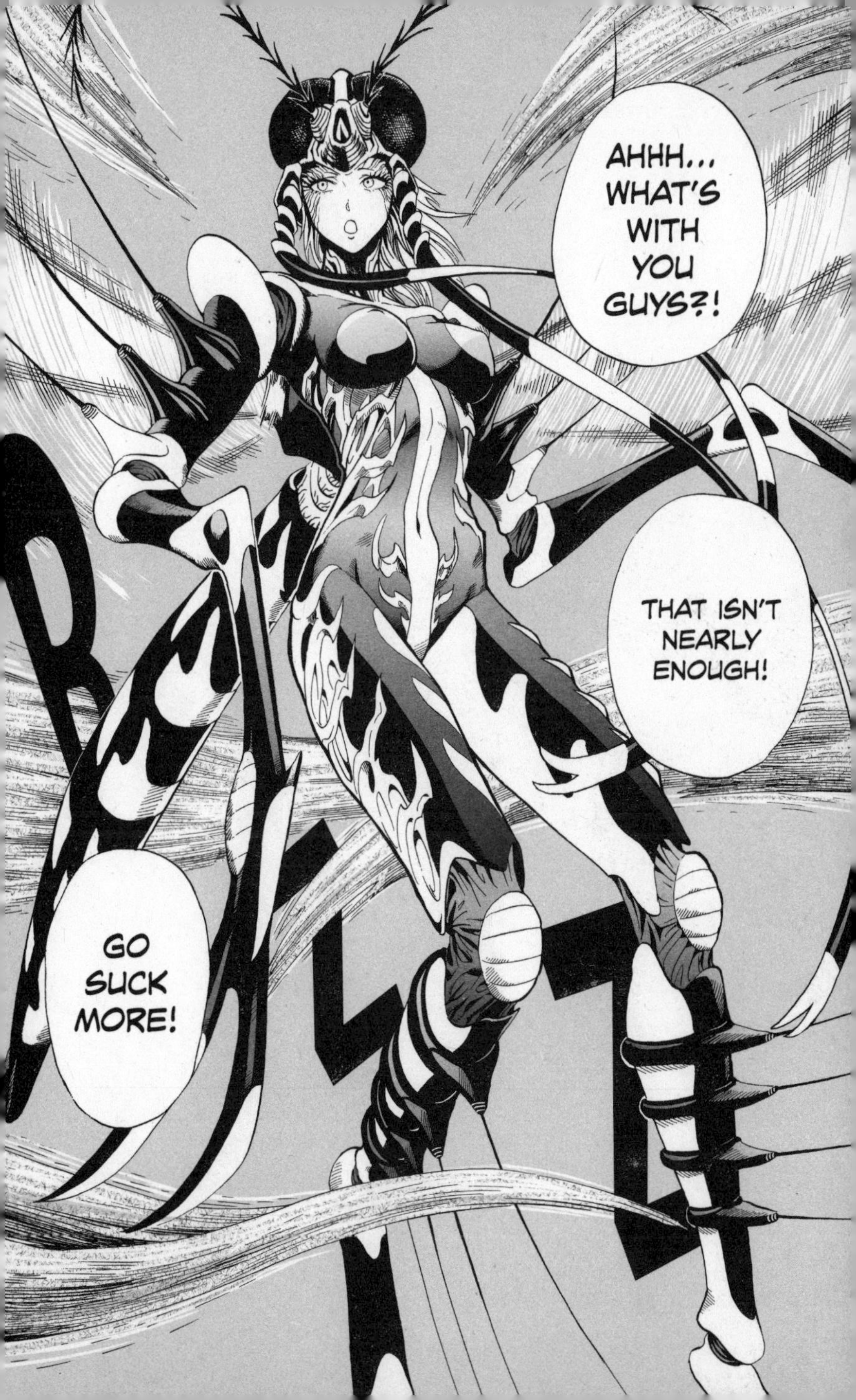
AHHH... WHAT'S WITH YOU GUYS?!
THAT ISN'T NEARLY ENOUGH!
GO SUCK MORE!

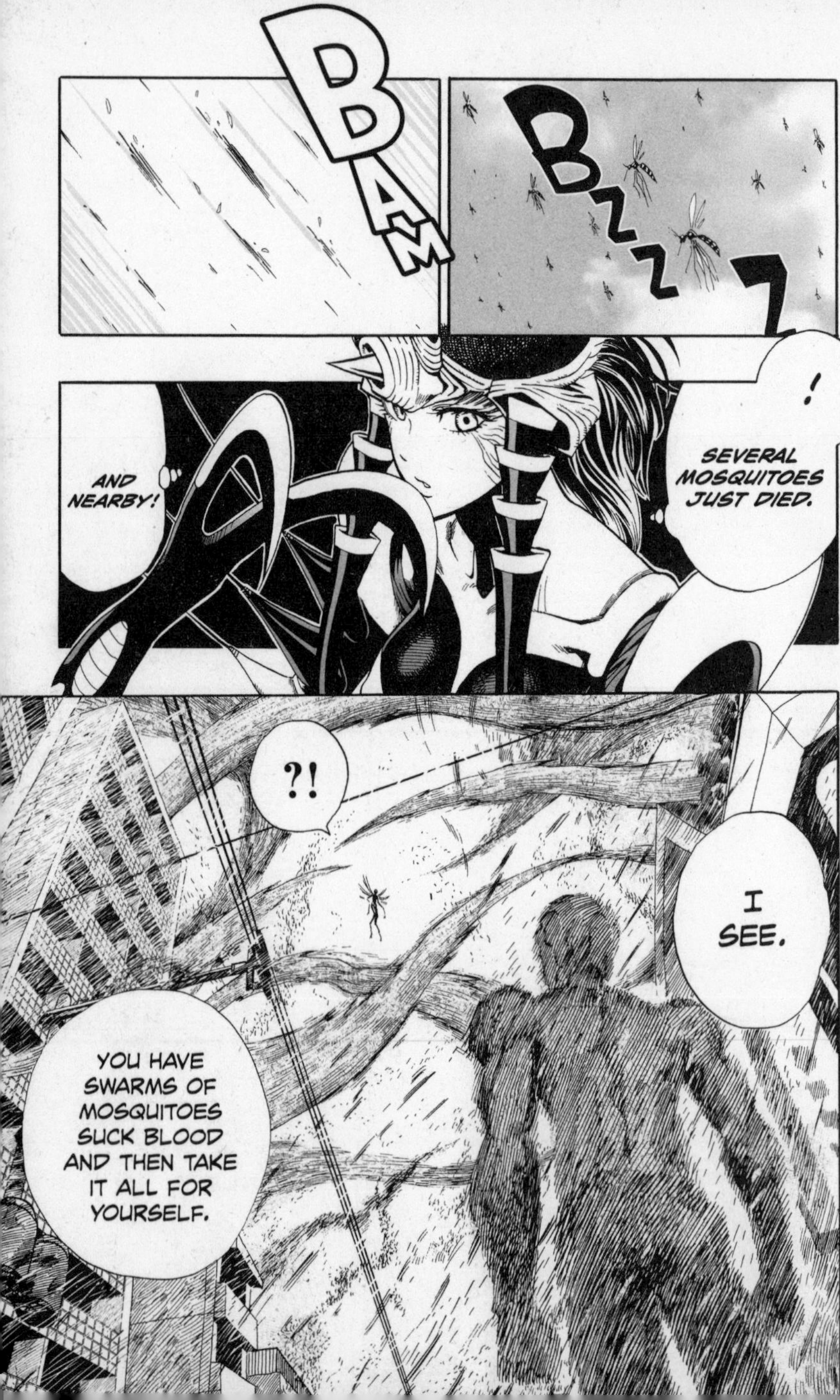
BZZZZ
BAM
!
SEVERAL MOSQUITOES JUST DIED.
AND NEARBY!
?!
I SEE.
YOU HAVE SWARMS OF MOSQUITOES SUCK BLOOD AND THEN TAKE IT ALL FOR YOURSELF.

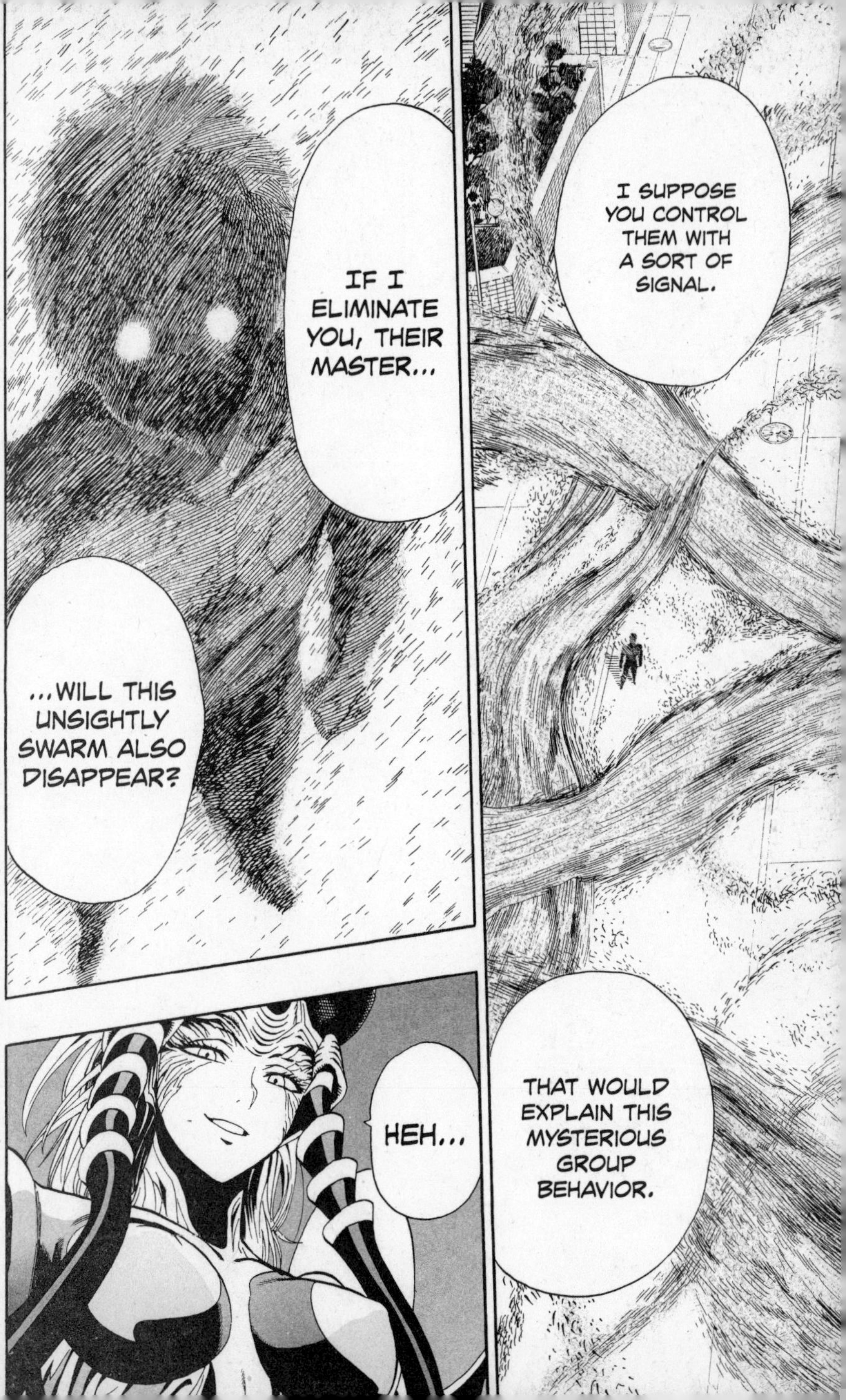
I SUPPOSE YOU CONTROL THEM WITH A SORT OF SIGNAL.
THAT WOULD EXPLAIN THIS MYSTERIOUS GROUP BEHAVIOR.
IF I ELIMINATE YOU, THEIR MASTER...
...WILL THIS UNSIGHTLY SWARM ALSO DISAPPEAR?
HEH...

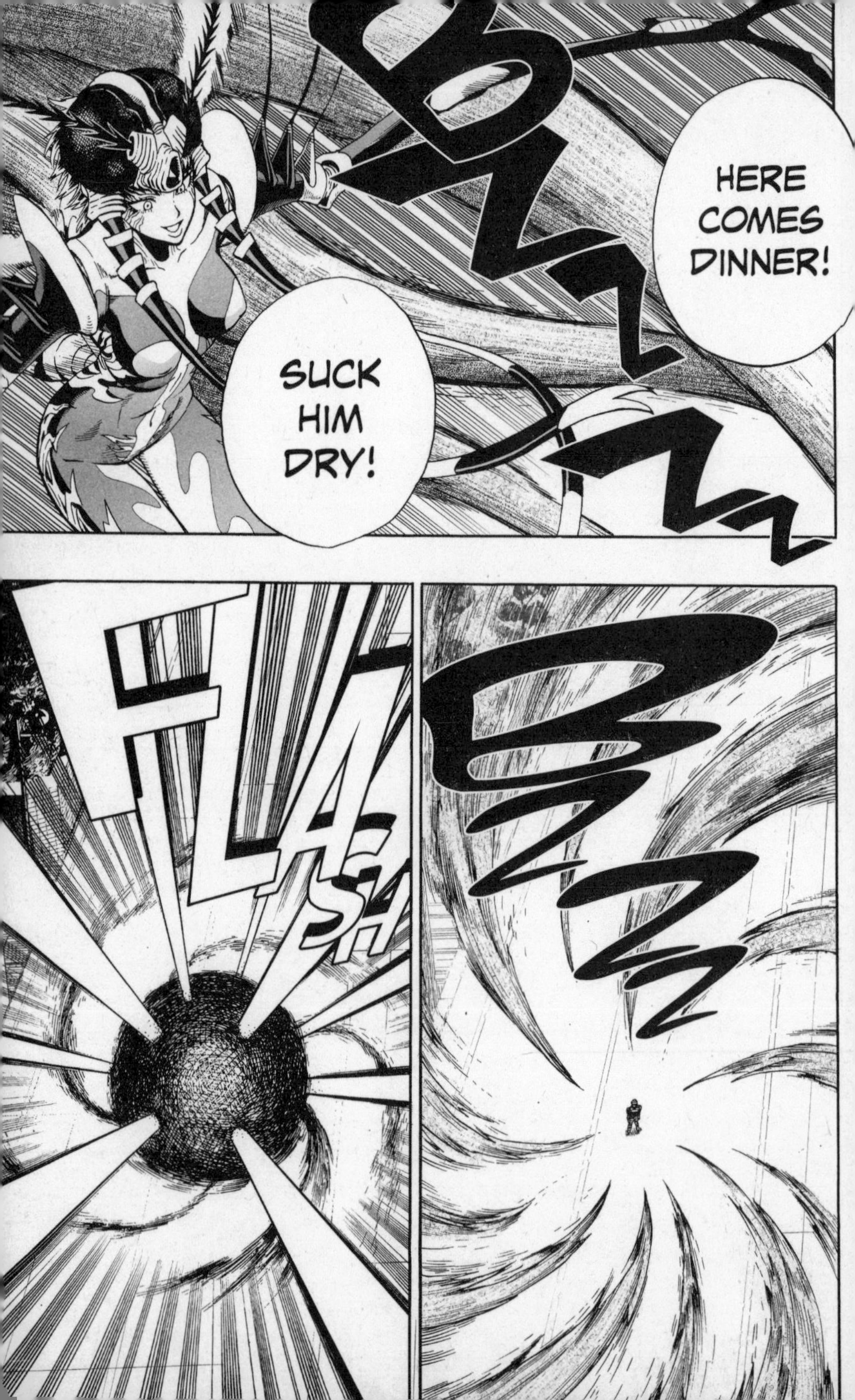
HERE COMES DINNER!
SUCK HIM DRY!
BZZZZZ
BZZZZZ
FLASH

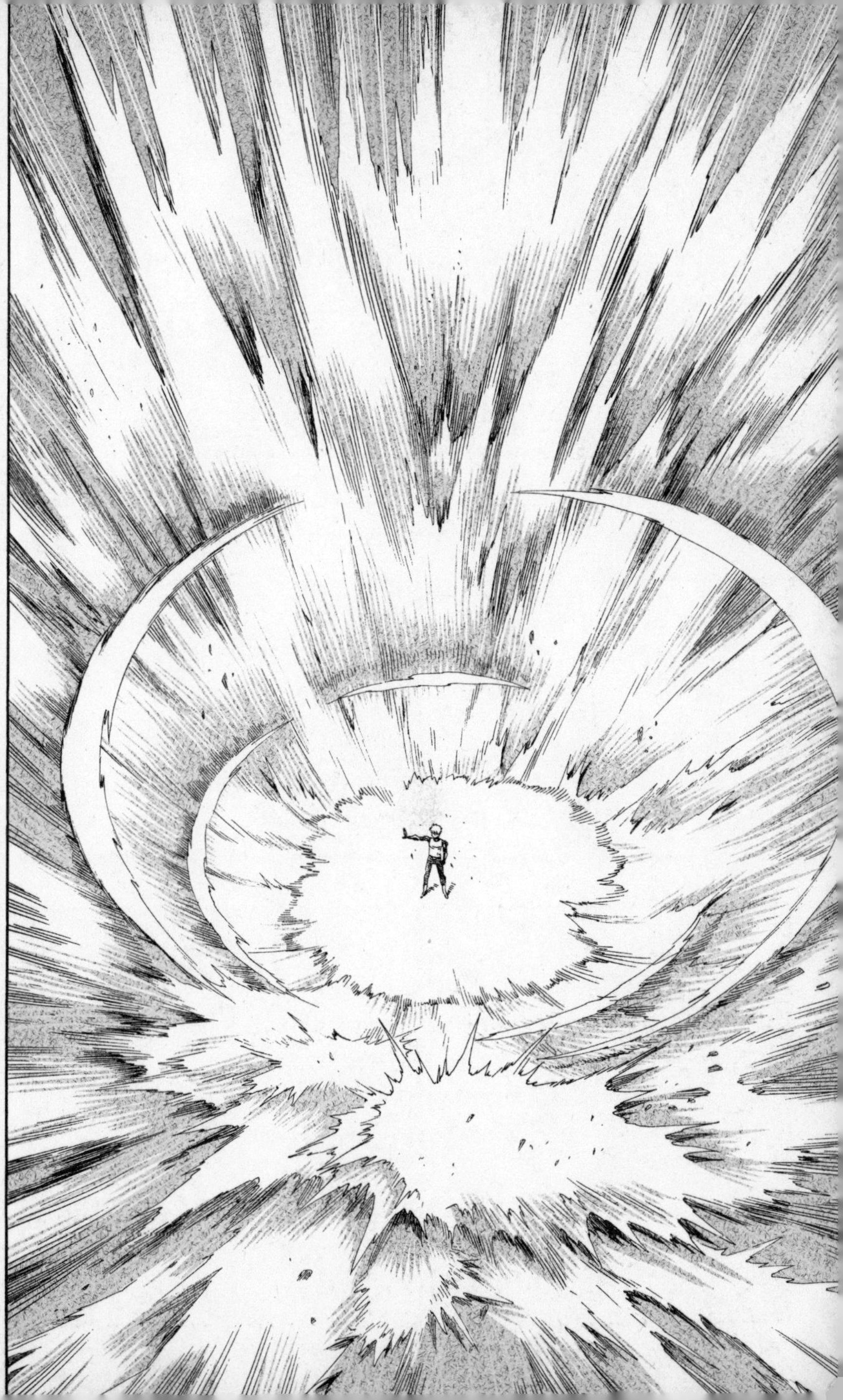

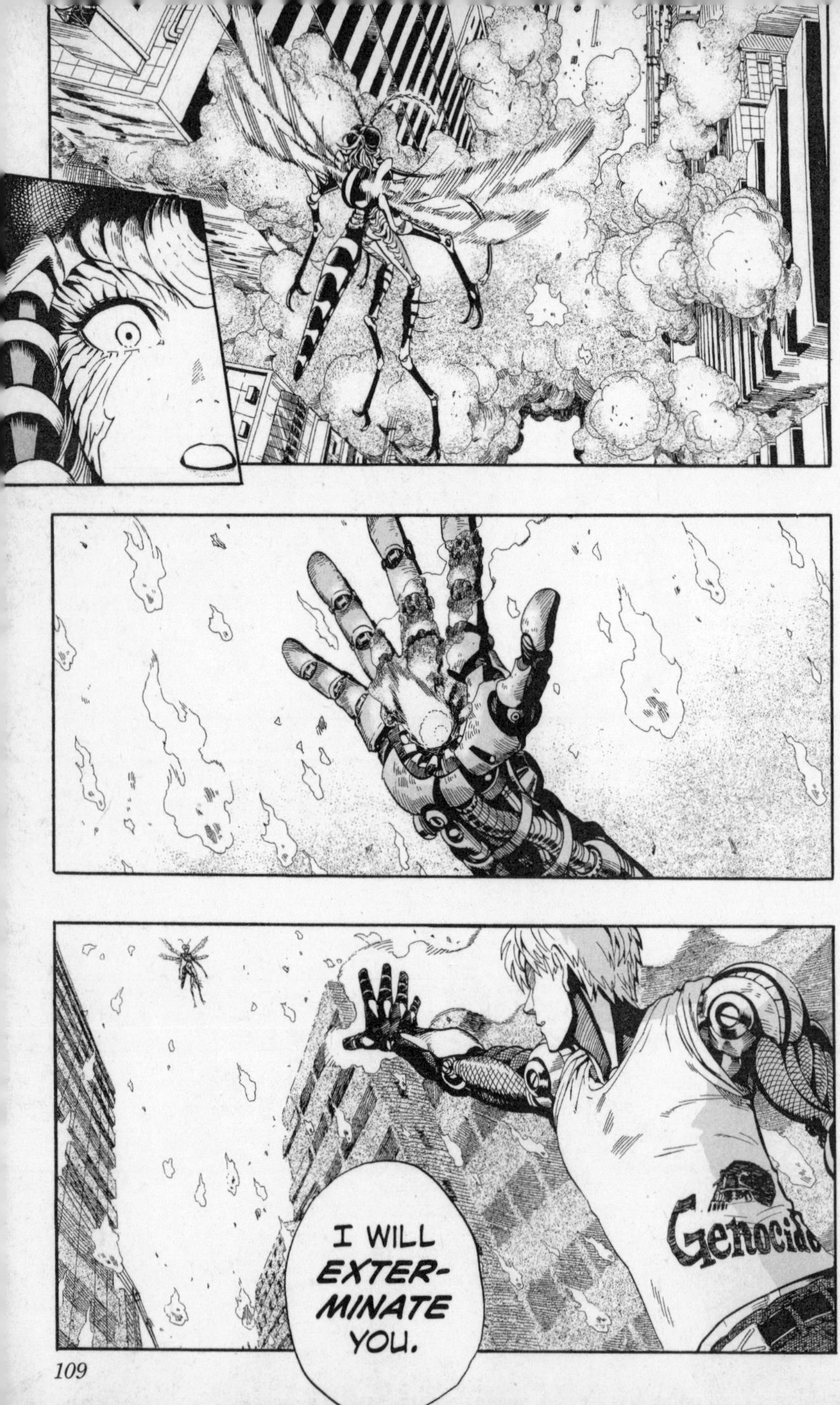
Genocide
I WILL EXTER-MINATE YOU.

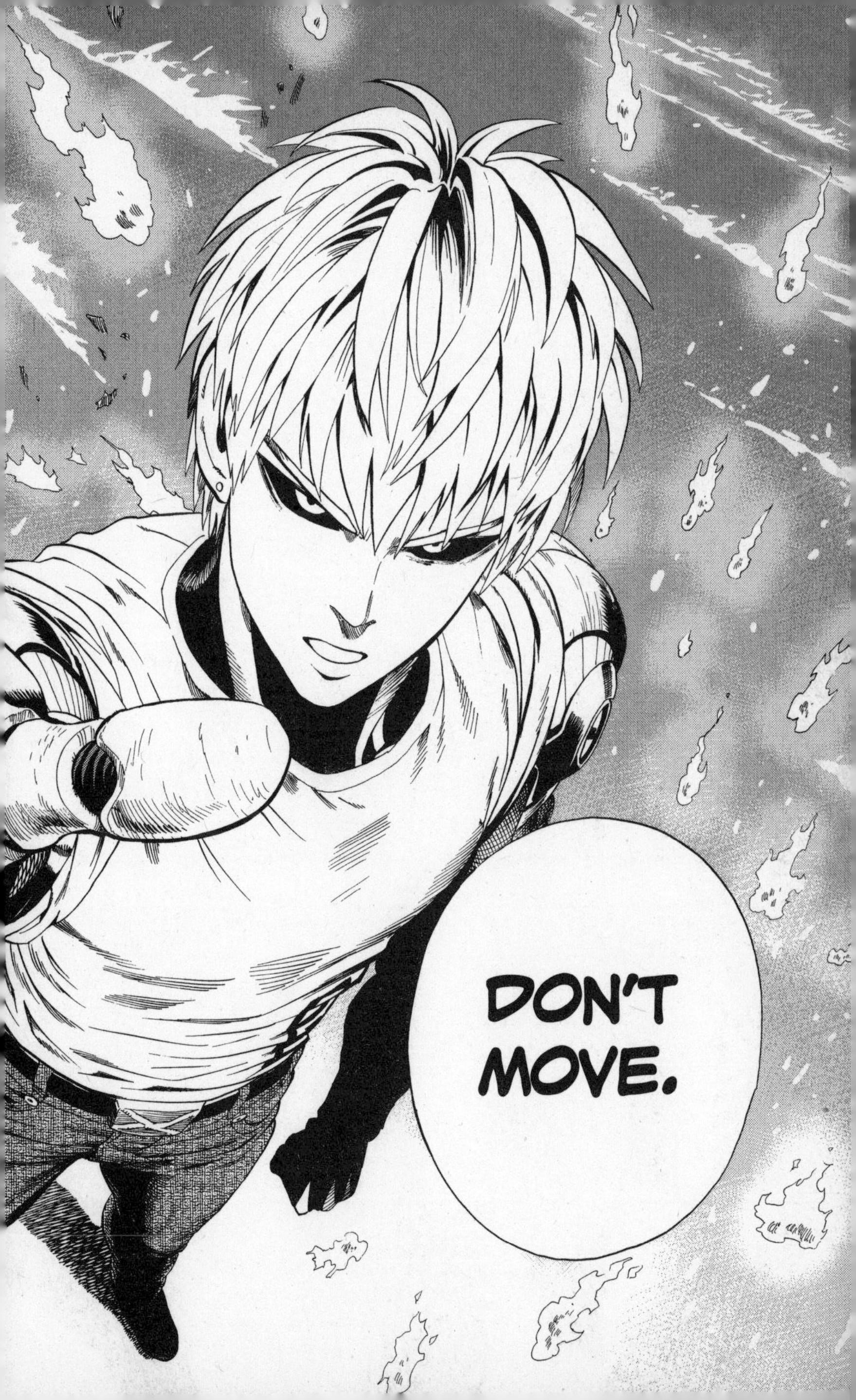
DON'T MOVE.

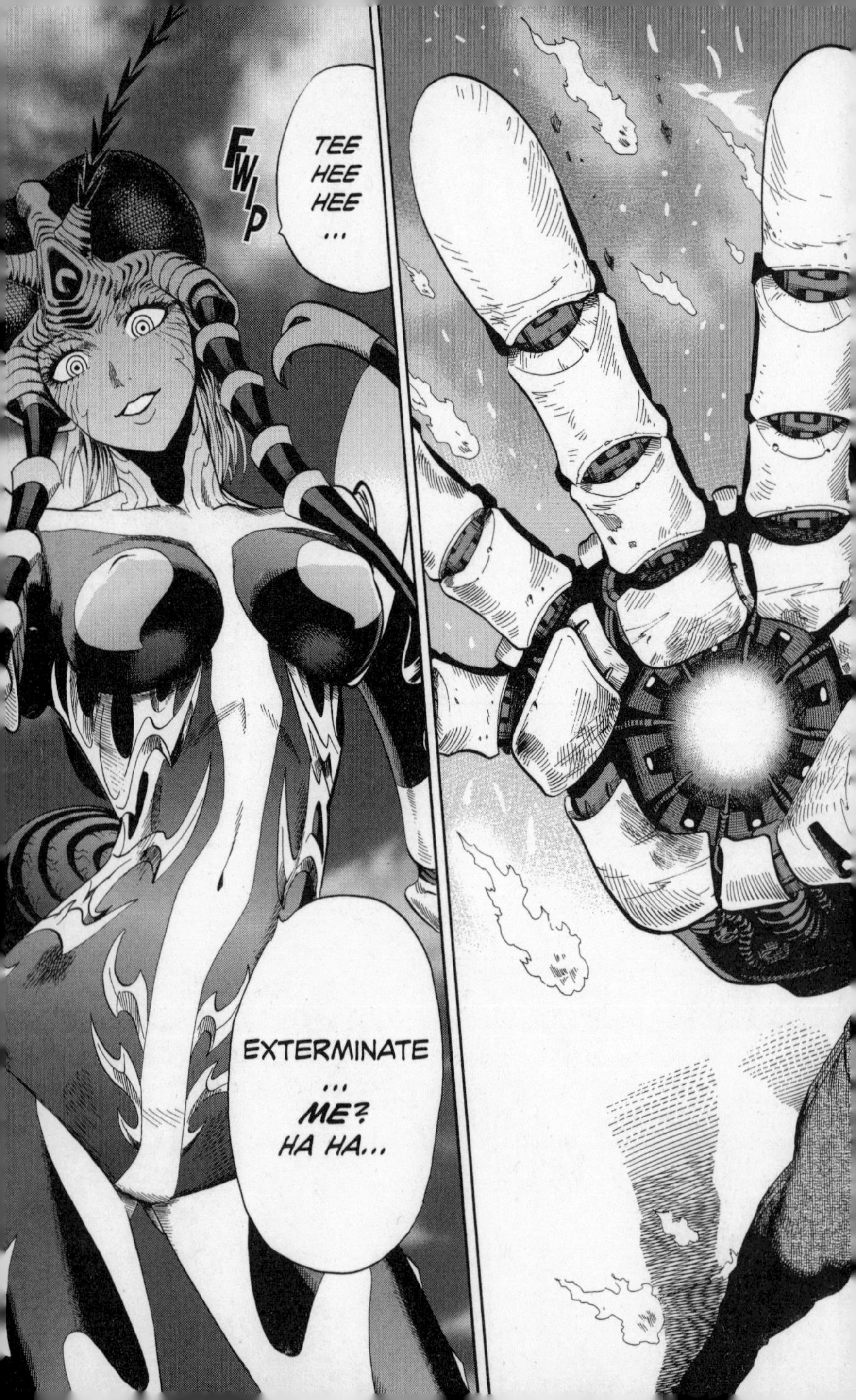
TEE HEE HEE ...
FWIP
EXTERMINATE ... ME? HA HA...

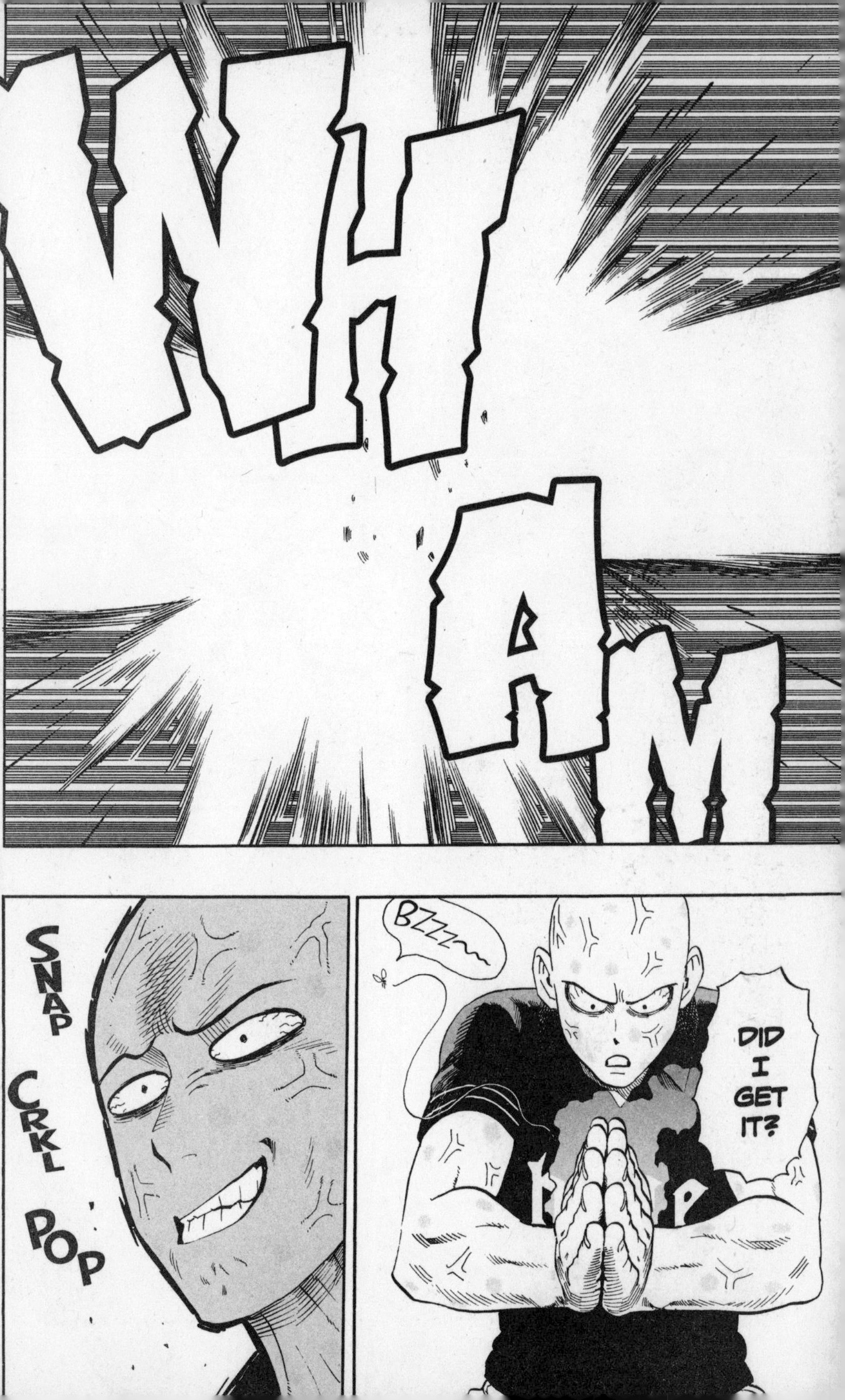
WHAM
BZZZ
DID I GET IT?
SNAP
CRKL
POP

PUNCH 6: SAITAMA

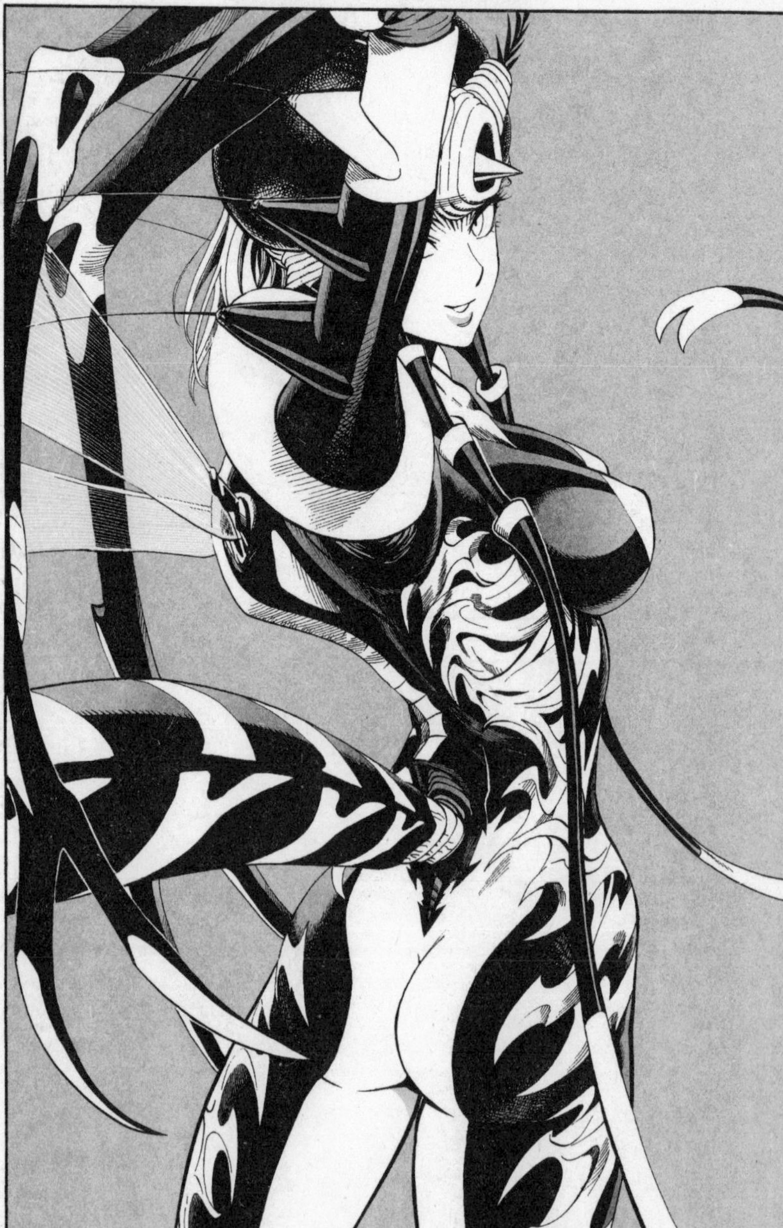

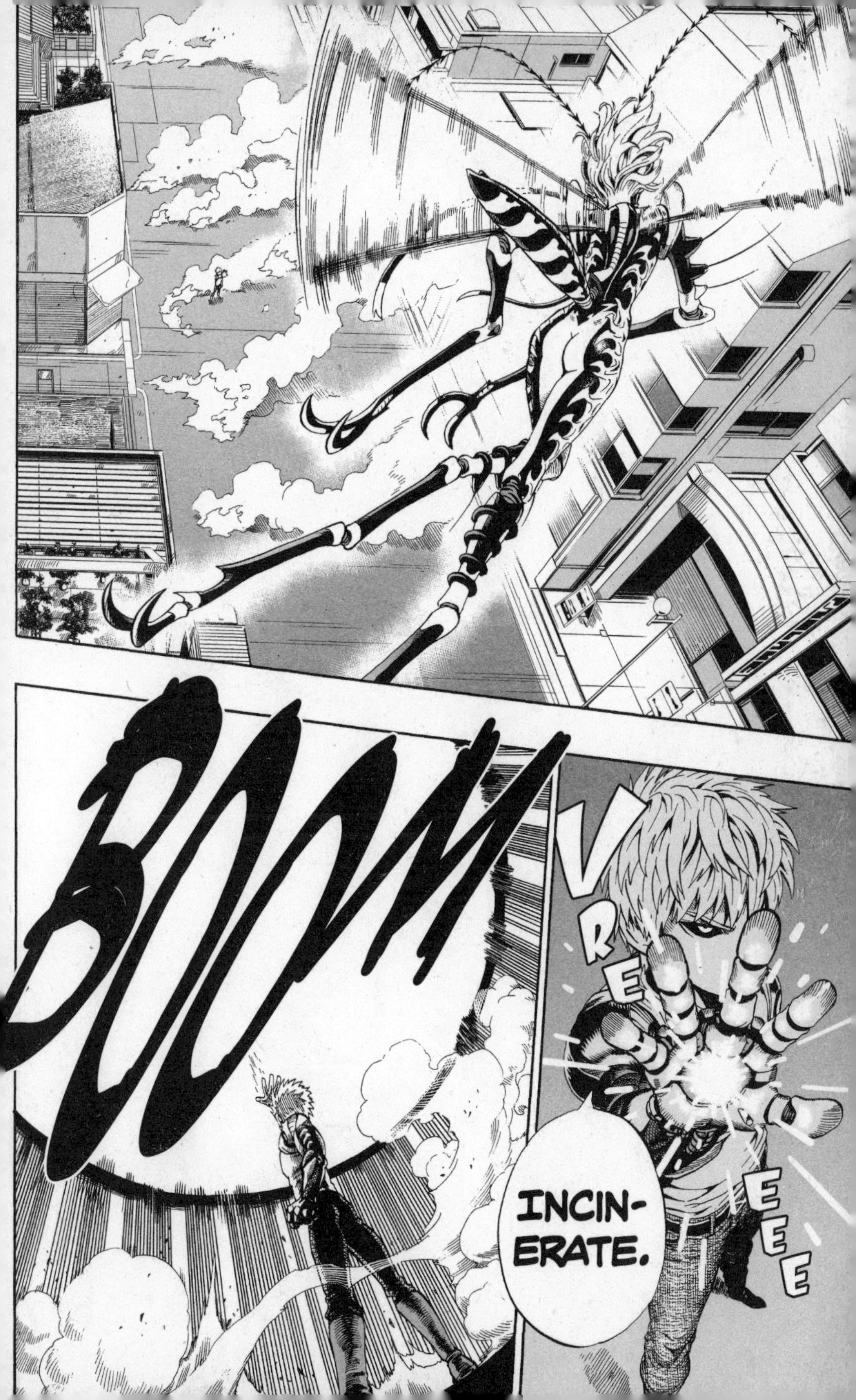
VREEEE
INCIN-ERATE.
BOOM

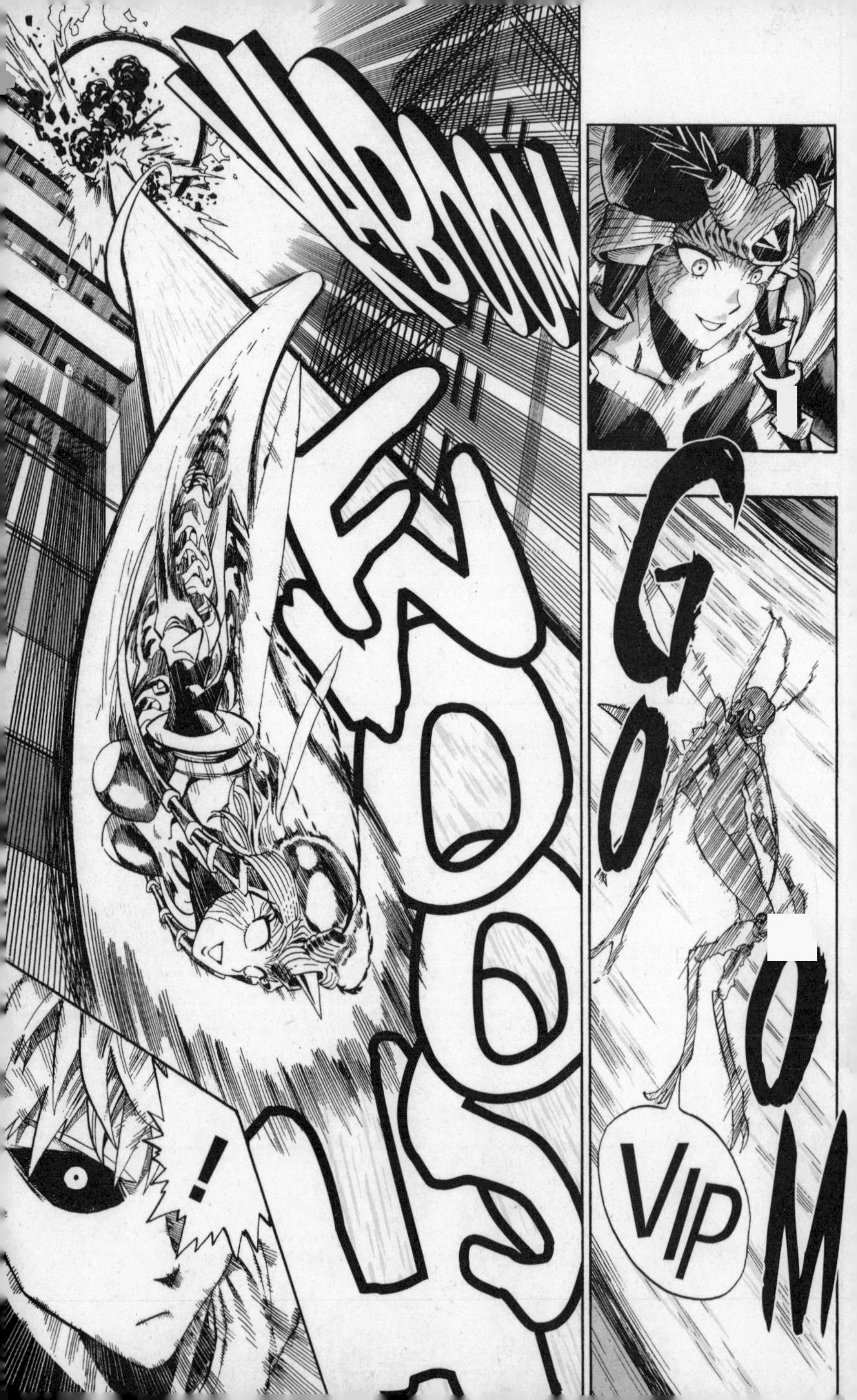
VIP
!

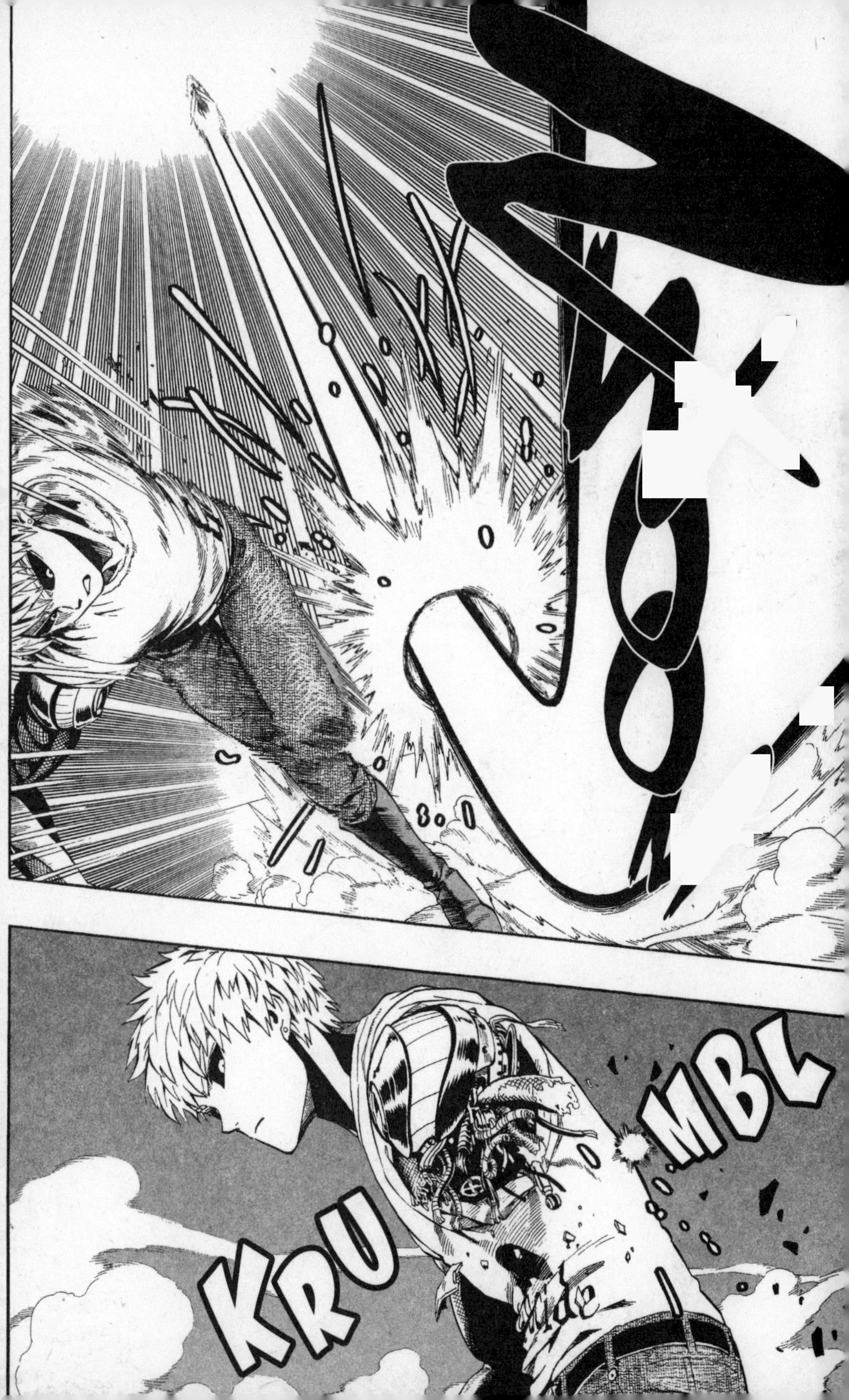
KRUMBL

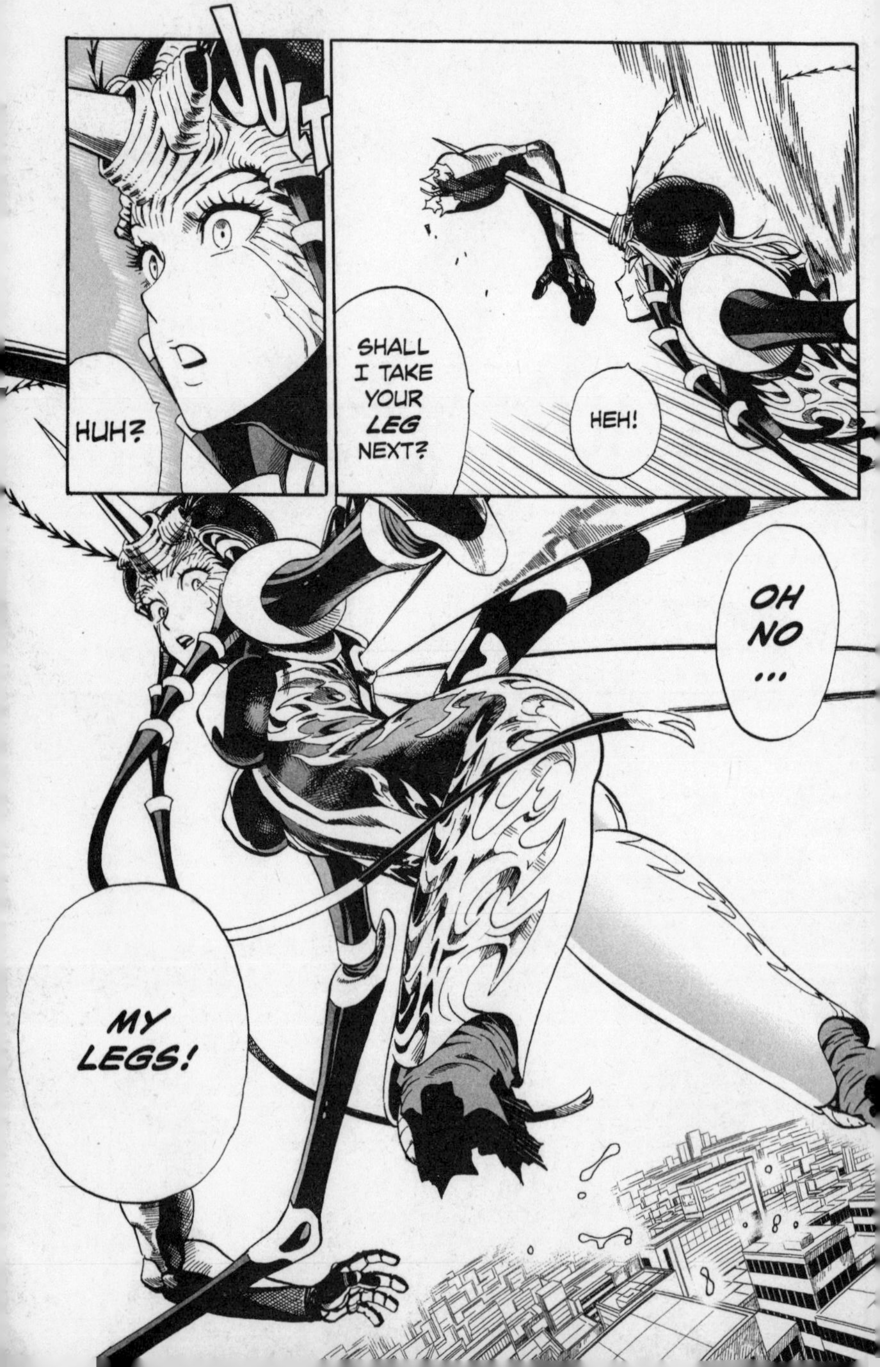
HEH!
SHALL I TAKE YOUR LEG NEXT?
JOLT
HUH?
OH NO ...
MY LEGS!

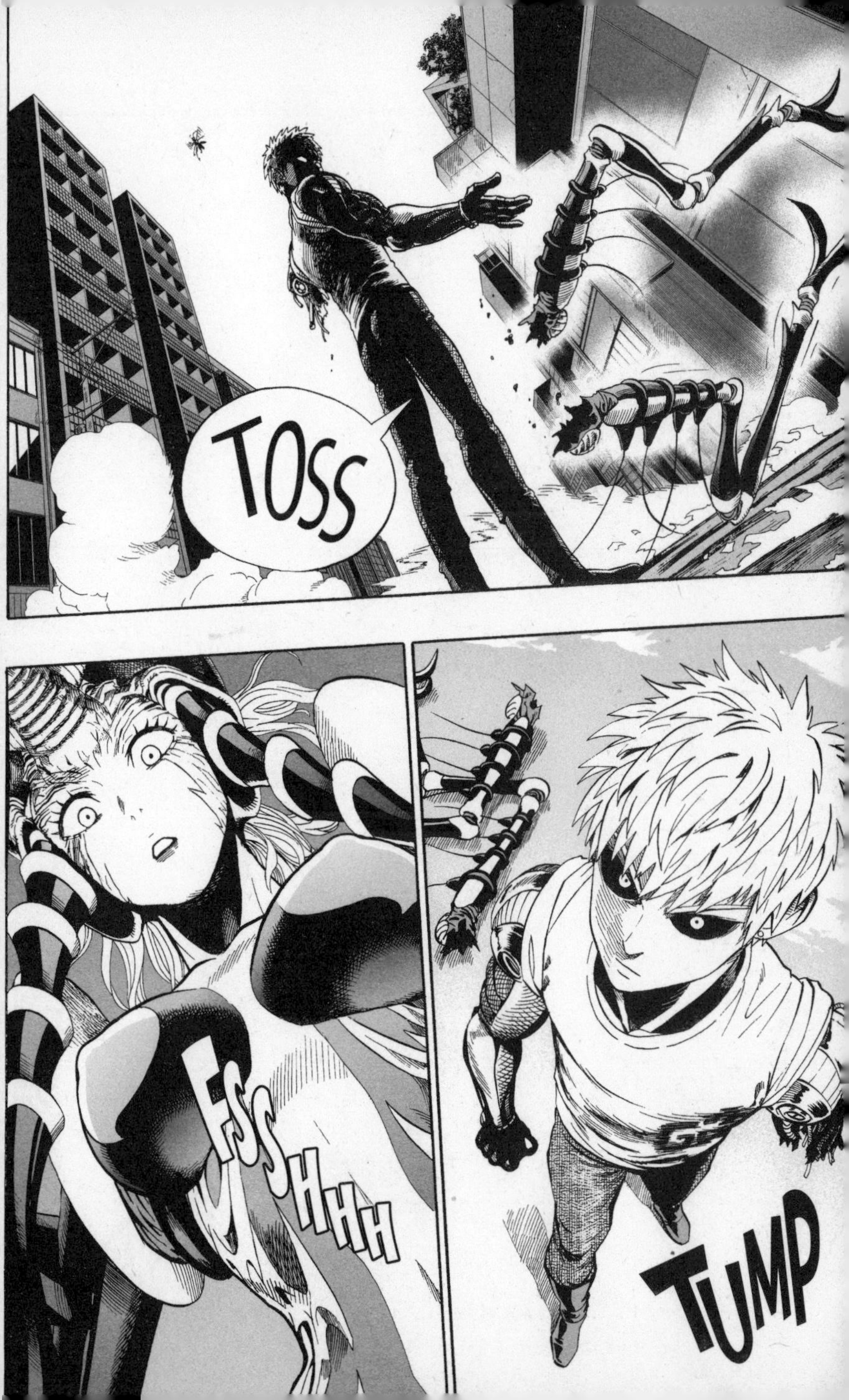
TOSS
TUMP
FSSHHHH

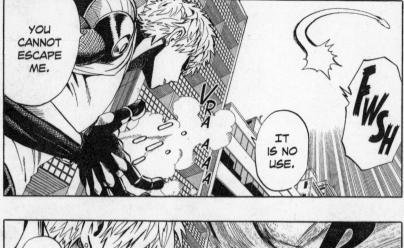

YOU CANNOT ESCAPE ME.

IT IS NO USE.

VRAAAAA

FWSH

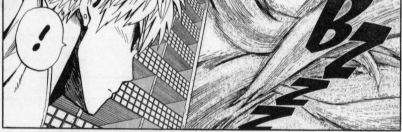

!

BZZZZ

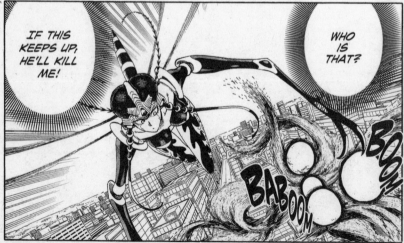

IF THIS KEEPS UP, HE'LL KILL ME!

WHO IS THAT?

BOOM

BABOOM

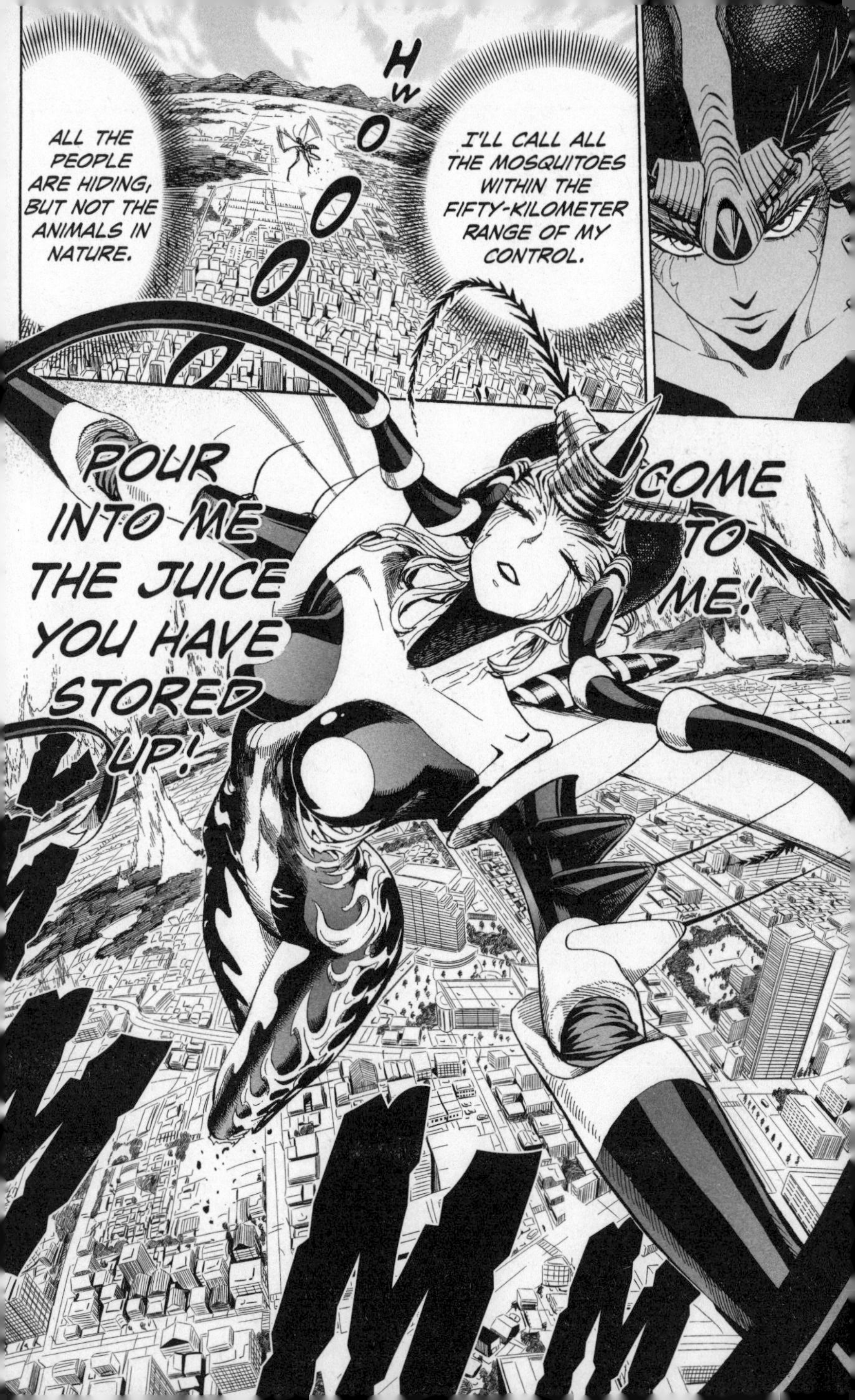
I'LL CALL ALL THE MOSQUITOES WITHIN THE FIFTY-KILOMETER RANGE OF MY CONTROL.
HWOOOO
ALL THE PEOPLE ARE HIDING, BUT NOT THE ANIMALS IN NATURE.
COME TO ME!
POUR INTO ME THE JUICE YOU HAVE STORED UP!

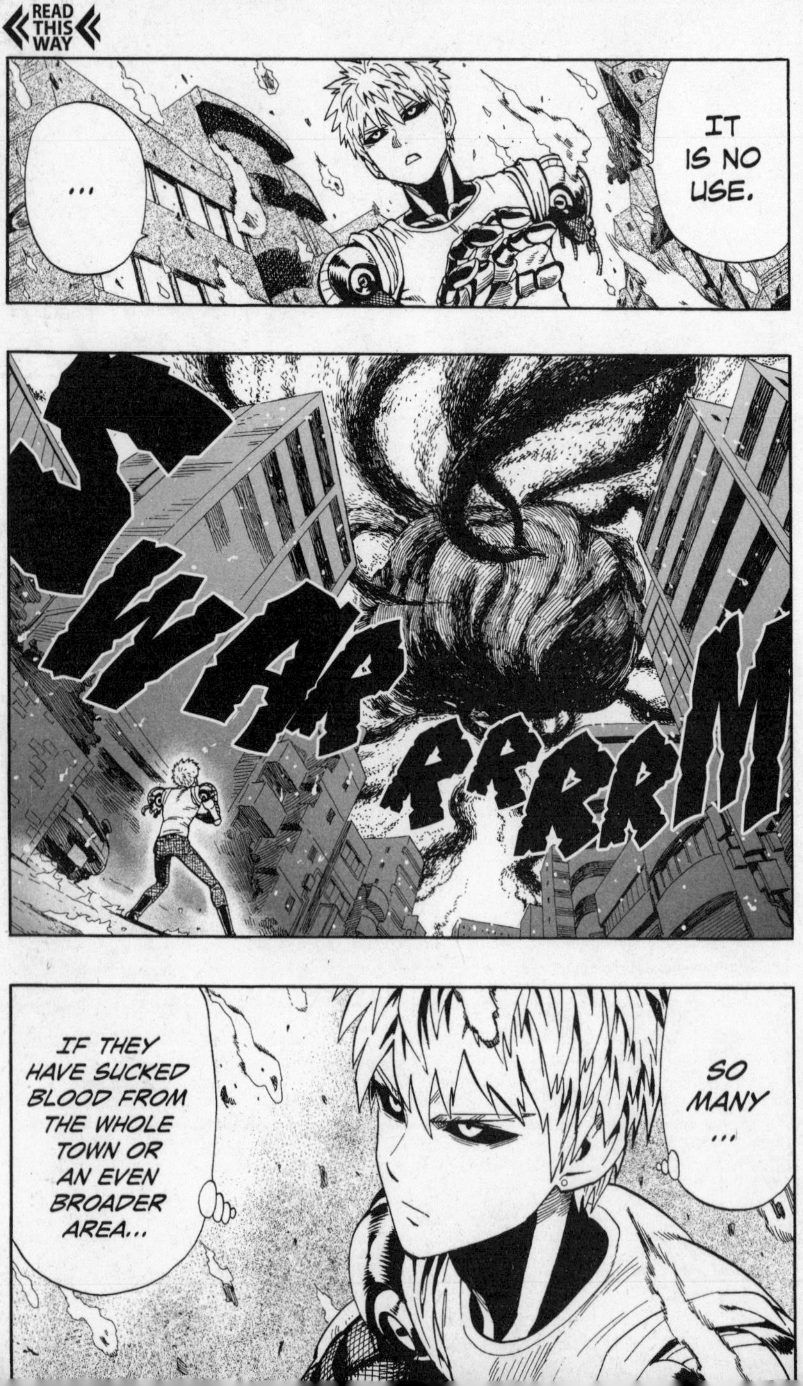
READ THIS WAY
IT IS NO USE.
...
WABRRRM
SO MANY ...
IF THEY HAVE SUCKED BLOOD FROM THE WHOLE TOWN OR AN EVEN BROADER AREA...

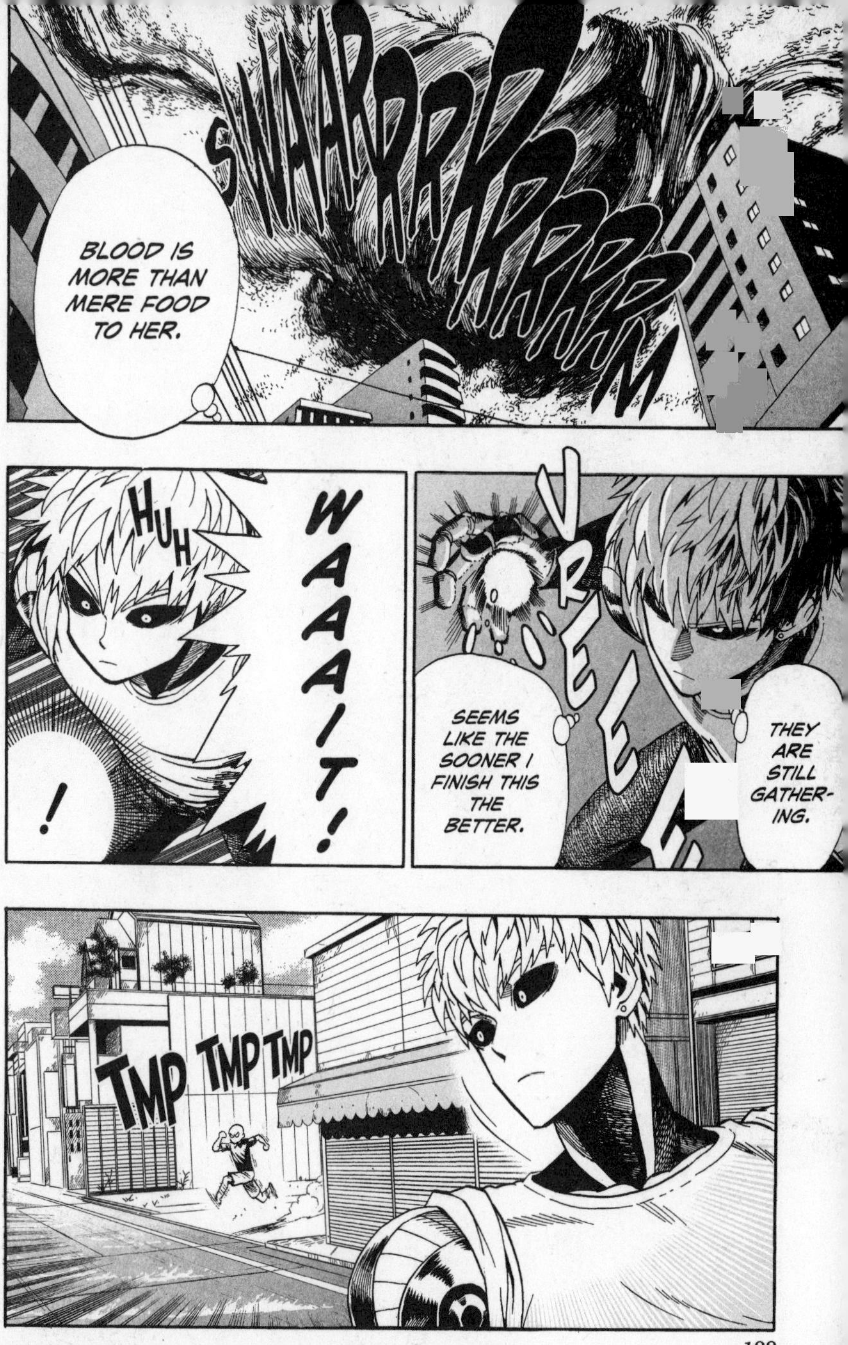

SWARRRKRRRRM
BLOOD IS MORE THAN MERE FOOD TO HER.
VREEE
THEY ARE STILL GATHER-ING.
SEEMS LIKE THE SOONER I FINISH THIS THE BETTER.
HUH
WAAAIT!
!
TMP TMP TMP

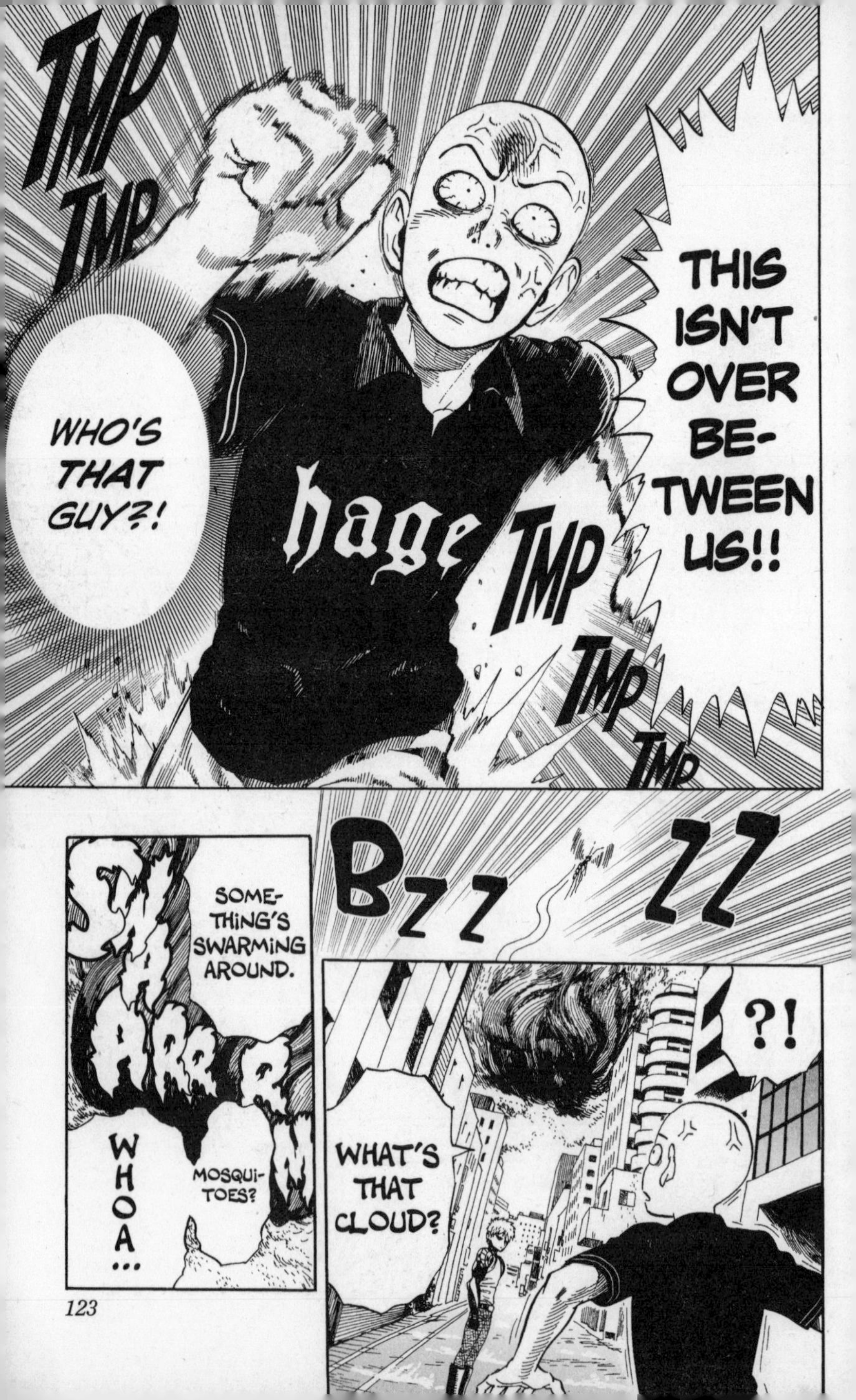
TMP TMP
THIS ISN'T OVER BE-TWEEN US!!
TMP TMP
WHO'S THAT GUY?!
BZZ ZZ
?!
WHAT'S THAT CLOUD?
SOME-THING'S SWARMING AROUND.
WHOA...
MOSQUI-TOES?

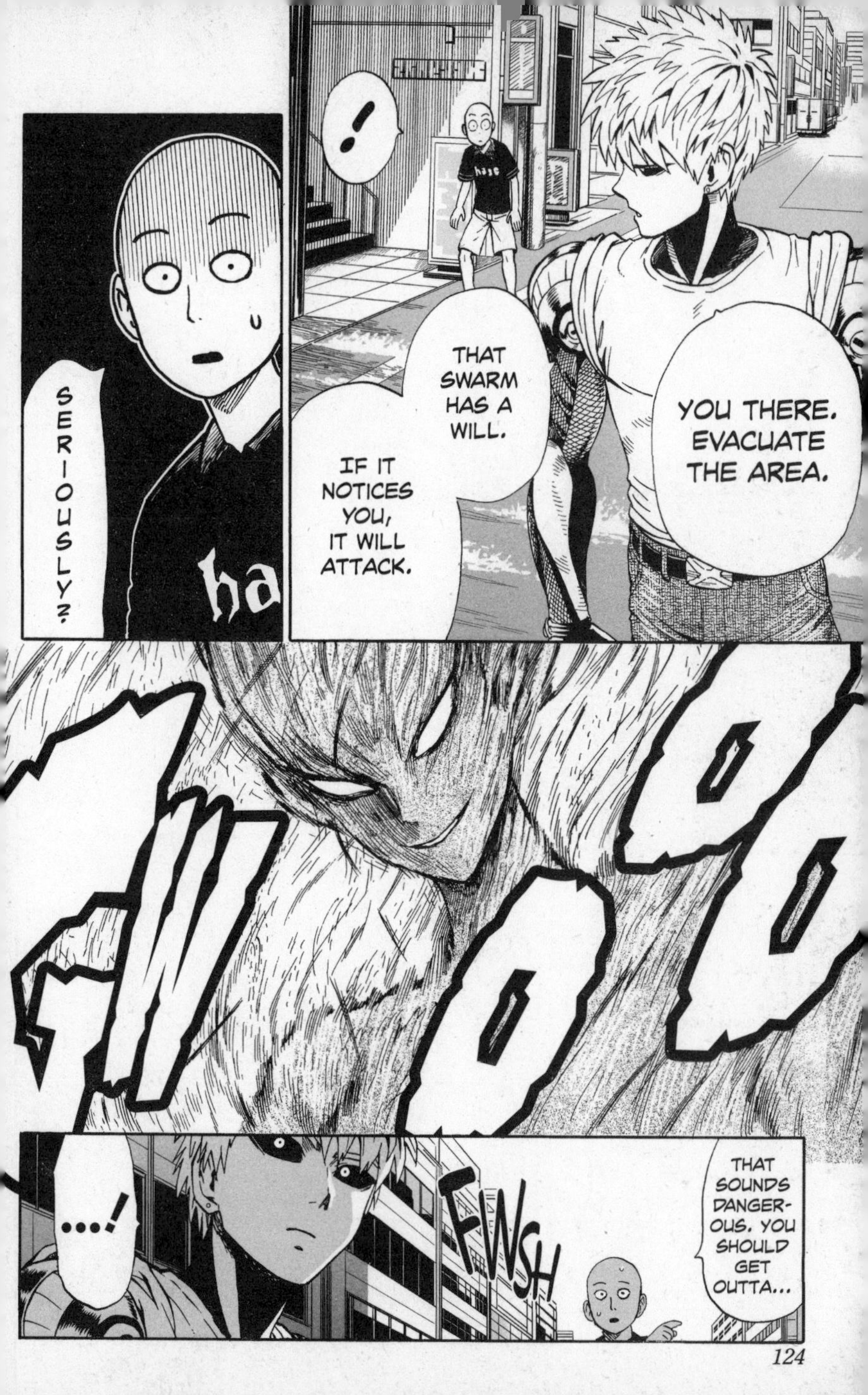
!
YOU THERE. EVACUATE THE AREA.
THAT SWARM HAS A WILL.
IF IT NOTICES YOU, IT WILL ATTACK.
SERIOUSLY?
THAT SOUNDS DANGER-OUS. YOU SHOULD GET OUTTA...
FWSH
...!

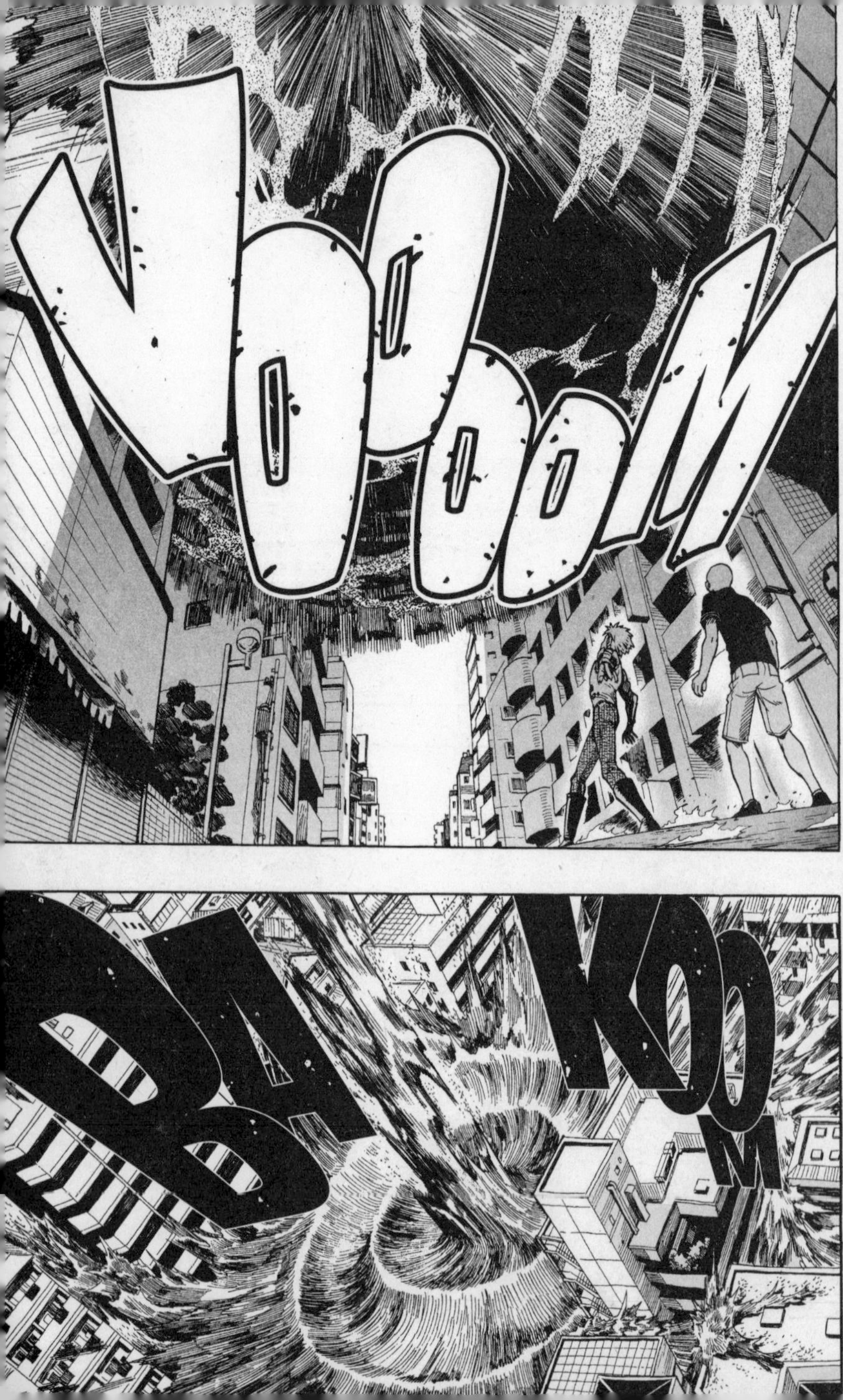
VOOOOM
BAKOOM

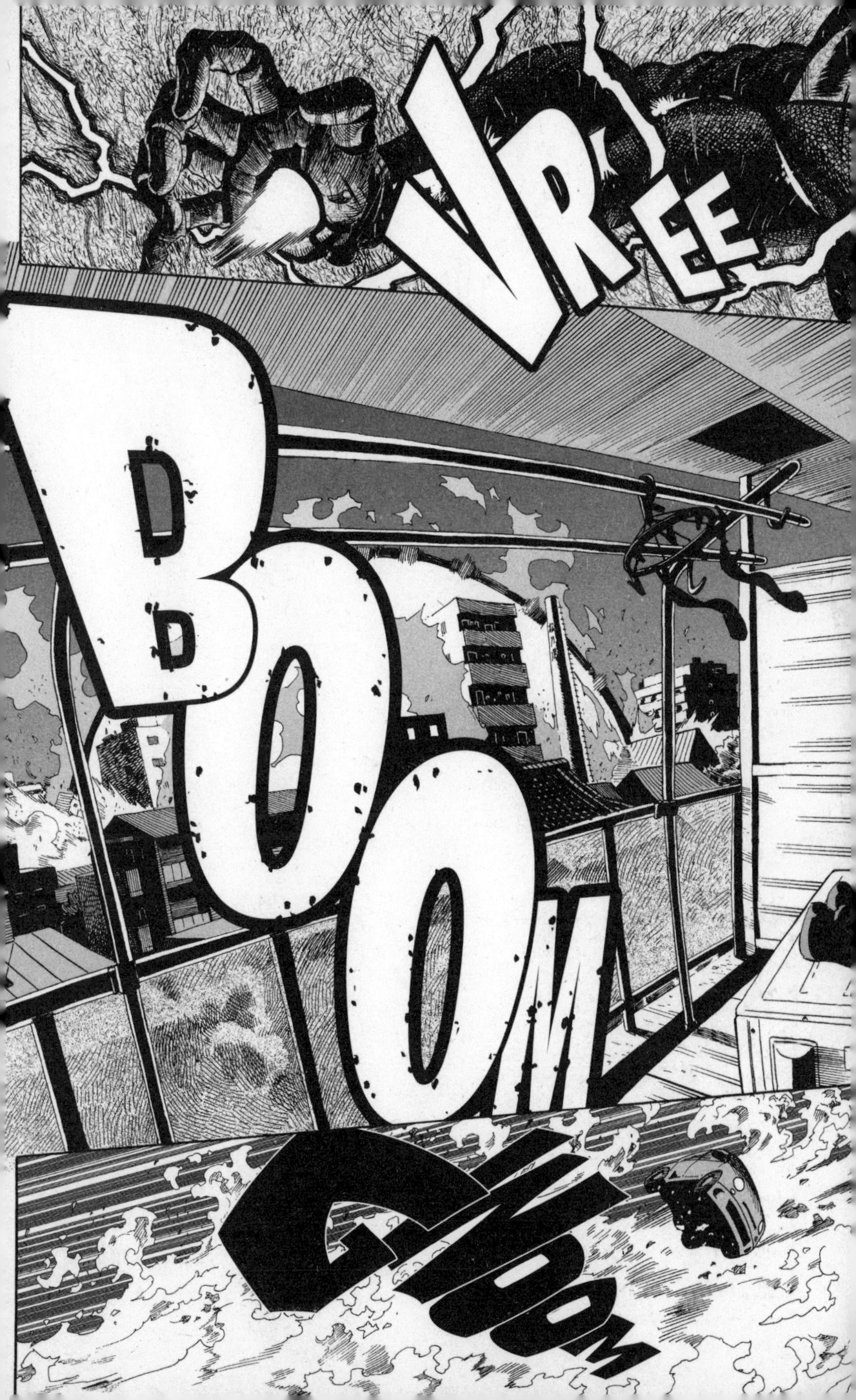
VREE
BOOM
GLOOM

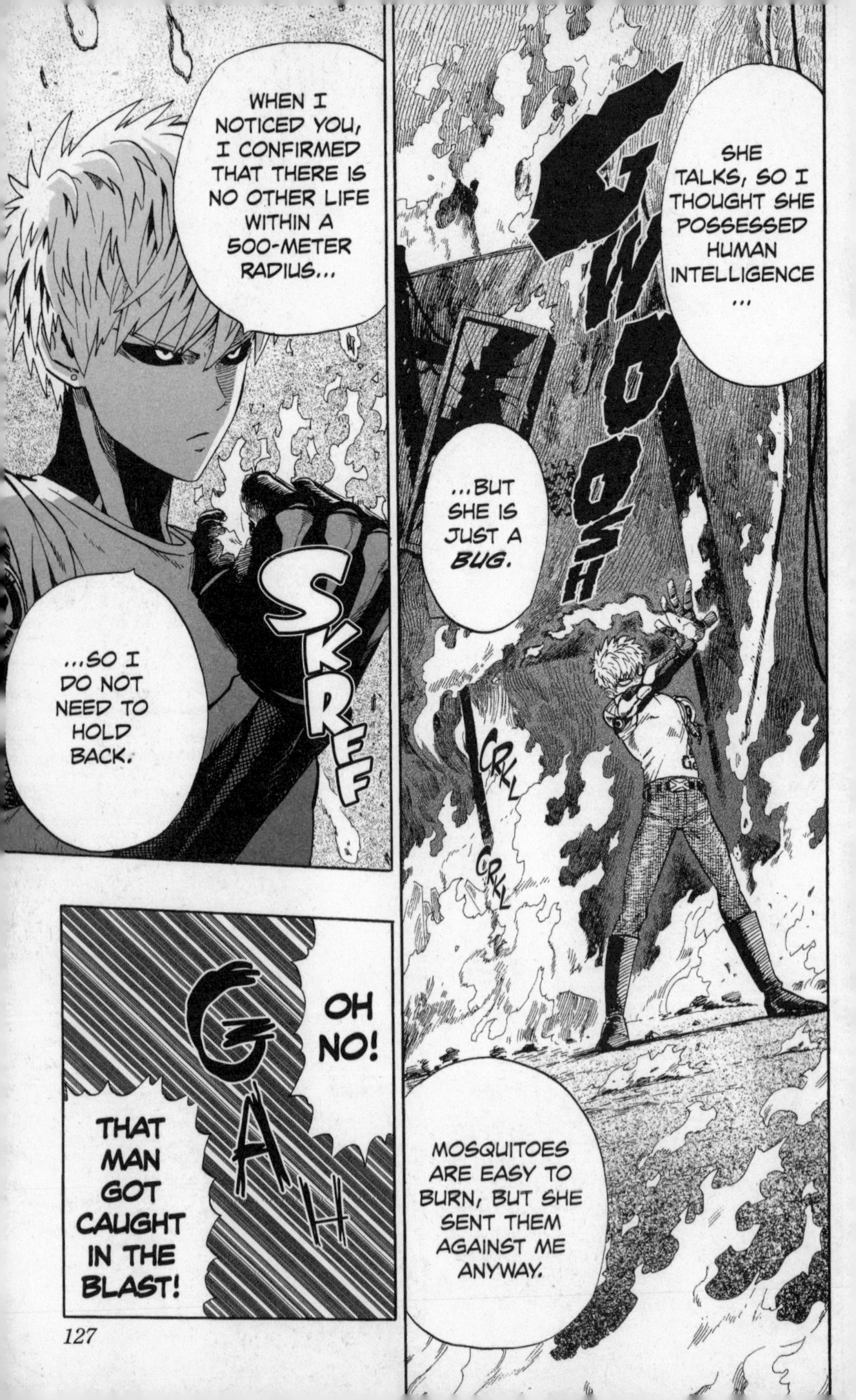
SHE TALKS, SO I THOUGHT SHE POSSESSED HUMAN INTELLIGENCE ...
GWOOOSH
...BUT SHE IS JUST A *BUG*.
CRKL
CRKL
MOSQUITOES ARE EASY TO BURN, BUT SHE SENT THEM AGAINST ME ANYWAY.
WHEN I NOTICED YOU, I CONFIRMED THAT THERE IS NO OTHER LIFE WITHIN A 500-METER RADIUS...
SKREFF
...SO I DO NOT NEED TO HOLD BACK.
OH NO!
GAH
THAT MAN GOT CAUGHT IN THE BLAST!

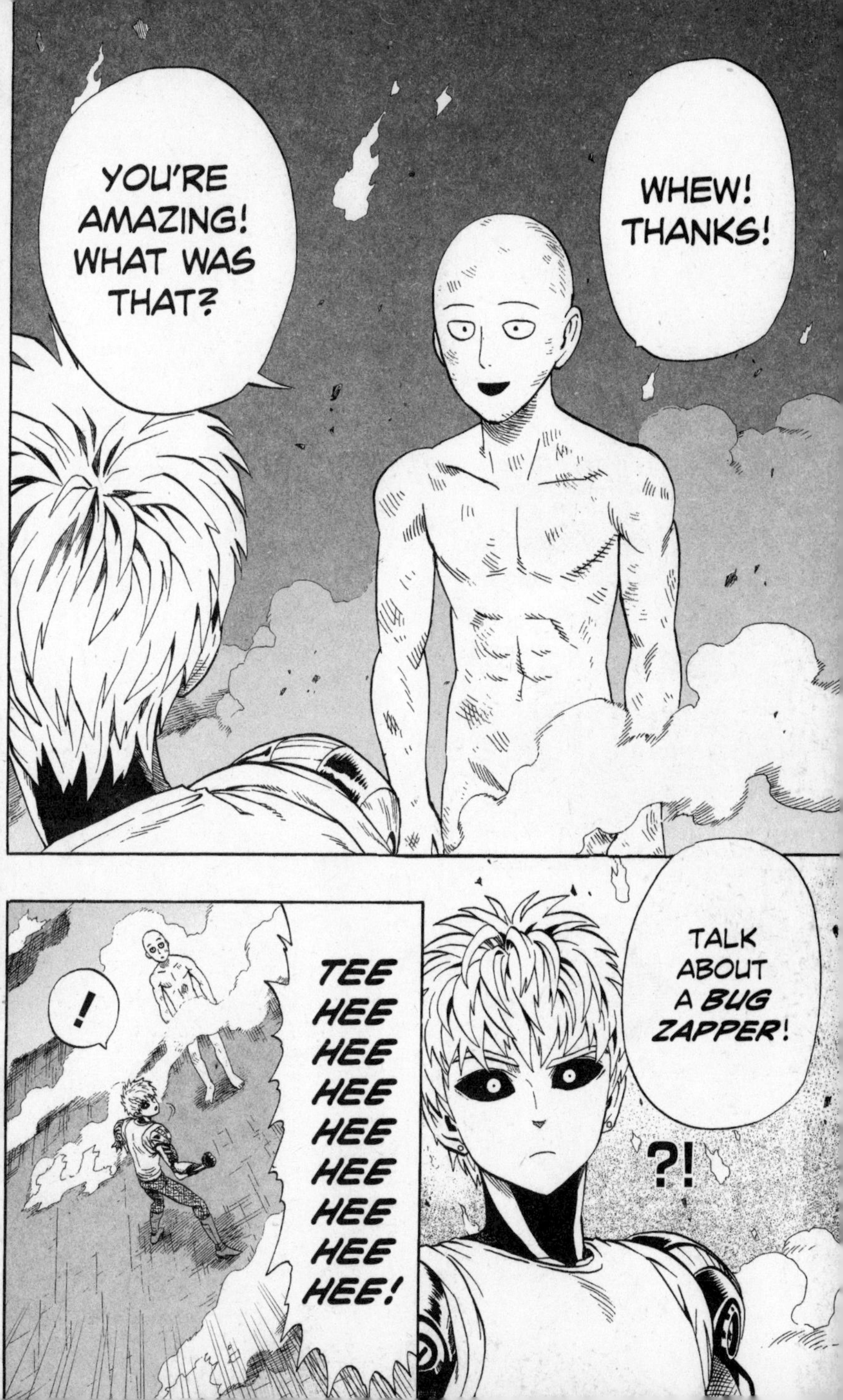
WHEW! THANKS!
YOU'RE AMAZING! WHAT WAS THAT?
TALK ABOUT A BUG ZAPPER!
?!
TEE HEE HEE HEE HEE HEE HEE HEE HEE!
!

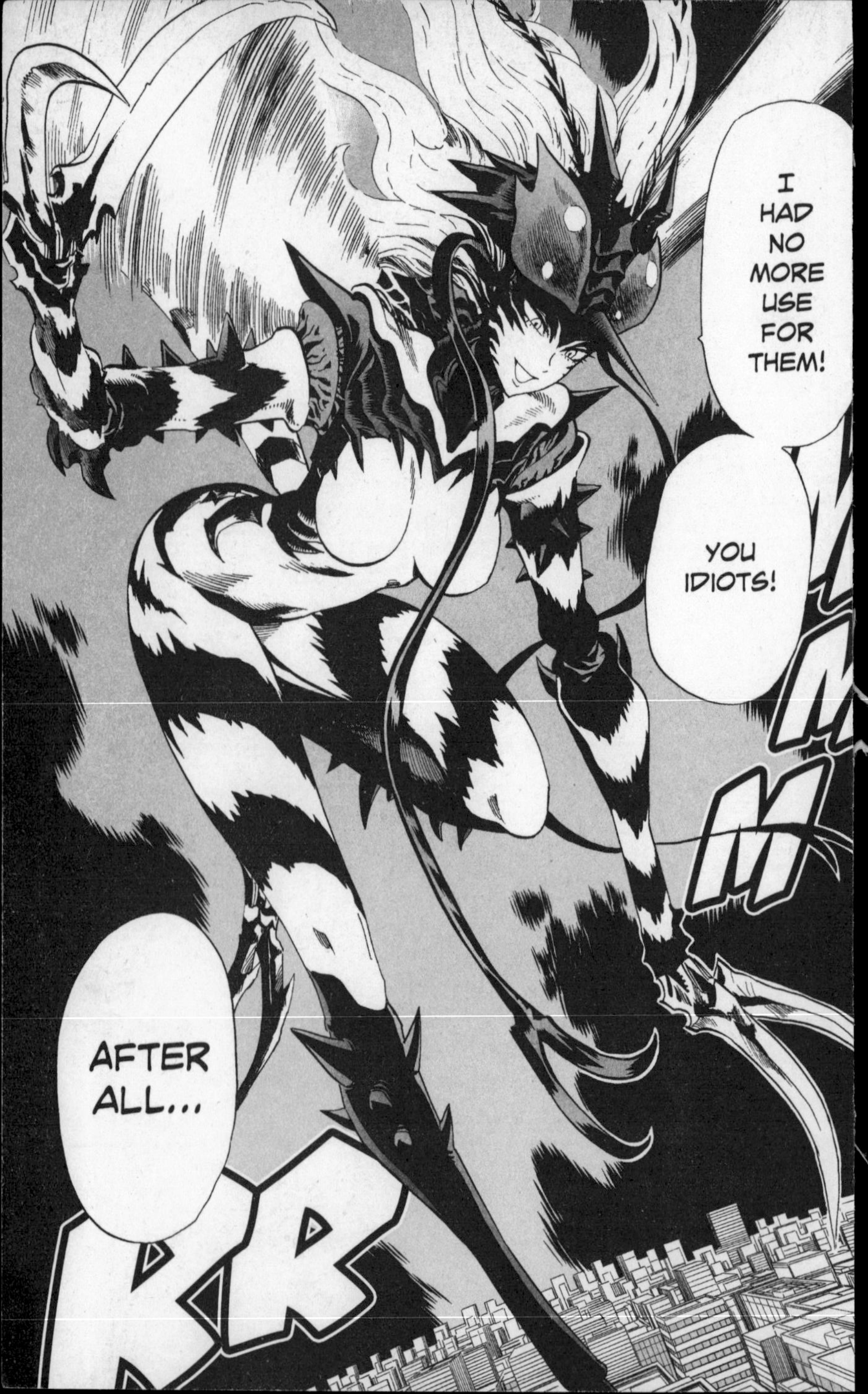
I HAD NO MORE USE FOR THEM!
YOU IDIOTS!
AFTER ALL...

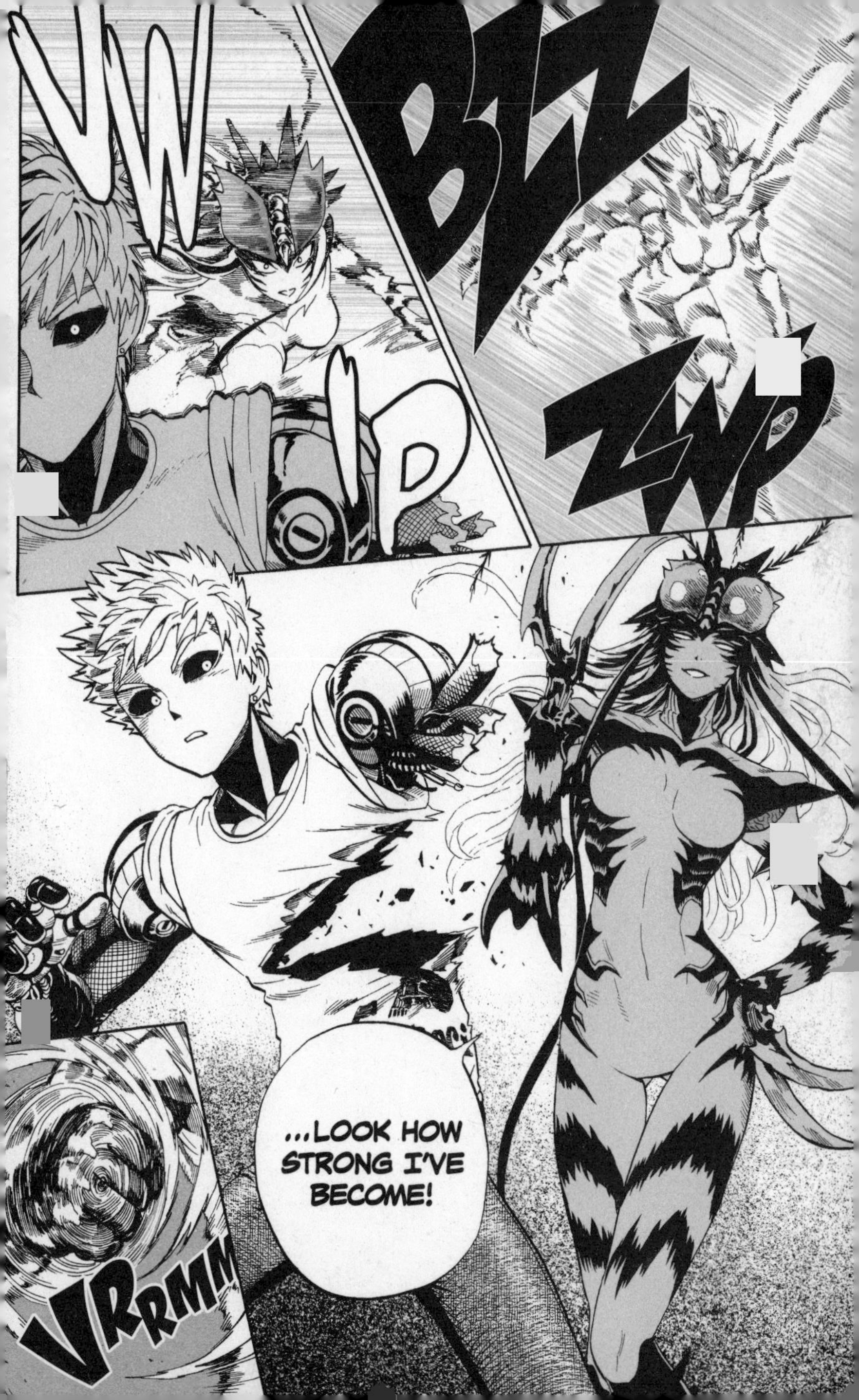
BZZ
ZWP
VWW
IP
...LOOK HOW STRONG I'VE BECOME!
VRRMM

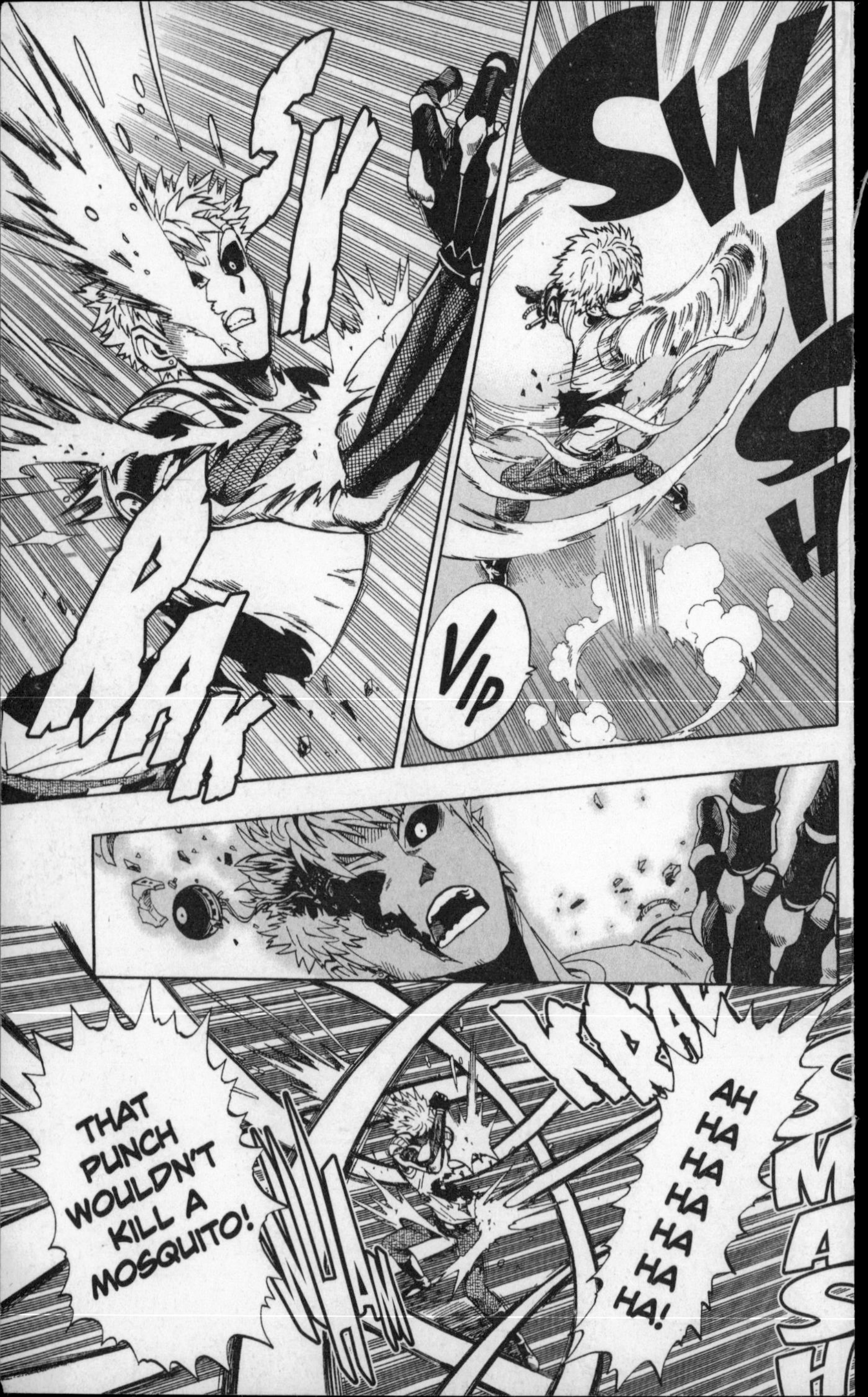
VIP
AH HA HA HA HA HA HA HA HA!
THAT PUNCH WOULDN'T KILL A MOSQUITO!

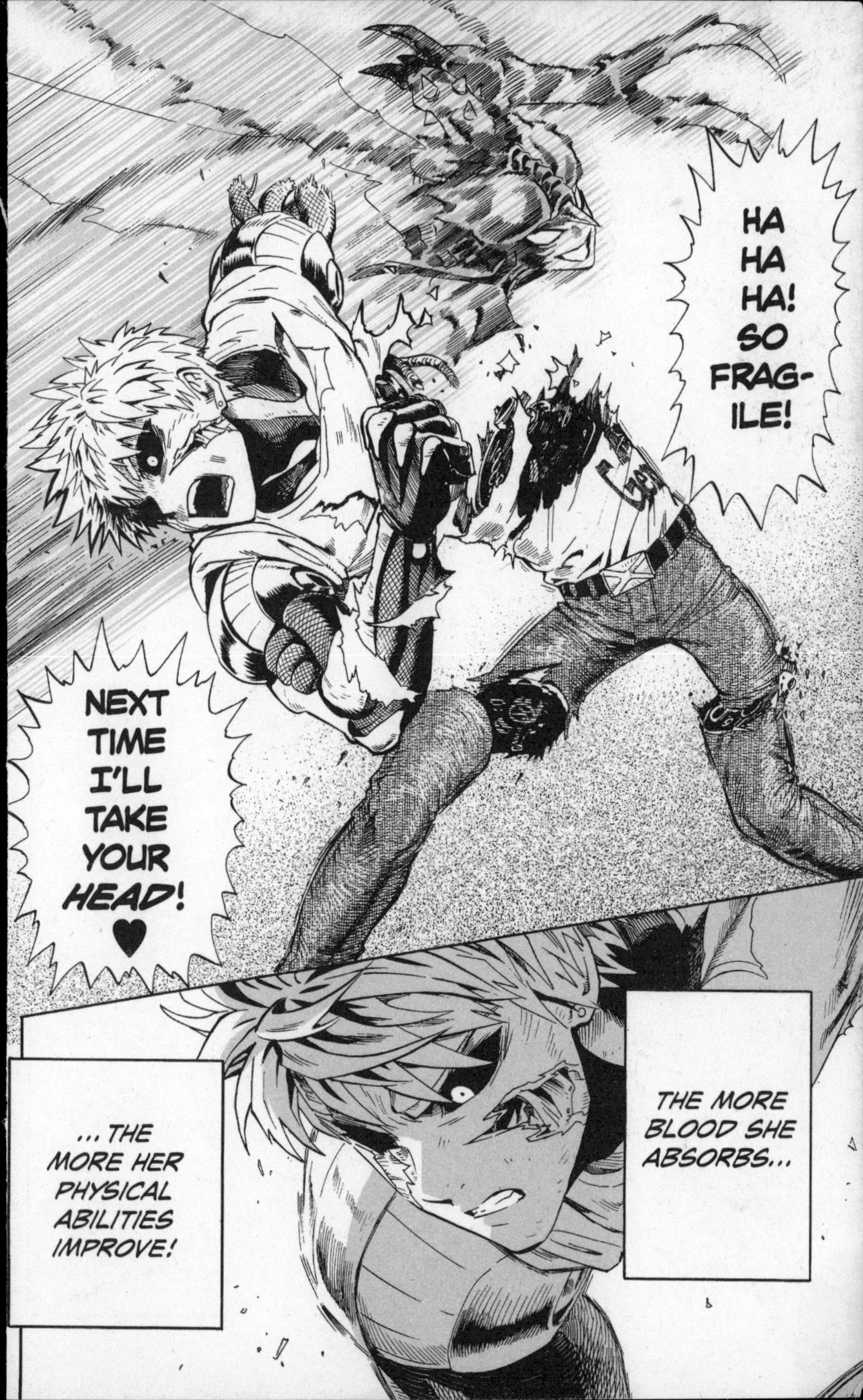
HA HA HA! SO FRAG-ILE!
NEXT TIME I'LL TAKE YOUR *HEAD!* ♥
THE MORE BLOOD SHE ABSORBS...
...THE MORE HER PHYSICAL ABILITIES IMPROVE!

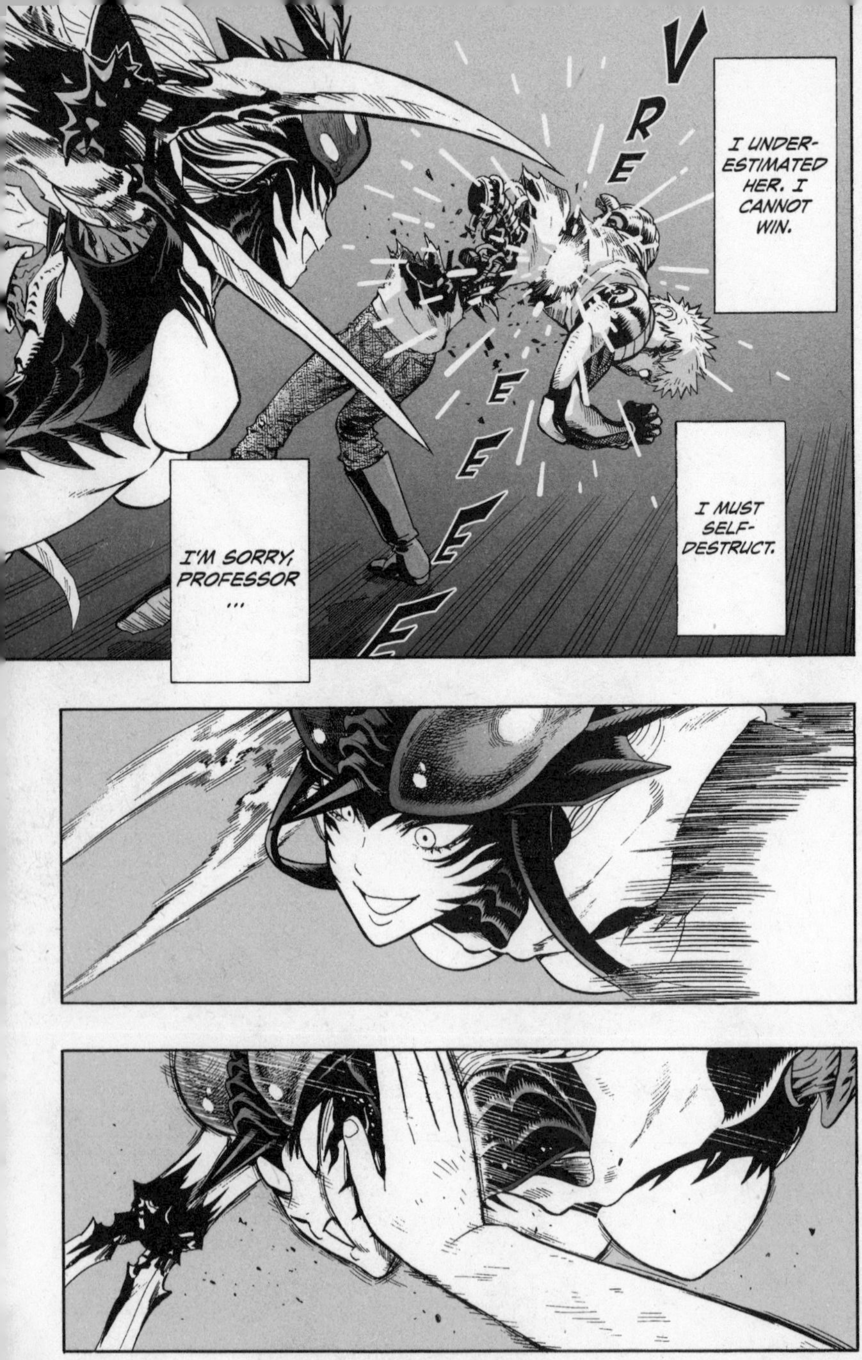
I UNDER-ESTIMATED HER. I CANNOT WIN.
VREEEEE
I MUST SELF-DESTRUCT.
I'M SORRY, PROFESSOR ...

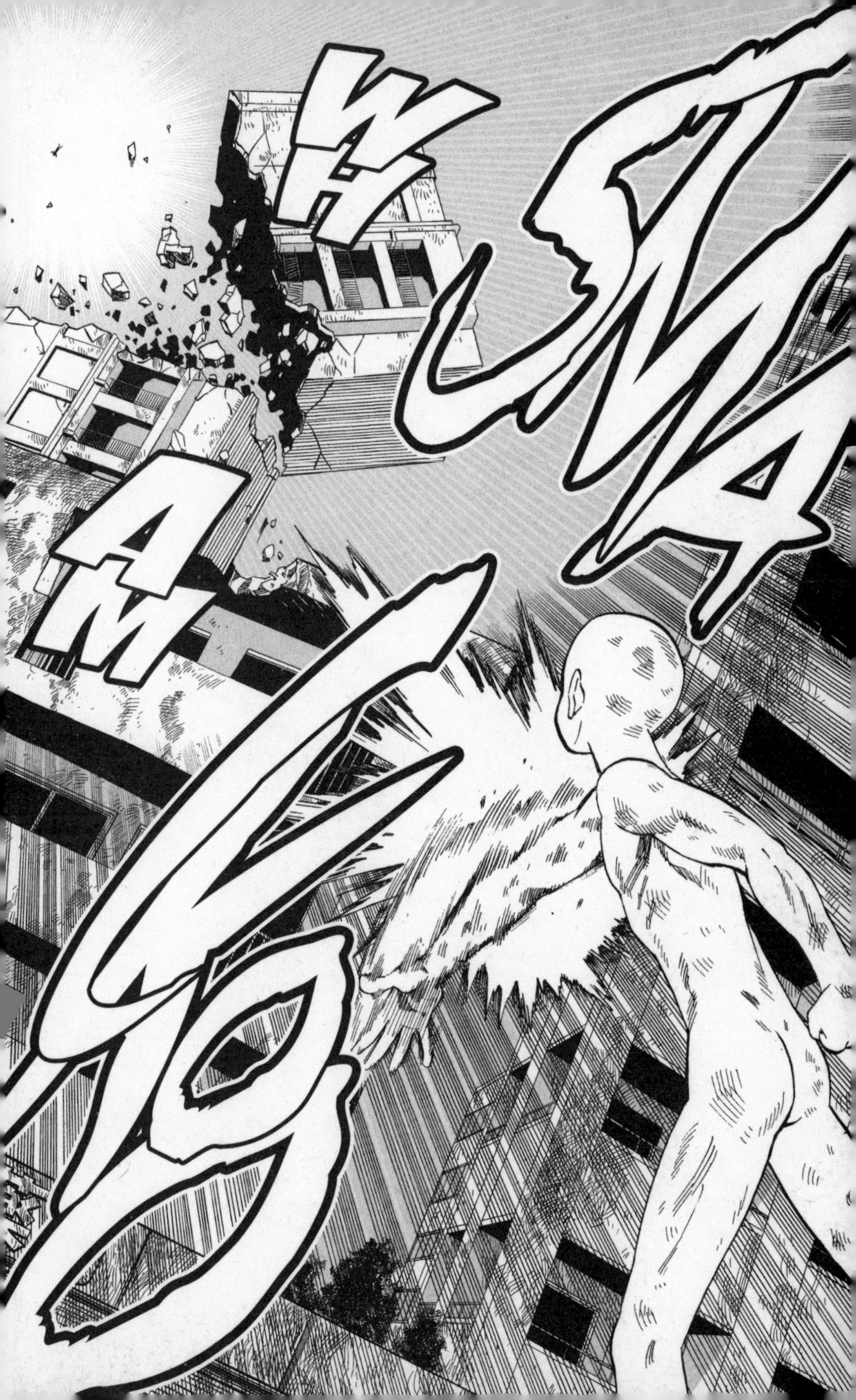
WHAM

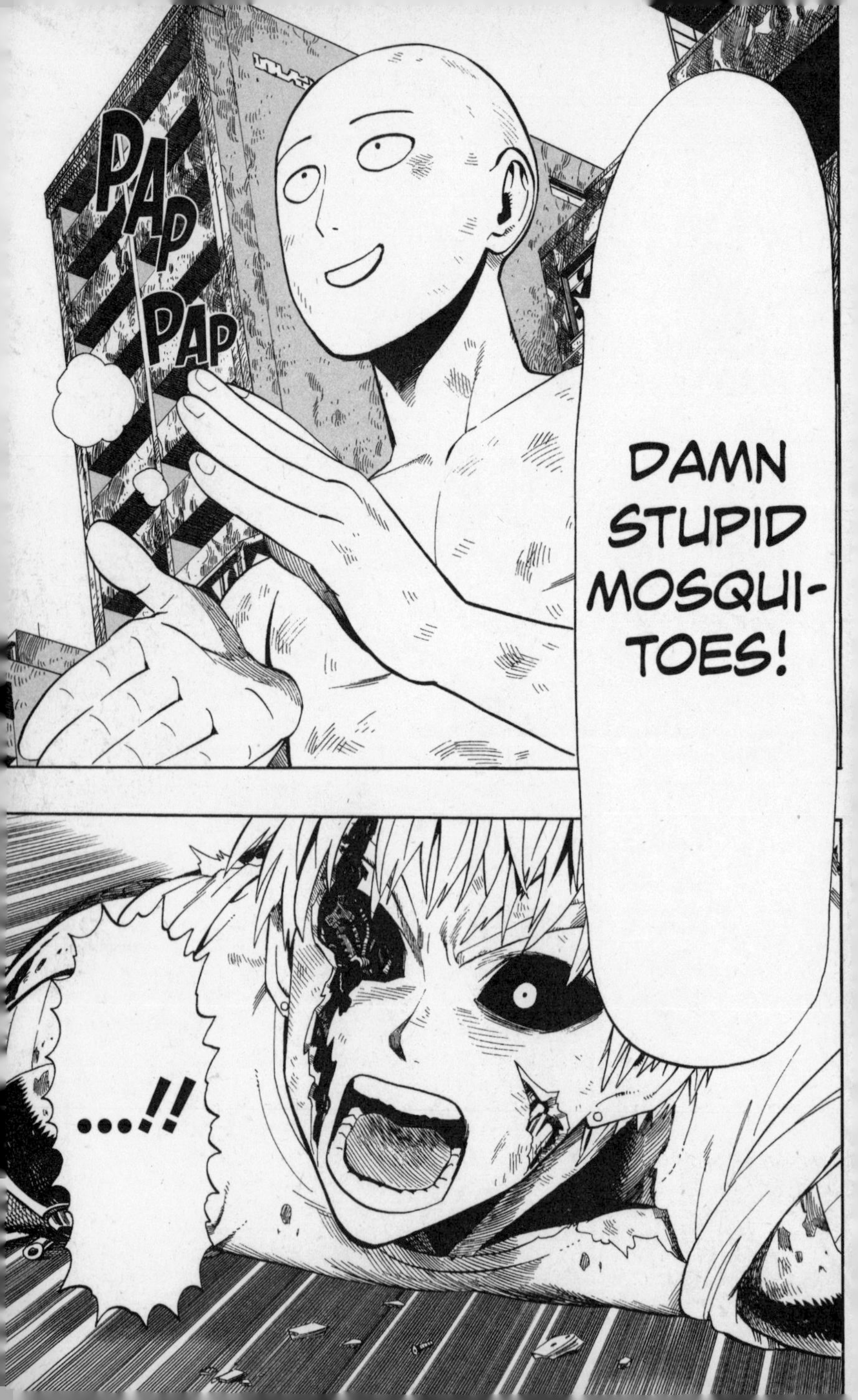
PAP PAP
DAMN STUPID MOSQUI- TOES!
...!!

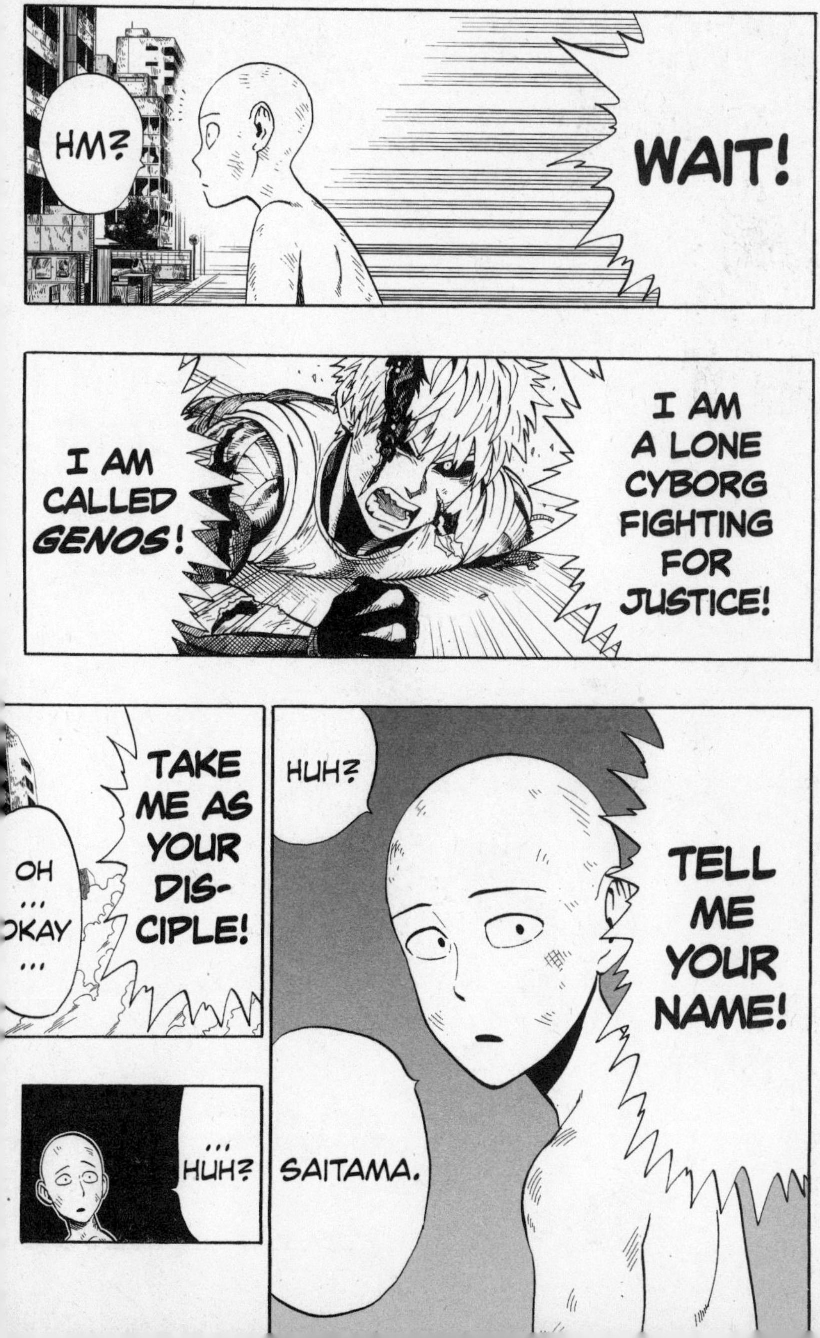
WAIT!
HM?
I AM A LONE CYBORG FIGHTING FOR JUSTICE!
I AM CALLED GENOS!
TELL ME YOUR NAME!
HUH?
SAITAMA.
TAKE ME AS YOUR DIS-CIPLE!
OH ... KAY ...
... HUH?

PUNCH 7: A MYSTERIOUS ATTACK

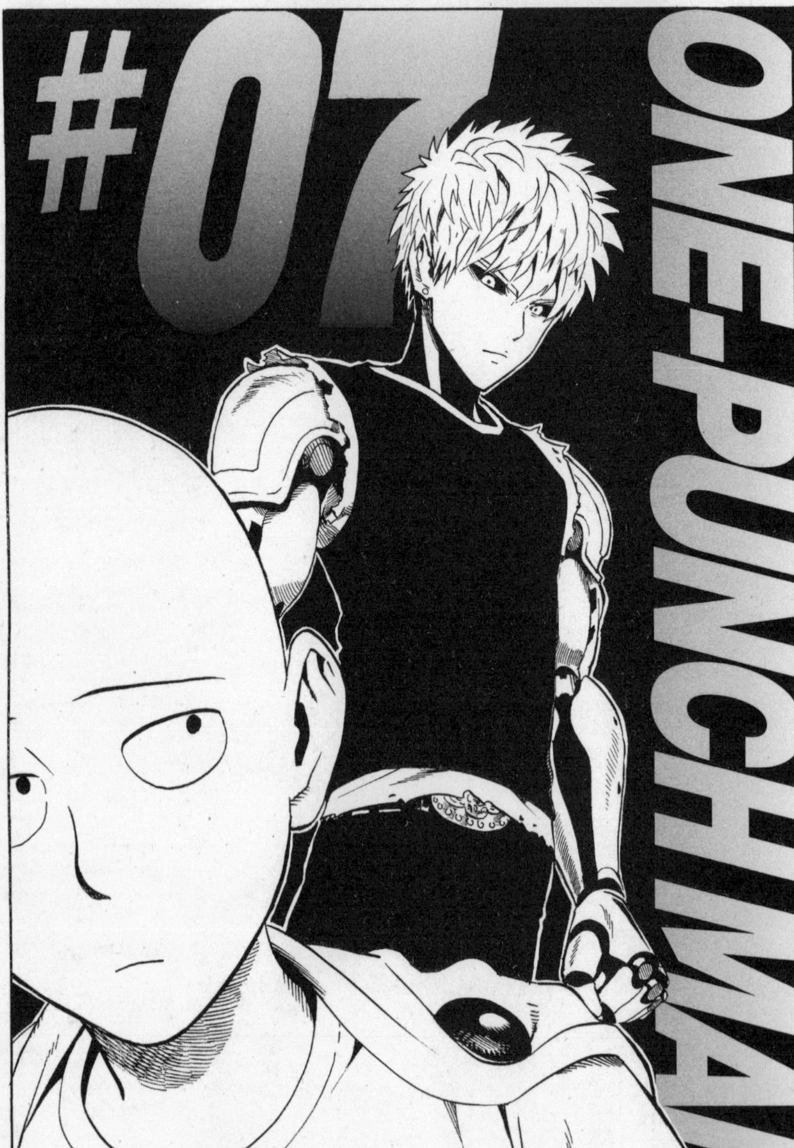
#07
ONE-PUNCH MAN

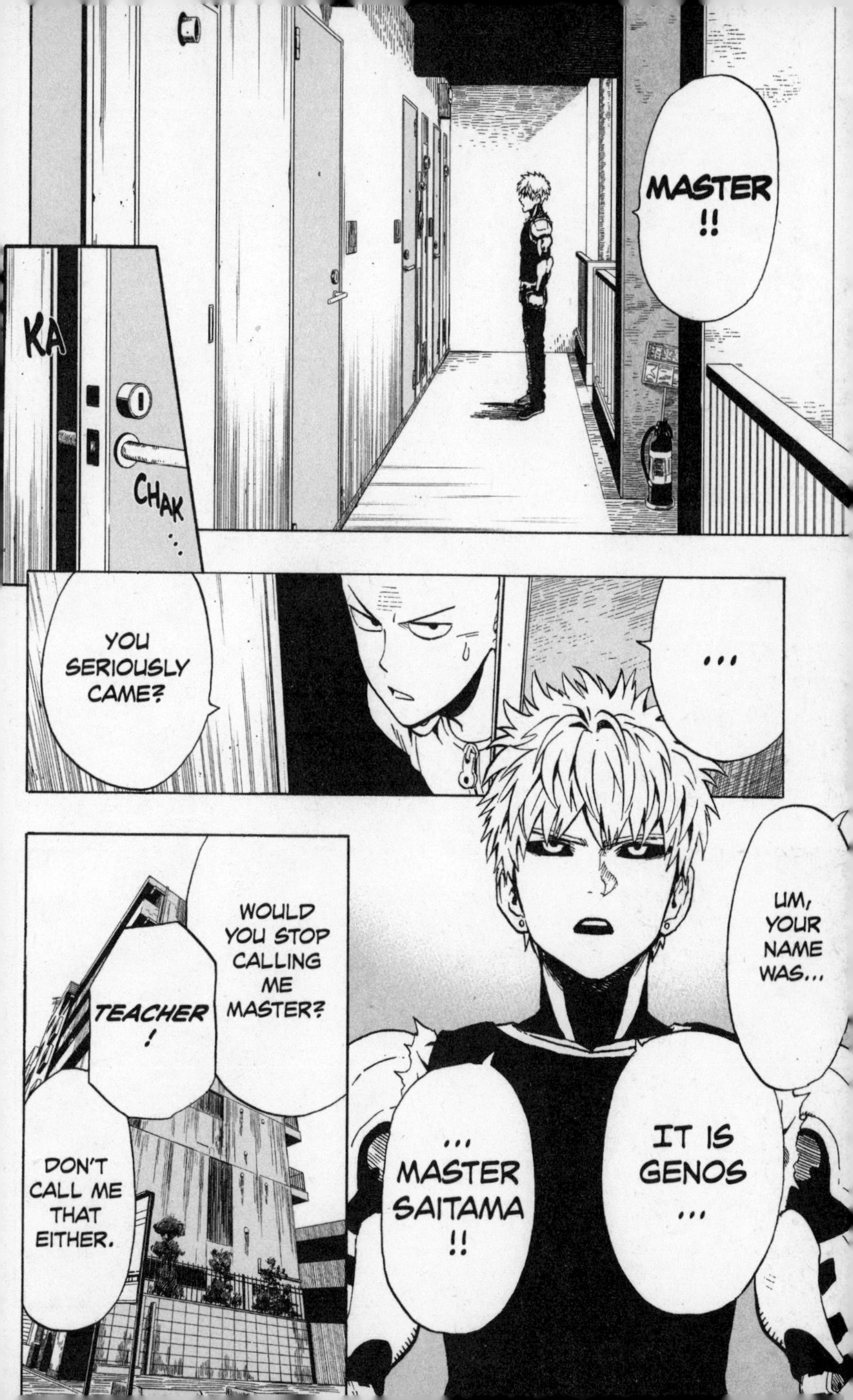
MASTER !!
KA
CHAK ...
...
YOU SERIOUSLY CAME?
UM, YOUR NAME WAS...
IT IS GENOS ...
... MASTER SAITAMA !!
WOULD YOU STOP CALLING ME MASTER?
TEACHER !
DON'T CALL ME THAT EITHER.

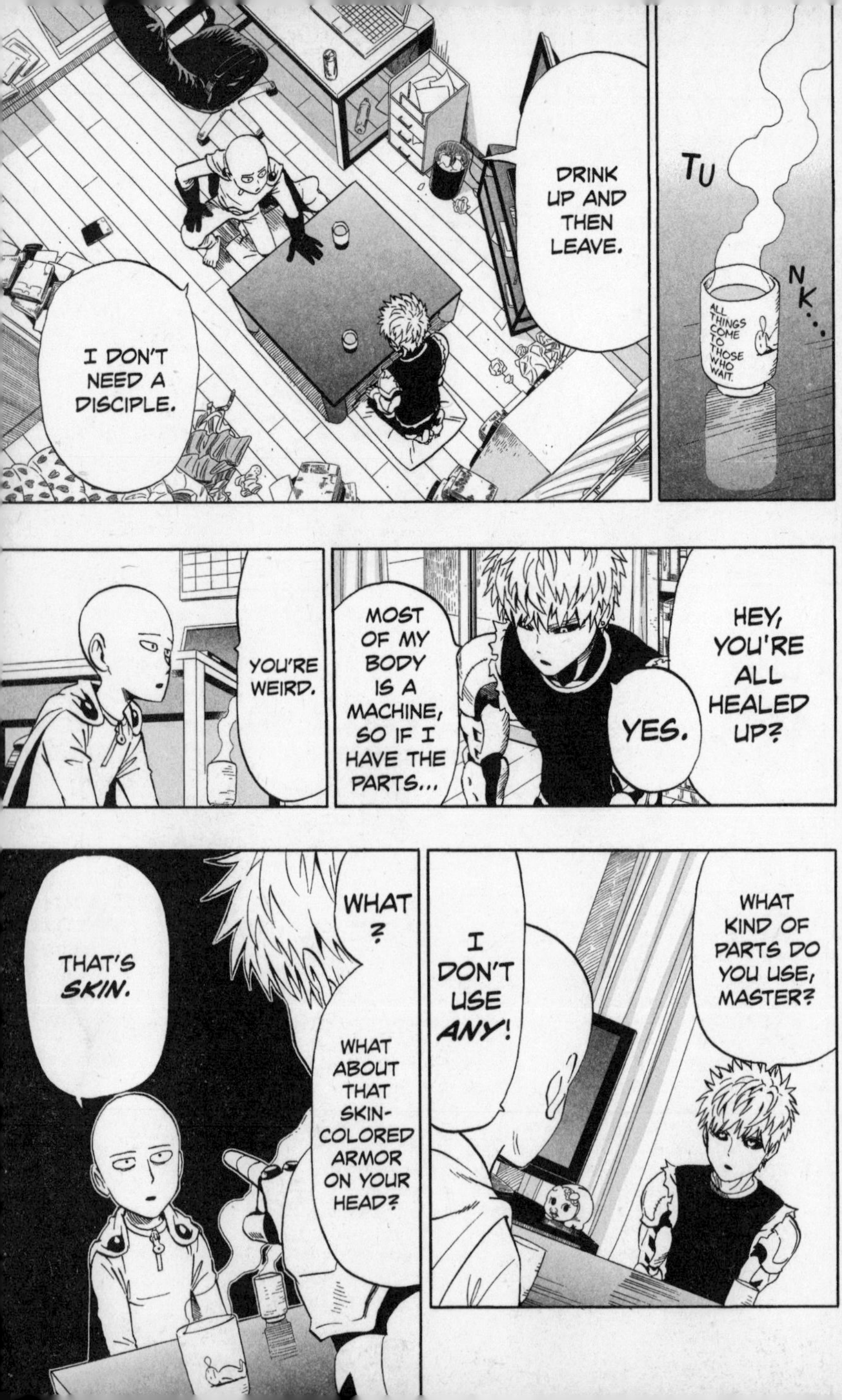
TU
NK...
ALL THINGS COME TO THOSE WHO WAIT.
DRINK UP AND THEN LEAVE.
I DON'T NEED A DISCIPLE.
HEY, YOU'RE ALL HEALED UP?
YES.
MOST OF MY BODY IS A MACHINE, SO IF I HAVE THE PARTS...
YOU'RE WEIRD.
WHAT KIND OF PARTS DO YOU USE, MASTER?
I DON'T USE *ANY*!
WHAT?
WHAT ABOUT THAT SKIN-COLORED ARMOR ON YOUR HEAD?
THAT'S *SKIN*.

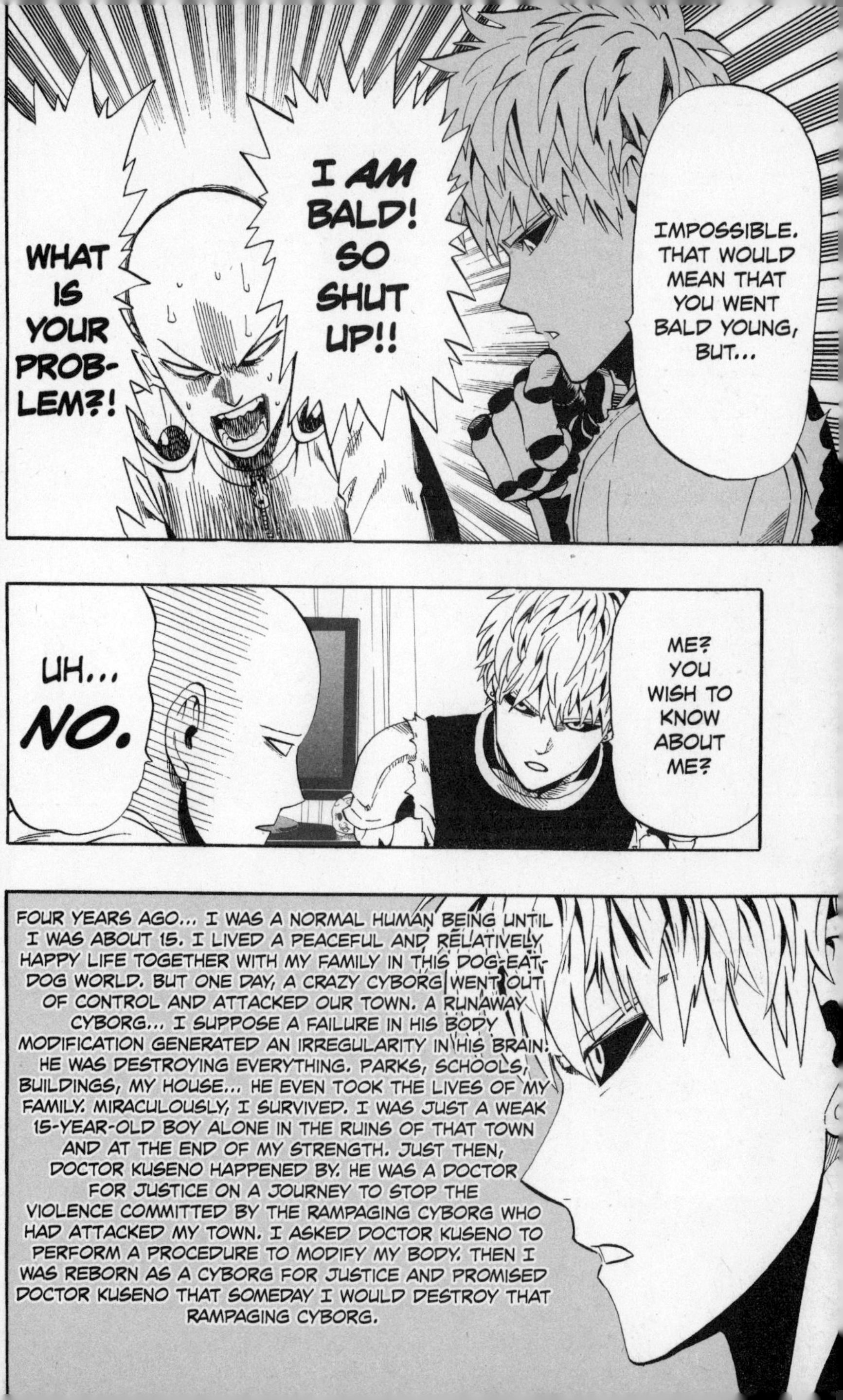
IMPOSSIBLE. THAT WOULD MEAN THAT YOU WENT BALD YOUNG, BUT...
I AM BALD! SO SHUT UP!!
WHAT IS YOUR PROB-LEM?!
ME? YOU WISH TO KNOW ABOUT ME?
UH... NO.
FOUR YEARS AGO... I WAS A NORMAL HUMAN BEING UNTIL I WAS ABOUT 15. I LIVED A PEACEFUL AND RELATIVELY HAPPY LIFE TOGETHER WITH MY FAMILY IN THIS DOG-EAT-DOG WORLD. BUT ONE DAY, A CRAZY CYBORG WENT OUT OF CONTROL AND ATTACKED OUR TOWN. A RUNAWAY CYBORG... I SUPPOSE A FAILURE IN HIS BODY MODIFICATION GENERATED AN IRREGULARITY IN HIS BRAIN. HE WAS DESTROYING EVERYTHING. PARKS, SCHOOLS, BUILDINGS, MY HOUSE... HE EVEN TOOK THE LIVES OF MY FAMILY. MIRACULOUSLY, I SURVIVED. I WAS JUST A WEAK 15-YEAR-OLD BOY ALONE IN THE RUINS OF THAT TOWN AND AT THE END OF MY STRENGTH. JUST THEN, DOCTOR KUSENO HAPPENED BY. HE WAS A DOCTOR FOR JUSTICE ON A JOURNEY TO STOP THE VIOLENCE COMMITTED BY THE RAMPAGING CYBORG WHO HAD ATTACKED MY TOWN. I ASKED DOCTOR KUSENO TO PERFORM A PROCEDURE TO MODIFY MY BODY. THEN I WAS REBORN AS A CYBORG FOR JUSTICE AND PROMISED DOCTOR KUSENO THAT SOMEDAY I WOULD DESTROY THAT RAMPAGING CYBORG.

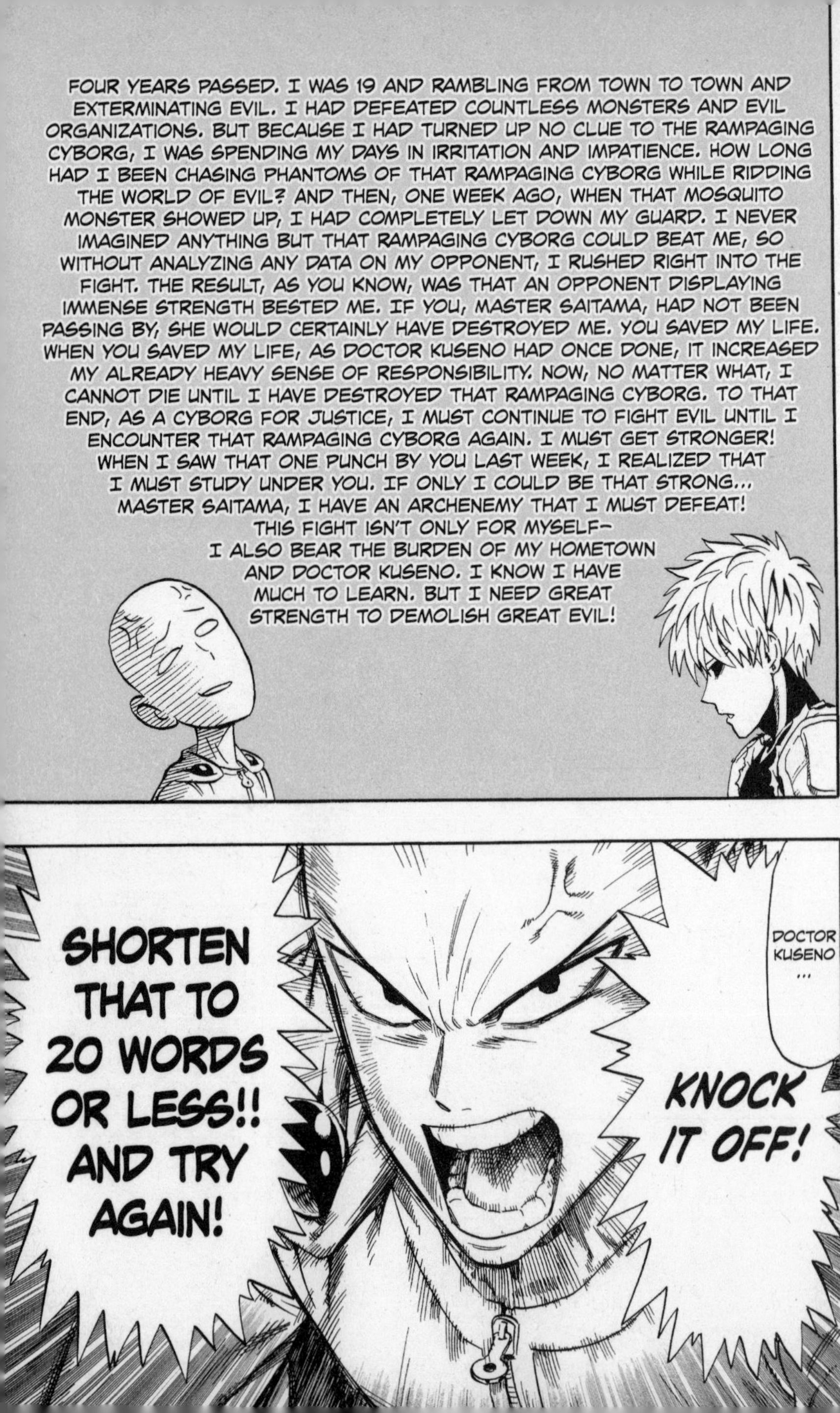
FOUR YEARS PASSED. I WAS 19 AND RAMBLING FROM TOWN TO TOWN AND EXTERMINATING EVIL. I HAD DEFEATED COUNTLESS MONSTERS AND EVIL ORGANIZATIONS. BUT BECAUSE I HAD TURNED UP NO CLUE TO THE RAMPAGING CYBORG, I WAS SPENDING MY DAYS IN IRRITATION AND IMPATIENCE. HOW LONG HAD I BEEN CHASING PHANTOMS OF THAT RAMPAGING CYBORG WHILE RIDDING THE WORLD OF EVIL? AND THEN, ONE WEEK AGO, WHEN THAT MOSQUITO MONSTER SHOWED UP, I HAD COMPLETELY LET DOWN MY GUARD. I NEVER IMAGINED ANYTHING BUT THAT RAMPAGING CYBORG COULD BEAT ME, SO WITHOUT ANALYZING ANY DATA ON MY OPPONENT, I RUSHED RIGHT INTO THE FIGHT. THE RESULT, AS YOU KNOW, WAS THAT AN OPPONENT DISPLAYING IMMENSE STRENGTH BESTED ME. IF YOU, MASTER SAITAMA, HAD NOT BEEN PASSING BY, SHE WOULD CERTAINLY HAVE DESTROYED ME. YOU SAVED MY LIFE. WHEN YOU SAVED MY LIFE, AS DOCTOR KUSENO HAD ONCE DONE, IT INCREASED MY ALREADY HEAVY SENSE OF RESPONSIBILITY. NOW, NO MATTER WHAT, I CANNOT DIE UNTIL I HAVE DESTROYED THAT RAMPAGING CYBORG. TO THAT END, AS A CYBORG FOR JUSTICE, I MUST CONTINUE TO FIGHT EVIL UNTIL I ENCOUNTER THAT RAMPAGING CYBORG AGAIN. I MUST GET STRONGER! WHEN I SAW THAT ONE PUNCH BY YOU LAST WEEK, I REALIZED THAT I MUST STUDY UNDER YOU. IF ONLY I COULD BE THAT STRONG... MASTER SAITAMA, I HAVE AN ARCHENEMY THAT I MUST DEFEAT! THIS FIGHT ISN'T ONLY FOR MYSELF— I ALSO BEAR THE BURDEN OF MY HOMETOWN AND DOCTOR KUSENO. I KNOW I HAVE MUCH TO LEARN. BUT I NEED GREAT STRENGTH TO DEMOLISH GREAT EVIL!
DOCTOR KUSENO ...
KNOCK IT OFF!
SHORTEN THAT TO 20 WORDS OR LESS!! AND TRY AGAIN!

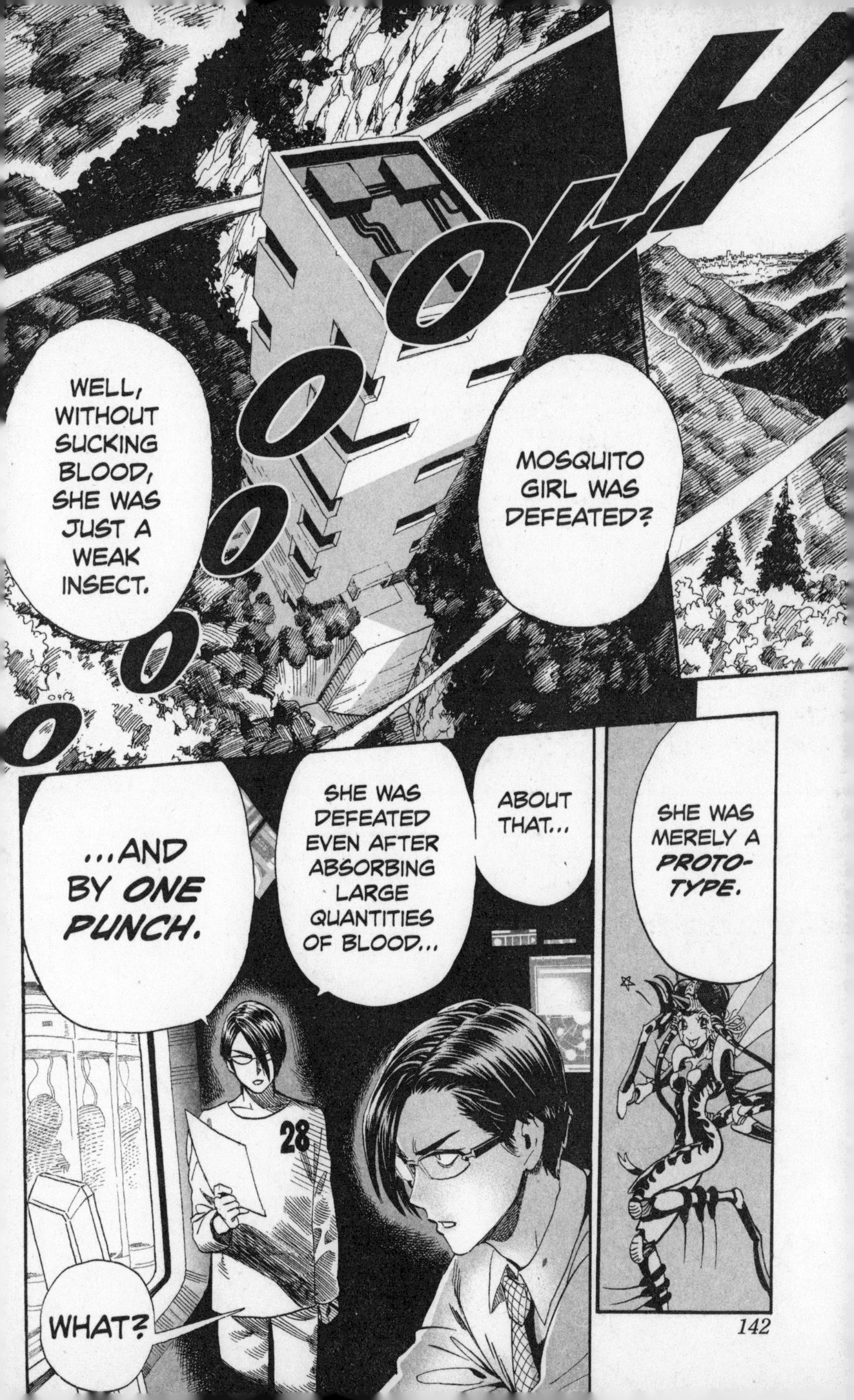
MOSQUITO GIRL WAS DEFEATED?
WELL, WITHOUT SUCKING BLOOD, SHE WAS JUST A WEAK INSECT.
SHE WAS MERELY A *PROTO-TYPE.*
ABOUT THAT...
SHE WAS DEFEATED EVEN AFTER ABSORBING LARGE QUANTITIES OF BLOOD...
...AND BY *ONE PUNCH.*
WHAT?
28

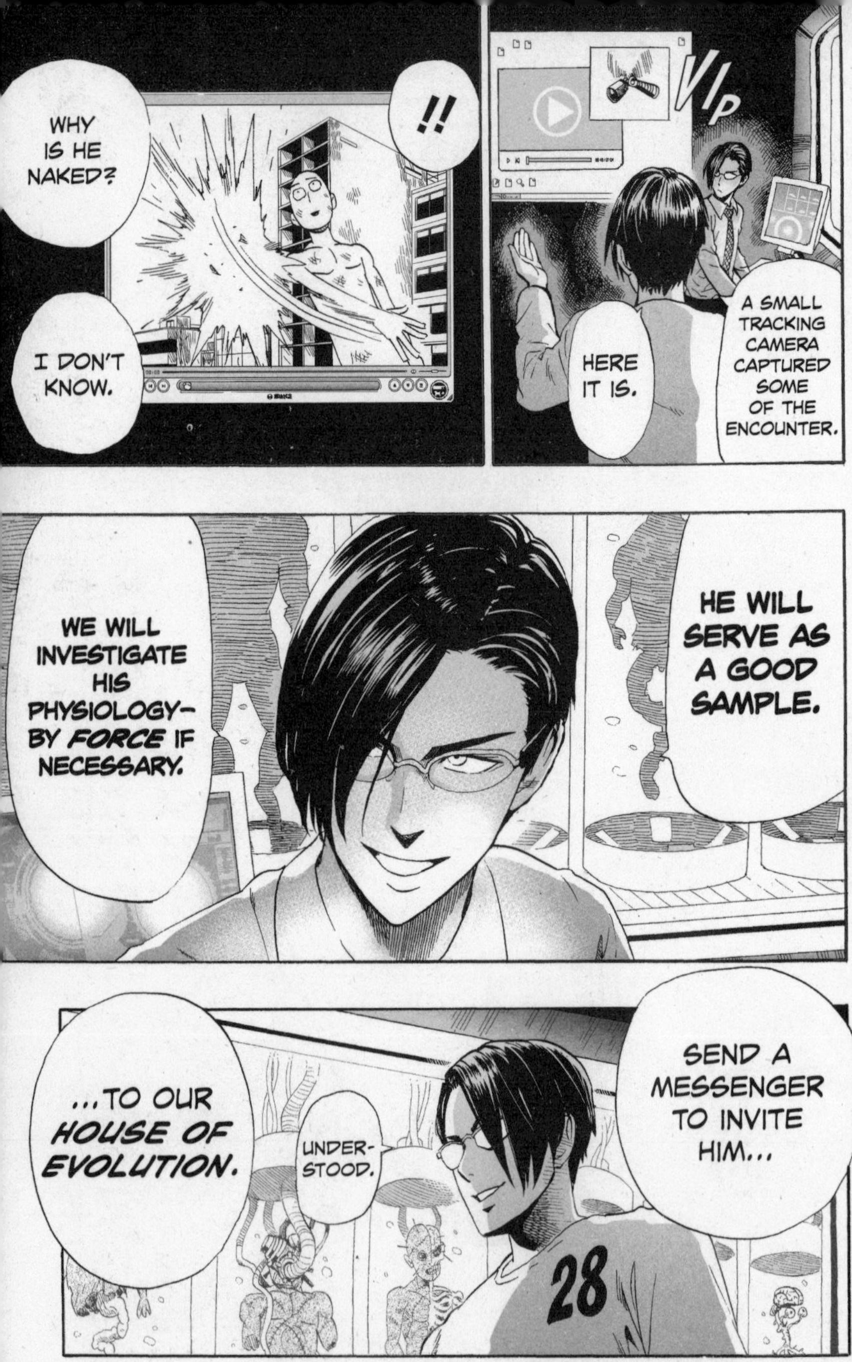
A SMALL TRACKING CAMERA CAPTURED SOME OF THE ENCOUNTER.
HERE IT IS.
VIP
!!
WHY IS HE NAKED?
I DON'T KNOW.
HE WILL SERVE AS A GOOD SAMPLE.
WE WILL INVESTIGATE HIS PHYSIOLOGY—BY *FORCE* IF NECESSARY.
SEND A MESSENGER TO INVITE HIM...
UNDERSTOOD.
...TO OUR *HOUSE OF EVOLUTION.*
28

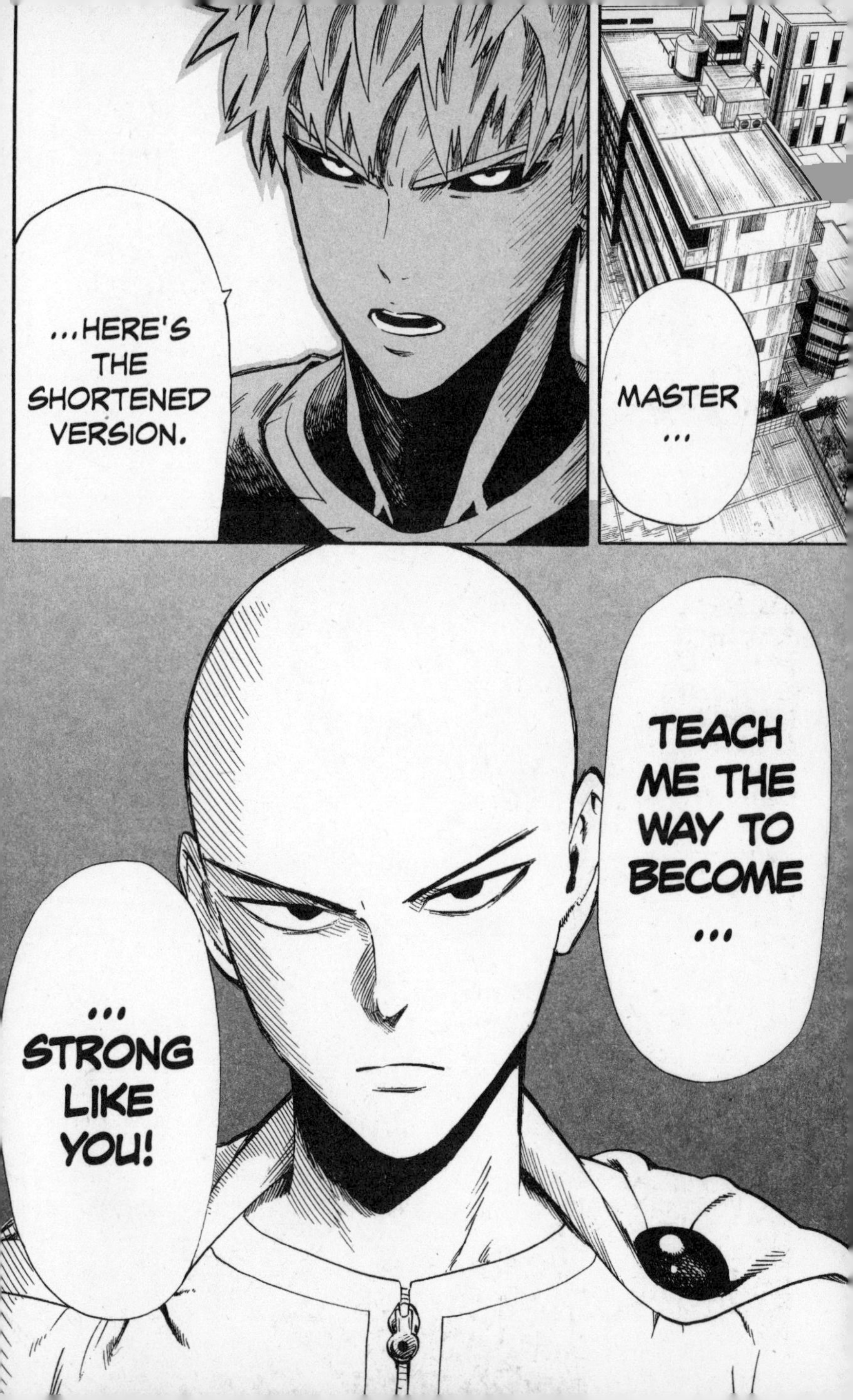
MASTER ...
...HERE'S THE SHORTENED VERSION.
TEACH ME THE WAY TO BECOME ...
... STRONG LIKE YOU!

READ THIS WAY

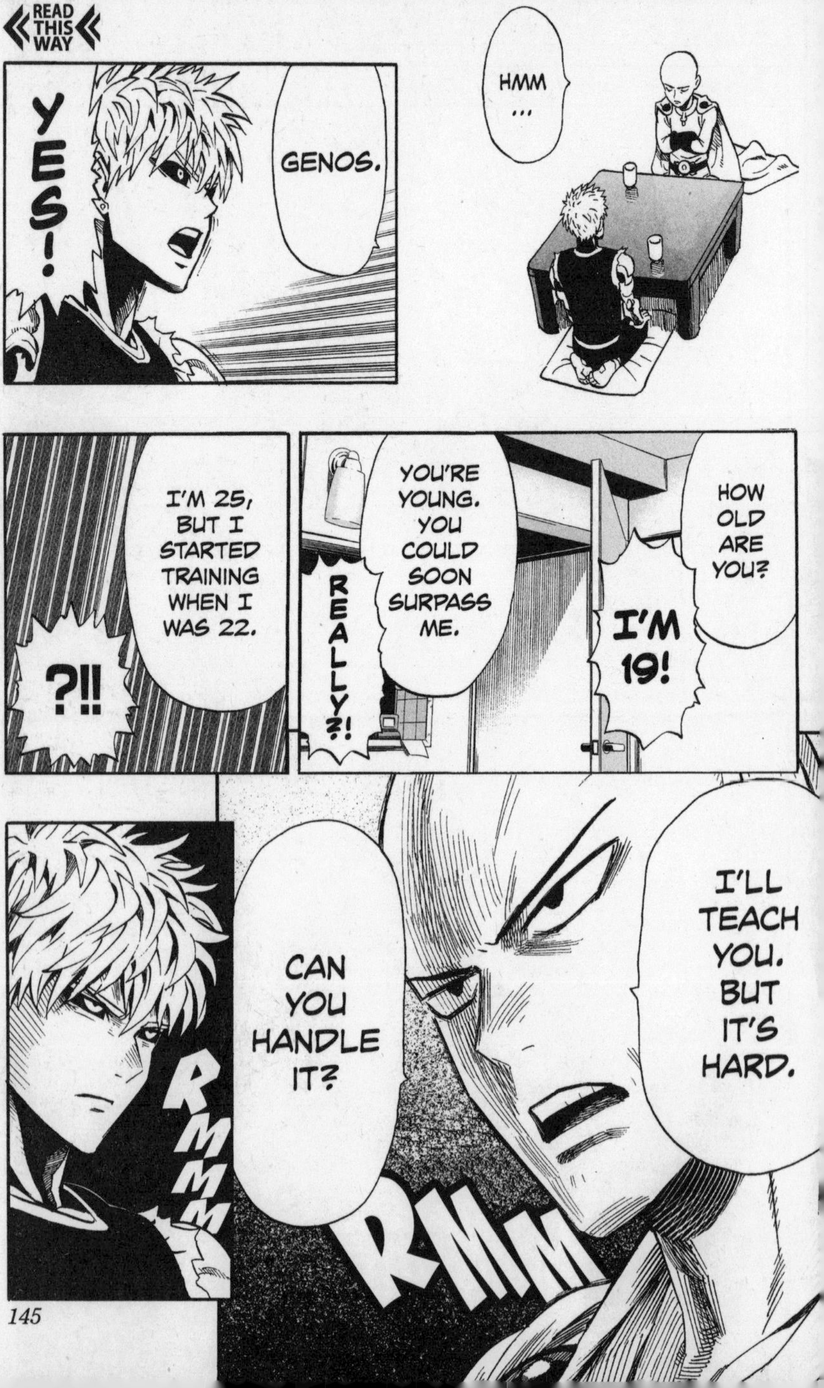

HMM ...
GENOS.
YES!
HOW OLD ARE YOU?
I'M 19!
YOU'RE YOUNG. YOU COULD SOON SURPASS ME.
REALLY?!
I'M 25, BUT I STARTED TRAINING WHEN I WAS 22.
?!!
I'LL TEACH YOU. BUT IT'S HARD.
CAN YOU HANDLE IT?
RMMM
RMMMM

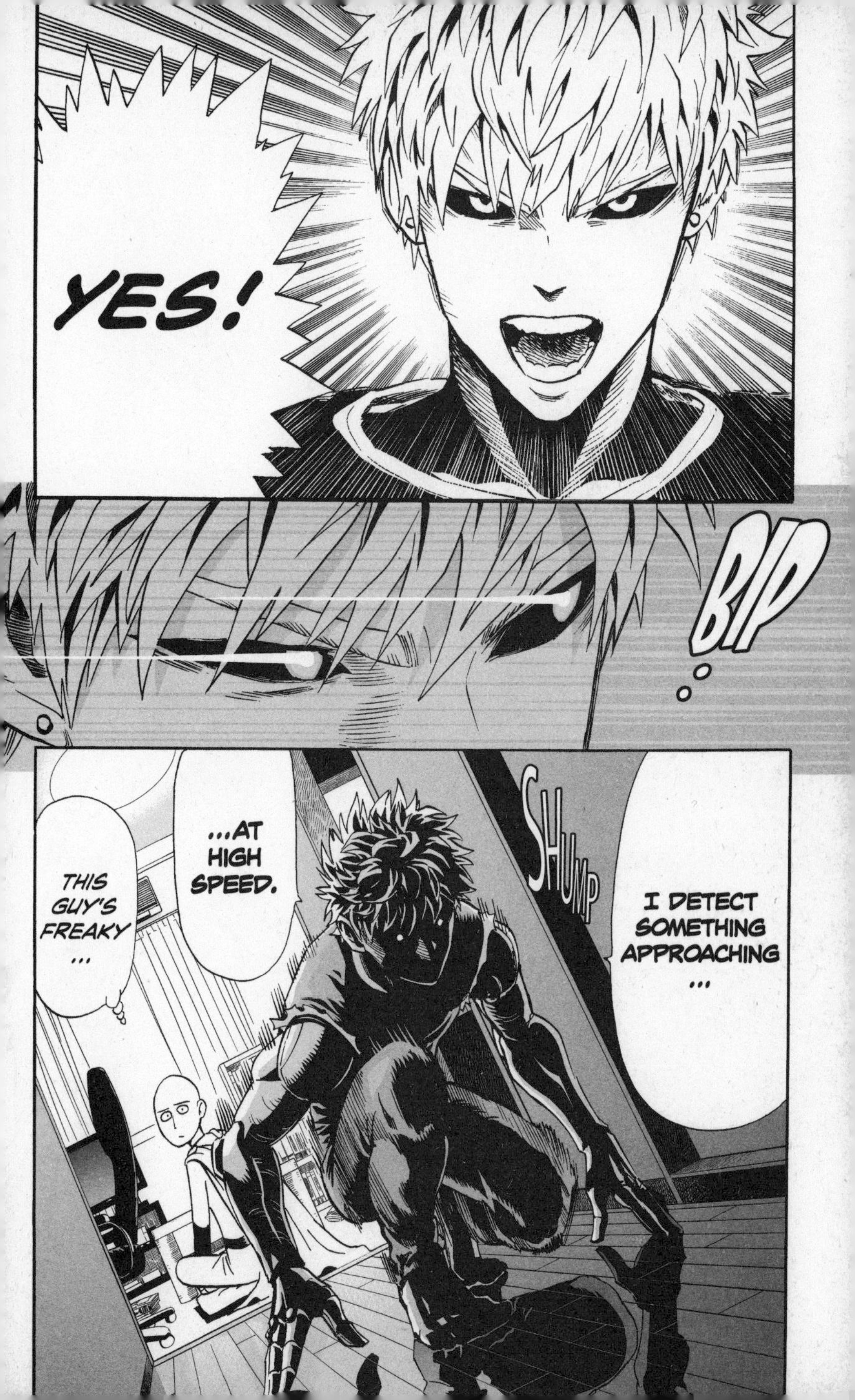
YES!
BIP
I DETECT SOMETHING APPROACHING ...
SHUMP
...AT HIGH SPEED.
THIS GUY'S FREAKY ...

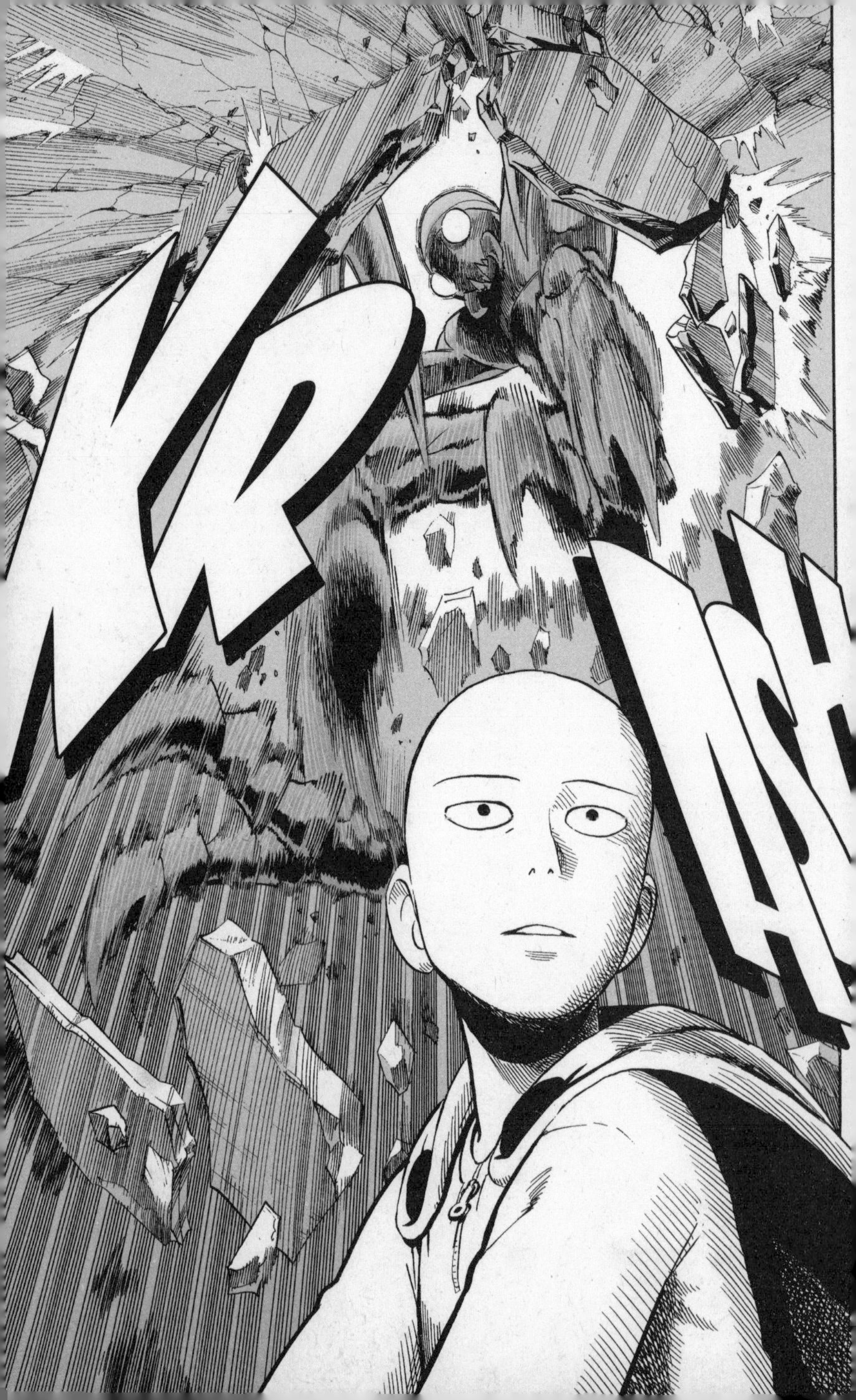

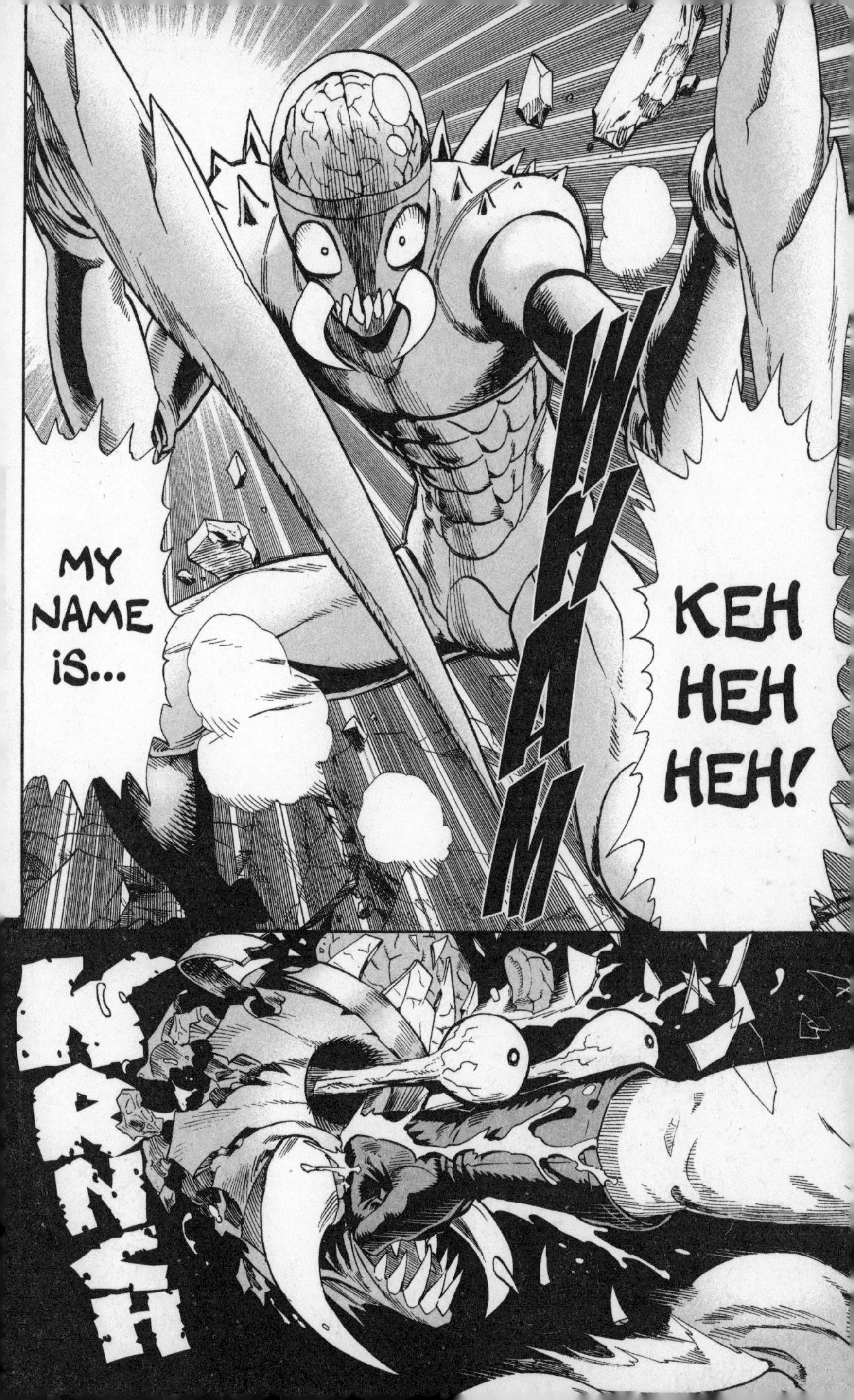
KEH HEH HEH!
WHAM
MY NAME IS...
KRNCH

READ THIS WAY

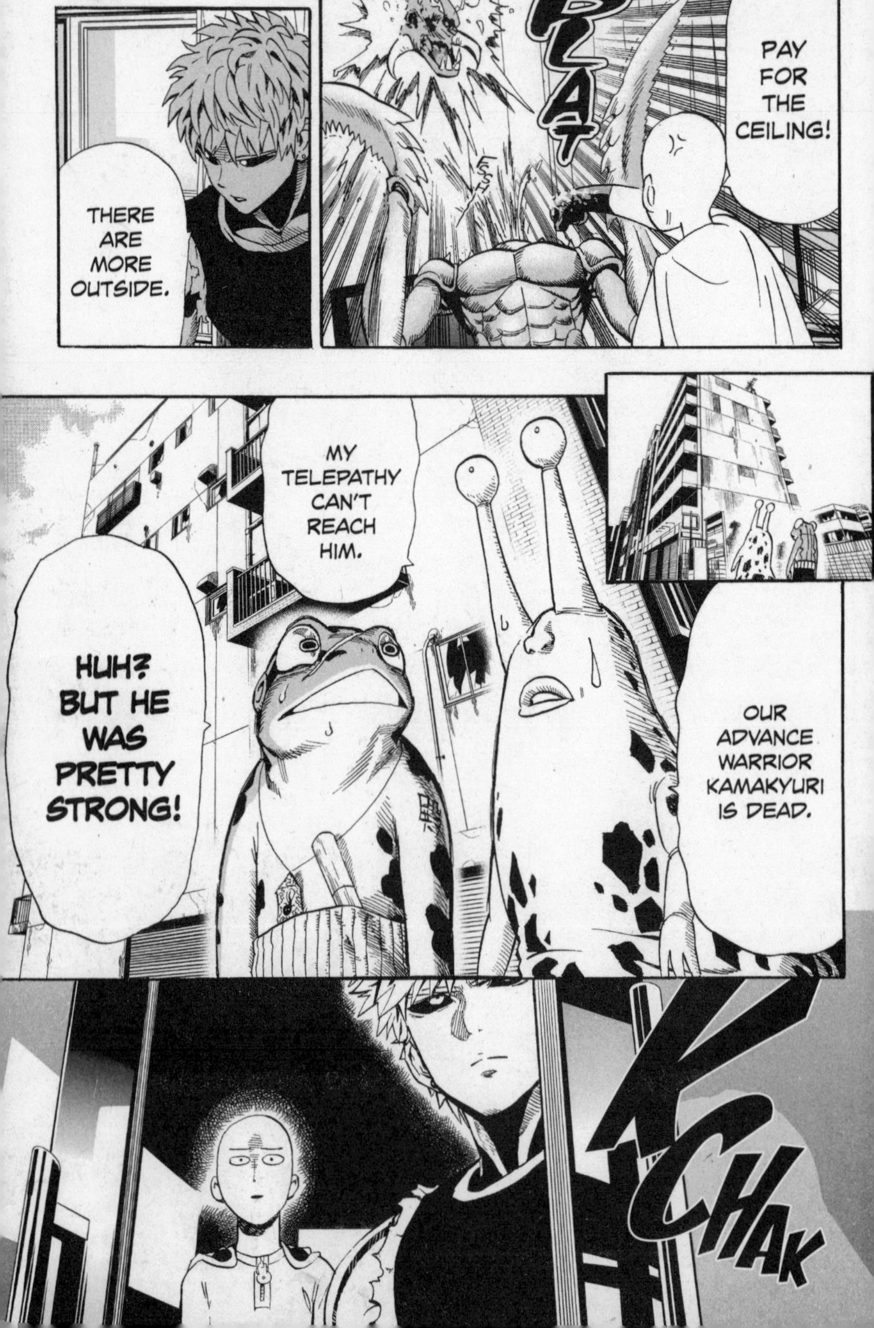
SPLAT
PAY FOR THE CEILING!
FSSH
THERE ARE MORE OUTSIDE.
OUR ADVANCE WARRIOR KAMAKYURI IS DEAD.
MY TELEPATHY CAN'T REACH HIM.
HUH? BUT HE WAS PRETTY STRONG!
KCHAK

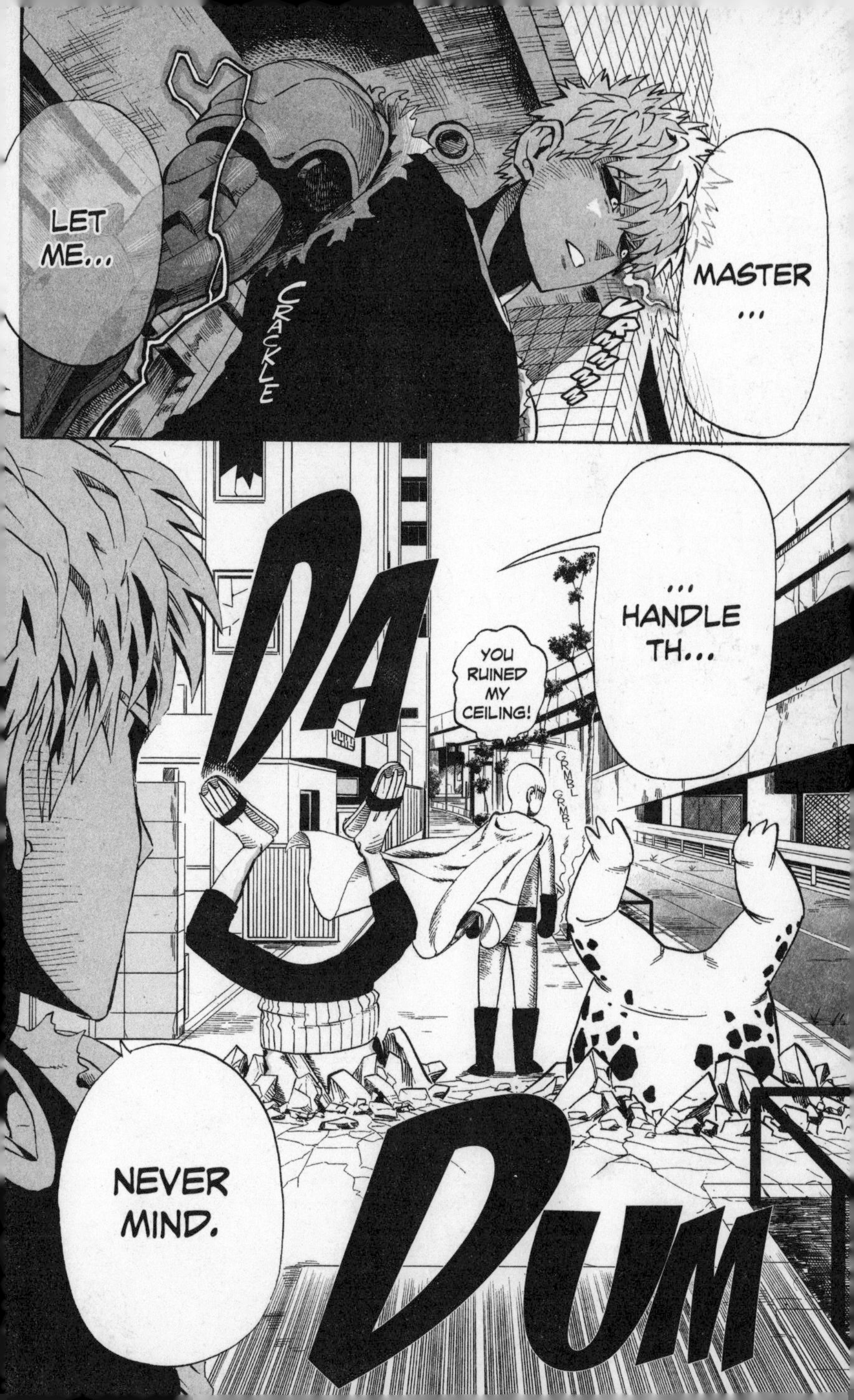
MASTER ...
VRMMMM
CRACKLE
LET ME...
... HANDLE TH...
YOU RUINED MY CEILING!
GRMBL GRMBL
DA
NEVER MIND.
DUM

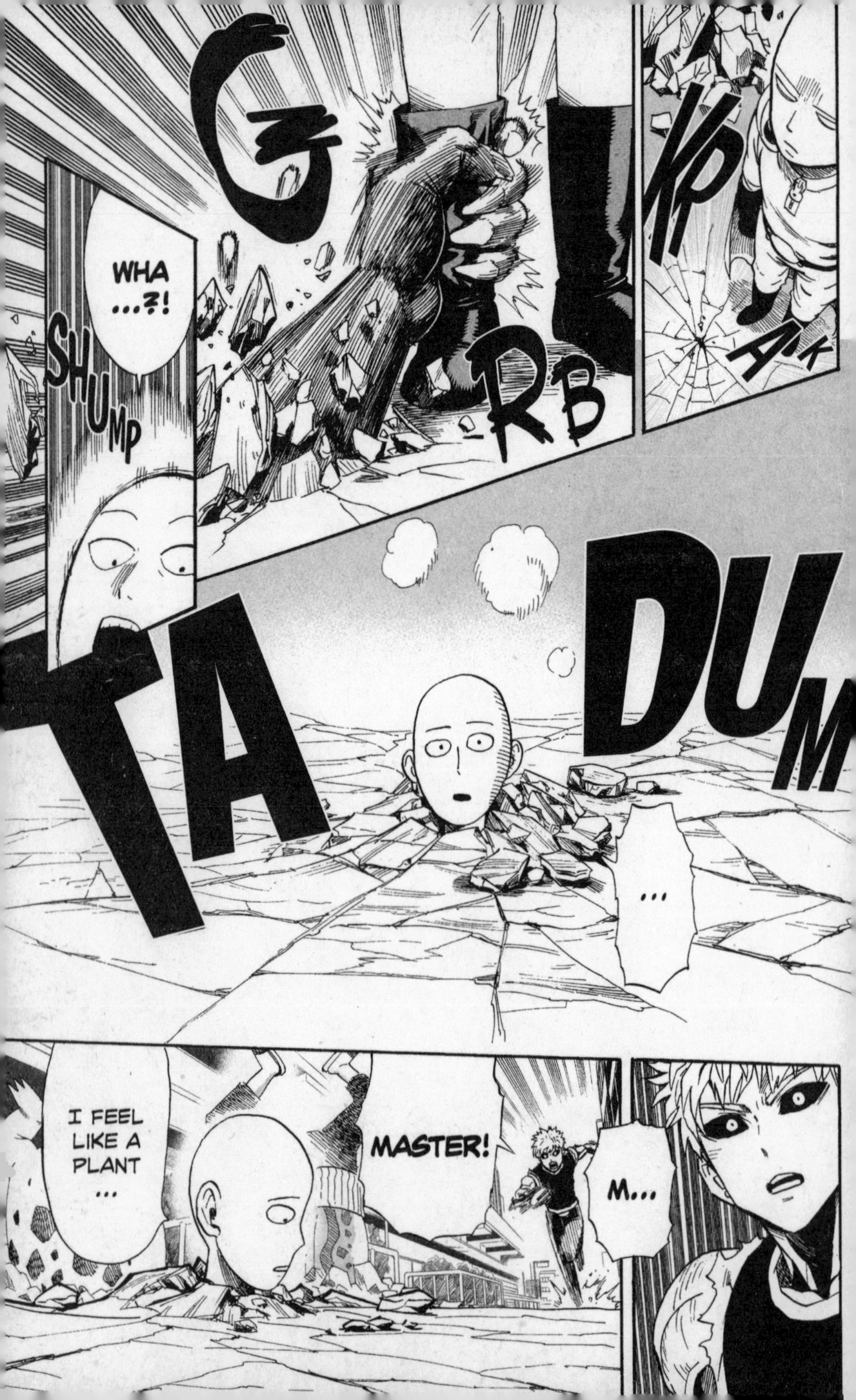
KRAK
GRB
WHA ...?!
SHUMP
TADUM
...
M...
MASTER!
I FEEL LIKE A PLANT ...

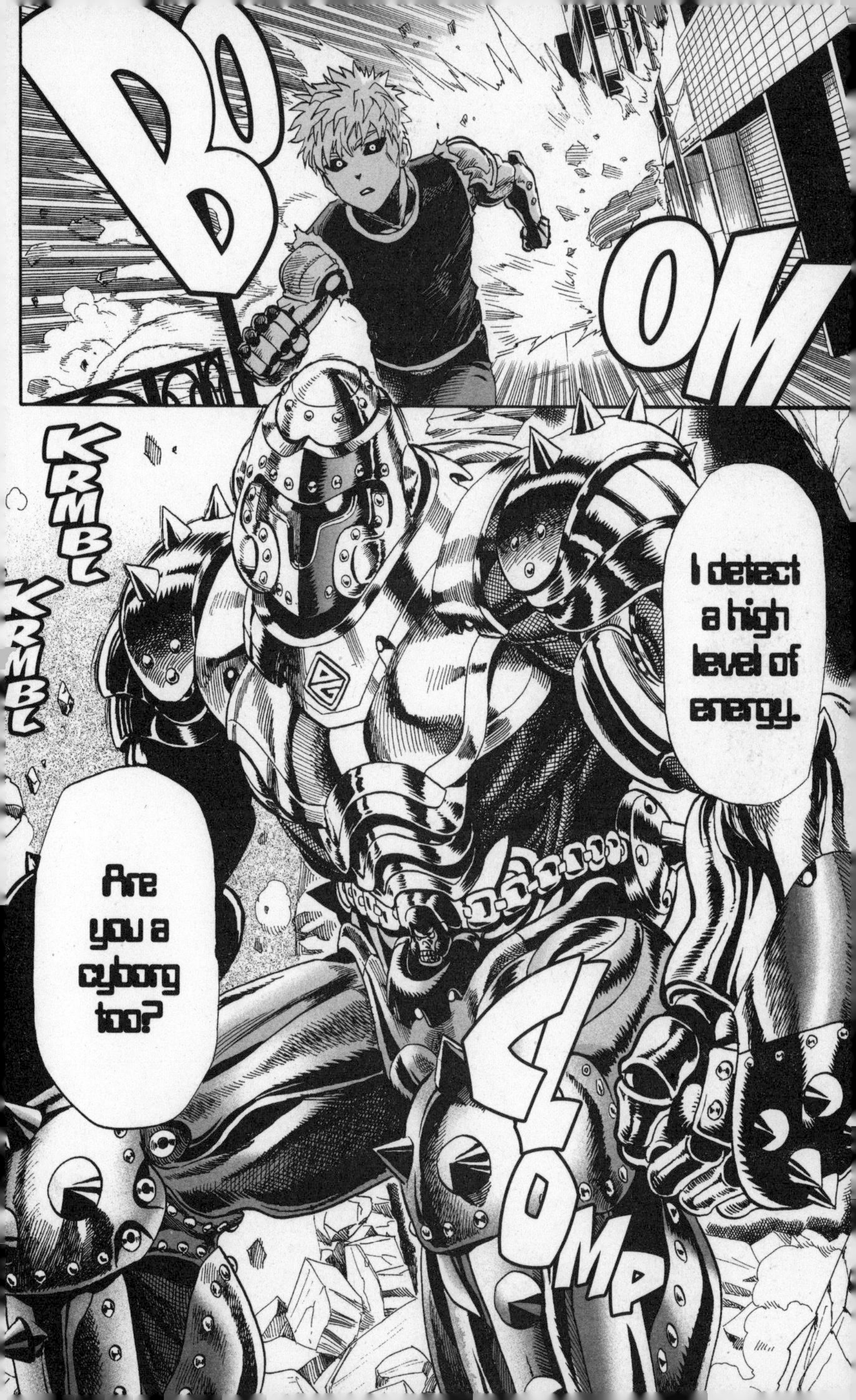
BOOM
I detect a high level of energy.
KRMBL
KRMBL
Are you a cyborg too?
STOMP

PUNCH 8: THIS GUY?

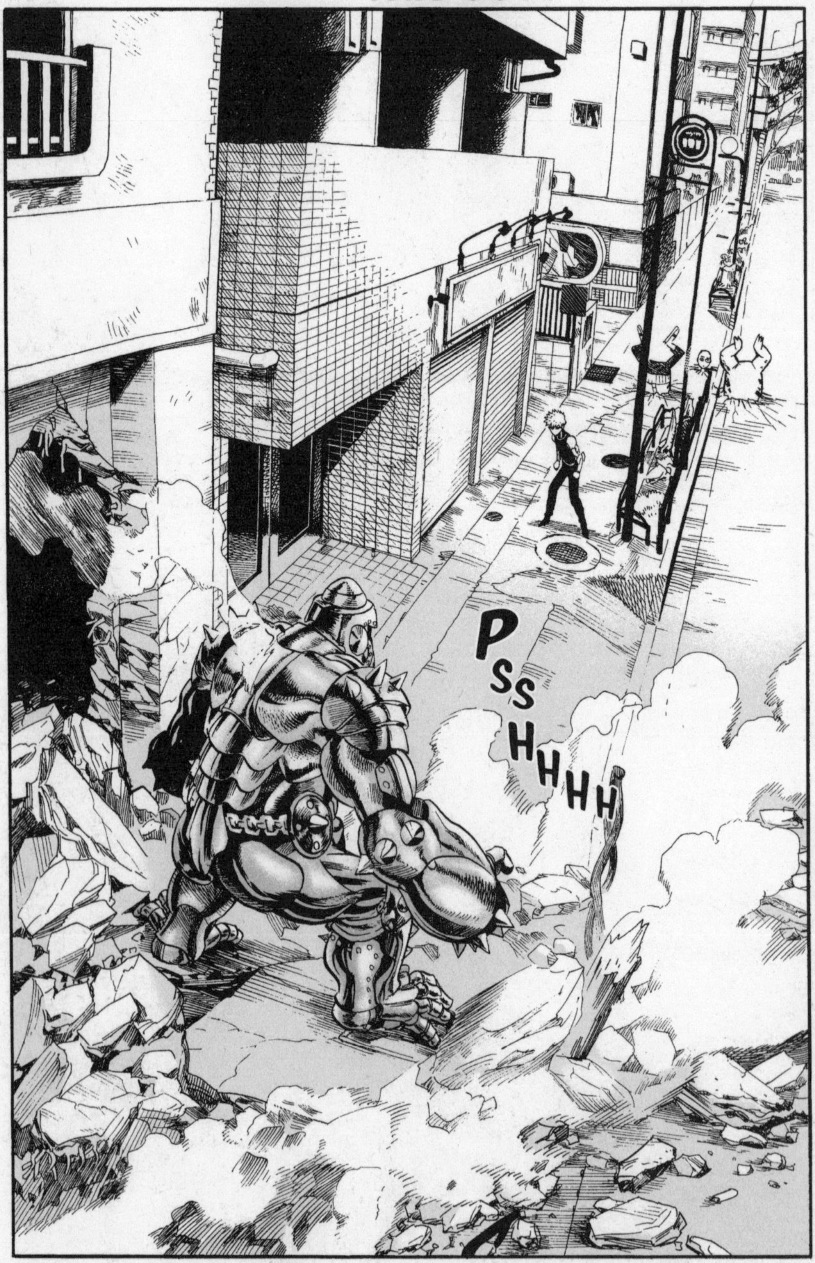
PSSHHHHH

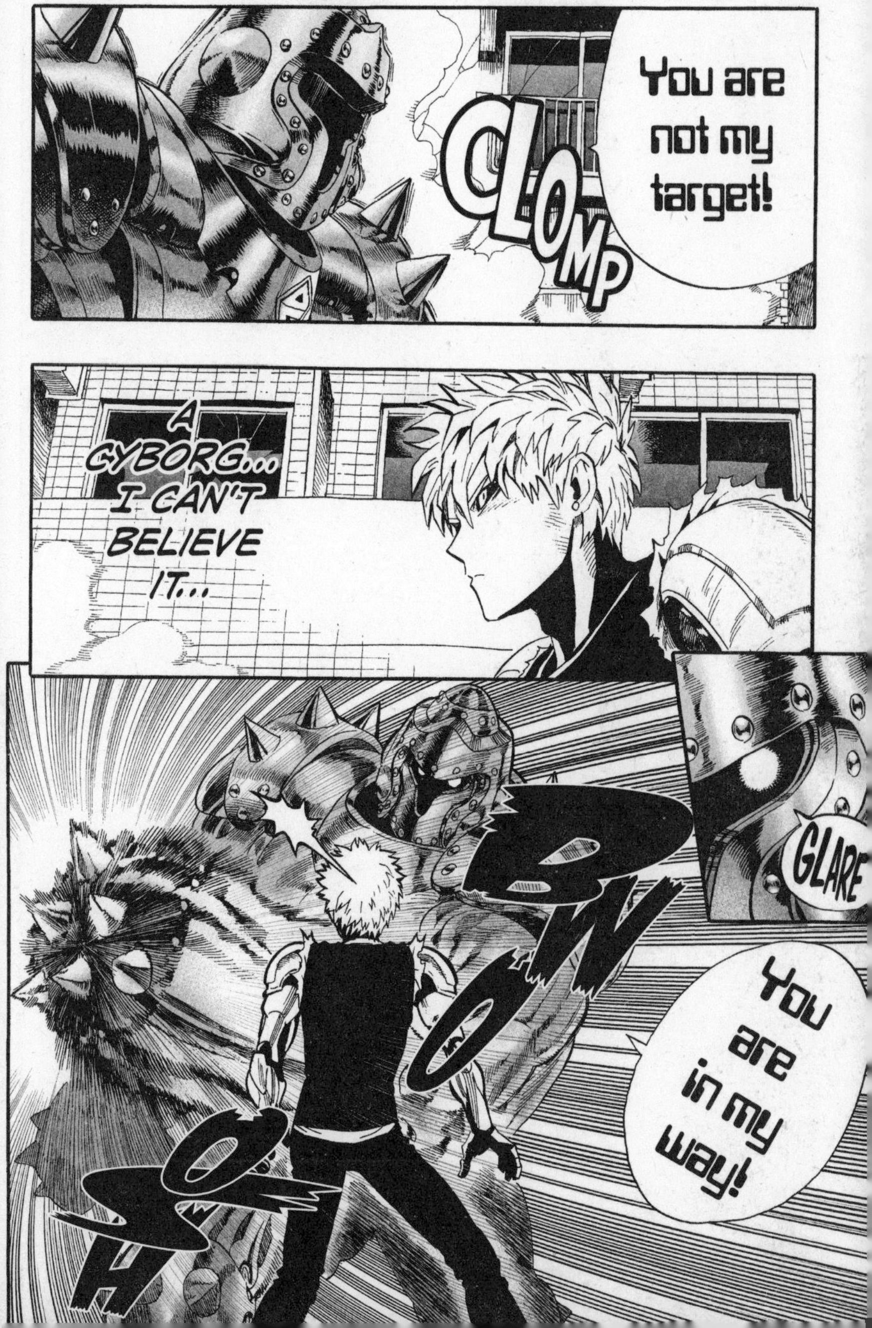
You are not my target!
CLOMP
A CYBORG... I CAN'T BELIEVE IT...
GLARE
You are in my way!

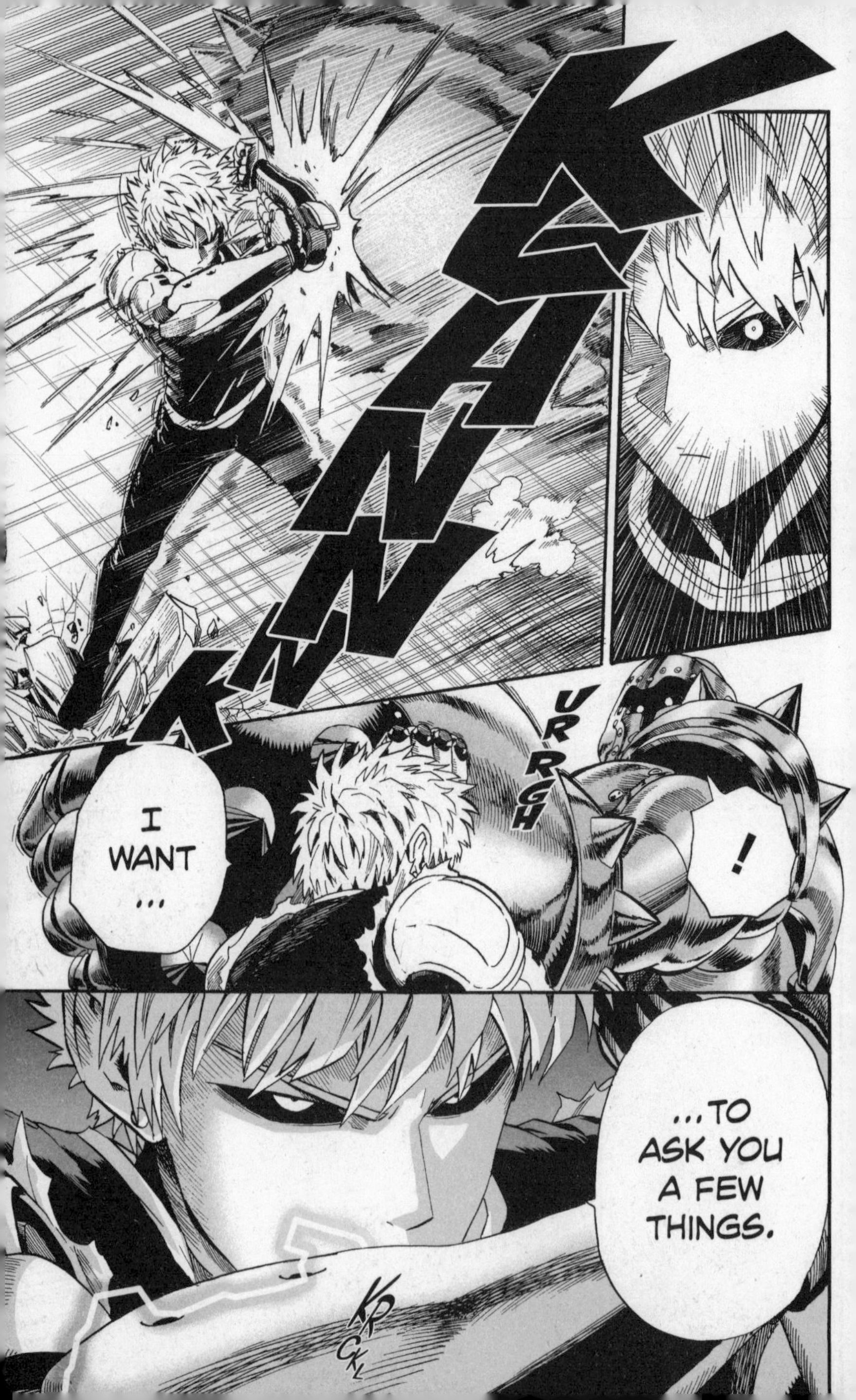
KANNN
!
URRRGH
I WANT ...
...TO ASK YOU A FEW THINGS.
KRCKL

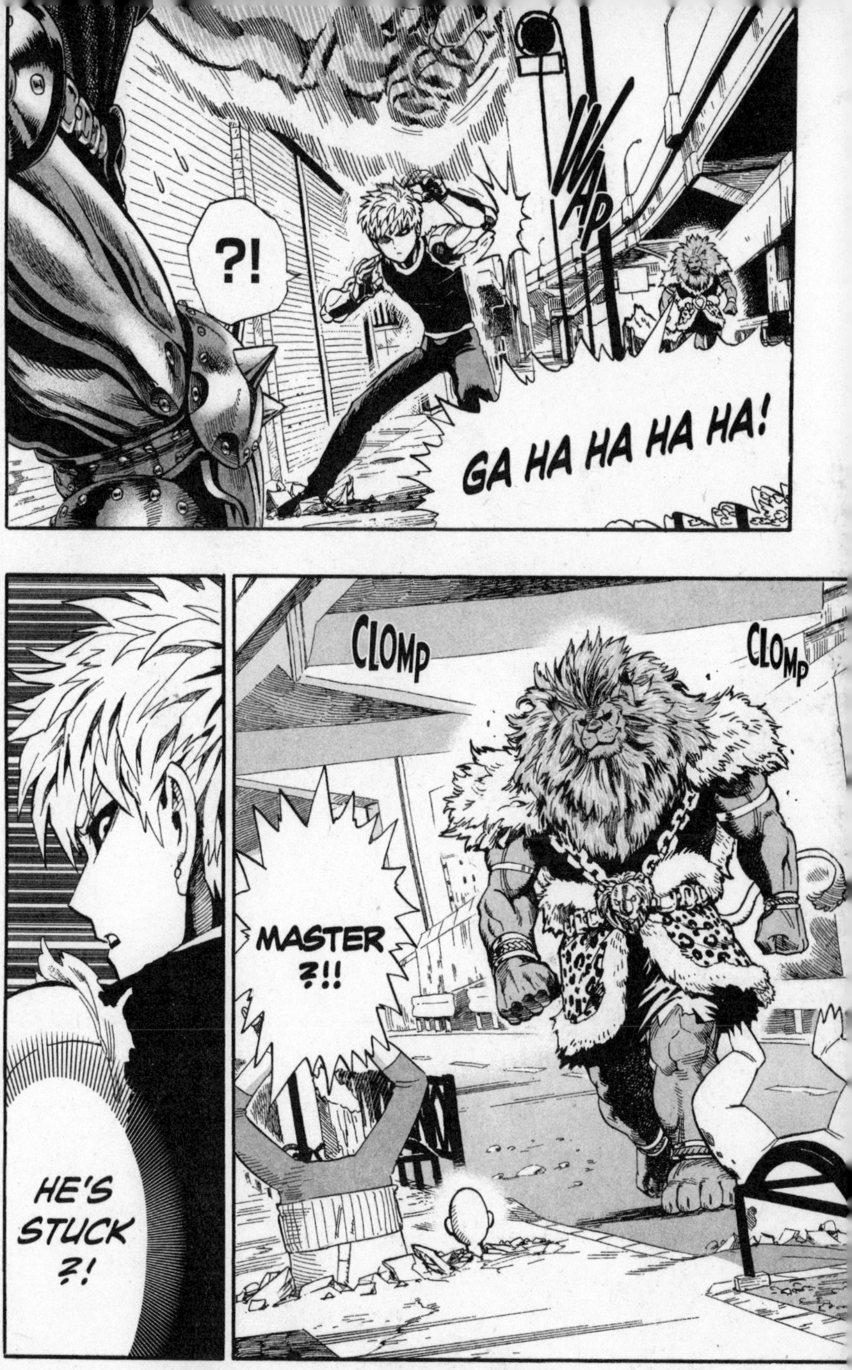
WAP
?!
GA HA HA HA HA!
CLOMP
CLOMP
MASTER ?!!
HE'S STUCK ?!

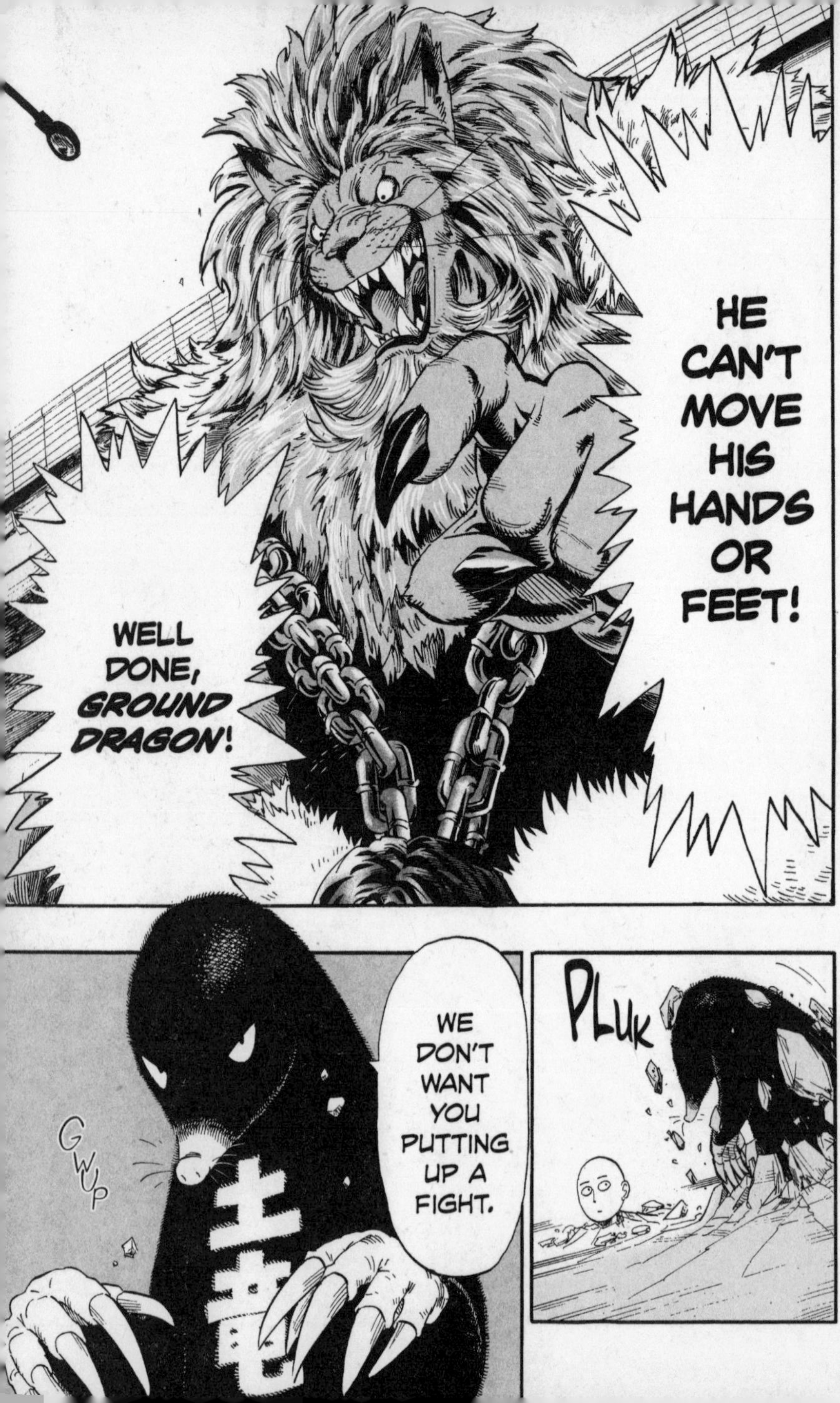
HE CAN'T MOVE HIS HANDS OR FEET!
WELL DONE, GROUND DRAGON!
PLUK
WE DON'T WANT YOU PUTTING UP A FIGHT.
GWUP
土竜

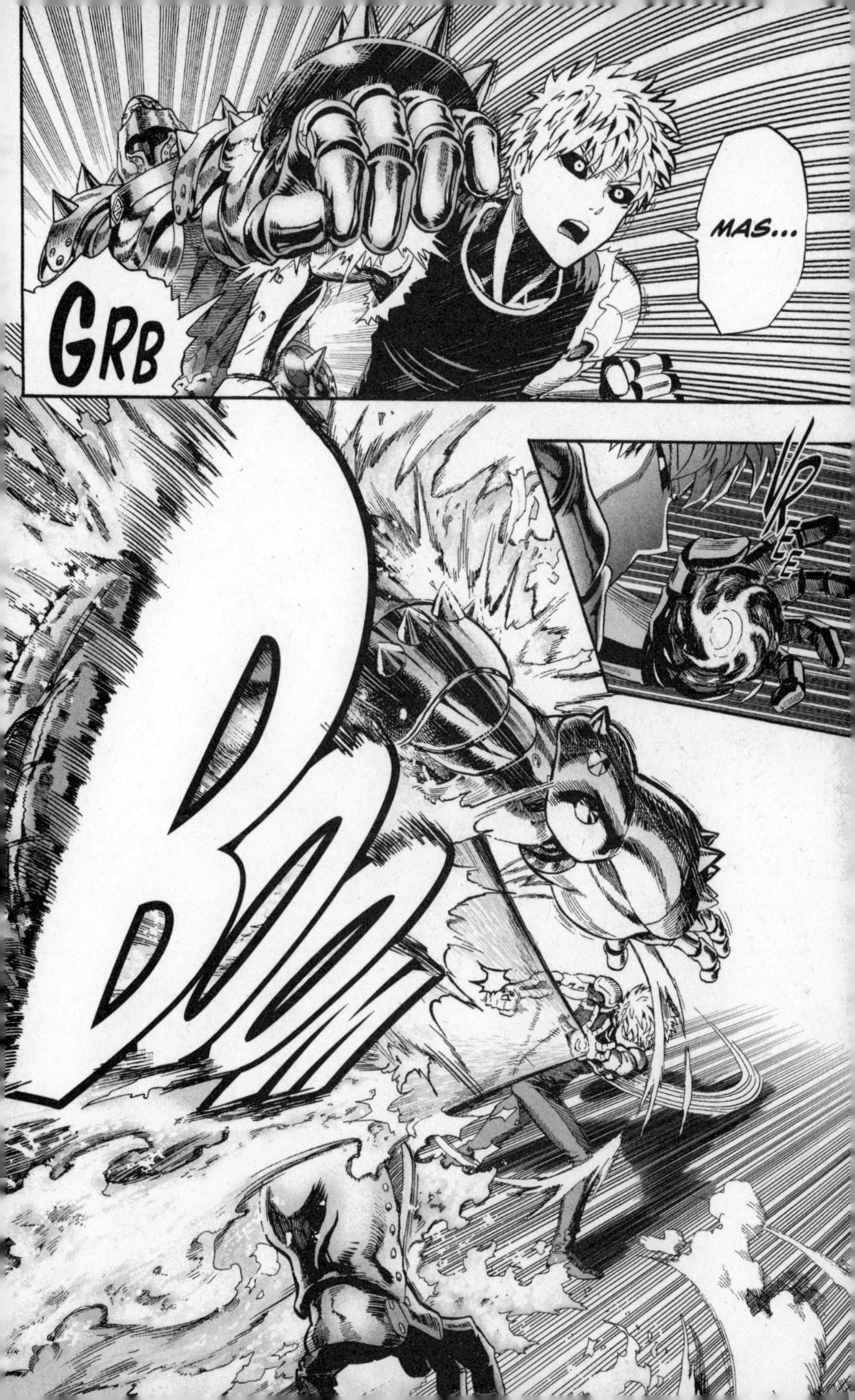
MAS...
GRB
VREEE
BOOM

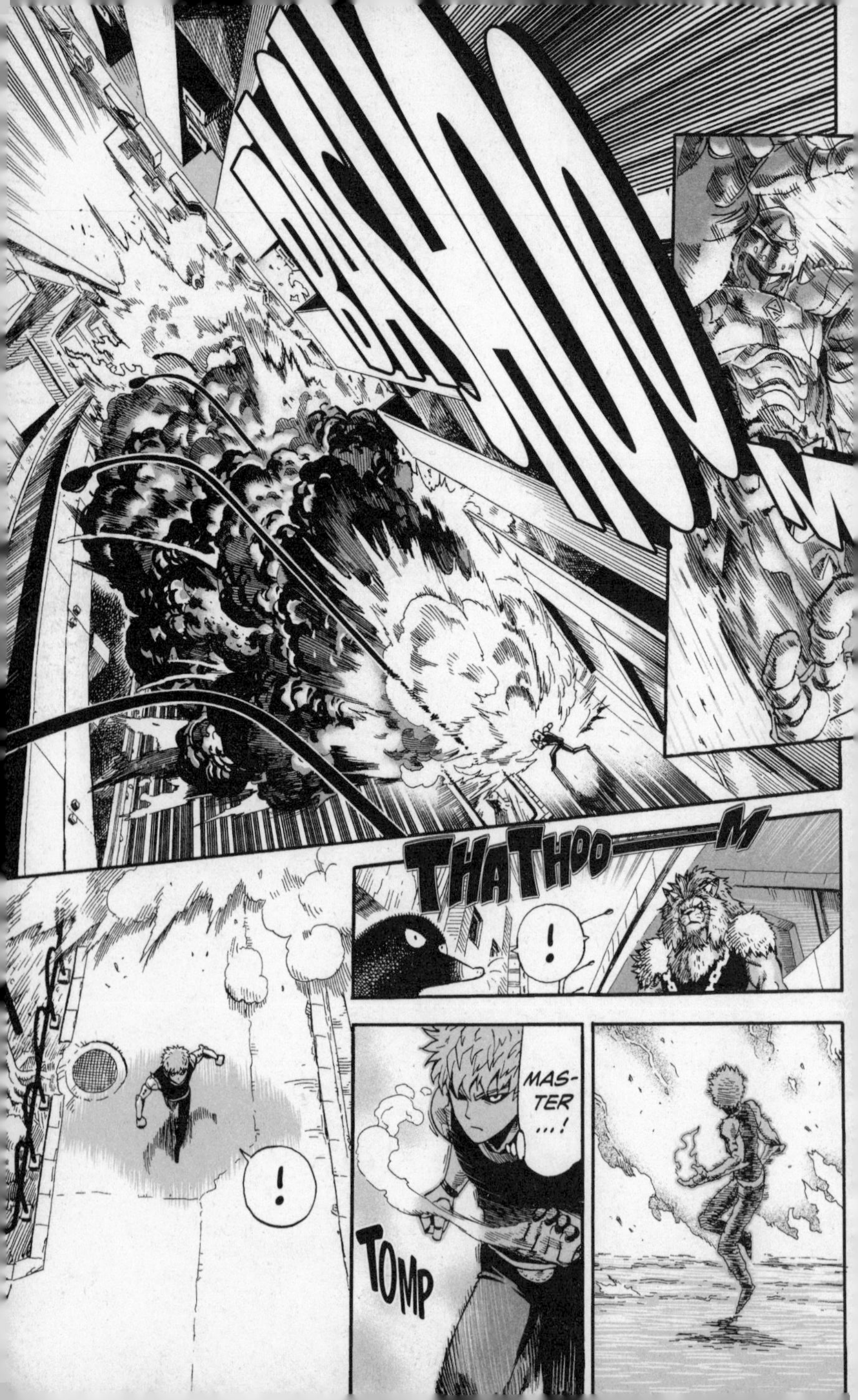
THATHOOM
!
MASTER...!
TOMP
!

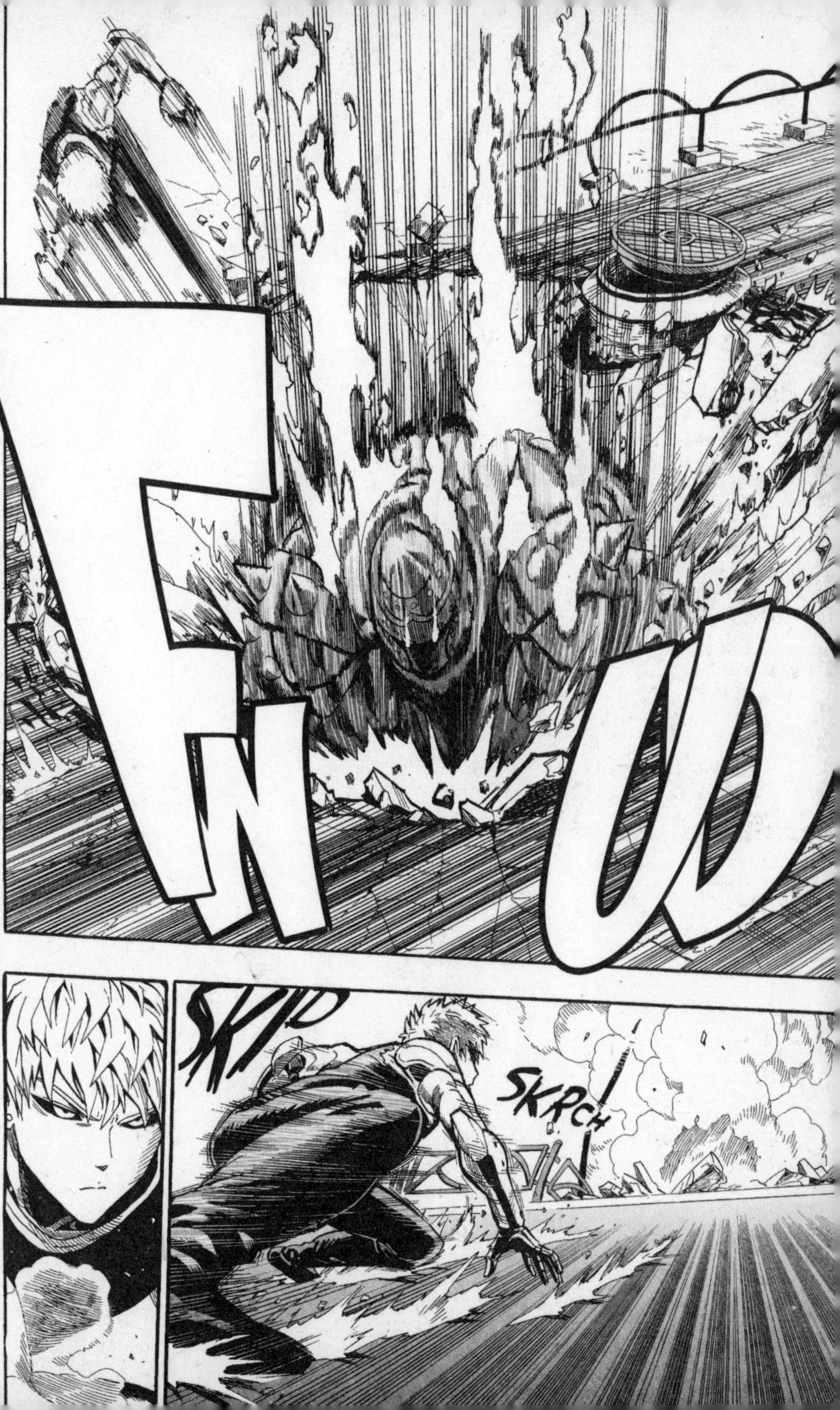
SKRCH

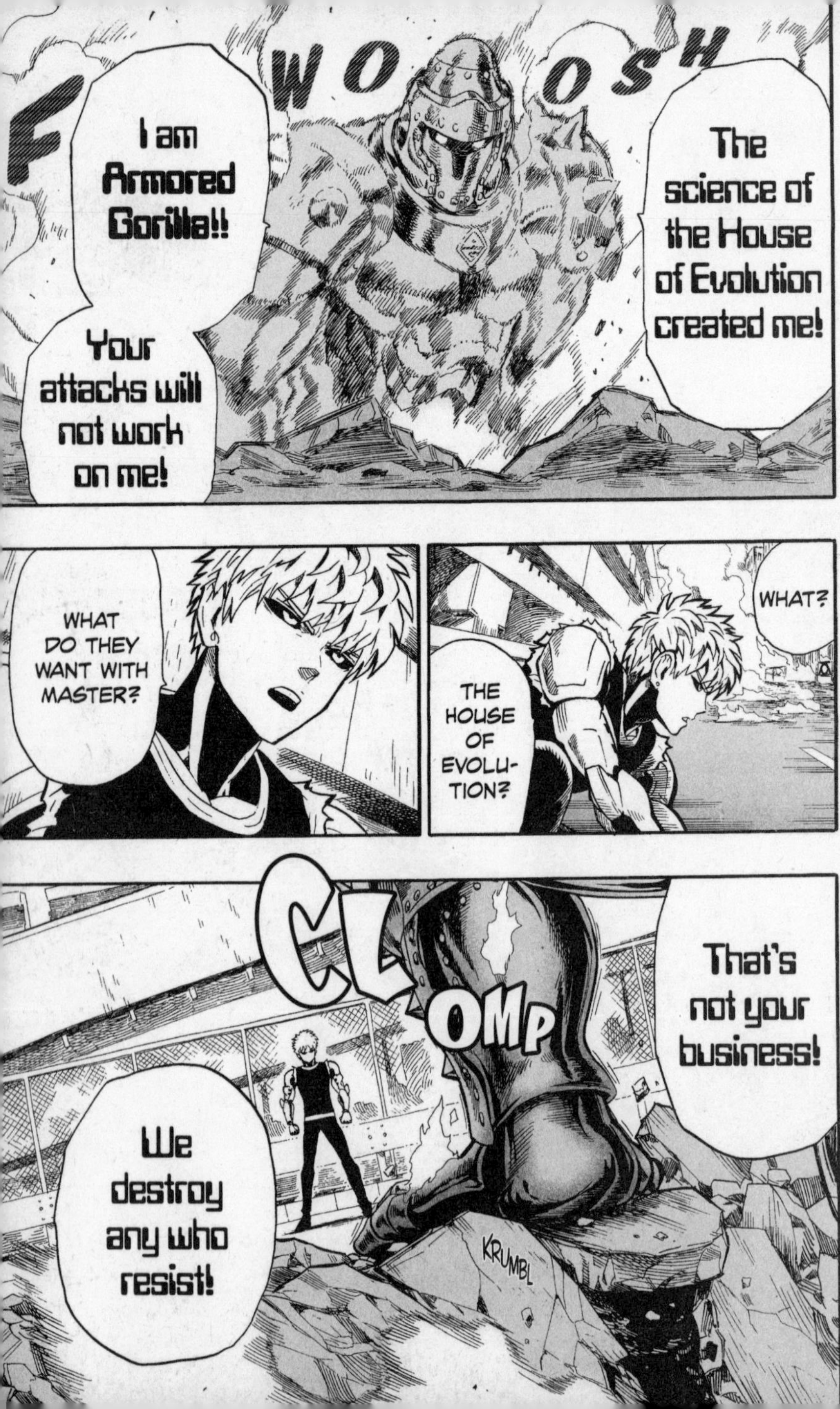
FWOOSH
The science of the House of Evolution created me!
I am Armored Gorilla!!
Your attacks will not work on me!
WHAT?
THE HOUSE OF EVOLUTION?
WHAT DO THEY WANT WITH MASTER?
CLOMP
That's not your business!
We destroy any who resist!
KRUMBL

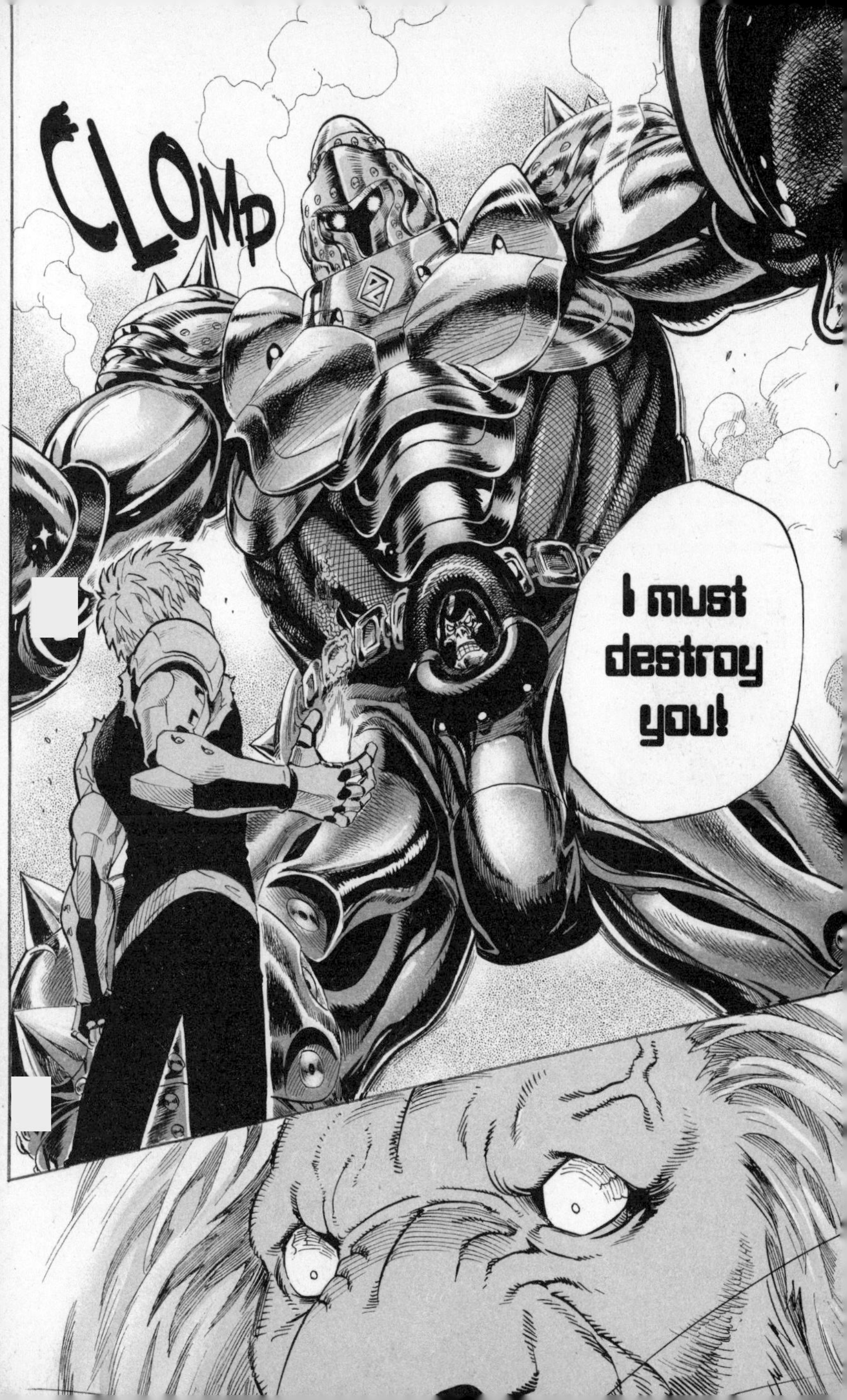
CLOMP
I must destroy you!

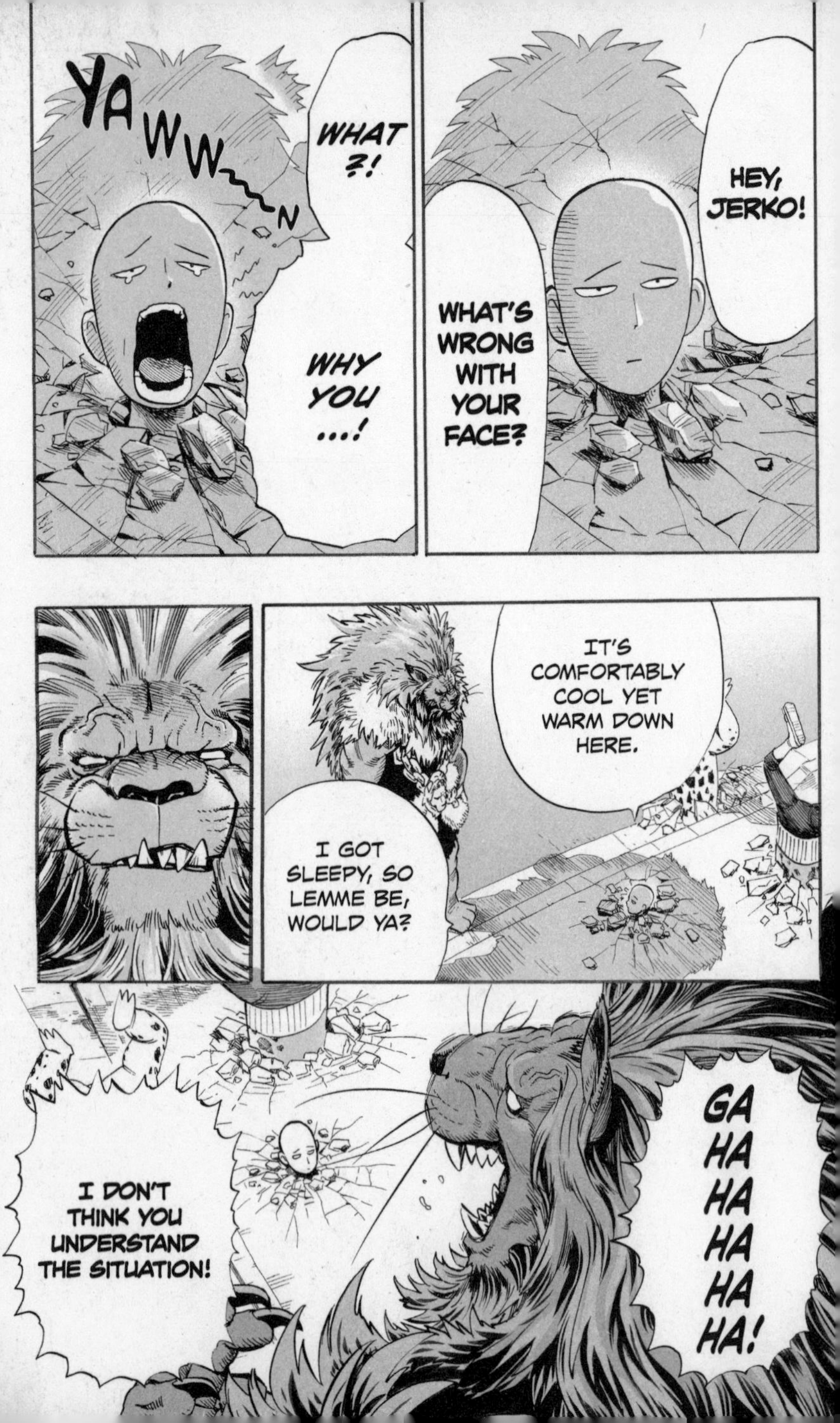
HEY, JERKO!
WHAT'S WRONG WITH YOUR FACE?
WHAT ?!
YAWWN
WHY YOU ...!
IT'S COMFORTABLY COOL YET WARM DOWN HERE.
I GOT SLEEPY, SO LEMME BE, WOULD YA?
GA HA HA HA HA HA HA!
I DON'T THINK YOU UNDERSTAND THE SITUATION!

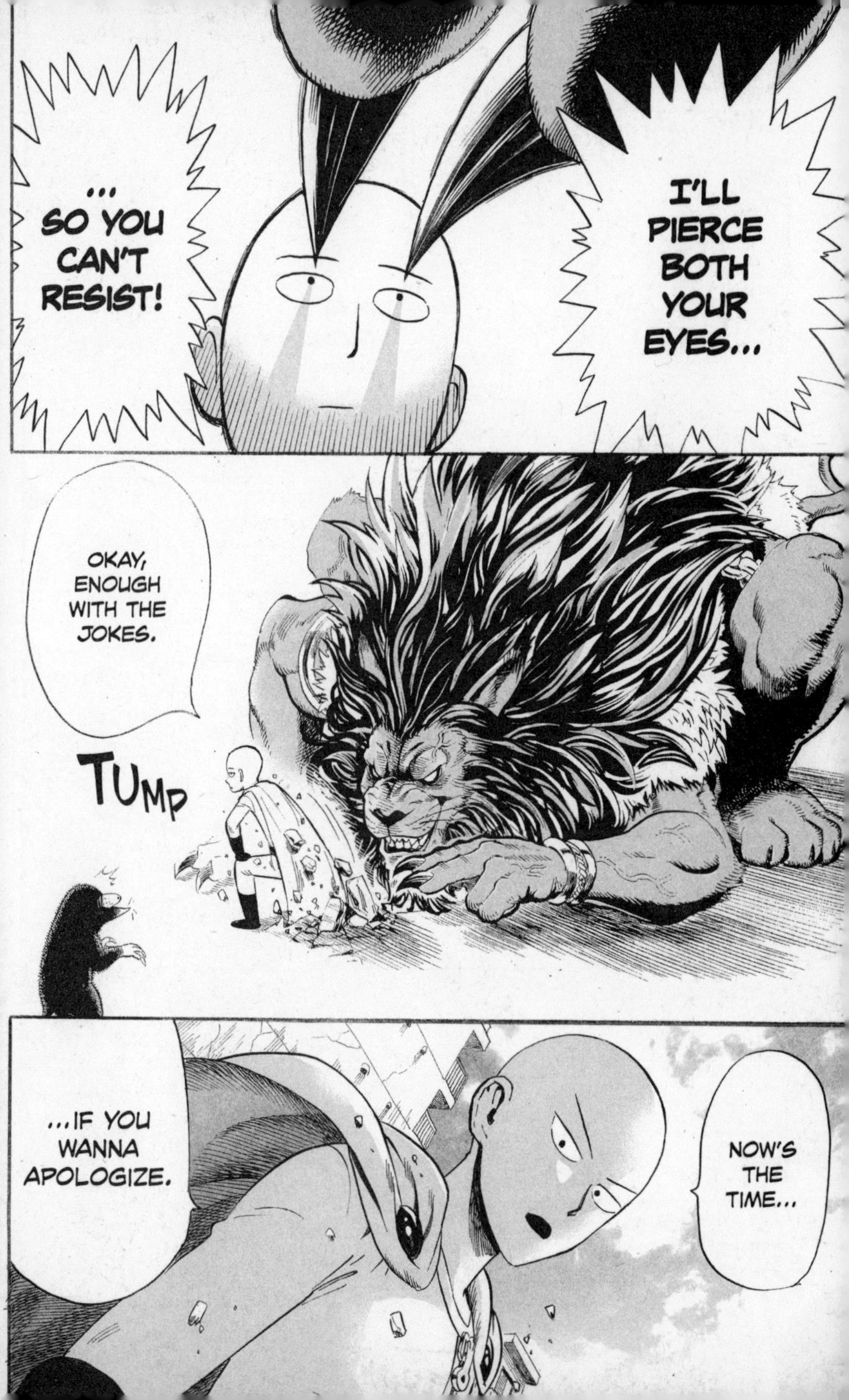
I'LL PIERCE BOTH YOUR EYES...
... SO YOU CAN'T RESIST!
OKAY, ENOUGH WITH THE JOKES.
TUMP
NOW'S THE TIME...
...IF YOU WANNA APOLOGIZE.

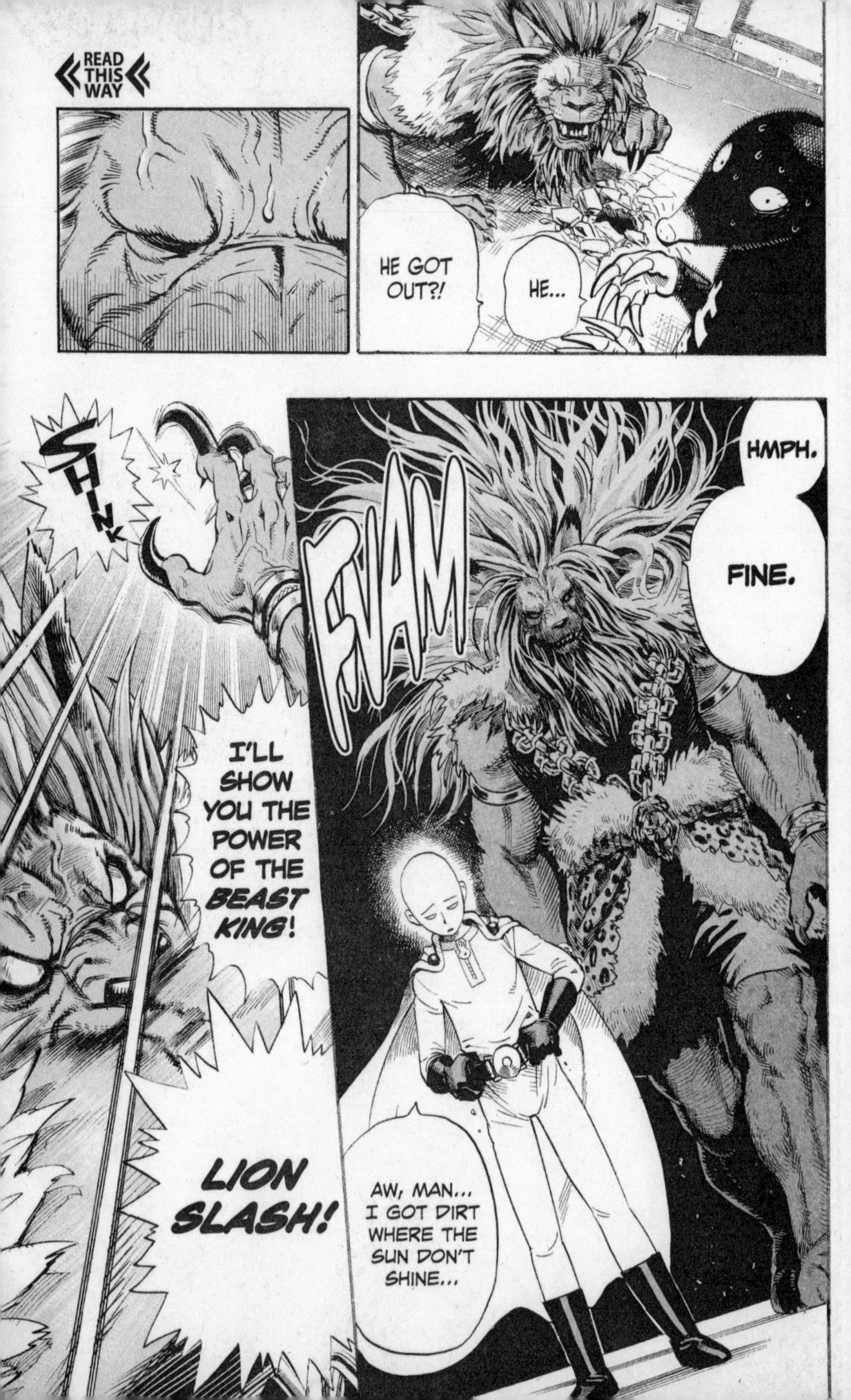
READ THIS WAY
HE...
HE GOT OUT?!
HMPH.
FINE.
FWAM
AW, MAN... I GOT DIRT WHERE THE SUN DON'T SHINE...
SHINK
I'LL SHOW YOU THE POWER OF THE *BEAST KING*!
LION SLASH!

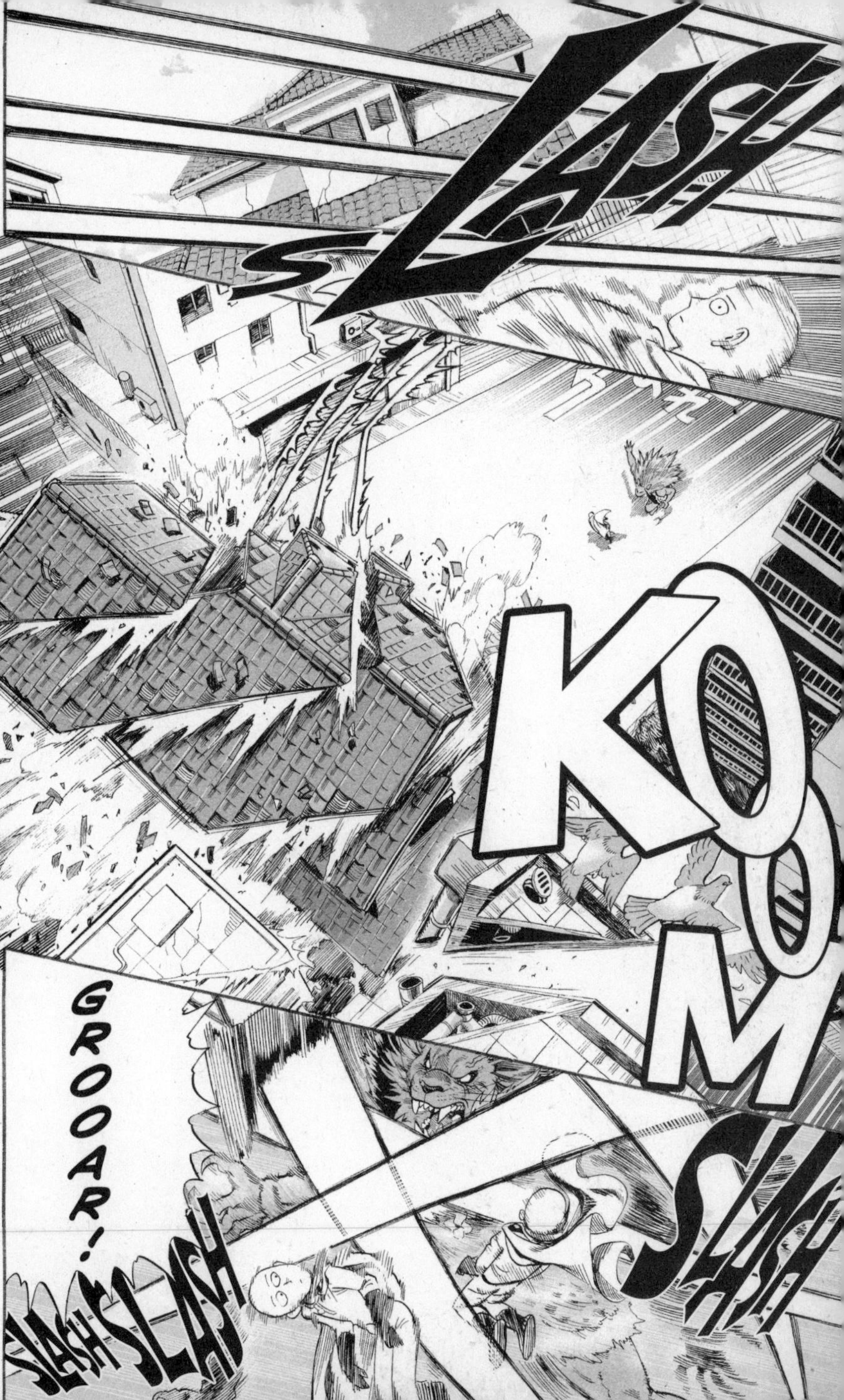
SLASH
KOOM
SLASH
GROOOAR!!
SLASH SLASH

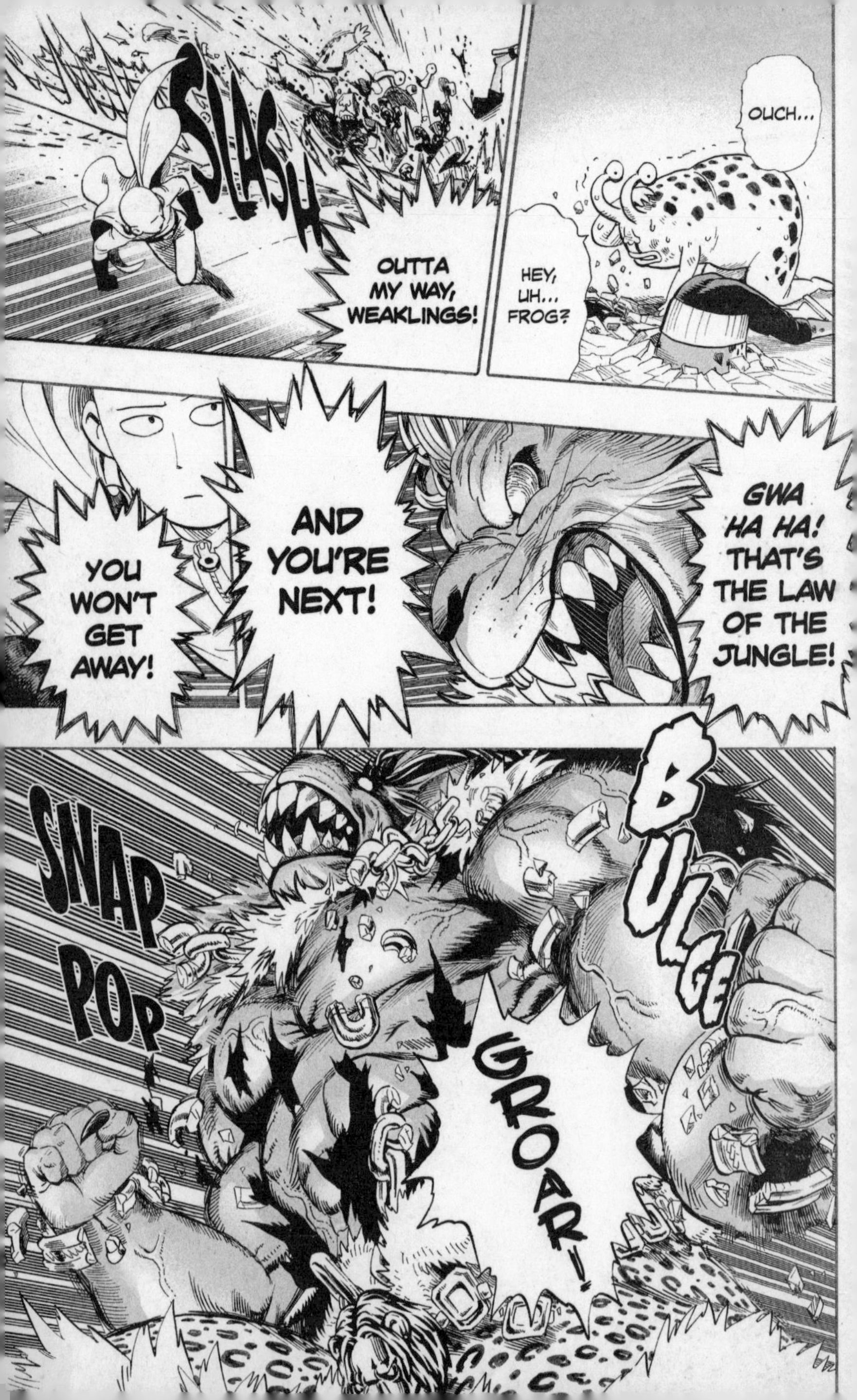
OUCH...
HEY, UH... FROG?
SLASH
OUTTA MY WAY, WEAKLINGS!
GWA HA HA! THAT'S THE LAW OF THE JUNGLE!
AND YOU'RE NEXT!
YOU WON'T GET AWAY!
BULGE
GROAR!
SNAP
POP

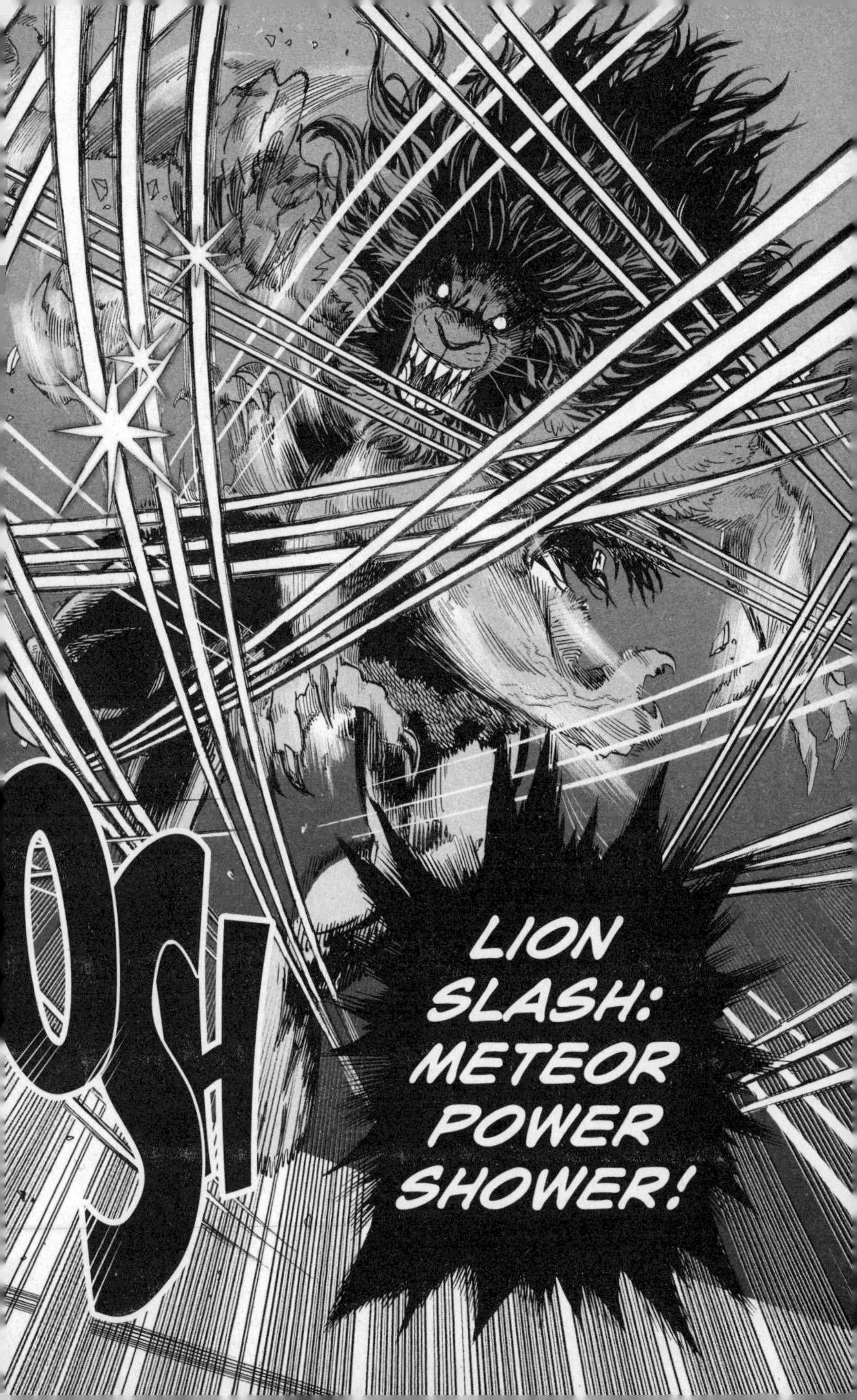
OSH
LION SLASH: METEOR POWER SHOWER!

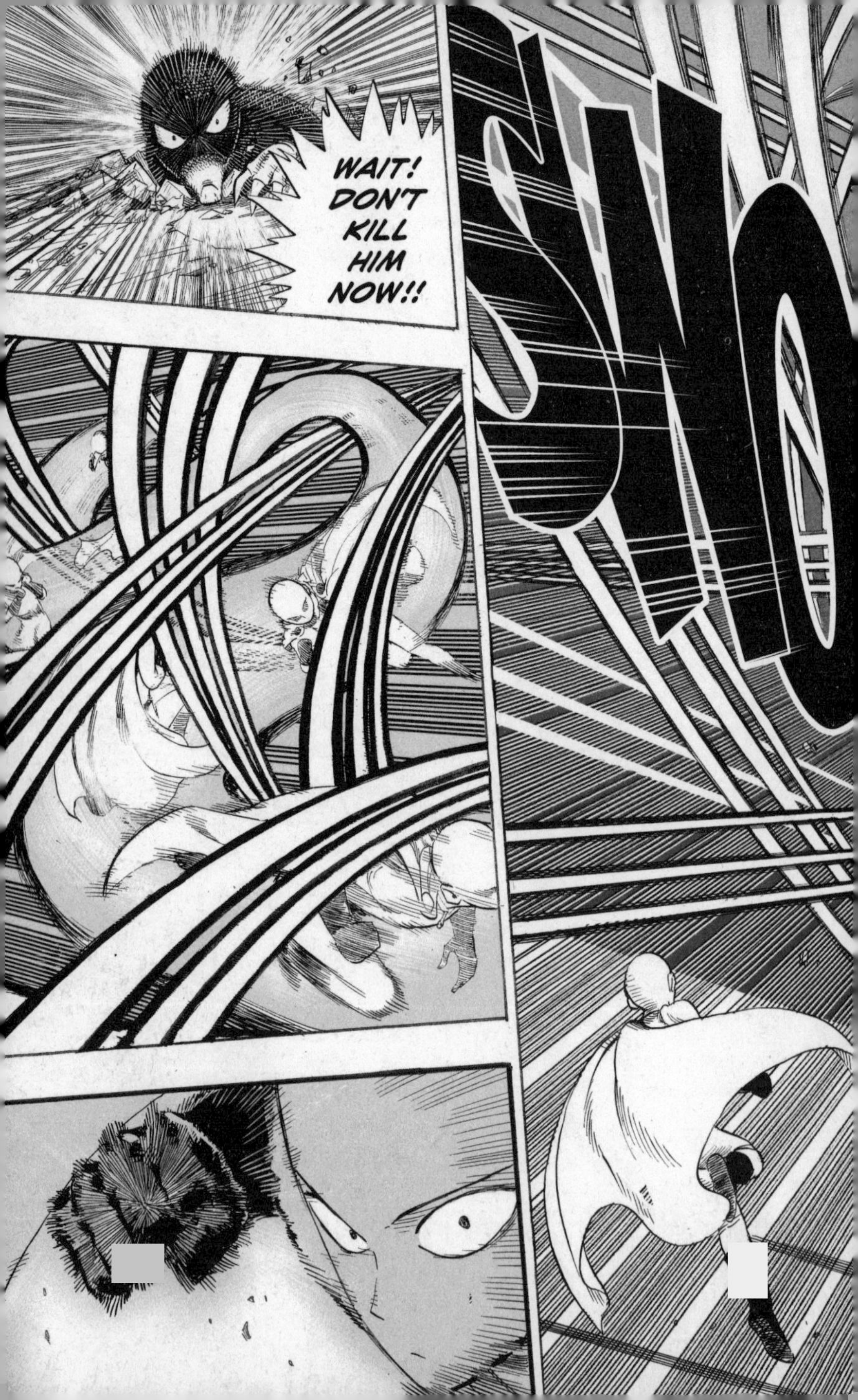
WAIT! DON'T KILL HIM NOW!!

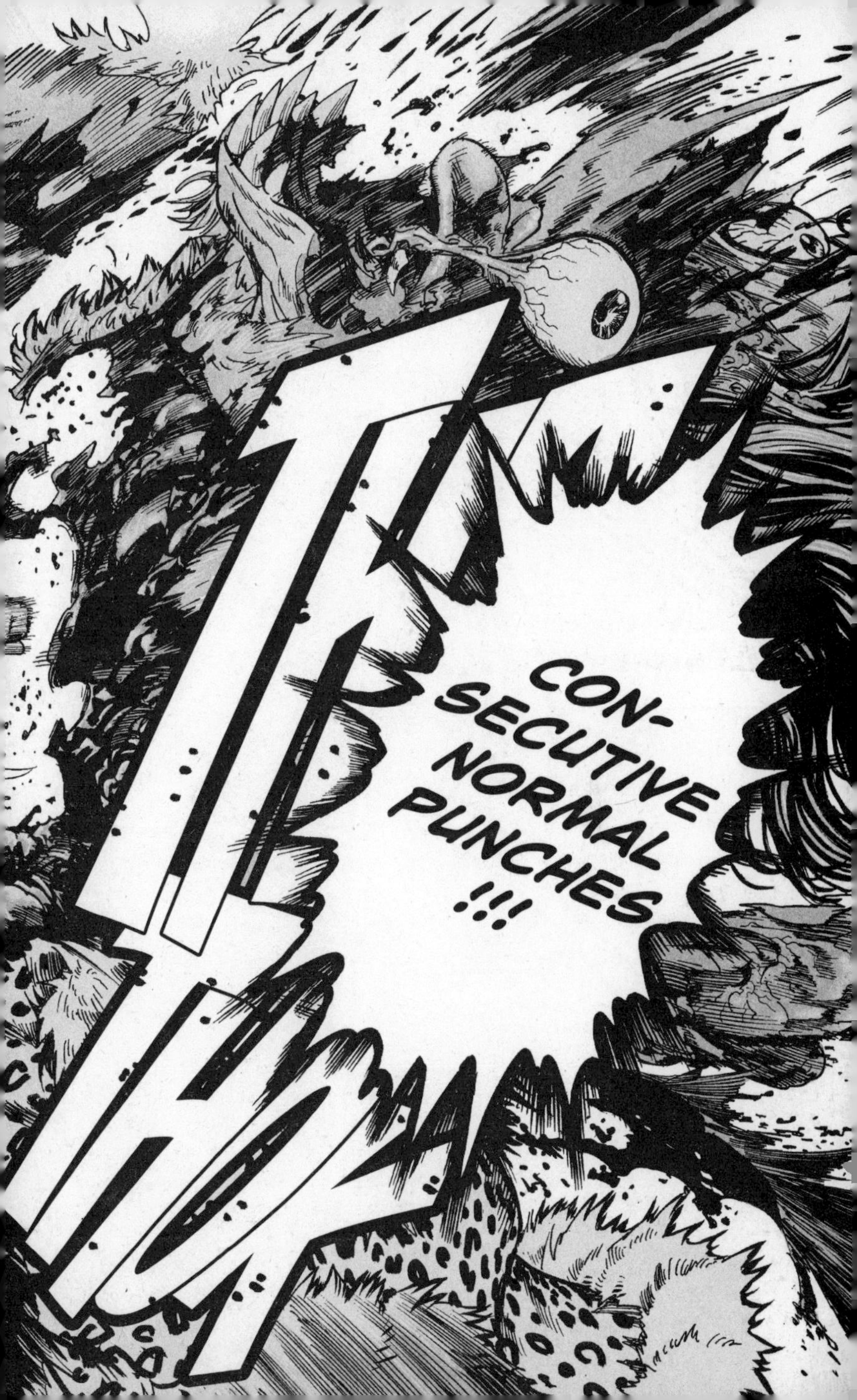
CON-
SECUTIVE
NORMAL
PUNCHES
!!!

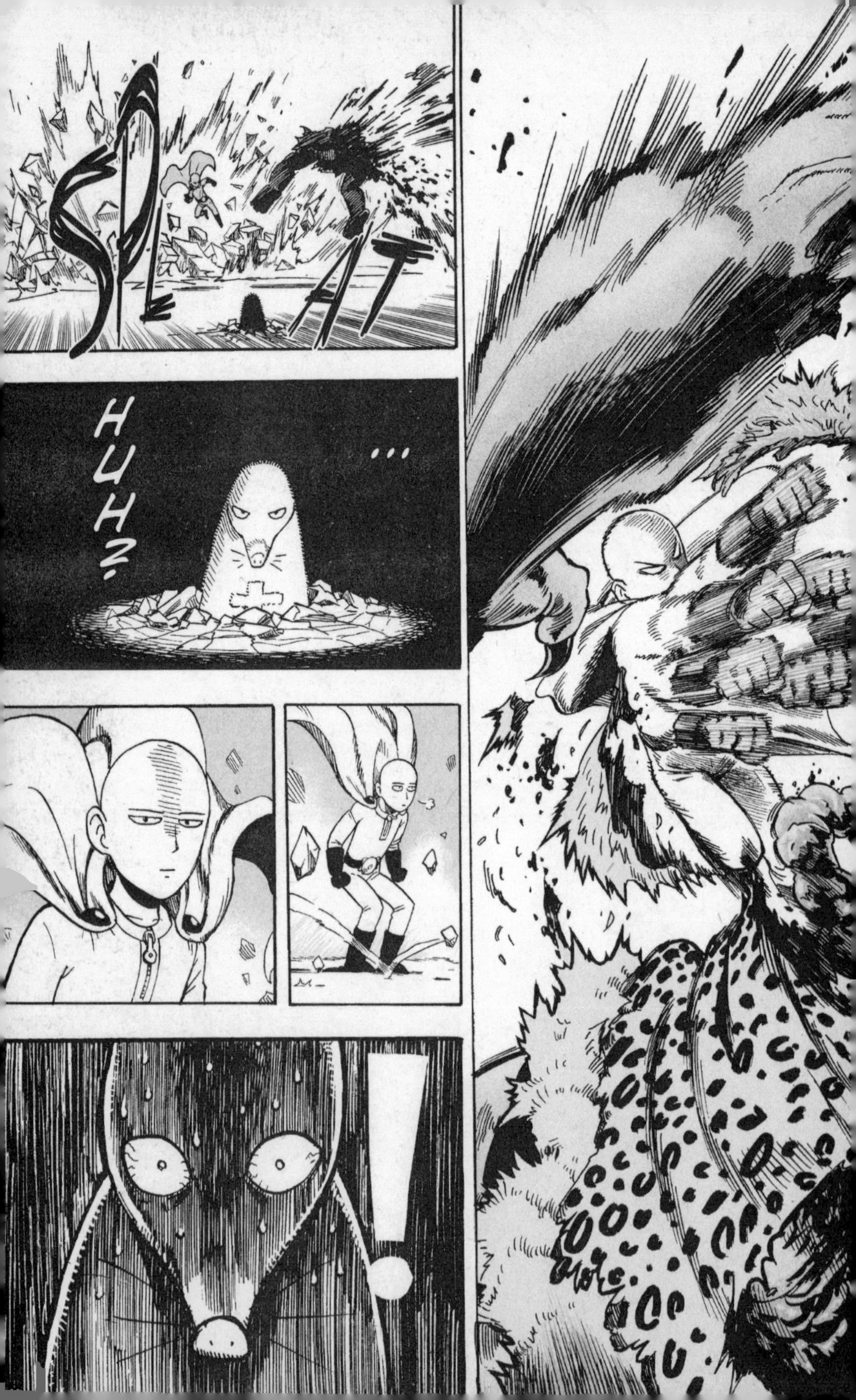
SPLAT
...
HUH?
!

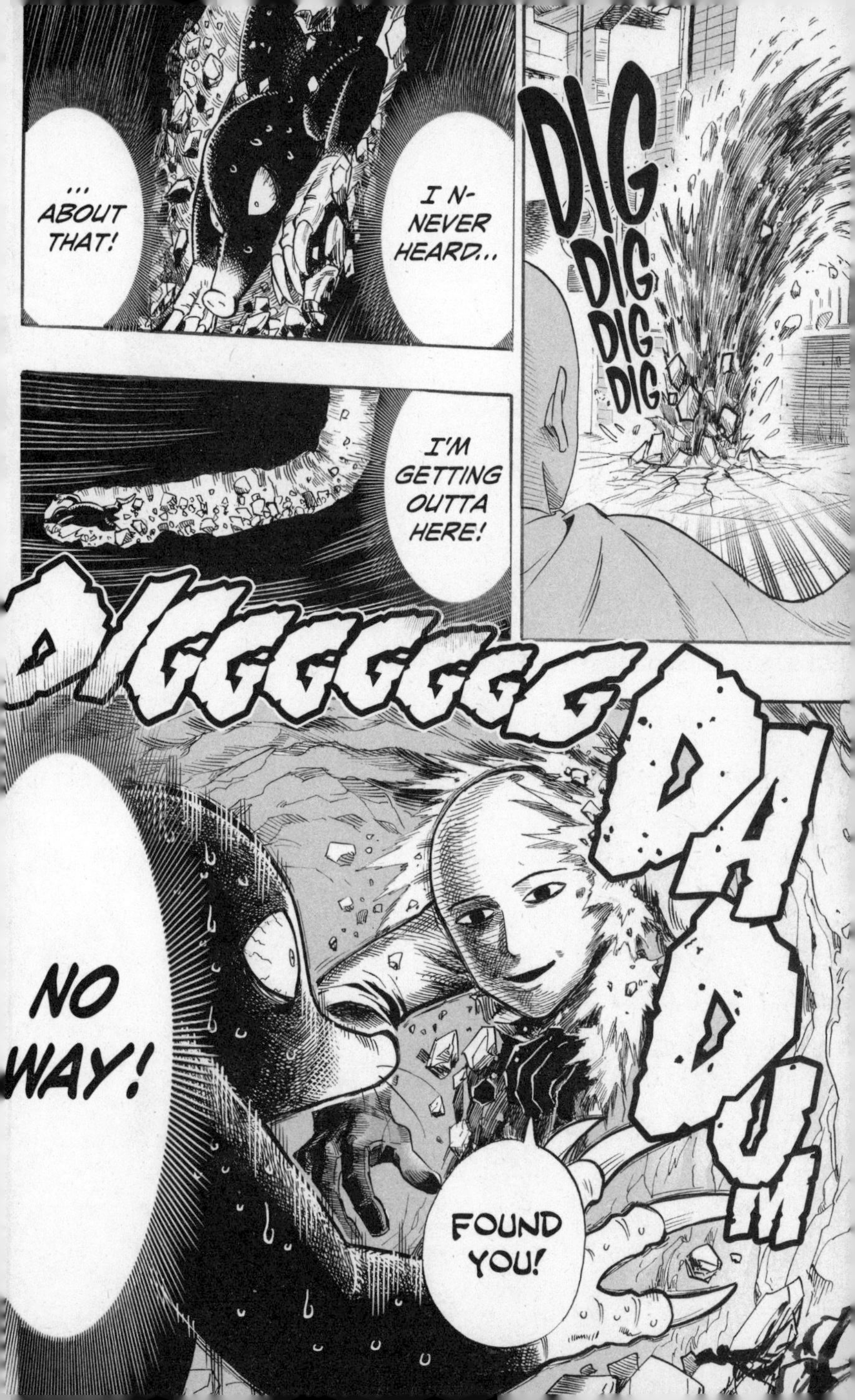

DIG DIG DIG DIG
I N-NEVER HEARD...
...ABOUT THAT!
I'M GETTING OUTTA HERE!
DIGGGGGGG
DADUM
FOUND YOU!
NO WAY!

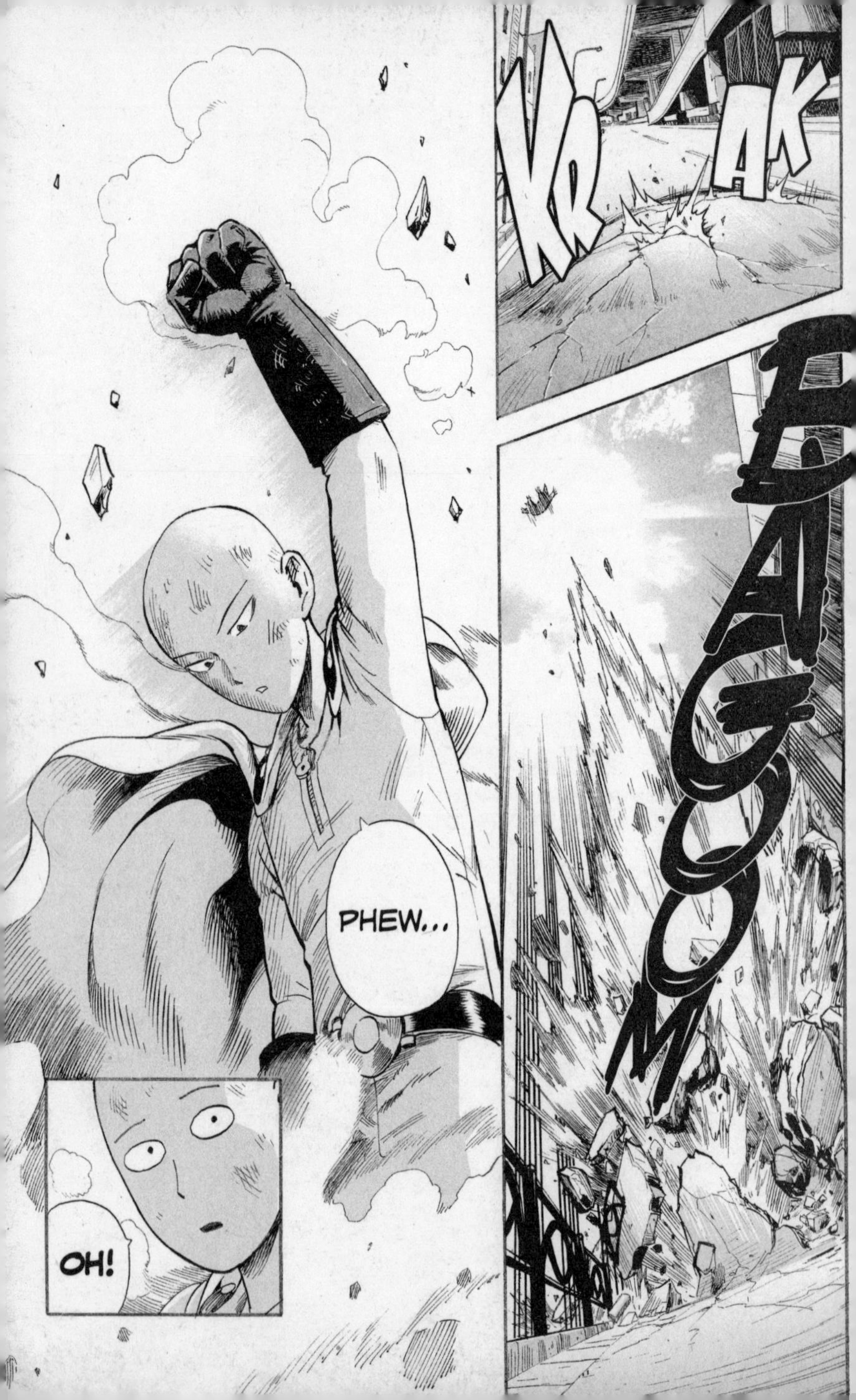
KRAK
AGOOM
PHEW...
OH!

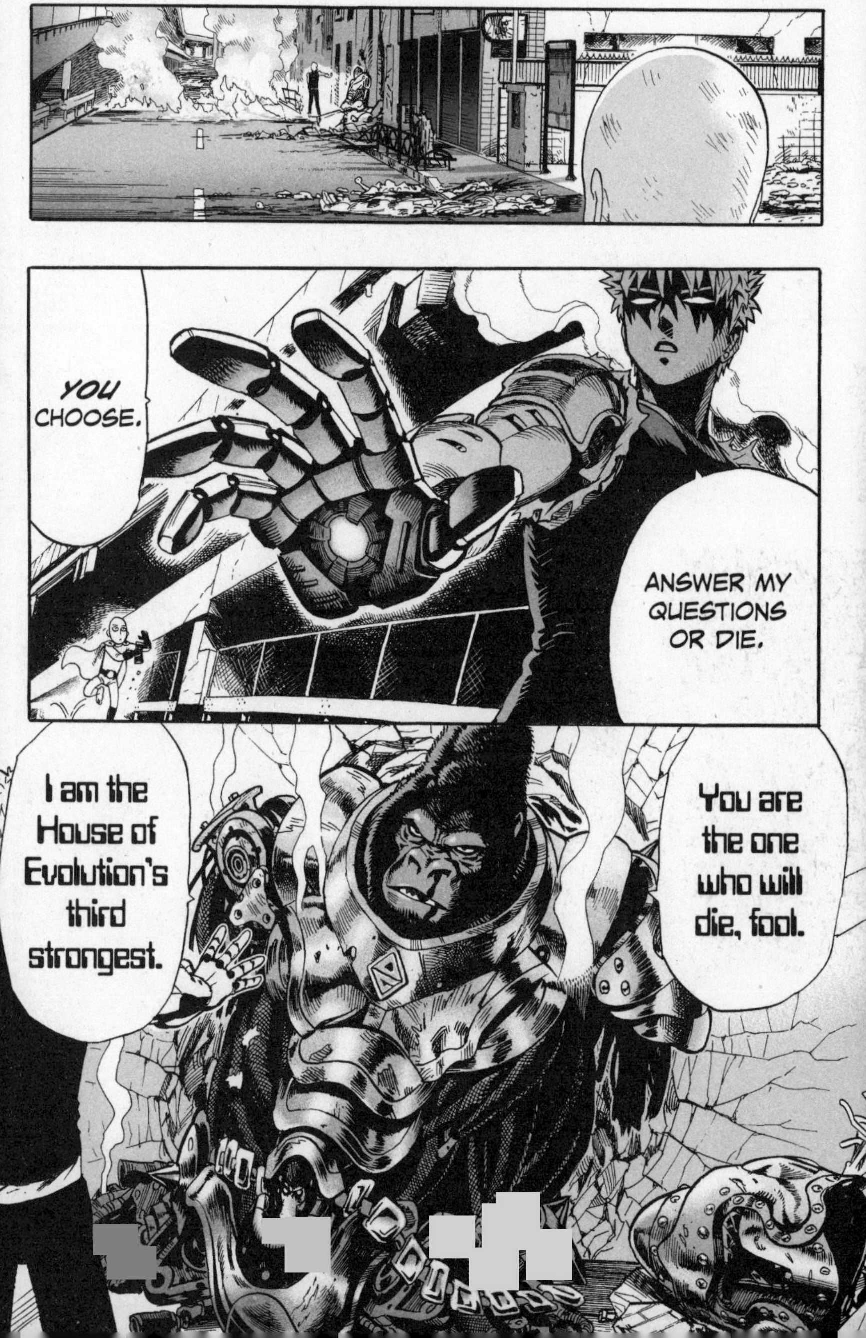
ANSWER MY QUESTIONS OR DIE.
YOU CHOOSE.
You are the one who will die, fool.
I am the House of Evolution's third strongest.

READ THIS WAY

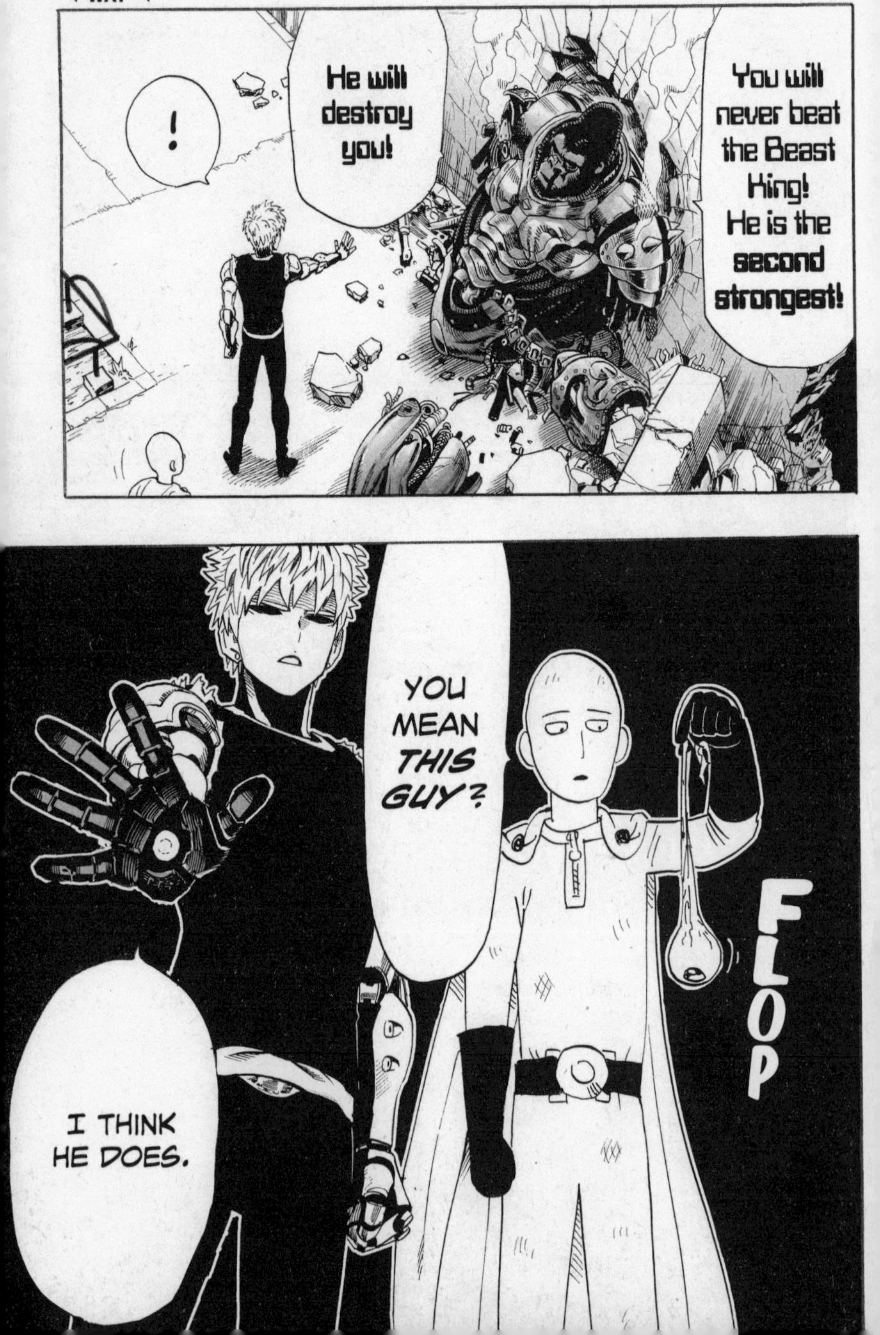
You will never beat the Beast King! He is the second strongest!
He will destroy you!
!
YOU MEAN THIS GUY?
FLOP
I THINK HE DOES.

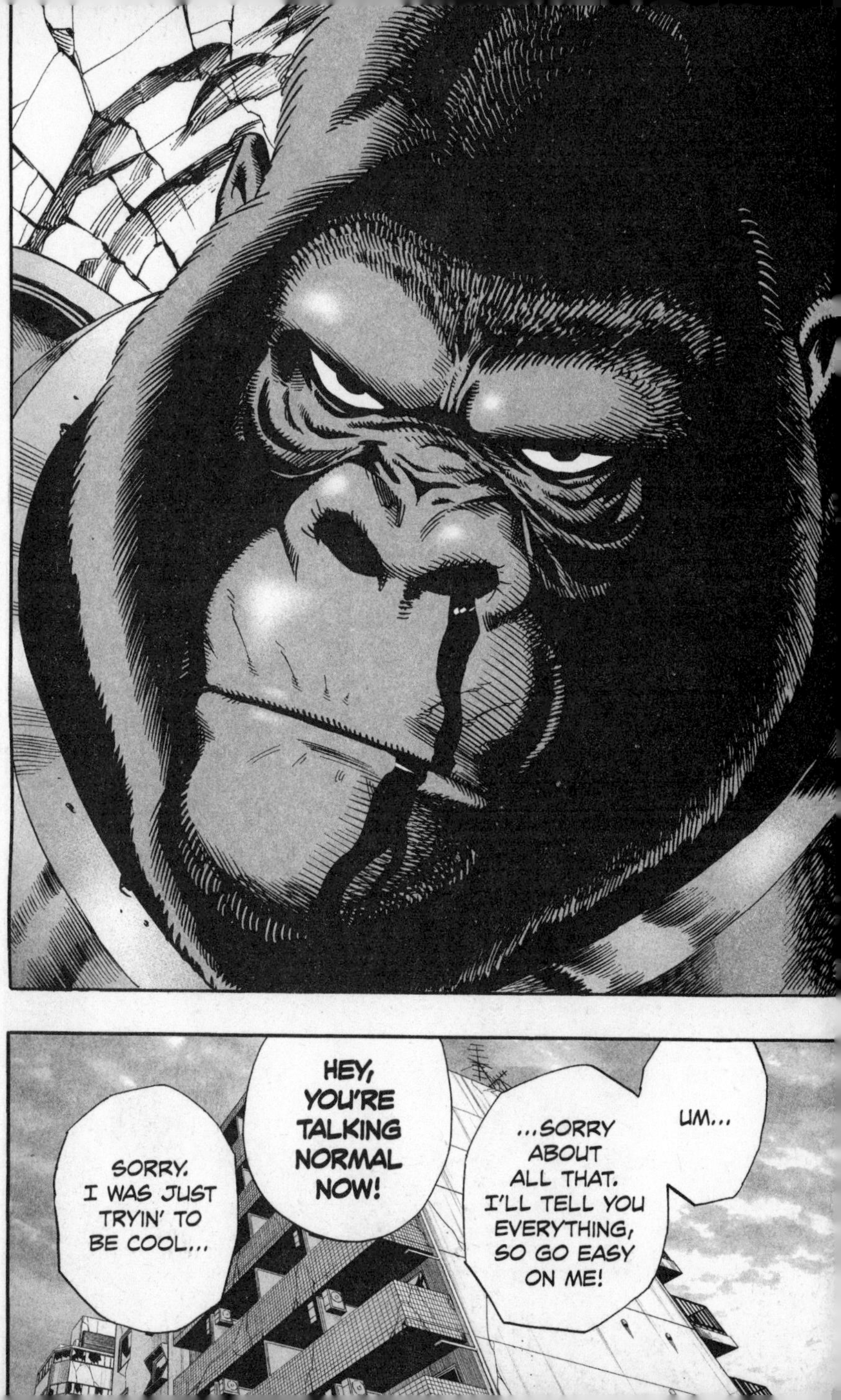
UM...
...SORRY ABOUT ALL THAT. I'LL TELL YOU EVERYTHING, SO GO EASY ON ME!
HEY, YOU'RE TALKING NORMAL NOW!
SORRY. I WAS JUST TRYIN' TO BE COOL...

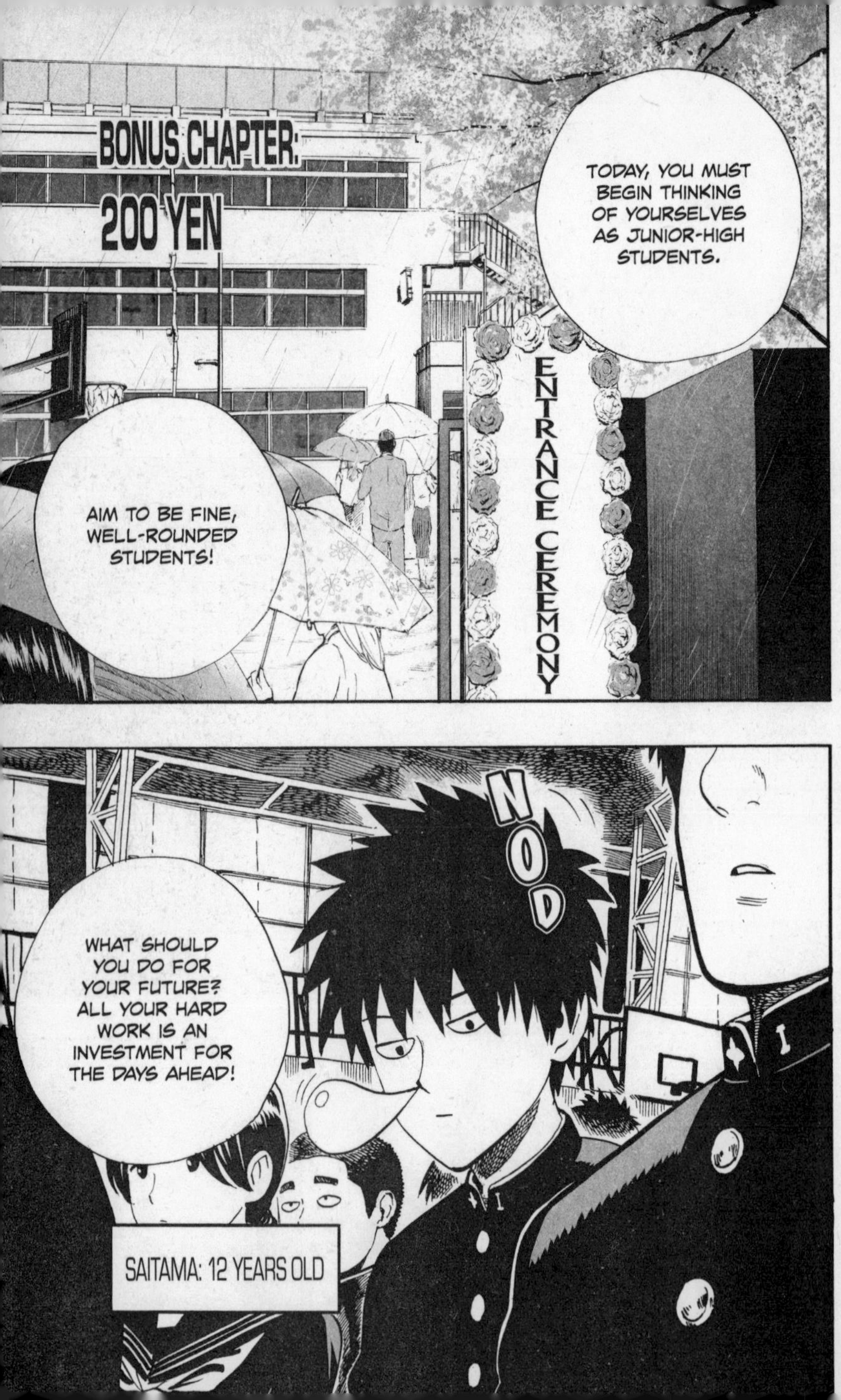
BONUS CHAPTER: 200 YEN
TODAY, YOU MUST BEGIN THINKING OF YOURSELVES AS JUNIOR-HIGH STUDENTS.
ENTRANCE CEREMONY
AIM TO BE FINE, WELL-ROUNDED STUDENTS!
NOD
WHAT SHOULD YOU DO FOR YOUR FUTURE? ALL YOUR HARD WORK IS AN INVESTMENT FOR THE DAYS AHEAD!
SAITAMA: 12 YEARS OLD

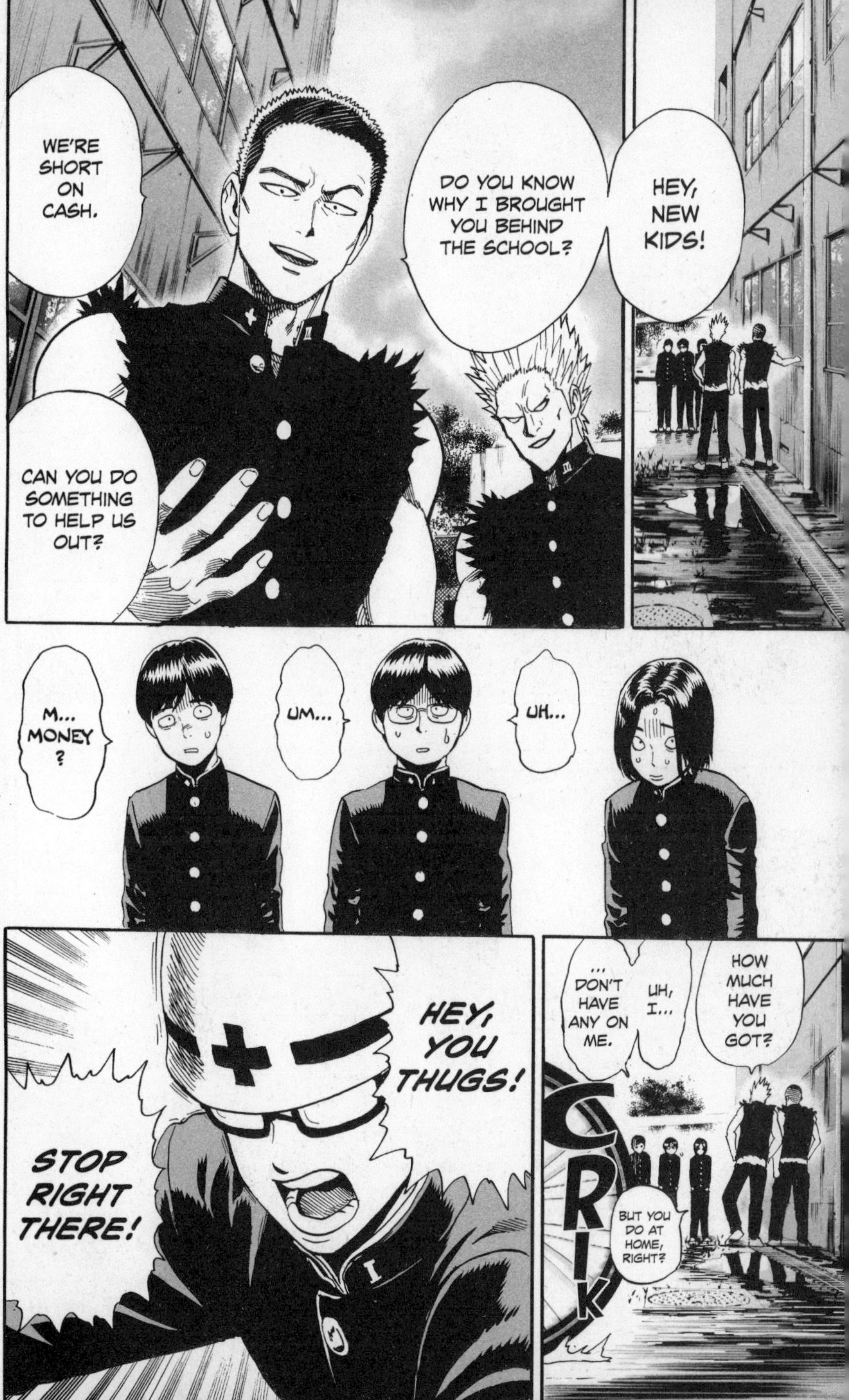
HEY, NEW KIDS!
DO YOU KNOW WHY I BROUGHT YOU BEHIND THE SCHOOL?
WE'RE SHORT ON CASH.
CAN YOU DO SOMETHING TO HELP US OUT?
UH...
UM...
M... MONEY?
HOW MUCH HAVE YOU GOT?
UH, I...
... DON'T HAVE ANY ON ME.
CRIK
BUT YOU DO AT HOME, RIGHT?
HEY, YOU THUGS!
STOP RIGHT THERE!

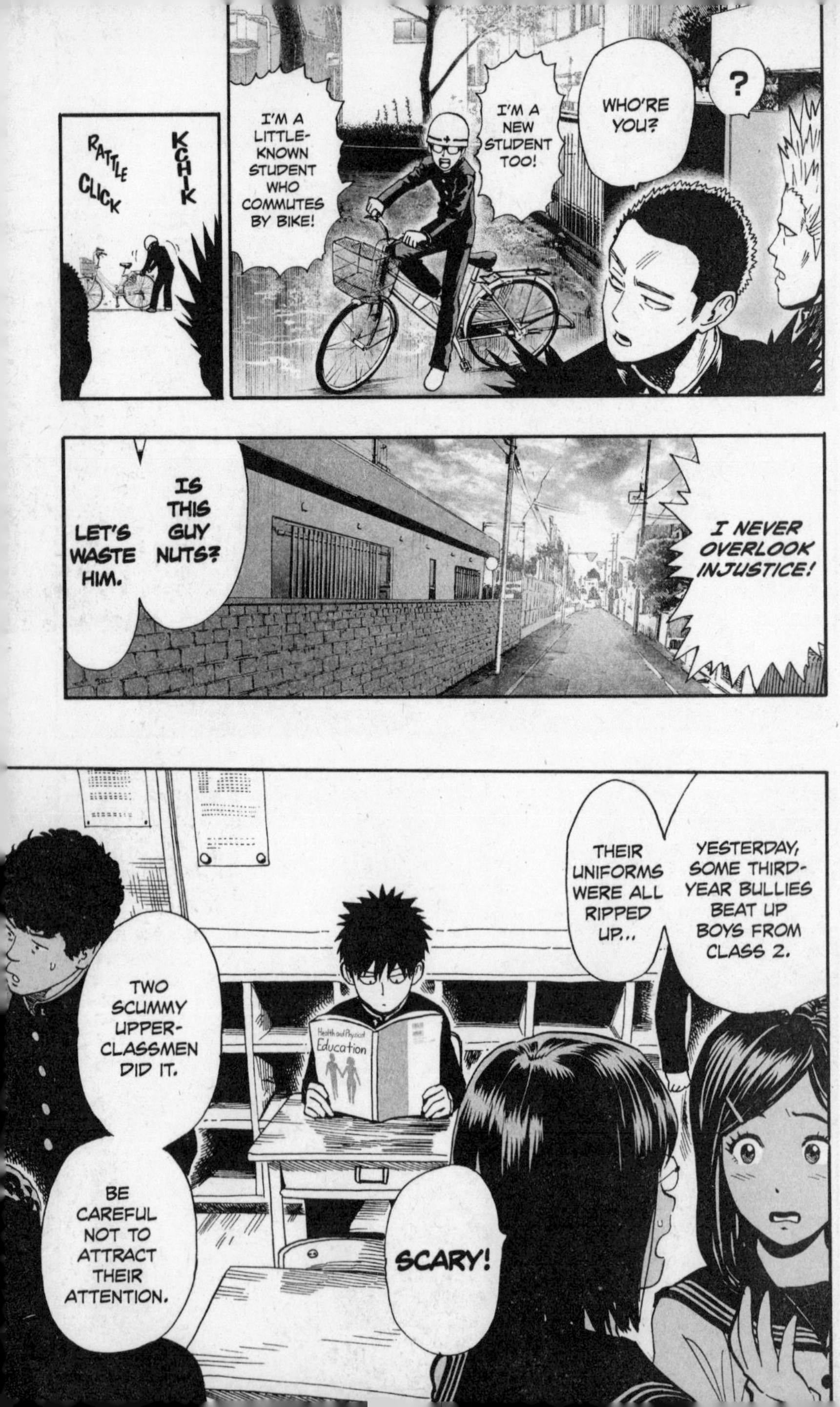
?
WHO'RE YOU?
I'M A NEW STUDENT TOO!
I'M A LITTLE-KNOWN STUDENT WHO COMMUTES BY BIKE!
KCHIK
RATTLE CLICK
I NEVER OVERLOOK INJUSTICE!
IS THIS GUY NUTS?
LET'S WASTE HIM.
YESTERDAY, SOME THIRD-YEAR BULLIES BEAT UP BOYS FROM CLASS 2.
THEIR UNIFORMS WERE ALL RIPPED UP...
SCARY!
Health and Physical Education
TWO SCUMMY UPPERCLASSMEN DID IT.
BE CAREFUL NOT TO ATTRACT THEIR ATTENTION.

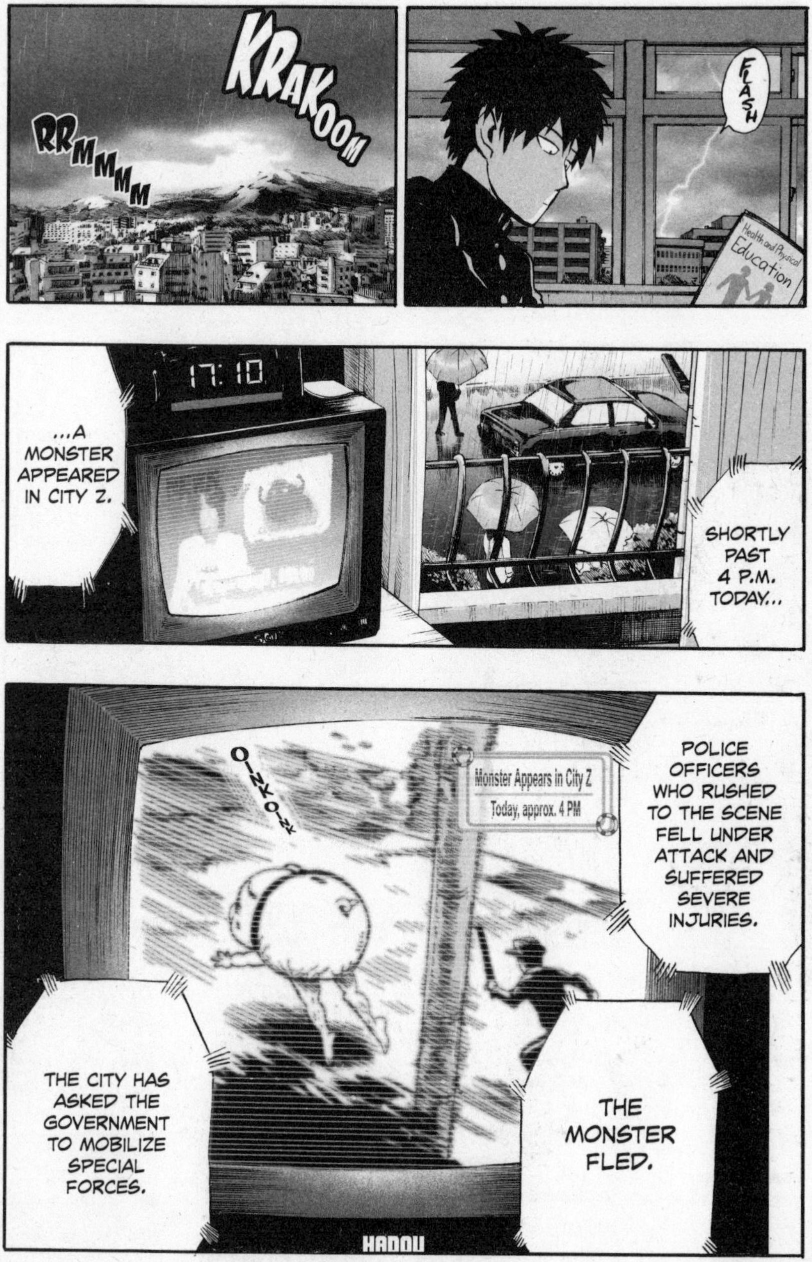
FLASH
Health and Physical Education
KRAKOOM
RRMMMM
SHORTLY PAST 4 P.M. TODAY...
17:10
...A MONSTER APPEARED IN CITY Z.
POLICE OFFICERS WHO RUSHED TO THE SCENE FELL UNDER ATTACK AND SUFFERED SEVERE INJURIES.
Monster Appears in City Z
Today, approx. 4 PM
OINK OINK
THE MONSTER FLED.
THE CITY HAS ASKED THE GOVERNMENT TO MOBILIZE SPECIAL FORCES.
HADOU

READ THIS WAY

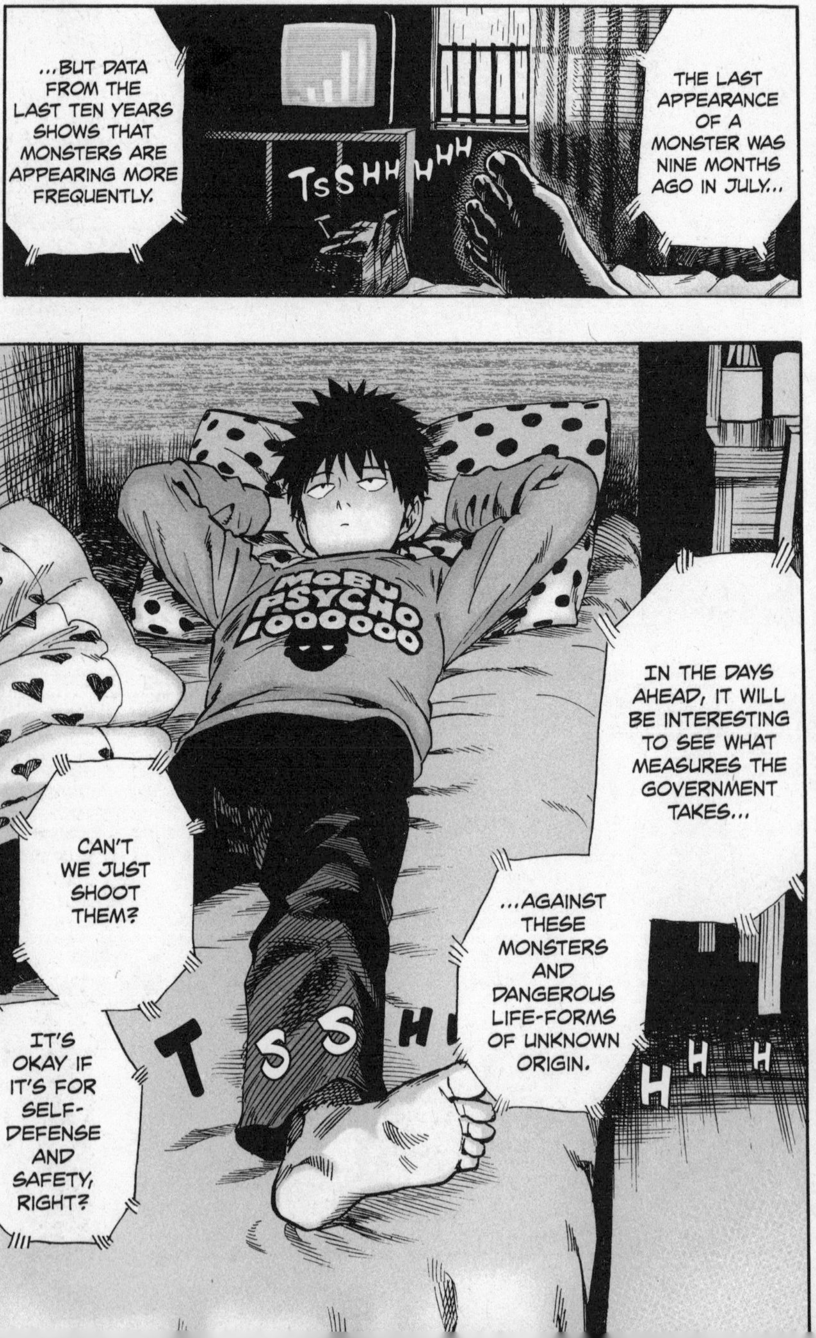
THE LAST APPEARANCE OF A MONSTER WAS NINE MONTHS AGO IN JULY...
...BUT DATA FROM THE LAST TEN YEARS SHOWS THAT MONSTERS ARE APPEARING MORE FREQUENTLY.
TSSHHHHHH
IN THE DAYS AHEAD, IT WILL BE INTERESTING TO SEE WHAT MEASURES THE GOVERNMENT TAKES...
...AGAINST THESE MONSTERS AND DANGEROUS LIFE-FORMS OF UNKNOWN ORIGIN.
MOBU PSYCHO 1000000
CAN'T WE JUST SHOOT THEM?
IT'S OKAY IF IT'S FOR SELF-DEFENSE AND SAFETY, RIGHT?
TSSHHHHH

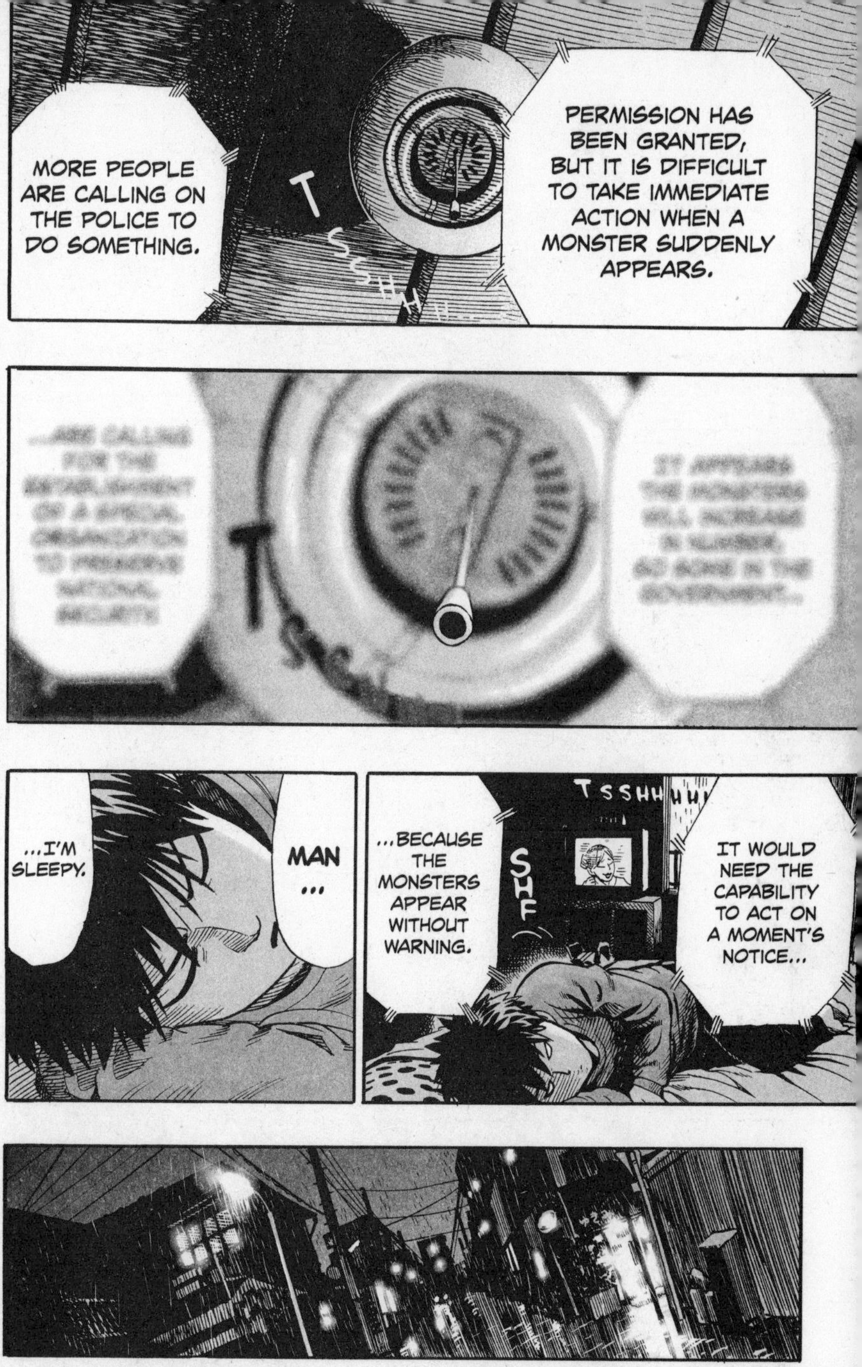
PERMISSION HAS BEEN GRANTED, BUT IT IS DIFFICULT TO TAKE IMMEDIATE ACTION WHEN A MONSTER SUDDENLY APPEARS.
TSSHH...
MORE PEOPLE ARE CALLING ON THE POLICE TO DO SOMETHING.
TSSHHHHH
IT WOULD NEED THE CAPABILITY TO ACT ON A MOMENT'S NOTICE...
SHF
...BECAUSE THE MONSTERS APPEAR WITHOUT WARNING.
MAN...
...I'M SLEEPY.

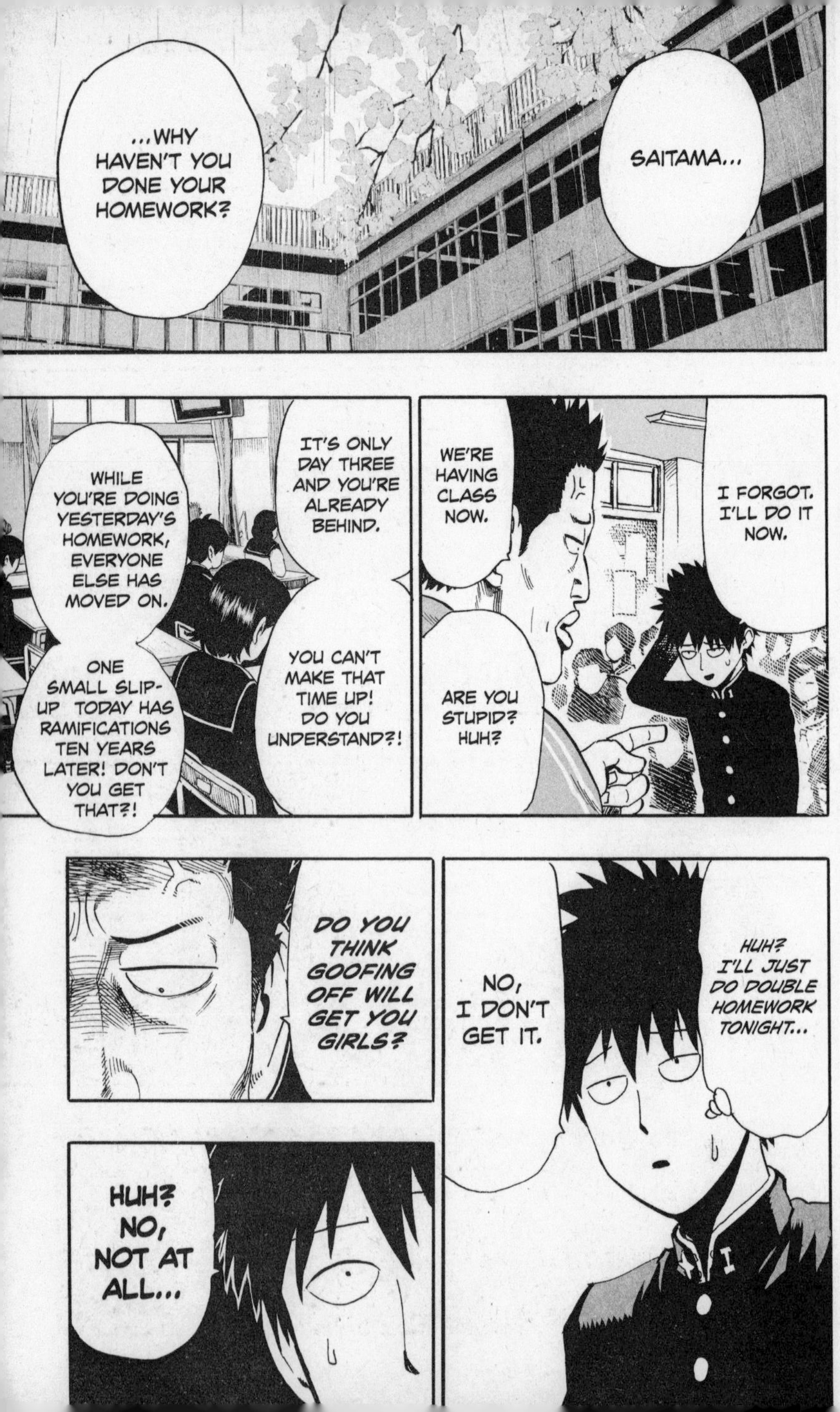
SAITAMA...
...WHY HAVEN'T YOU DONE YOUR HOMEWORK?
I FORGOT. I'LL DO IT NOW.
WE'RE HAVING CLASS NOW.
ARE YOU STUPID? HUH?
IT'S ONLY DAY THREE AND YOU'RE ALREADY BEHIND.
WHILE YOU'RE DOING YESTERDAY'S HOMEWORK, EVERYONE ELSE HAS MOVED ON.
YOU CAN'T MAKE THAT TIME UP! DO YOU UNDERSTAND?!
ONE SMALL SLIP-UP TODAY HAS RAMIFICATIONS TEN YEARS LATER! DON'T YOU GET THAT?!
HUH? I'LL JUST DO DOUBLE HOMEWORK TONIGHT...
NO, I DON'T GET IT.
DO YOU THINK GOOFING OFF WILL GET YOU GIRLS?
HUH? NO, NOT AT ALL...

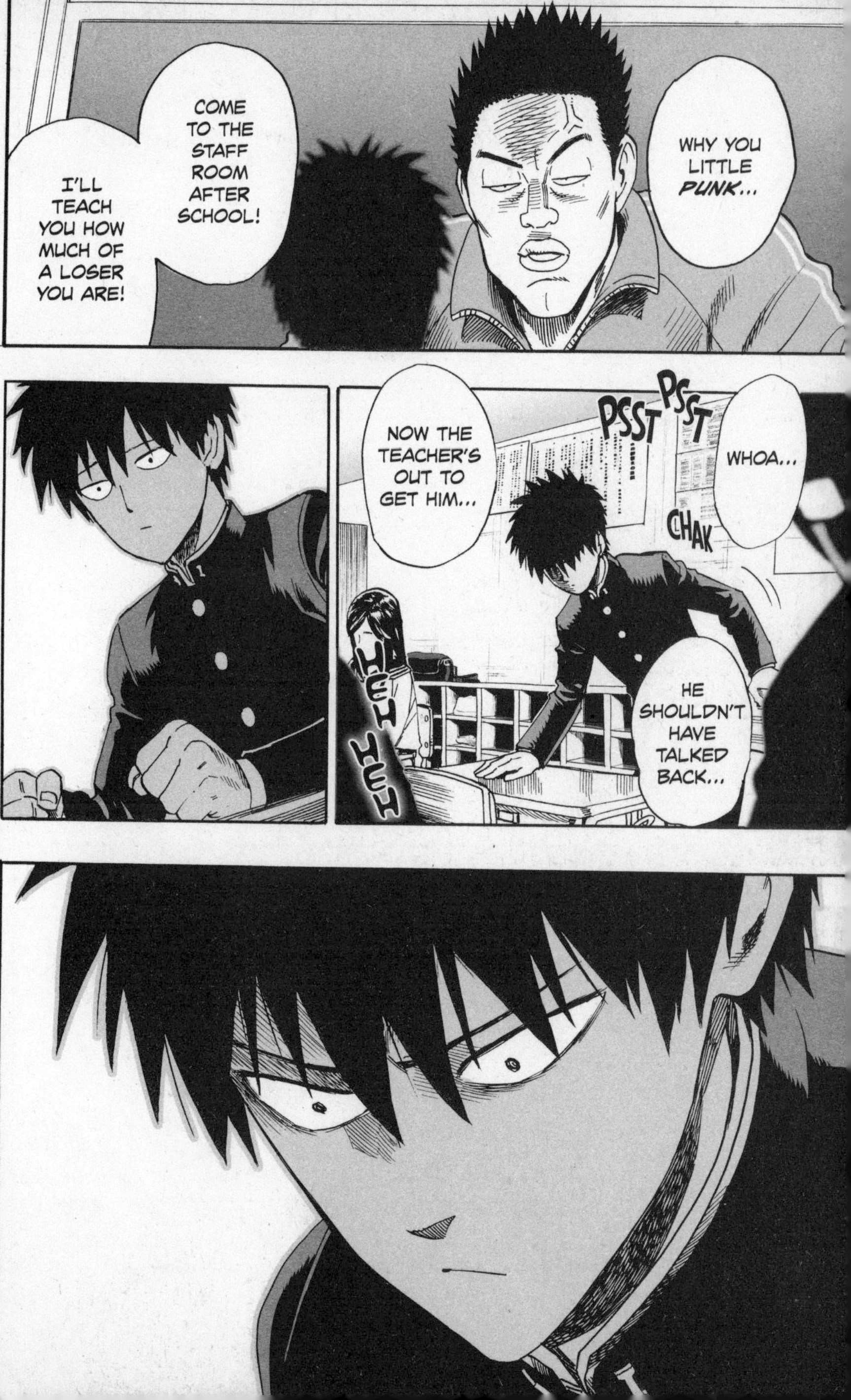
WHY YOU LITTLE *PUNK*...
COME TO THE STAFF ROOM AFTER SCHOOL!
I'LL TEACH YOU HOW MUCH OF A LOSER YOU ARE!
PSST PSST
WHOA...
CHAK
NOW THE TEACHER'S OUT TO GET HIM...
HEH HEH
HE SHOULDN'T HAVE TALKED BACK...

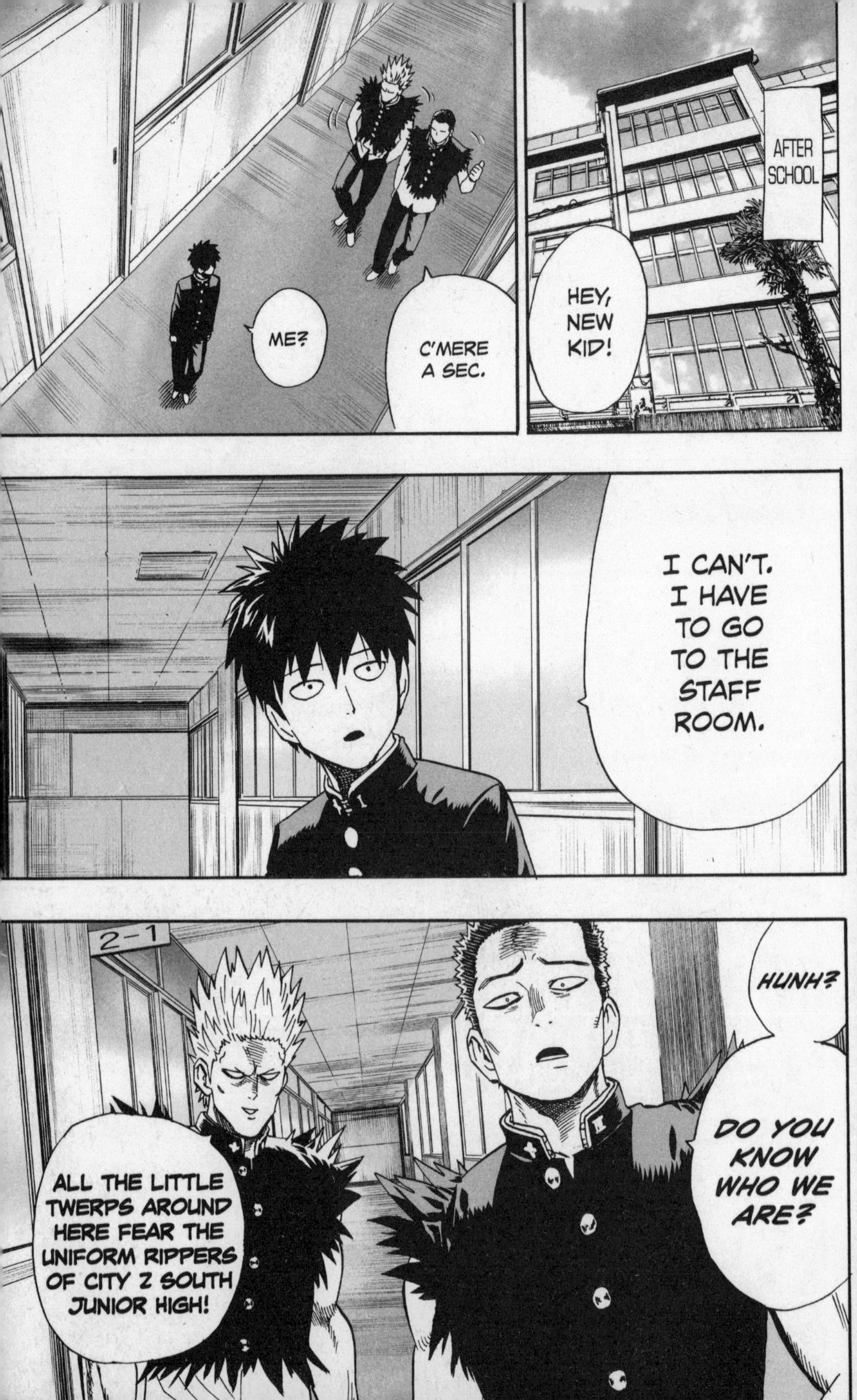
AFTER SCHOOL
HEY, NEW KID!
C'MERE A SEC.
ME?
I CAN'T. I HAVE TO GO TO THE STAFF ROOM.
HUNH?
DO YOU KNOW WHO WE ARE?
2-1
ALL THE LITTLE TWERPS AROUND HERE FEAR THE UNIFORM RIPPERS OF CITY Z SOUTH JUNIOR HIGH!

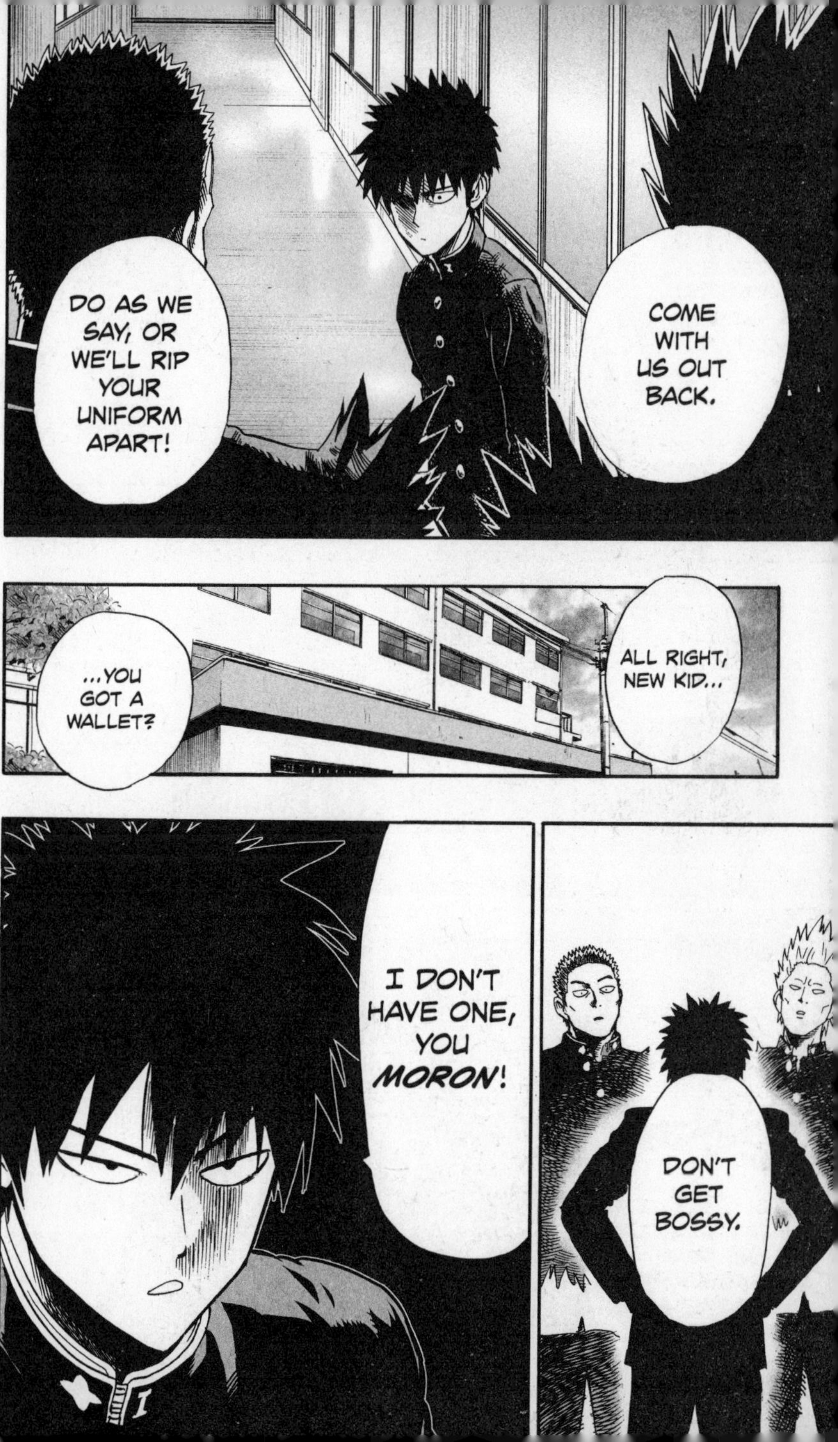
COME WITH US OUT BACK.
DO AS WE SAY, OR WE'LL RIP YOUR UNIFORM APART!
ALL RIGHT, NEW KID...
...YOU GOT A WALLET?
DON'T GET BOSSY.
I DON'T HAVE ONE, YOU *MORON*!

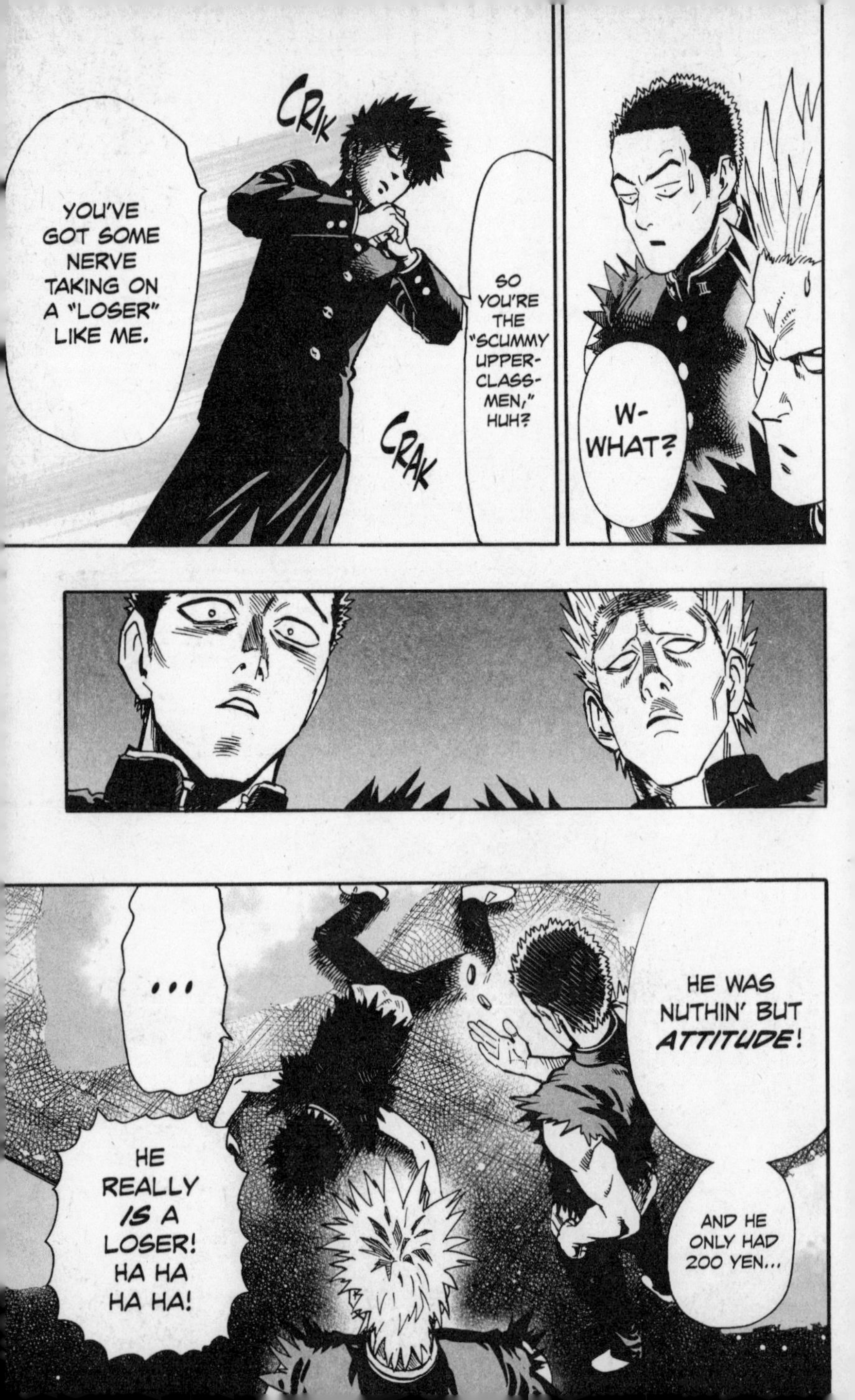
W-WHAT?
SO YOU'RE THE "SCUMMY UPPER-CLASSMEN," HUH?
CRIK
CRAK
YOU'VE GOT SOME NERVE TAKING ON A "LOSER" LIKE ME.
HE WAS NUTHIN' BUT *ATTITUDE*!
...
AND HE ONLY HAD 200 YEN...
HE REALLY *IS* A LOSER! HA HA HA HA!

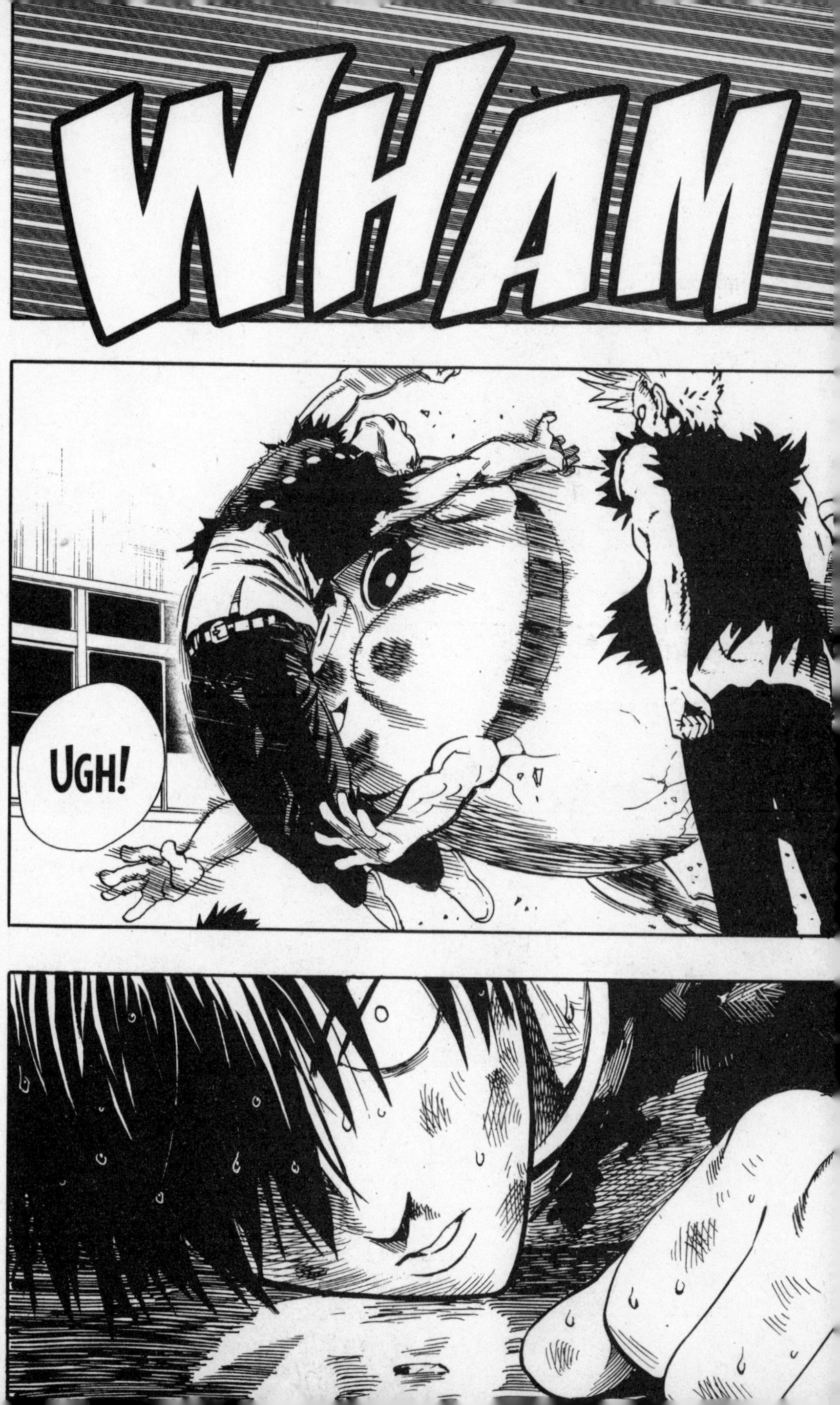
WHAM
UGH!

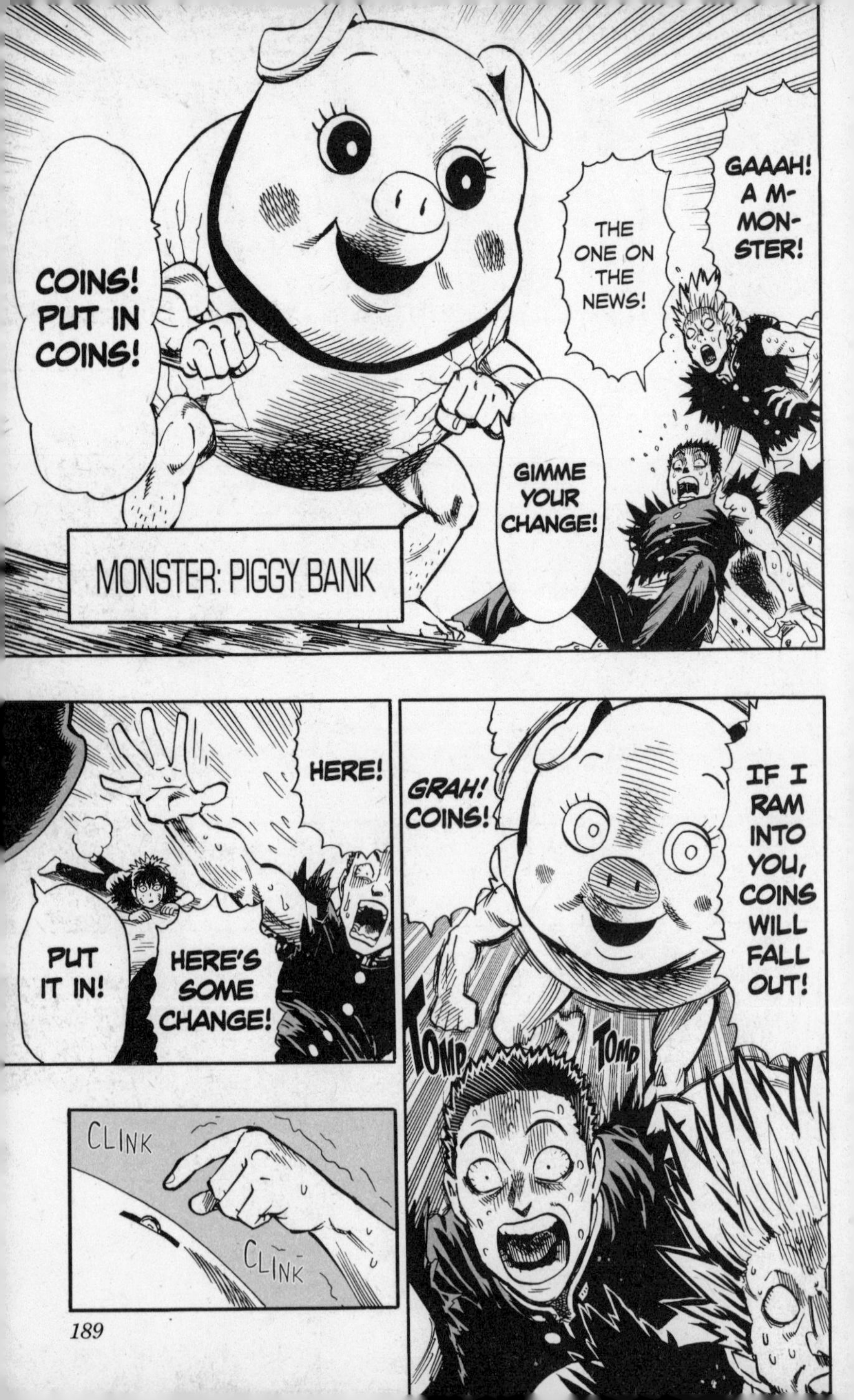
GAAAH! A M-MONSTER!
THE ONE ON THE NEWS!
GIMME YOUR CHANGE!
MONSTER: PIGGY BANK
COINS! PUT IN COINS!
IF I RAM INTO YOU, COINS WILL FALL OUT!
GRAH! COINS!
TOMP
TOMP
HERE!
HERE'S SOME CHANGE!
PUT IT IN!
CLINK
CLINK

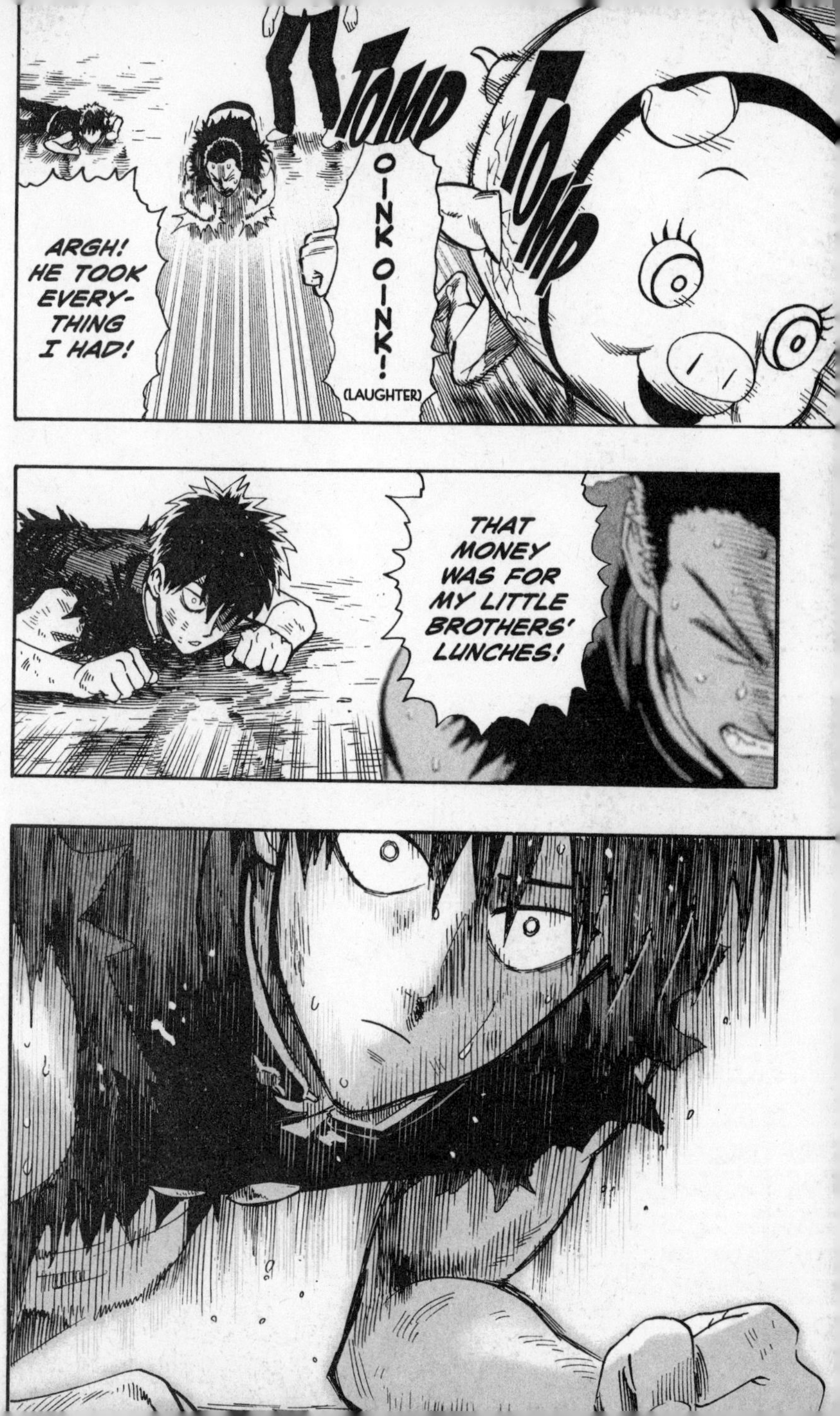
TOMP TOMP
TOMP
OINK OINK!
(LAUGHTER)
ARGH! HE TOOK EVERY-THING I HAD!
THAT MONEY WAS FOR MY LITTLE BROTHERS' LUNCHES!

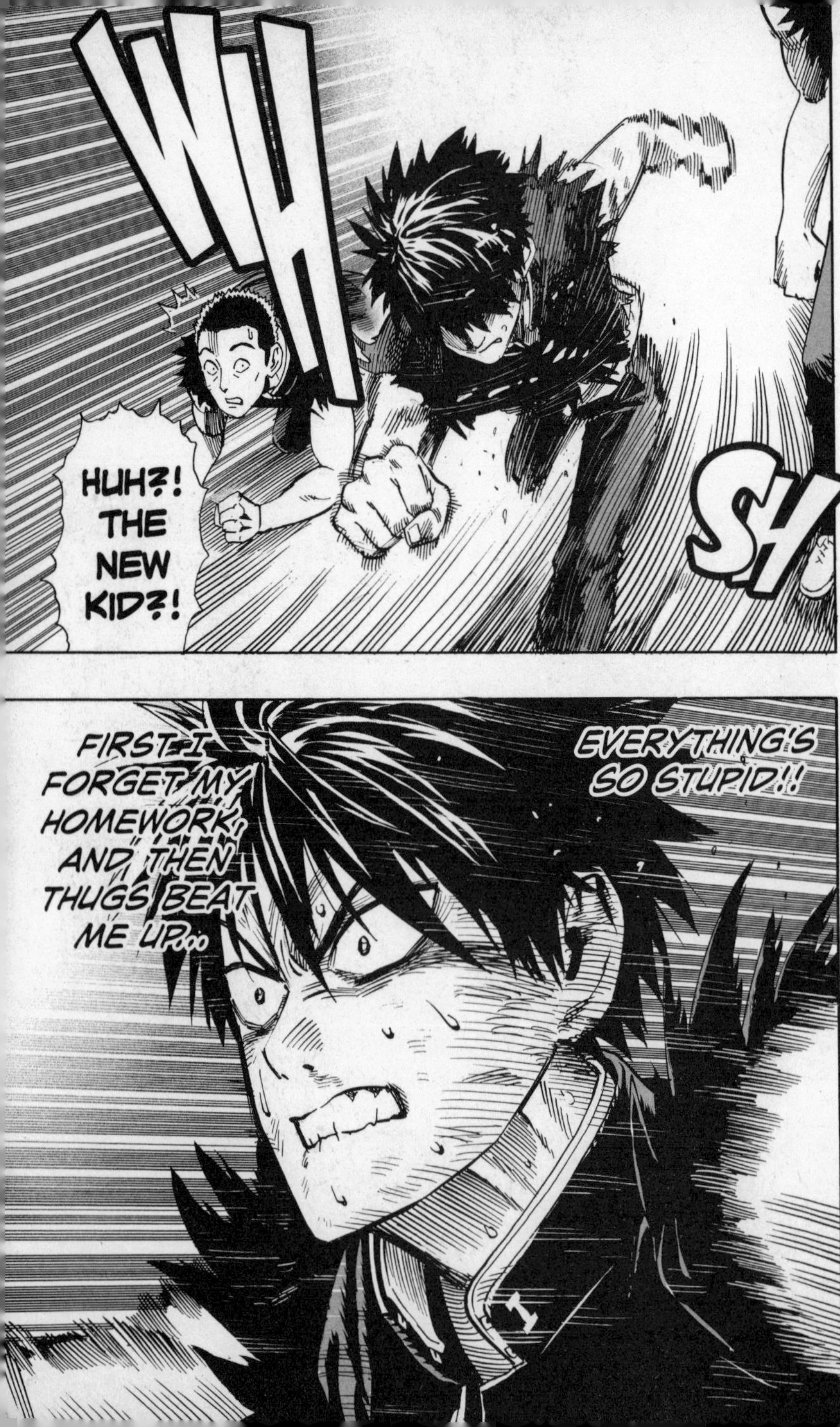
WHA
SH
HUH?! THE NEW KID?!
EVERYTHING'S SO STUPID!!
FIRST I FORGET MY HOMEWORK, AND THEN THUGS BEAT ME UP...

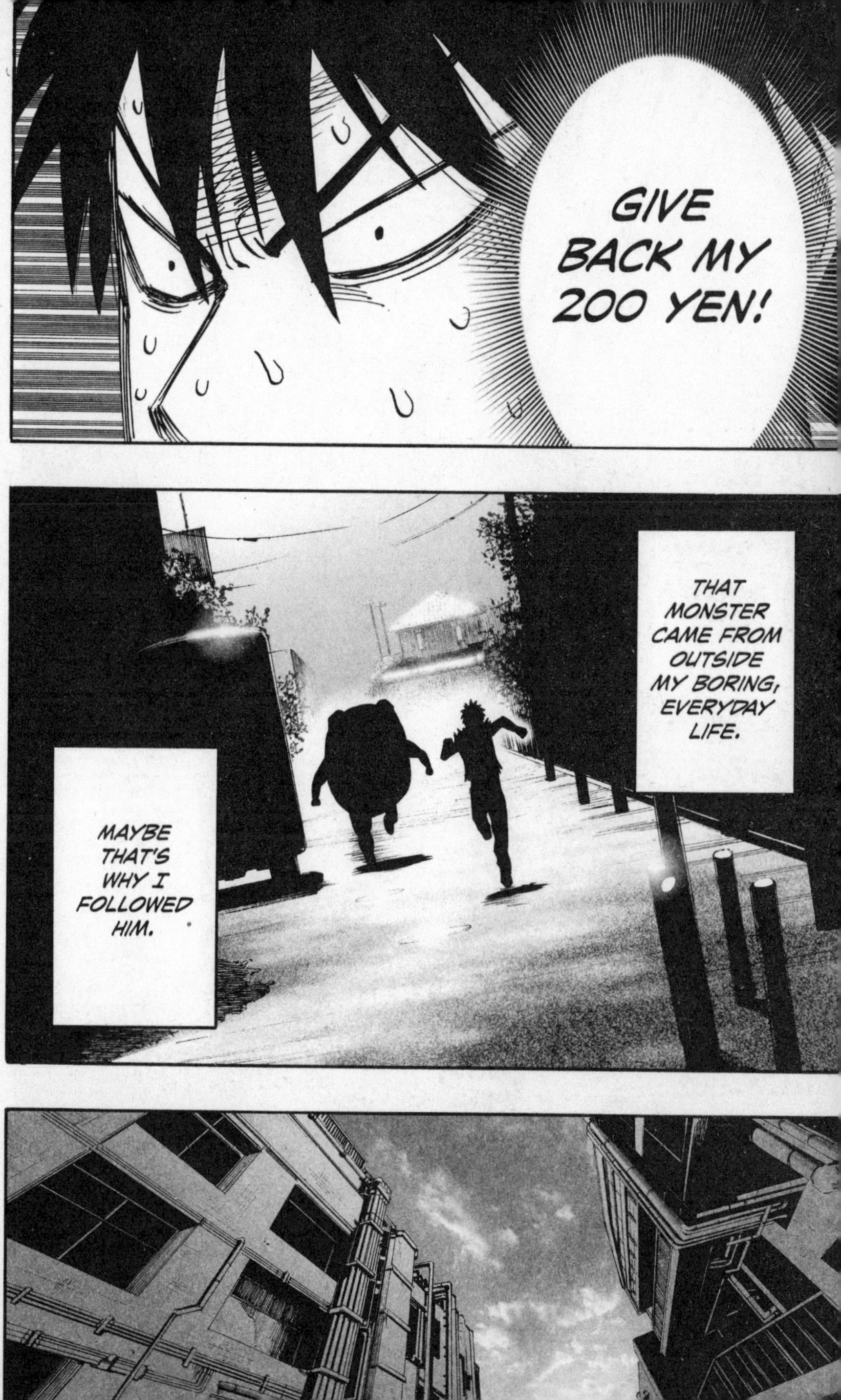
GIVE BACK MY 200 YEN!
THAT MONSTER CAME FROM OUTSIDE MY BORING, EVERYDAY LIFE.
MAYBE THAT'S WHY I FOLLOWED HIM.

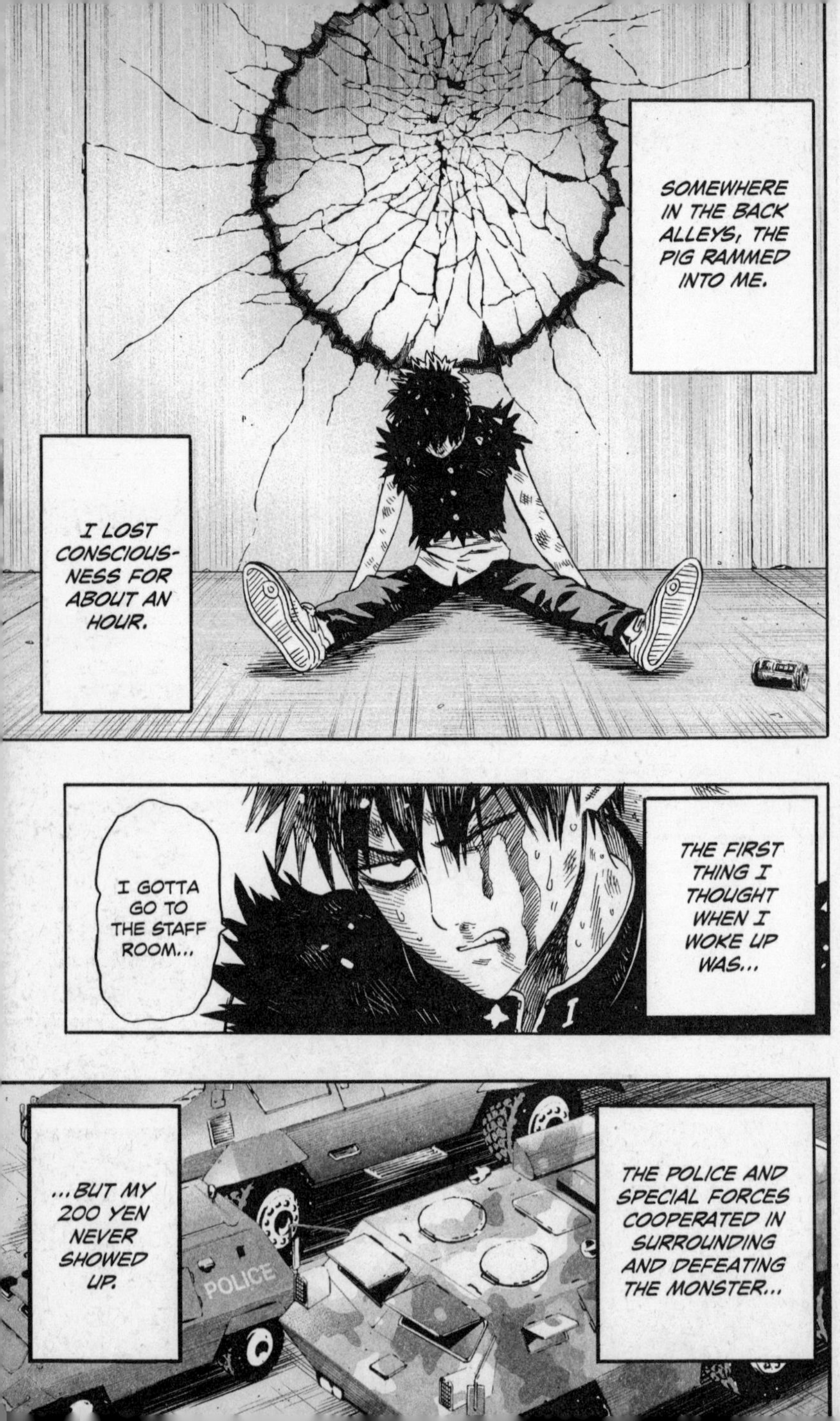
SOMEWHERE IN THE BACK ALLEYS, THE PIG RAMMED INTO ME.
I LOST CONSCIOUS-NESS FOR ABOUT AN HOUR.
THE FIRST THING I THOUGHT WHEN I WOKE UP WAS...
I GOTTA GO TO THE STAFF ROOM...
THE POLICE AND SPECIAL FORCES COOPERATED IN SURROUNDING AND DEFEATING THE MONSTER...
...BUT MY 200 YEN NEVER SHOWED UP.
POLICE

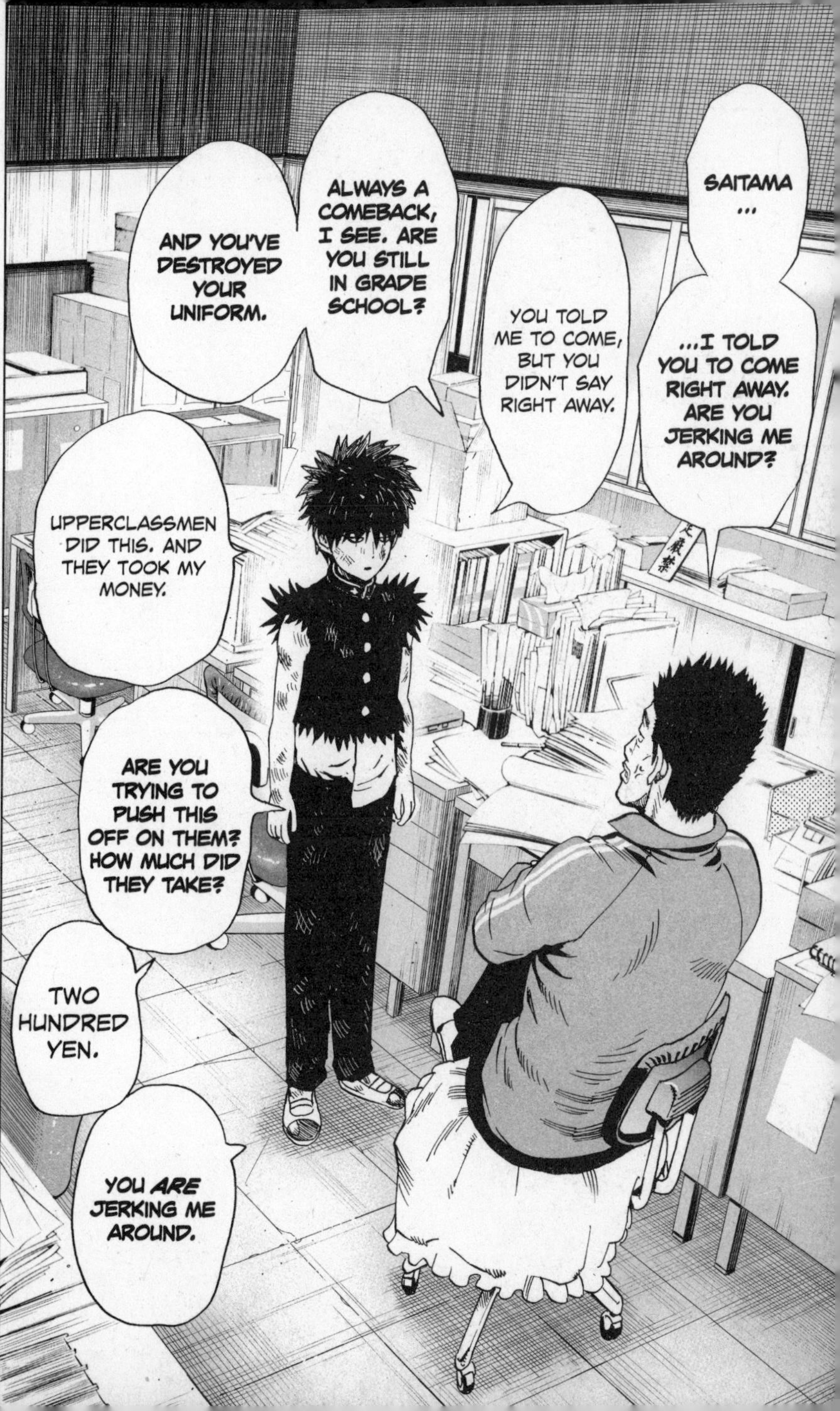
SAITAMA ...
...I TOLD YOU TO COME RIGHT AWAY. ARE YOU JERKING ME AROUND?
YOU TOLD ME TO COME, BUT YOU DIDN'T SAY RIGHT AWAY.
ALWAYS A COMEBACK, I SEE. ARE YOU STILL IN GRADE SCHOOL?
AND YOU'VE DESTROYED YOUR UNIFORM.
UPPERCLASSMEN DID THIS. AND THEY TOOK MY MONEY.
ARE YOU TRYING TO PUSH THIS OFF ON THEM? HOW MUCH DID THEY TAKE?
TWO HUNDRED YEN.
YOU *ARE* JERKING ME AROUND.

READ THIS WAY

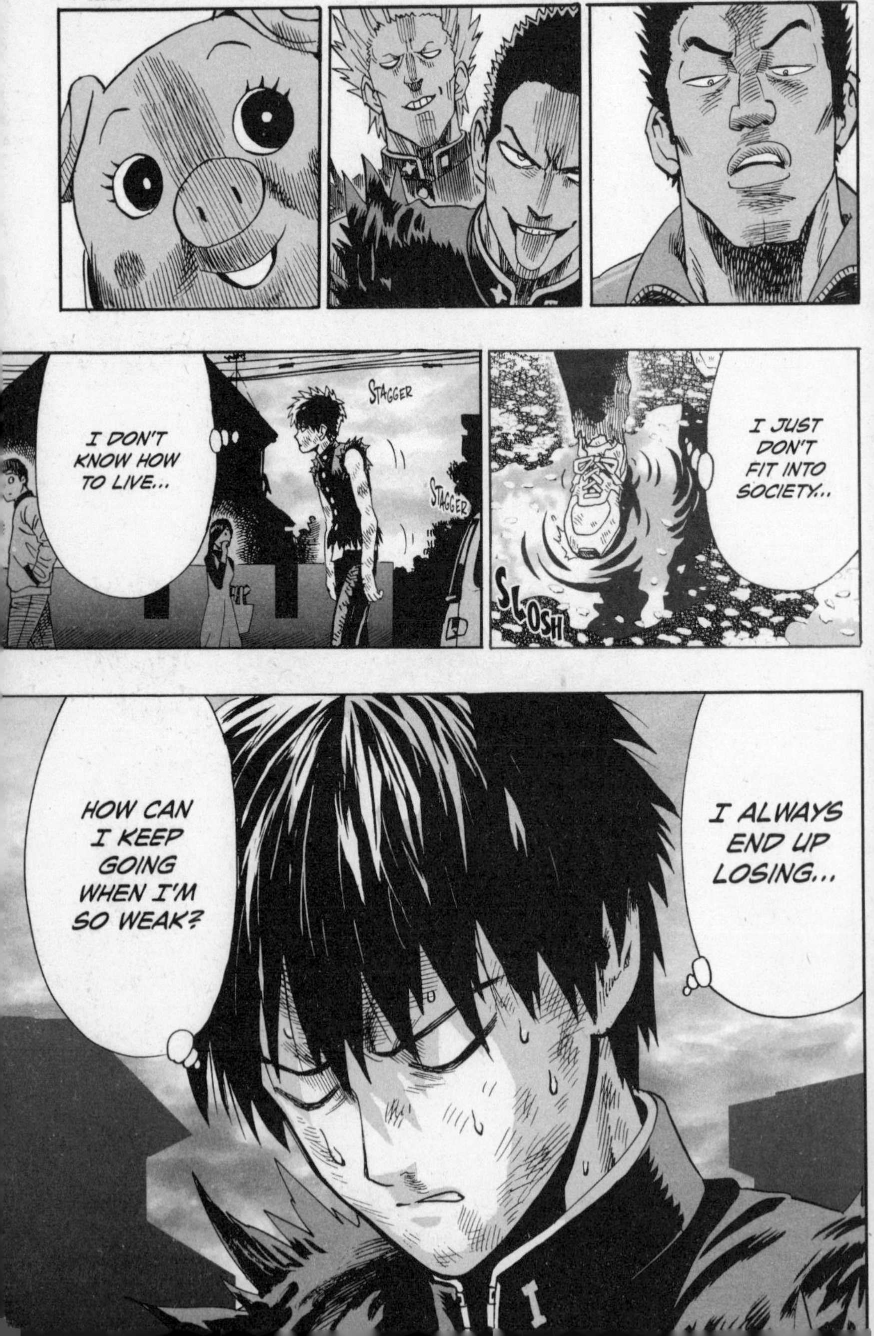
I JUST DON'T FIT INTO SOCIETY...
SLOSH
I DON'T KNOW HOW TO LIVE...
STAGGER
STAGGER
I ALWAYS END UP LOSING...
HOW CAN I KEEP GOING WHEN I'M SO WEAK?

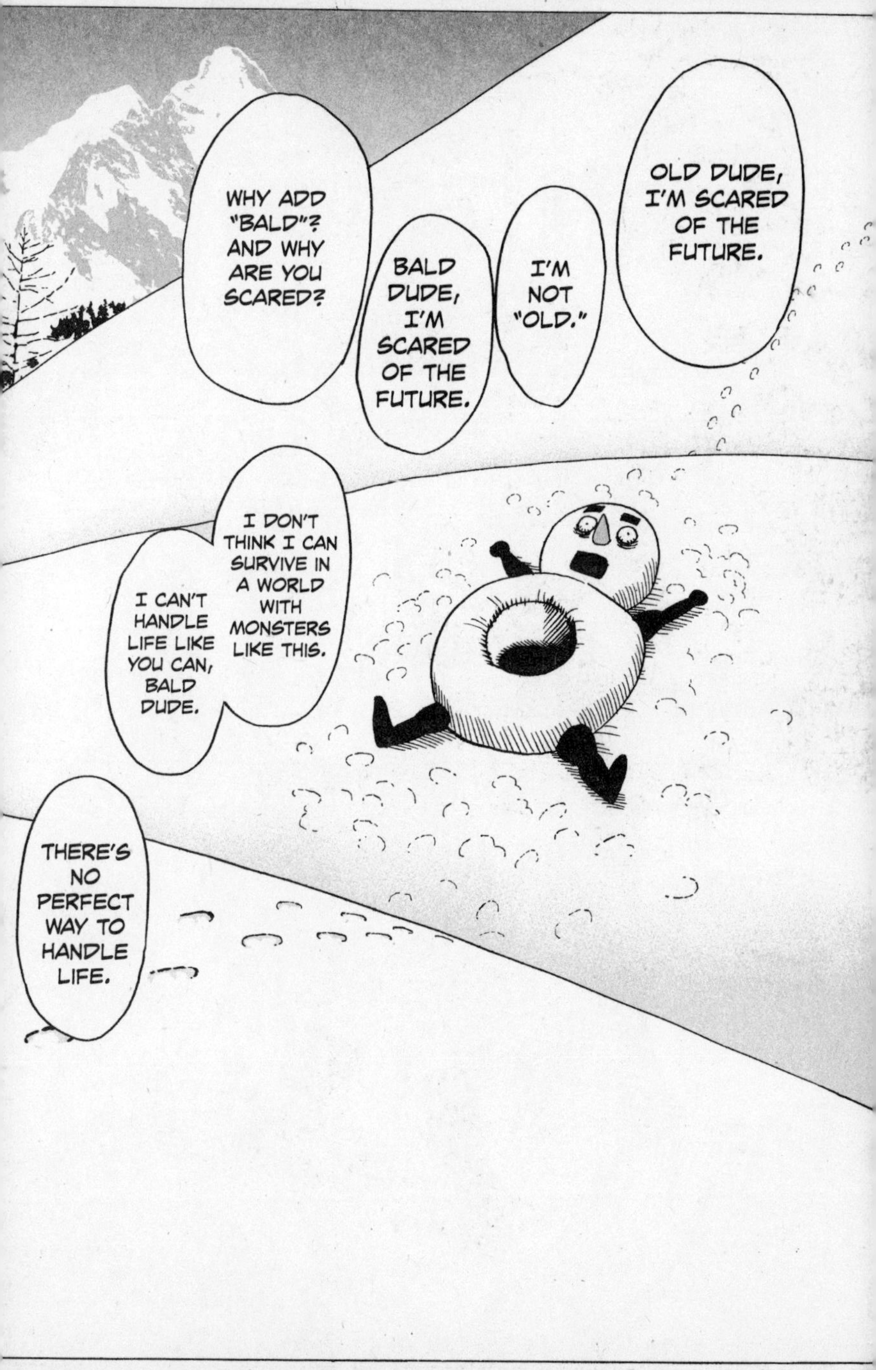
OLD DUDE, I'M SCARED OF THE FUTURE.
I'M NOT "OLD."
BALD DUDE, I'M SCARED OF THE FUTURE.
WHY ADD "BALD"? AND WHY ARE YOU SCARED?
I DON'T THINK I CAN SURVIVE IN A WORLD WITH MONSTERS LIKE THIS.
I CAN'T HANDLE LIFE LIKE YOU CAN, BALD DUDE.
THERE'S NO PERFECT WAY TO HANDLE LIFE.

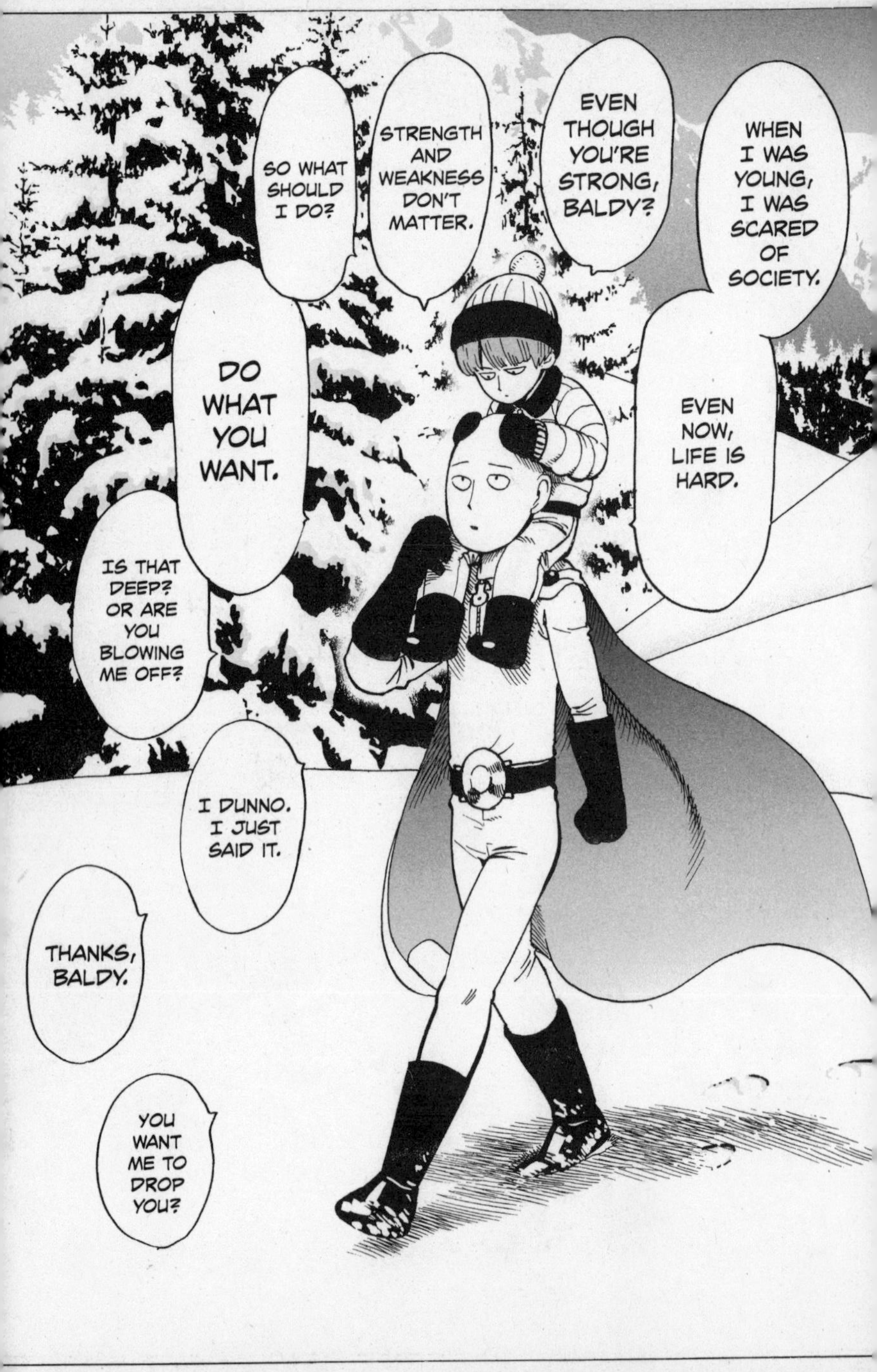
WHEN I WAS YOUNG, I WAS SCARED OF SOCIETY.
EVEN NOW, LIFE IS HARD.
EVEN THOUGH YOU'RE STRONG, BALDY?
STRENGTH AND WEAKNESS DON'T MATTER.
SO WHAT SHOULD I DO?
DO WHAT YOU WANT.
IS THAT DEEP? OR ARE YOU BLOWING ME OFF?
I DUNNO. I JUST SAID IT.
THANKS, BALDY.
YOU WANT ME TO DROP YOU?

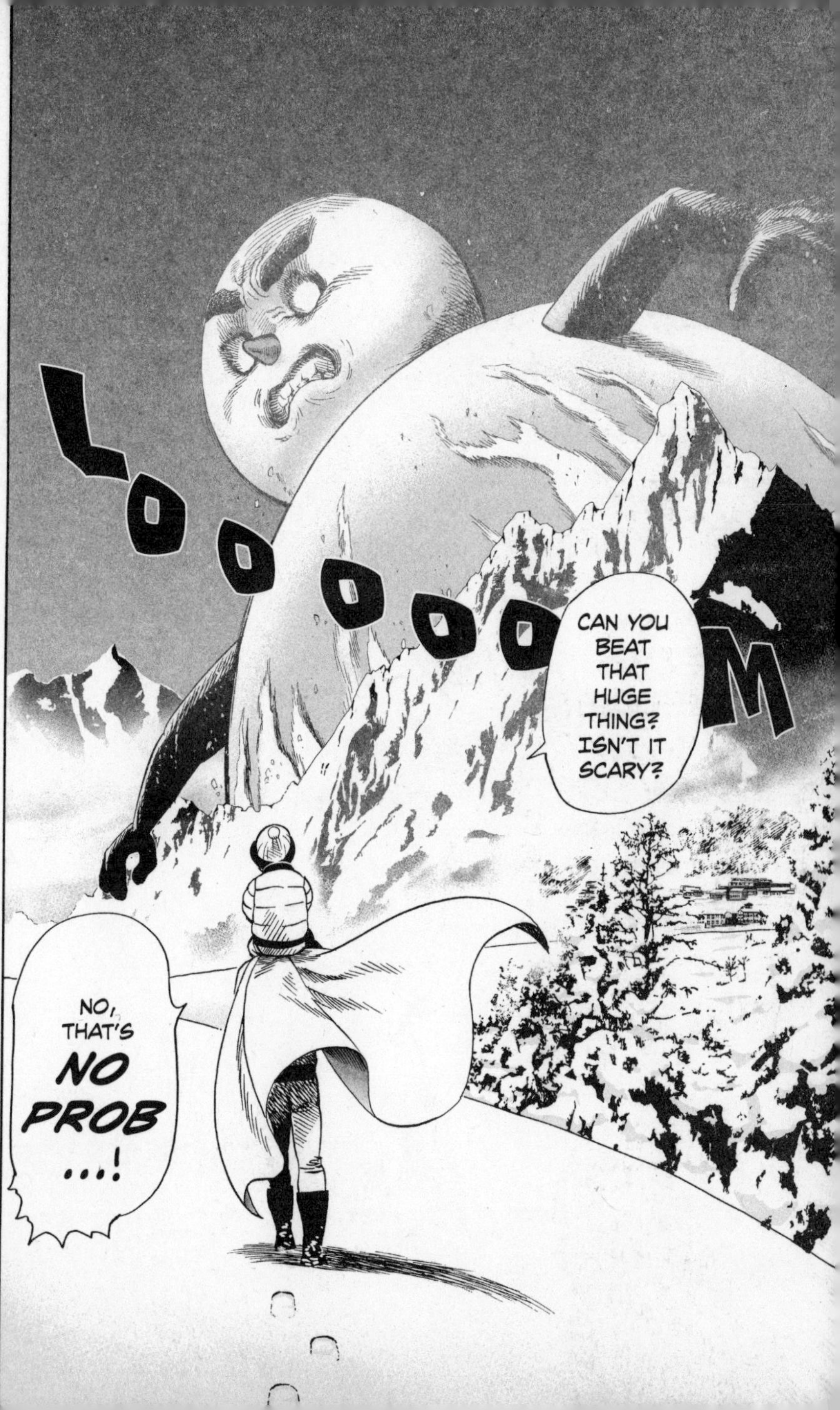
LOOOOOOM
CAN YOU BEAT THAT HUGE THING? ISN'T IT SCARY?
NO, THAT'S NO PROB...!

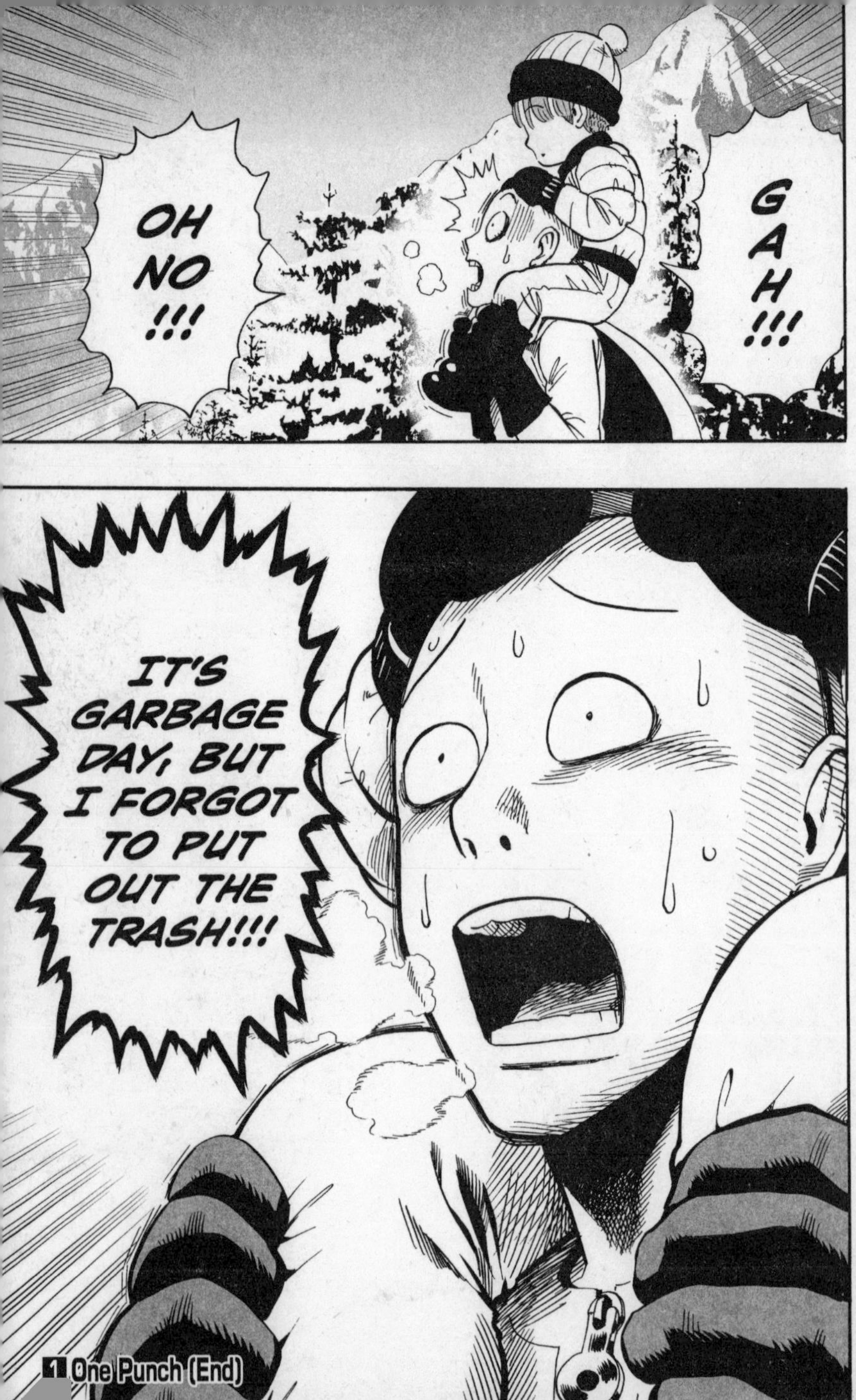
GAH!!!
OH NO!!!
IT'S GARBAGE DAY, BUT I FORGOT TO PUT OUT THE TRASH!!!

1 One Punch (End)

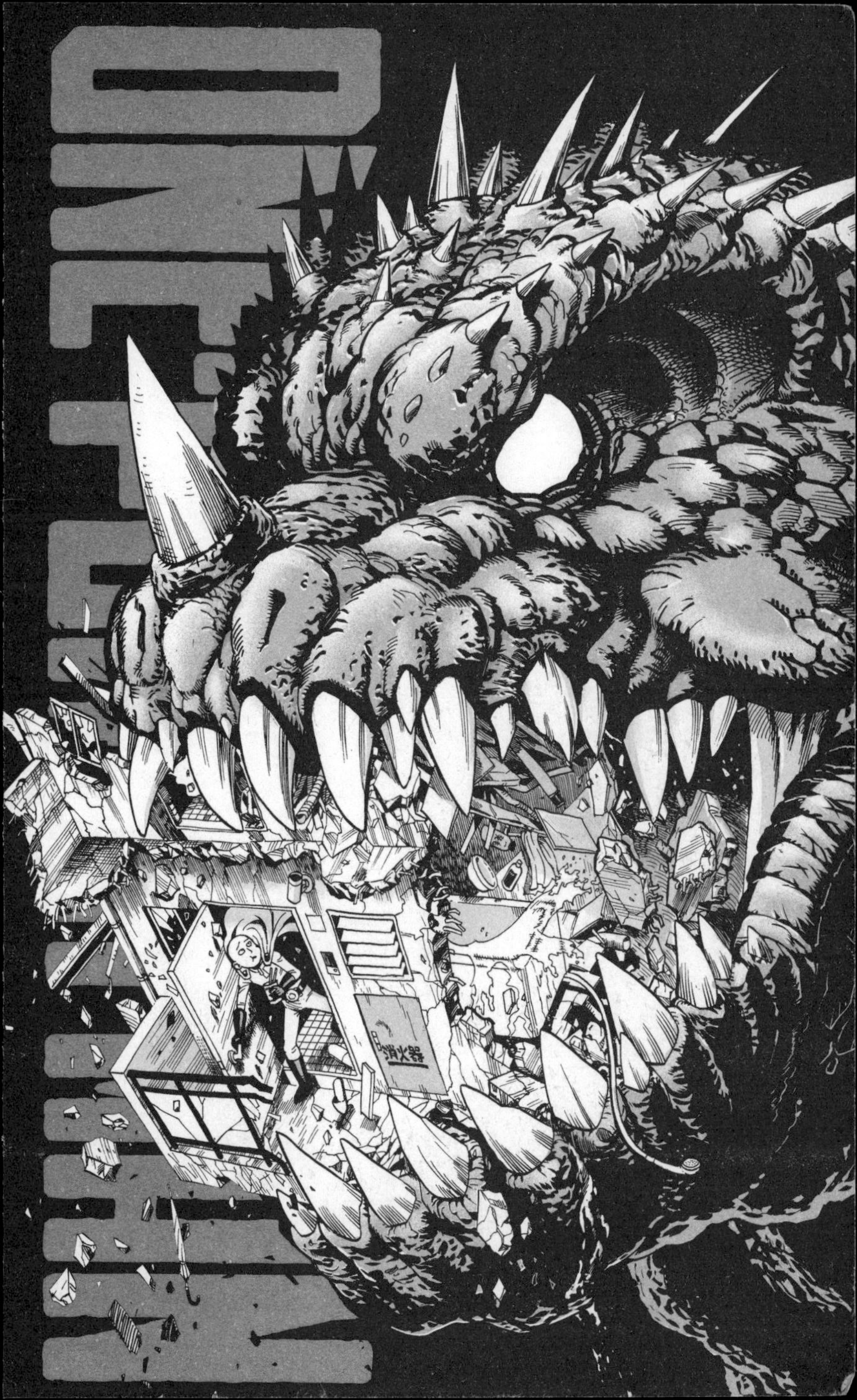
消火器

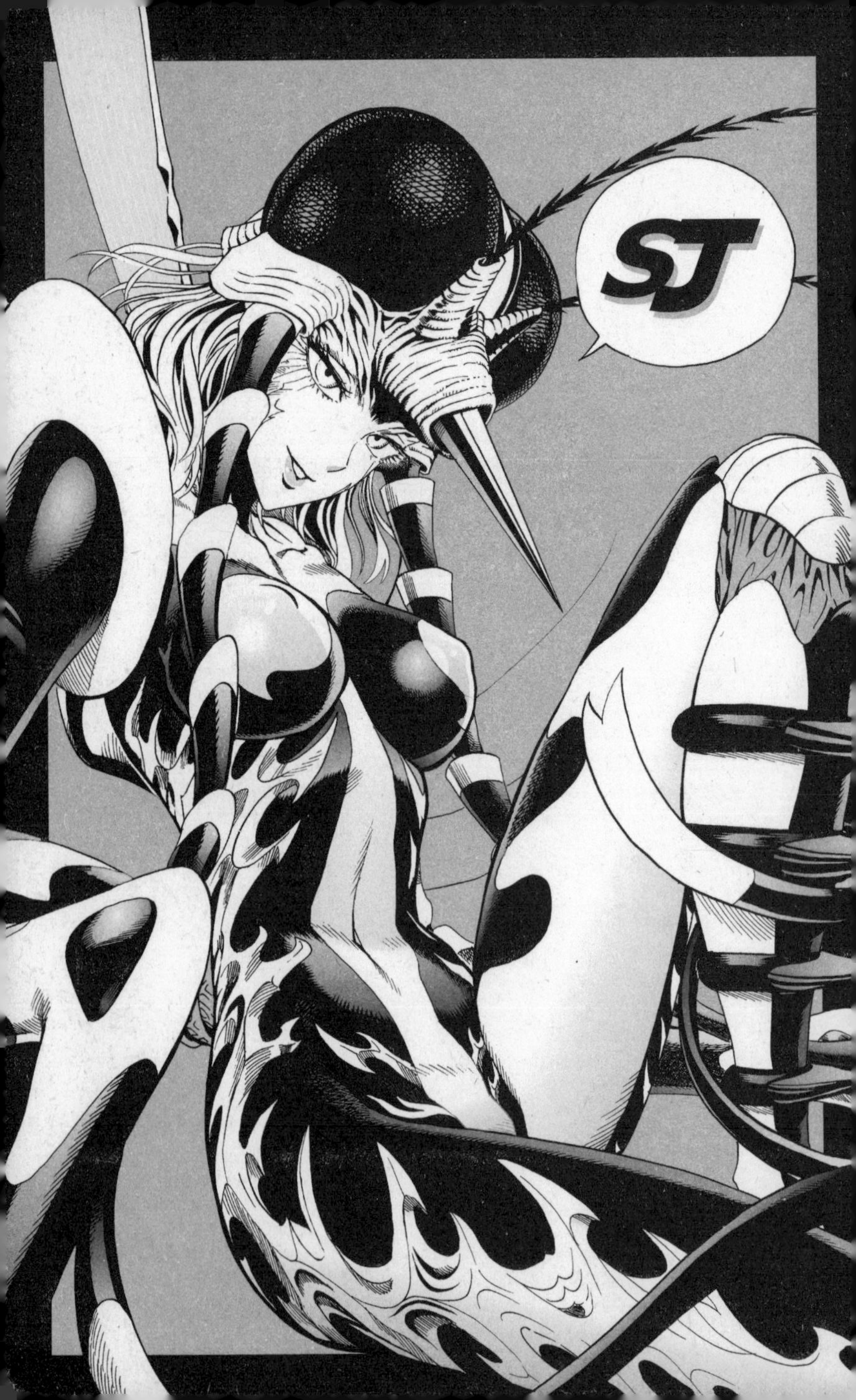
SJ

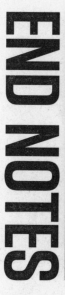

END NOTES

PAGE 149, PANEL 4:
The tattoo on the frog's shoulder says "Tono,"
which means "Master."

PAGE 157, PANEL 3:
The kanji on the mole's chest means "Ground Dragon,"
which is another way to write "mole" in japanese.

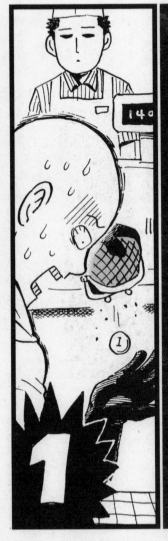

ONE-PUNCH MAN
VOLUME 1
SHONEN JUMP MANGA EDITION

STORY BY | **ONE**
ART BY | **YUSUKE MURATA**

TRANSLATION | JOHN WERRY
TOUCH-UP ART AND LETTERING | JAMES GAUBATZ
DESIGN | FAWN LAU
SHONEN JUMP SERIES EDITOR | JOHN BAE
GRAPHIC NOVEL EDITOR | JENNIFER LEBLANC

ONE-PUNCH MAN © 2012 by ONE, Yusuke Murata
All rights reserved.
First published in Japan in 2012 by SHUEISHA Inc., Tokyo.
English translation rights arranged by SHUEISHA Inc.

Printed in the U.S.A.

Published by VIZ Media, LLC
P.O. Box 77010
San Francisco, CA 94107

10 9 8 7 6 5
First printing, September 2015
Fifth printing, March 2017

www.viz.com

www.shonenjump.com

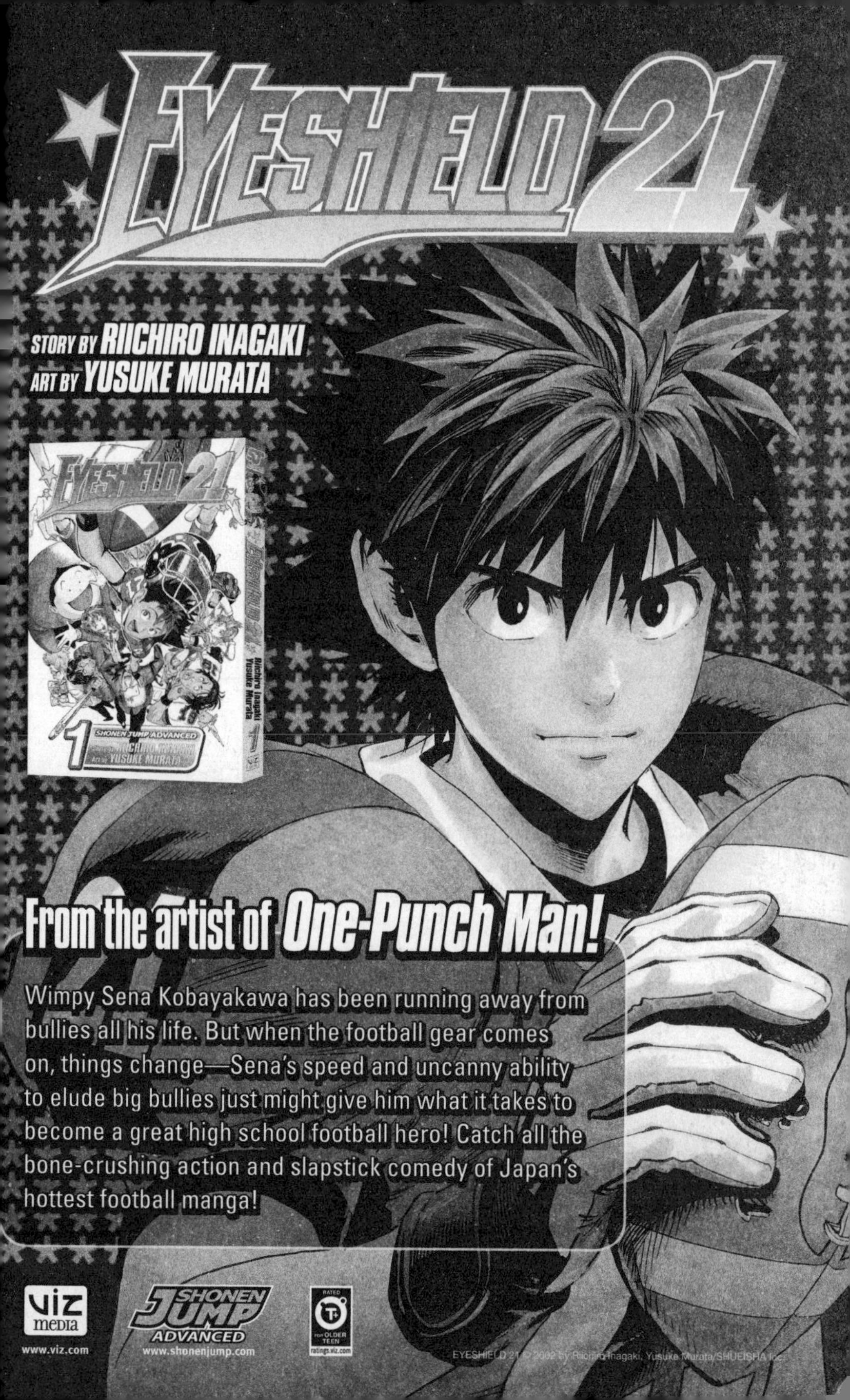
EYESHIELD 21
STORY BY RIICHIRO INAGAKI
ART BY YUSUKE MURATA
EYESHIELD 21
Riichiro Inagaki Yusuke Murata
1 SHONEN JUMP ADVANCED
From the artist of One-Punch Man!
Wimpy Sena Kobayakawa has been running away from bullies all his life. But when the football gear comes on, things change—Sena's speed and uncanny ability to elude big bullies just might give him what it takes to become a great high school football hero! Catch all the bone-crushing action and slapstick comedy of Japan's hottest football manga!
viz media
www.viz.com
SHONEN JUMP ADVANCED
www.shonenjump.com
RATED T+ FOR OLDER TEEN
ratings.viz.com
EYESHIELD 21 © 2002 by Riichiro Inagaki, Yusuke Murata/SHUEISHA Inc.

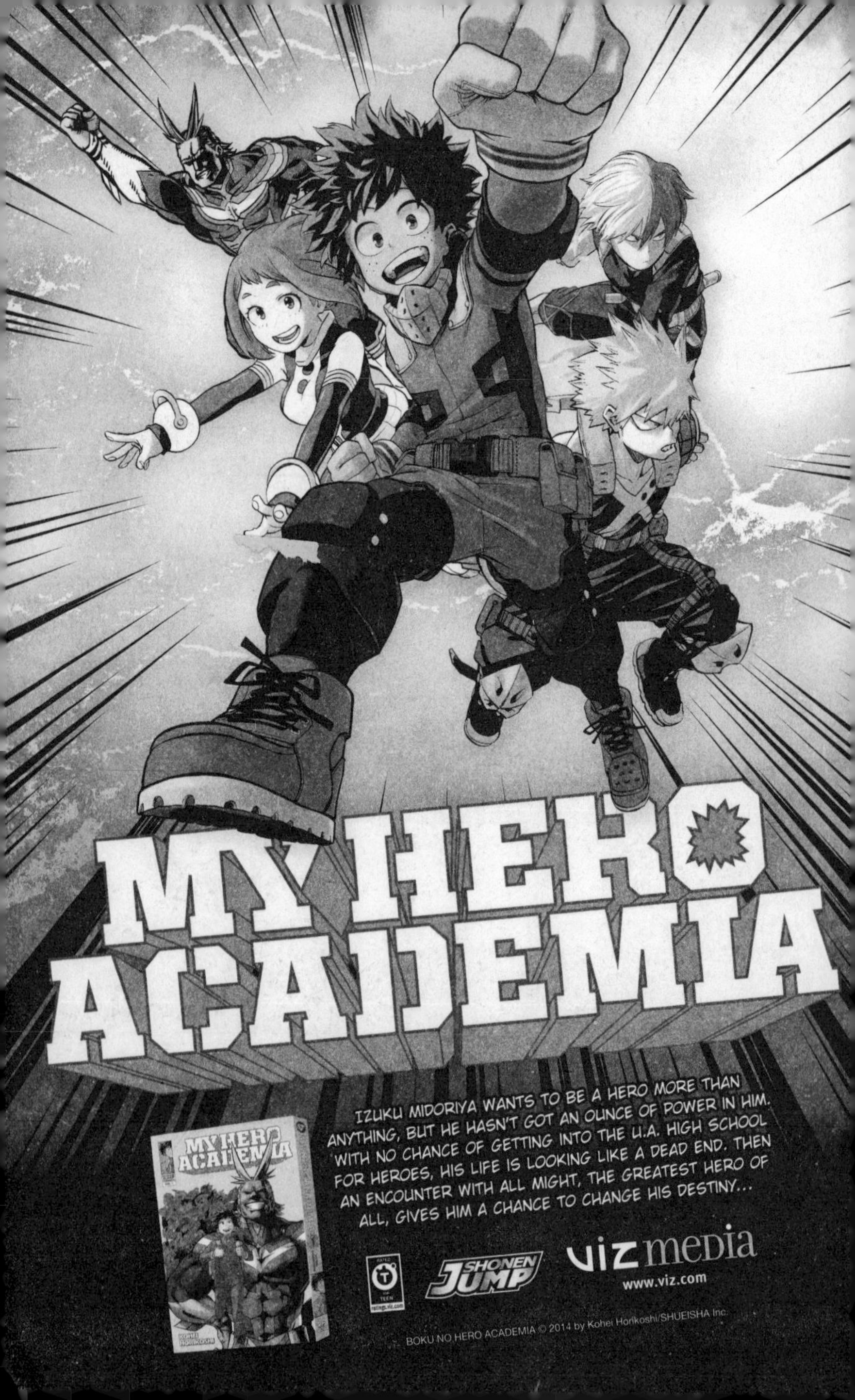
MY HERO ACADEMIA
IZUKU MIDORIYA WANTS TO BE A HERO MORE THAN ANYTHING, BUT HE HASN'T GOT AN OUNCE OF POWER IN HIM. WITH NO CHANCE OF GETTING INTO THE U.A. HIGH SCHOOL FOR HEROES, HIS LIFE IS LOOKING LIKE A DEAD END. THEN AN ENCOUNTER WITH ALL MIGHT, THE GREATEST HERO OF ALL, GIVES HIM A CHANCE TO CHANGE HIS DESTINY...
MY HERO ACADEMIA
KOHEI HORIKOSHI
SHONEN JUMP
viz media
www.viz.com
BOKU NO HERO ACADEMIA © 2014 by Kohei Horikoshi/SHUEISHA Inc.

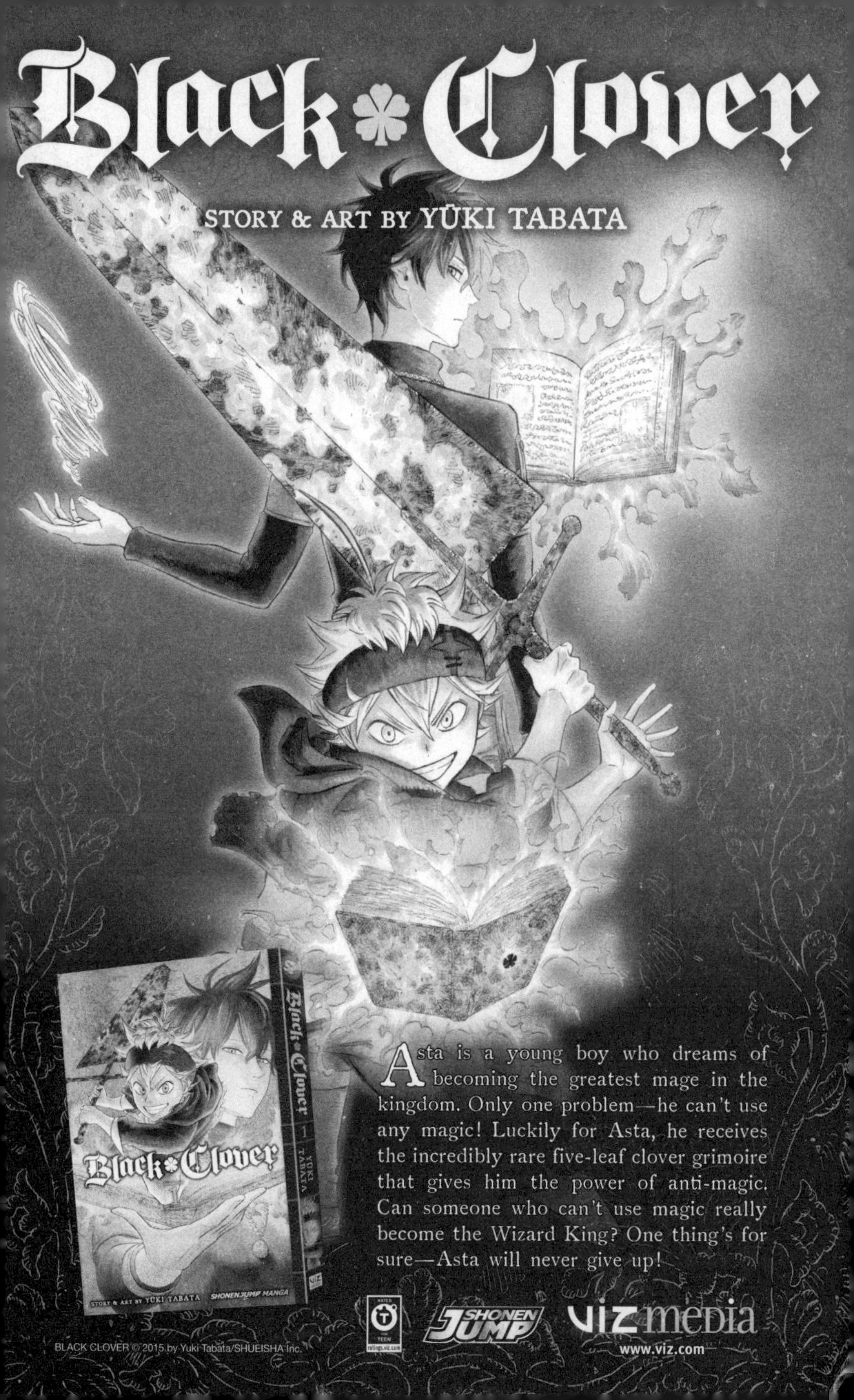
Black Clover
STORY & ART BY YŪKI TABATA
Asta is a young boy who dreams of becoming the greatest mage in the kingdom. Only one problem—he can't use any magic! Luckily for Asta, he receives the incredibly rare five-leaf clover grimoire that gives him the power of anti-magic. Can someone who can't use magic really become the Wizard King? One thing's for sure—Asta will never give up!
Black Clover
1
YUKI TABATA
STORY & ART BY YUKI TABATA
SHONENJUMP MANGA
RATED T FOR TEEN
ratings.viz.com
SHONEN JUMP
VIZ media
www.viz.com
BLACK CLOVER © 2015 by Yuki Tabata/SHUEISHA Inc.

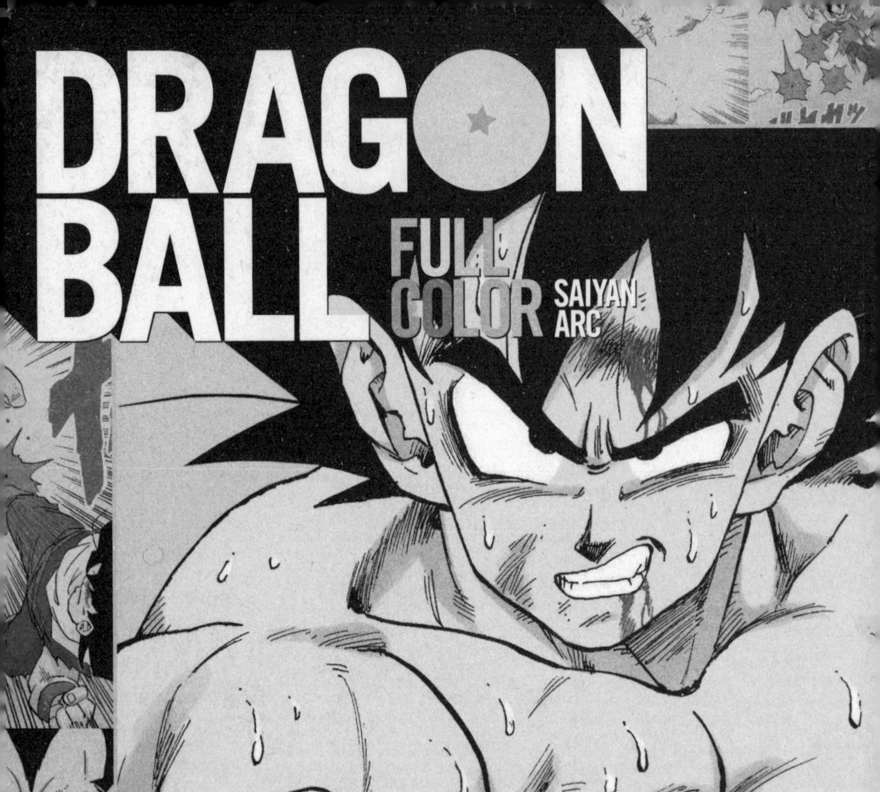
DRAGON BALL
FULL COLOR
SAIYAN ARC

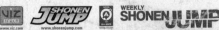

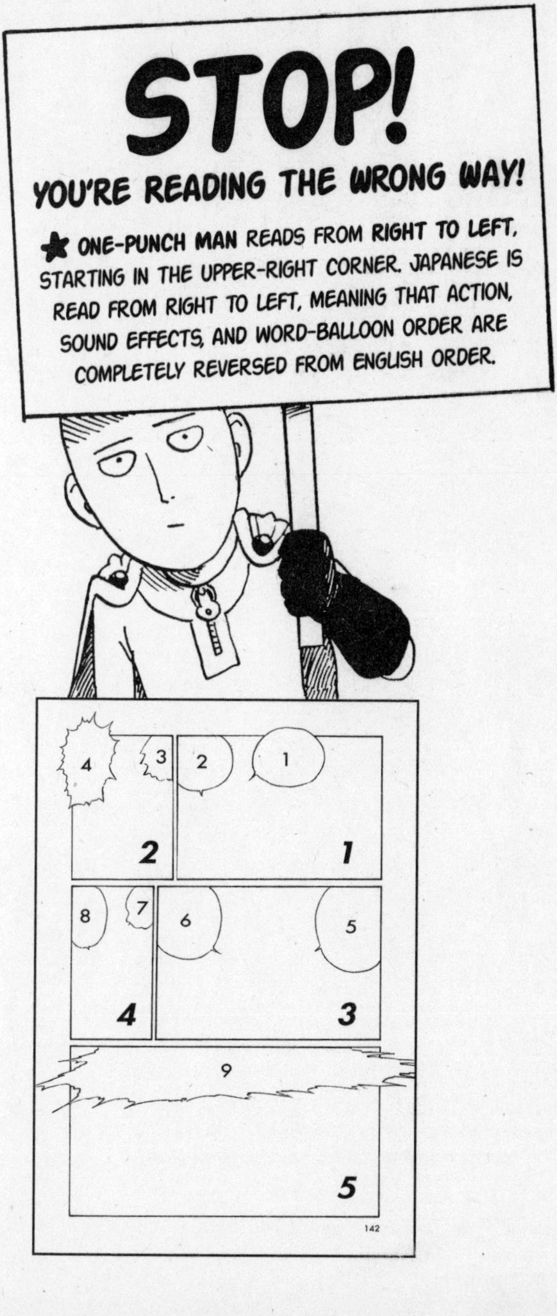
STOP!
YOU'RE READING THE WRONG WAY!
ONE-PUNCH MAN READS FROM RIGHT TO LEFT, STARTING IN THE UPPER-RIGHT CORNER. JAPANESE IS READ FROM RIGHT TO LEFT, MEANING THAT ACTION, SOUND EFFECTS, AND WORD-BALLOON ORDER ARE COMPLETELY REVERSED FROM ENGLISH ORDER.